The Wild Swan

by the same author

novels

LOVERS AREN'T COMPANY
DRESS REHEARSAL
LADIES WITH A UNICORN
THE BOY IN BLUE
SOME DARLING FOLLY
SIGH FOR A STRANGE LAND
SNIPER IN THE HEART

short stories

ADVENTURERS PLEASE ABSTAIN
JOURNEYS WE SHALL NEVER MAKE

biography

THE FINE AND THE WICKED
The Life and Times of Ouida
A PRIDE OF LIONS
A Portrait of Napoleon's Mother

The Wild Swan

The Life and Times of
Hans Christian Andersen
by
Monica Stirling

A Helen and Kurt Wolff Book
Harcourt, Brace & World, Inc.
New York

In Memory of
KAREN BLIXEN

Contents

Illustrations

The tailpieces to the chapters are reproduced from paper cut-outs made by Hans Christian Andersen

The endpapers show some of the illustrations by Vilhelm Pedersen for the first German collected edition of Hans Christian Andersen's Fairy Tales

Acknowledgments

For generous help, hospitality, and permission to use texts and information, I want to thank:

Dr Erik Dal and the staff of the Royal Library, Copenhagen, Dr Topsøe-Jensen of the University Library, Copenhagen, the late Svend Larsen of the Hans Christian Andersen Museum at Odense, the Count and Countess Moltke-Huitfeldt, Mr and Mrs H. Stein Christensen, Miss Melchior, Mrs Aagot Christensen, Mrs Neiiendam of the Christiansborg Theatre Museum, Mr Helge Henrichsen, the Danish Embassy and the Danish Tourist Bureau in Paris, Mrs Anne Anderson, the Librairie Galignani in Paris, Miss Clara Svendsen, Miss Anne-Marie Riedlinger, Dr Semadeni, Dr Isabelle Timmermans-Roget, Miss Elisabeth Vogelsanger, Mrs St George Saunders, Mrs Fuoss, Madame Odette Arnaud, Miss Cyrilly Abels, Mrs Edith Killerich, Mr and Mrs Robert Knittel, and particularly my friends Miss Margaret Rawlings, Madame Patrice de la Selle, Mrs Roe and Mr and Mrs Jørgen Skjerk, now Danish correspondents for Writer's and Speaker's Research, without whose devoted assistance I should not have been able to consult all the Danish documentation listed in the bibliography.

The translation of Andersen's Tales used throughout is that of the late Jean Hersholt, the only one that exists in English containing all 168 tales, copyright 1942 and 1949 by The Limited Editions Club for the George Macy Companies, Inc., New York. Thanks for permission to use this are due to Mrs Helen Macy, The Limited Editions Club, New York.

Extracts from *The Fairy Tale of My Life* are taken from the translation by W. Glyn Jones, published by Nyt Nordisk Forlag, Copenhagen. Acknowledgment is also made for permission to quote from the following: *Rumour and Reflection* by Bernard Berenson—Constable and Co., Ltd., Simon and Schuster Inc. and Miss E. Mariano; *Hans Andersen and Charles Dickens* by Professor Elias Bredsdorff—the author; *The Song of the Lark* by Willa Cather—The Houghton Mifflin Co., Inc.; *The March of Literature* by Ford Madox Ford—Allen and Unwin Ltd., *Studies in the Literature of Northern Europe* by Edmund Gosse—Routledge and Kegan Paul, Ltd,; *Two Visits to Denmark* by Edmund Gosse—John Murray, Ltd.; *Markings* by Dag Hammarskjøld, translated from the Swedish by Leif Sjöberg and W. H. Auden, © 1964 by Alfred A. Knopf, Inc. and Faber and Faber, Ltd.; *Portrait of an Age* by G. M. Young—All Souls College, Oxford.

Prologue: Seasons in Copenhagen

Between the Baltic and the North Sea lies an old Swan's nest and it is called Denmark. In it have been born, and will be born hereafter, Swans whose names shall never die.

Hans Christian Andersen, *The Swan's Nest*, 1852

Hans Christian Andersen died before I was born, yet I have the feeling that I know him well, and that he has been a friend of mine.

Karen Blixen, 1962

*

HANS CHRISTIAN ANDERSEN. I cannot remember a time when this name meant nothing to me, but the moment is still vivid when I first associated it with an individual man as well as with the stories that until then I had taken for granted as having always existed, by divine dispensation, like Shakespeare and the Bible. In the corner of a railway carriage the child I then was sits looking out of the window to hide her tears from her fellow travellers. The train is taking her away to boarding-school and she longs fiercely to turn the clock back and capture yesterday. The muscular effort to stop crying makes her clutch more and more tightly the already much-handled book in her lap. Presently she opens this book. At first she sees the letters indistinctly. Then she reads: 'Far out at sea, the water is as blue as the loveliest cornflower, and as clear as the purest glass; but it is very deep, deeper than any anchor lines can go, and many a church steeple would have to be placed one on top of another to reach from the bottom to the surface. Down there live the sea people.' Immediately the child forgets her own troubles for those of *The Little Mermaid.*

The world of the child's daily life is full of alarming mysteries, but in the world of Hans Christian Andersen everything seems

13

comprehensible. She understands little Karen's immoderate love of her Red Shoes, for she herself finds just such an insensate pride in the black woollen stockings – the first stockings she has ever worn – that are part of her new school uniform. The Emperor of China is as real to her as Joseph and his coat of many colours; the Ugly Duckling is her favourite brother; the Snow Queen is her idea of wilful fascination and the Nightingale of natural music; Thumbelina is as real as Moses in the bulrushes. Everything in this world touches that depth of unconsciousness that is half of her being, and when she reads in *The Marsh King's Daughter* that 'love brings life. The greatest love brings the greatest life', she suddenly realizes that Hans Christian Andersen is an individual, one person on his own, and wishes passionately that he were alive now and that she might turn to him.

Later I paid the first of many visits to Denmark. It was Christmas weather, 'the time when the white bees swarm', snow underfoot, sunshine overhead, and the copper roofs and spires of Copenhagen outlined against a pale Tiepolo sky. The ramparts had vanished, but despite electricity and motor traffic Copenhagen is still recognizably the city described by Andersen in *Godfather's Picture-book*, with its Round Tower and Church of Our Lady. Masts of ships still sway in canals beside streets the colour of Danish silver, sea, stone and sky merging into one great lightness like that of Paul Klee's 'Paysage Polaire'. Glittering white bells hang across Strøget, the street that links Raadhuspladen (Town Hall Square) to Kongens Nytorv (the King's New Market-place). Blonde children in scarlet woollen caps press their neat noses against shop windows behind which Father Christmas and his reindeer gyrate. Snatches of recorded carols drift out from music shops – 'Good King Wenceslaus looked out', 'God rest you merry, Gentlemen', 'Silent Night'. 'Such dreadful crowds!' says a Danish friend just in from the country and unacquainted with the ferocious struggle for survival that already marks the rush hours in New York, Paris, London. Many of Copenhagen's waterways are frozen over. Breadcrumbs attract hosts of sea-gulls, their screeching both plaintive and threatening, and when an imprudent swan is found imprisoned in the ice sympathetic bystanders promptly summon an ambulance to the rescue. On the pavement outside the railings of the Church of the Holy Ghost a man in a fur cap and ear-muffs sells straw reindeer and stars swaying inside wreaths of straw, all decorated with red ribbons. In the churchyard immediately behind the vendor stands a spectral figure of Death with his Scythe, sculpted by Niels Hansen Jacobsen to illustrate Hans Christian Andersen's *The Story of a Mother*, in which Death 'flies faster than the wind. And he never brings back what he has taken away'. Suddenly I realize that all over the city are places associated with the man who has made his version of Denmark the imaginary homeland of all the world's children; and not only children.

Here is the still flourishing Hôtel d'Angleterre, of which Andersen wrote, as an elderly man who never lost his wanderlust, that merely to set foot in it made him feel young again; there is the Grand Magasin du Nord, the fashionable department store on the former site of the old Hôtel du Nord where Andersen met Jenny Lind for the first time; there is the new Royal Theatre which Andersen saw inaugurated the year before his death; and across Holmens Canal is the museum devoted to the work of Andersen's friend Thorvaldsen, the sculptor, who is buried there amid a marble population that he himself created. Behind it, in Christiansborg palace, was the old Royal Court Theatre of Andersen's youth, in whose ballet school he once danced with ungainly zeal. Near by is the Royal Library, full of Anderseniana, books by and about Andersen, diaries, letters, manuscripts, daguerreotypes, photographs, clippings, scrapbooks, the phosphorescent sediment of greatness.

Years later, I was invited to stay with a Danish writer in her seventeenth-century manor house a hundred yards from the sea, midway between Copenhagen and Hamlet's Elsinore. Its name is Rungstedlund, tulips grow alongside the white walls, wistaria climbs to the red roofs. Across the sea with its moving frieze of white swans, the coast of Sweden is visible. Behind the house stretch great woods, a paradise for birds whose sanctuary they are. At the front door stands a beautiful woman who was born at Rungstedlund in 1885. This is its owner, Baroness Blixen, who sometimes wrote under the pseudonym of Isak Dinesen. Small, aquiline, with mighty eyes and the map of her life etched on her face in delicate lines, she has the bone structure that enables beauty to defy old age. Her grandfather had known Andersen well and it was in manor houses such as this one, with its farming, military and poetic traditions, that Andersen spent much of his adult life. Originally an inn where wagoners changed horses, Rungstedlund had housed the eighteen-year-old Charles XII of Sweden when he led his army ashore in 1700. Seventy-three years later Denmark's greatest lyric poet, Johannes Ewald, accomplished his finest work there. A bench marks his favourite retreat in the woods.

By this time I had read and re-read Andersen's novels for adults, his travel books, his autobiographies and many of his poems. Returning from the unhappy Ewald's bench to the house dominated by Karen Blixen, I remembered a moment in Andersen's fourth novel, *The Two Baronesses*: ' "Long may she live!" shouted Holger, "original people must not die out, for they create as good an effect in the world as uniforms in the theatre." '

Thanks to Karen Blixen, I visited other such houses: her niece's eighteenth-century farmhouse, full of children, trophies, tractors and peacocks; the Øregaard museum, formerly the home of her maternal great-grandfather who married a French beauty from Guernsey and when she felt homesick sent a ship to her island for gravel so that she might walk on Guernsey soil in her Danish park; Count and Countess Schulin's classic white manor house, their family coat of arms carved over the door, thatched farm buildings in front, and behind the house a great lawn studded with magnolia trees and sloping down to a lake. In one room of particularly noble proportions was a vast Aubusson carpet, green and yellow, with fleurs-de-lis and two pastoral scenes; it had been made specially for this room when the house was new. None of these peacefully beautiful houses had changed much since Andersen wrote in *The Ugly Duckling*, 'It was so beautiful out in the country. It was summer – the wheatfields were golden, the oats were green, and down among the green meadows the hay was stacked. There the stork minced about on his red legs, clacking away in Egyptian, which was the language his mother had taught him. Round about the fields and meadowlands rose vast forests, in which deep lakes lay hidden. Yes, it was indeed lovely out there in the country. In the midst of the sunshine stood an old manor house that had a deep moat around it.'

Later I visited Glorup, a baroque castle built over medieval ruins, which Andersen visited about thirty times. From the outside it has the numbing beauty of the Snow Queen's palace, but inside the harmoniously proportioned rooms display the influence of eighteenth-century French art. Glorup still belongs to the Moltke-Huitfeldt family whose great-grandparents befriended Andersen, and the rooms he occupied are still kept much as they were kept for him in his lifetime. From their windows can be seen the waterways and lime avenues he loved.

The descendants of the friends in whose houses he wrote still read him – not only as children but throughout their lives. Men have always needed contact with the marvellous to nourish their imagination and help them deal with the difficulties of daily life. The earliest civilizations, notably those of Greece and Rome, found satisfaction in religion for their need of magic, myths and philosophical symbols. Long before the invention of printing, public story-tellers transformed reality into something rich and strange that was handed on by word of mouth and often subtly changed in the process. The Orient and medieval Europe produced every kind of fantasy from the Greek *Iliad* to the *Nibelungenlied* and Nordic sagas, the French *chansons de geste*, the Spanish *romanceros* – and during the Renaissance Christian and pagan mysteries flowered side by side. Paradoxically, the acknowledgment of the inevitability of mystery seems essential to the psyche's balance. Today the millions who watch royal weddings on television are seeking for compensatory magic, and readers of thrillers and westerns, in which justice triumphs in the person of a hero who instinctively leaps to defend the innocent, are hungry for what only the genuine myth, springing from the innermost life of the psyche, can produce.

Every period creates its own myths but is also created by them; it is a two-way process, and Andersen was the greatest mythmaker of the nineteenth century, a century strikingly rich in myths. Even when he used traditional material, he transformed it by his own sensibility into something uniquely personal that had the power to cross the frontiers of age, time and space. He had many ways of creating magic. In his drawings, paper cut-outs and scrap-books one sees in the so-called childishness and simplicity of his highly personal landscapes, his wild birds that symbolize release, his animals, trees, plants and objects each endowed with a richly individualized personality, proof of the power in him that was beyond his conscious control and relates his world to that of Marc Chagall and the earliest drawings of Paul Klee. Nor did Andersen produce this by turning away from the times in which he lived. His work shows a devotion to science, a belief in the value of its progress, as keen as Jules Verne's and particular to the nineteenth century, before over-population and the disintegration of the atom had made the world itself seem as fragile as its imprudent inhabitants.

Before leaving the hospitable Royal Library in Copenhagen for Andersen's birthplace, Odense, I paid two visits. First to Rungstedlund where I walked among bare-branched trees, my steps almost silent in the snow, to Ewald's bench overlooking the two-hundred-year-old beech tree beside which Karen Blixen's grave now lies. No birds sang that day, but they were nevertheless rustlingly present in that bird sanctuary that made it possible to say of her 'the birds of the heaven shall live through thy strength'. From Rungstedlund I returned to Copenhagen and drove past the park named after Andersen's friend, the great physicist Ørsted, to the Assistens Cemetery of which Andersen wrote in his fifth novel, *To Be or Not to Be*: 'The story is told of an English family who were travelling by steamer to St Petersburg that, having some hours to spend in Copenhagen, they hired a coachman and said, "Drive us to a place where there is something beautiful to see." The most beautiful place known to the coachman was not a picture-gallery or a museum. No, it was the Assistens Churchyard. So he drove them out there and it is said that they were highly delighted and promised to return in order to be buried there, as it *was* the most beautiful place in the world.' Eighteen years after writing this, Andersen was himself buried there and the day I saw it his grave was certainly a beautiful place, with its blanket of sunlit snow covered with Christmas wreaths and crosses of fir branches, pale grey-green lichen and scarlet berries. Here was the end of Andersen's mortal story. Yet as I stood among the dead I heard two voices still very much alive: Karen Blixen's asking for a book on her way to bed, 'Where's my Andersen?' and Andersen's own voice beginning his auto-biography with the words 'My life is a fairy tale.' There are indeed fairy-tale elements in the story of the penniless cobbler's son who, after slaying many a dragon, won fame, fortune and the friendship of princes, but it is also a tragic story, in some ways the archetype of the artist's life-story.

1. *Childhood in Odense*

1805-19.

> There is no work of art so big or so beautiful that it was not once all contained in some youthful body.
>
> Willa Cather, *The Song of the Lark*

> I wonder at times whether art of any kind, poetry, painting, music, sculpture and architecture, can flower and ripen on a humus entirely free from the state of mind that lies open to superstition.
>
> Bernard Berenson, *Rumour and Reflection*

*

HANS CHRISTIAN ANDERSEN was born on April 2, 1805 in Odense, capital of Fyn, the second largest of Denmark's four hundred and eighty-three islands. His father, called variously Hans Andersen and Hansen, was a twenty-three-year-old cobbler, slightly built, imaginative and febrile; his mother Anne-Marie Andersdatter was a robust and superstitious washer-woman of about thirty-eight. They were married only two months before the birth of their son, Hans Christian Andersen, which took place, according to tradition, in the house at the corner of Hans Jensensstræde and Bangs Boder that is now the Hans Christian Andersen Museum; but they had no settled home of their own until 1806, when they moved into Munkemøllestræde, a cobbled street between Klingenberg market-place and the Odense river. Nearly half a century later Hans Christian wrote of this, the first home he could remember: 'Our little room, almost filled by the cobbler's bench, the bed and my crib, was the home of my childhood; on the chest of drawers were cups, glasses and ornaments, and over the workbench by the window was a shelf with books and songs. In the kitchen, above the cupboard where we kept the food, was a rack of plates; the little room seemed to me big and grand. The door itself, with landscapes

21

painted on the panels, was as much to me as a whole art gallery. From the kitchen we could go up a ladder to the roof and in the gutter between our house and the next was a box of earth with chives and parsley. This was all the garden my mother had; in my story *The Snow Queen* that garden still blooms.'

Odense was at the time of Hans Christian's birth a city of five thousand inhabitants, with its own castle, court, governor, provincial nobility and a garrison of dragoons who wore Greek helmets hung with flowing horsehair; but the hundred and thirty-seven kilometres as the crow flies between Odense and the Danish capital, Copenhagen, represented a two and a half days' journey by coach and ship. Remote from the main currents of European thought, Odense harboured gods older than Christianity. In a world without anæsthetics, electric light, telephones, motor-cars, radios and aeroplanes, this city was so ancient that Odin, the Nordic god of victory and the dead, was said to have founded it. In Hans Christian Andersen's second novel *O.T.* he wrote: 'The common people still tell a legend about the name of the city. Up on Næsbyhoved's hill there once stood a castle. Here lived King Odin and his wife. Odense did not yet exist, but work had begun on the first building. The court was undecided as to how the city was to be named. At last it was agreed that the first word spoken next morning by either the King or the Queen should decide the matter. Early next morning the Queen awoke and looked from her window and over the wood. The first house was built, all but the roof, and the masons had decorated it with a great garland, glittering with tinsel. "Odin, see!" exclaimed the Queen, and so the city was named.' Even in Andersen's day Odin's funeral mound could be seen outside the city walls and peasants still put out bundles of hay for Odin's eight-legged horse which could be heard galloping over the countryside during thunderstorms. In the twelfth century, long after Odin's rule, the murder of King Canute (descendant of the Canute who had made himself King of England) made a Christian shrine of Odense. As a child Hans Christian could never pass the beautiful Gothic church dedicated to St Canute without closing his eyes and imagining the dead king lying at the altar in bloodstained crown and robes.

Even in the nineteenth century, however, the saints and demons of medieval theology did not have full sway over the popular imagination. Scattered all over Fyn were boulders thrown there by witches from the Thorsing hills across the water. Mosses, banks, alder-trees and thickets were still inhabited by Ellefolk, descendants of Adam's first wife, Lilith. These Ellefolk could fly and swim, stole food and cats, and possessed singing voices so beautiful as to be dangerous to mortal children, whom they would help drive the cattle home of an evening only to lure them away afterwards. Less dangerous were the Nisses, tiny red-capped men in grey who made their homes in church steeples. Provided they were not laughed at, the Nisses were well disposed towards mortals and would settle down to help those farmers who put sweet porridge, cakes and ale for them in the barns on Thursday evenings and Christmas Eve. The spirits of water – no place in Denmark is more than fifty miles from the sea – had also to be propitiated lest they pursue mortals and transform them into animals or trees. Linking past to present, legend to history, the Odense trade guilds still held processions on feast days, carrying banners and swords decorated with lemons and ribbons and led by a belled Harlequin. Local marksmen still held annual contests. Every first Monday in Lent butchers led through the streets wreathed oxen, ridden by boys in white with wings. Sailors held wrestling matches on planks set across two boats, and the drum and fife corps, to which Hans Christian's father belonged, would regularly thrum and tootle the New Year in.

Hans Christian's small home was kept impeccably clean and neat by his mother, who was determined that he should have a better start in life than she herself had had. There was little of poverty and misery that Anne-Marie did not know from personal experience. She was the illegitimate daughter of one Anna Sørensdatter, who had borne three illegitimate children to different men and been sentenced to atone for her sins by spending a week on bread and water in Odense jail, after which she cheerfully married first a tailor, Jens Pedersen, himself just out of prison, and then, after Pedersen's death, Jørgen Rasmussen, a jack-of-all-trades who had been a glovemaker, mason, soldier, and night-watchman. Undeterred by her mother's example, Anne-

23

Marie herself had in 1799 borne an illegitimate daughter, Karen Marie, to a journeyman potter, Daniel Rosenvinge, who, when sentenced to support his diverse illegitimate children, ran away and joined the army. The half-concealed existence of this child, boarded out with her grandmother in Bogense, two days' walk from Odense, increased Anne-Marie's determination that her legitimate son should see as little as possible of the sordid aspects of poverty. She often told him how much luckier he was than she herself had been, and her account of her parents driving her out into the streets to beg was in her son's mind when he wrote one of the most famous of his tales, that of *The Little Match Girl*, bareheaded and barefoot in the snow on New Year's Eve.

As for Anne-Marie's husband, the melancholy and imaginative young cobbler, he was fiercely determined that his son should not be starved of education as he himself had been. According to what Hans Christian heard as a child, his paternal grandfather, Anders Hansen, had been a prosperous farmer at Killerup, south-east of Odense, until fire and cattle disease ruined him and obliged him to apprentice his son to a cobbler instead of sending him to school. At the time of Hans Christian's birth his grandfather had settled in Odense and was a local figure of fun, mildly but definitely insane. He spent his time going from door to door and out into the neighbouring countryside, selling the strange little wooden figures he carved – birds, winged animals, human beings with animals' heads; or else he drifted about Odense chatting and singing to himself, while his wife, still bright and energetic, earned their keep by looking after the garden of the Grey Friars' Hospital, a former monastery transformed during the Reformation into a home for the sick, old and indigent.

On the day of Hans Christian's birth his father sat reading aloud the plays of the great eighteenth-century dramatist Holberg beside what must have been one of the strangest of cribs for a baby – for in his poverty the young cobbler had been glad of the chance to build his marriage-bed out of trestles and a bier. Fragments of funeral crape still clung to the bed on which the newborn baby lay. The cobbler's enthusiasm for the theatre was fanatical but not unusual at that time, when the church and the theatre were the most cherished institutions in Denmark. Sermons and plays, fine points of theology and acting, excited people to an extent difficult to imagine in these days of multiple mass entertainment. Hans Christian was to admire Holberg extravagantly but on this occasion he howled, causing his father to wonder why the baby did not either go to sleep or listen quietly.

H. G. Olrik mentions the possibility that the writer's real father was his godfather, Nicolas Gomard, described in Andersen's autobiography as 'a poor French emigrant'. Nicolas Gomard enlisted in the Danish army in 1767 and subsequently settled in Odense, where he worked as a French teacher, a hairdresser, a tailor, and finally as doorkeeper at the Grey Friars' Hospital until his death in 1821. In 1936 Gomard's granddaughter said that Gomard's second wife had claimed that Hans Christian was her husband's son. This supposition led to another remarkably incongruous one, namely that Hans Christian Andersen was the cousin of Louis XV's mistress, Madame Du Barry, who had been born Jeanne Bécu, the illegitimate daughter of Anne Bécu and, possibly, of Jean-Jacques Gomard, brother of Hans Christian's godfather. However, once Andersen became famous, several families, particularly those for whom his mother had worked, claimed him as their own, so this supposition tells us less about Andersen than about the human tendency to ascribe exotic parentage to great men. Not only had the young cobbler every reason to believe that Hans Christian was his son, but the writer's fragile nervous constitution was clearly inherited in part from his unbalanced father and mad grandfather, just as his height and a strain of sturdy common sense came to him from his mother.

This play-reading, incomprehensible to the illiterate Anne-Marie, was the first of many treats provided for Hans Christian by his father. On a shelf over the cobbler's bench stood copies of Holberg, La Fontaine, Voltaire, the Bible and the *Arabian Nights* that soon became even more important to the child than the toys his father made for him – cut-out pictures manipulated by strings, a mill with a dancing miller and, best of all, a toy theatre of which Hans Christian could truly have said what the child Goethe said of his own toy theatre, that 'it created a new world in the house.'

The cobbler adored his little son and planned to give him, somehow, every educational advantage. His plans were not in the least tyrannical, however. He was determined that the boy should be free to choose his own path in life. The long evenings – in the depth of winter the darkness lasted for seventeen hours at a stretch – gave father and son plenty of time for reading and playing together. Sometimes they would press heated coins against the frosted window-panes to make peepholes through which to look at the snow surrounding their world of make-believe, a fragile world soon to be shaken by the Napoleonic campaigns that were carrying French power across Europe. A picture of Napoleon hung in the Andersens' home and the cobbler often pointed it out to his son and told him again and again the story of the poor Corsican boy who had sailed away from the island of his birth to become an Emperor and bestride the world like a colossus. This fairy tale made such an impression on the child that more than thirty years later he wrote in his novel *O.T.*: 'Beyond his own country, France was the only country that really interested Otto. Here Napoleon had ruled, and Napoleon's name had touched his heart – he had grown up whilst this name passed from mouth to mouth; the name and the deeds of the hero sounded to him, while yet a boy, like a great world adventure. How often had he heard his grandfather, shaking his head, say, "Yes, journalists can find little to say now that Napoleon is quiet." And then he had told his grandson of the hero at Arcola, and among the pyramids, of the great campaign against Europe, of the conflagration at Moscow and the return from Elba . . . Who has not written a play in his childhood? Otto's sole subject was Napoleon; the whole history of the hero, from the snow-batteries at Brienne to the rocky island in the ocean.'

When Hans Christian was two years old Napoleon and Alexander I of Russia met spectacularly, amid their assembled armies, on a raft on the river Niemen opposite Tilsit. One of their secret agreements was that, should England reject Russia's mediation, Russia would join in the Continental blockade while Sweden and Denmark (Denmark, Norway and Greenland had formed one kingdom since the fourteenth century) would be forced to close their ports to English ships. Should Sweden, which was then at war with France, refuse to comply, Denmark must abandon its neutrality and declare war on Sweden. The English promptly demanded that Denmark hand over its fleet to England 'for the duration of the present situation'. The Danes were thus in a cleft stick. If they satisfied the English they would be invaded by the French. So Danish ships took up stations north and south of Copenhagen to protect the capital from the English fleet in the Sound, and volunteer corps were hastily formed, while the main body of the army, led by the Crown Prince, went south to defend Denmark's land frontier. The Danes, however, were hopelessly outnumbered. An English corps of 20,000 Hanoverians landed in Denmark and easily routed 12,000 militia, 7,000 of whom were only volunteers equipped for the most part with halberds, lances and swords. Copenhagen was bombarded by the English fleet for three days. A thousand buildings were destroyed, including the three-hundred-year-old university, and the fire brigade could not master the flames. The English seized the royal dockyard, magazine and harbour, and destroyed what they could not take from the naval storehouses. Grief-stricken crowds watched in silence from the city ramparts as their captive fleet sailed away.

On October 21, 1807, Denmark made an alliance with Napoleon and early in 1808 Marshal Bernadotte entered Denmark with a French army and a corps of Spanish auxiliaries to attack Sweden, which had refused to close its ports to English ships. Some of these troops were billeted in Odense, and although Hans Christian was only three years old at the time, he never forgot the 'dark brown men making a din in the streets'. Odense was suddenly transformed. The dark brown men performed Spanish dances in the streets, slept on improvised pallets in schools, under ammunition wagons and among the ruins of the Grey Friars' Church. They brought their religion with them and the Danes, Lutheran Protestants since the Reformation, watched with alarmed curiosity when mass was openly celebrated out in the fields. The harsh music of the Spanish language gave Hans Christian his first contact with the world of the Mediterranean, and when the cannon boomed in Odense it seemed to him to be an echo of mighty battles fought far away by his father's hero Napoleon. One day a Spanish soldier picked Hans Christian up, showed him the silver medal that hung around his neck and held it out for the child to kiss. This frightened Anne-Marie, who considered Popery a form of black magic, but Hans Christian, who always welcomed even the small change of affection, the small courtesies of the heart, merely assumed that the foreign soldier must have a son of his own age in the distant country from which the holy medal had come. But another incident of the occupation was a traumatic experience for him. Since France had invaded Portugal the previous November and was threatening Spain, antagonism had sprung up between the French soldiers and their Spanish auxiliaries. Mild differences of opinion became dislike, and dislike swelled into hatred. The atmosphere became thunderous and one day Hans Christian saw a Spanish soldier led to execution for having killed a French comrade. The. child never forgot this and as a man wrote a poem about it, 'The Soldier', which became so popular in Germany that it ended by passing for an old German folksong.

French visitors to Odense at this time included Bernadotte's pretty wife, born Désirée Clary, with whom Napoleon had been in love before he met Joséphine. With Désirée was her nine-year-old son, Oscar, who owed his name to the admiration that his godfather Napoleon felt for Ossian's poetry. This was the first but not the last time that Hans Christian's and Oscar's paths crossed. In 1810 Oscar's father, Marshal Bernadotte, was elected heir apparent to the Swedish throne, and nearly forty years later the writer Hans Christian Andersen was to be the honoured guest of King Oscar I of Sweden.

The Spaniards did not remain long in Fyn. When they heard that their countrymen at home had revolted against the French, they seized the fortress and batteries of the port of Nyborg and held them until, with the help of the English fleet, blocking the passage between Denmark and Sweden, they were able to escape home to Spain. They left behind them legends that enriched the local tradition, according to which Nyborg had formerly been the lair of the dragon slain by St George. Twenty-six years later Hans Christian described the poppies of Nyborg in his novel *O.T.* as '. . . a proud colour! But they are manured by the blood of Andalusian horses . . . You know that in the year 1808 the Spaniards lay in Fyn; English ships were cruising in the Belt, and Romana fled with his whole army, but they could not take their horses on board. These were the most splendid Andalusian creatures ever seen. The Spaniards took off their bridles, and left them here to scamper about the fields like wild horses. It happened that the Nyborg horses also grazed here and as soon as the Andalusian horses became aware of ours they arranged themselves in rows and fell upon the Danish horses.' The surviving Spanish horses were captured by Danish peasants and long afterwards local horses still showed an unmistakably Andalusian strain.

With the departure of the Spaniards from Fyn, Hans Christian's first personal contact with the world as opposed to local history came to an end.

Even as a child Hans Christian was exceptionally tall and thin, with very large hands and feet that gave his appearance a touch of the grotesque. He had flaxen hair, light blue eyes, and a strong aquiline nose at variance with his disarming manners, so eager yet intimidated, so spontaneous yet ungainly, that as a boy he often impressed strangers as peculiarly articulated and over-emotional. Once when he and his mother were toiling with a group of gleaners, a bailiff known for his savage tempers advanced on them with upraised whip. Everyone fled except Hans Christian, who, absorbed by thoughts of the Biblical story of Ruth and Naomi gleaning in the fields of Boaz, was delayed by the loss of his wooden clogs. Faced with the angry bailiff, the child asked incredulously, 'How can you dare to strike me when God can see you?' To the onlookers' amazement the bailiff patted the boy's cheek, asked his name and gave him some money. Accustomed to harsh conduct, Anne-Marie was perplexed. She told her neighbours, 'He's an odd child, my Hans Christian, everyone is good to him, even that bad fellow . . .'

Thanks to his parents' love for him, Hans Christian's childhood never lacked affection and simple treats. On Sundays, in fine weather, father and son went to the woods, where the cobbler would sit absorbed in the fiercely laborious thoughts of a self-educated man while the child ran about caressing the noble old beech-trees, their trunks the colour of wet seals, picking wild strawberries or sailing the delicate little boats he constructed from the rushes. Like his father and grandfather, he had imaginatively deft fingers. Once a year, in May, Anne-Marie would accompany them to the woods to welcome spring that plays so dazzling a part in Nordic mythology and was heralded by the return of the storks. Hans Christian had a passion for these birds that, according to Scandinavian legend, owe their name to the fact that at the Crucifixion a stork flew around the Cross and cried out to Christ, '*Styrket, styrket!* (Be strong!)'. From childhood he felt a particular sympathy for these birds, and indeed the stork's combination of domestic piety (storks are monogamous, devoted to their young, and careful of their aged parents) with a love of venturesome travels did indeed suggest his own temperament.

For these ritual outings Anne-Marie wore her churchgoing dress of brown print and prepared a picnic of sandwiches and beer. Together the family would gather birch branches to put behind their porcelain stove, and sprigs of St John's wort to be tucked into the beams of their room and reveal, by the way they grew, whether their owners' lives would be long or short. Superstition was strong in Anne-Marie. She trusted wise-women, parsons and old wives' tales impartially and believed that the ubiquitous spirits of earth, air, fire and water required constant propitiation. She communicated enough of her beliefs to Hans Christian to make him as fearful as herself the day his father closed the Bible and said, 'Christ was a man like ourselves, but an extraordinary man.' On another occasion the cobbler said, 'There is no devil save the one we have in our own hearts,' and denied the divine origin of the Bible and the existence of hell. Whereupon Anne-Marie pulled Hans Christian out to the woodshed, threw her apron over his head and said, 'It was the Devil who was talking like that in our cottage, Hans Christian, not your father, and you must forget what he said'; after which they wept together and recited the Lord's Prayer. As an adult, Hans Christian was to share his father's views without losing either his very personal belief in a fatherly God or his responsiveness to the superstitions that had been the poetry of the poor among whom he had grown up.

Hans Christian did not know his maternal grandparents, and his mad grandfather terrified him, but he dearly loved his paternal

grandmother, Anne Catherine Nommensdatter, who visited him
daily and of whom he later wrote, 'She brought everything to me;
she loved me from the bottom of her heart; I knew and understood this.' An attractive figure with her bright blue eyes, upright
bearing and affectionate ways, she was the daughter of an
Odense town drummer, but, feeling a need for romantic ancestors,
told Hans Christian that her maternal grandmother had been a
German noblewoman who had run away from Kassel to marry an
actor and thus brought misfortune on the family. She urged Hans
Christian to remember that he shared this fictitious noble blood
(her maternal grandmother had in fact respectably married the
Assens post-rider) and, since Hans Christian was raised on stories
of kings, queens, prophets and genii, and had a passion for plays,
he found nothing incredible in his grandmother's stories of lost
grandeur. People's names were very fluid in Denmark at that
time, when the ordinary commoner took his father's Christian
name as surname, Lars Petersen's son Niels becoming Niels
Larsen, for example. It was not until 1828 that surnames were
handed on.

His grandmother used to bring him flowers from the hospital
garden and, twice a year, when she had to make a bonfire of
weeds and trash, he spent the day with her, helping to pick
weeds, playing with flowers and enjoying richer food than he had
at home. He liked visiting the old women who spent their last
years there spinning. Once, when he had just learnt something
about anatomy and was longing, as usual, to share his discoveries, he gave the old pensioners an impromptu lecture on the
subject, using a door as a blackboard on which to draw his
idiosyncratic notions of the human heart, intestines and kidneys.
The old women were delighted, declared him 'too clever to live',
and in exchange told him 'stories of bygone times, of memories
that whistle in the old willow tree' that became an integral part
of his imagination. One of his last stories, *What Old Johanne Told*,
written more than half a century later, was based on tales he had
heard as a child from those old women.

These visits also had horrific aspects. Part of the hospital was
occupied by lunatics, and the little boy would see the harmless
ones walking in the courtyard. Their disjointed talk and songs

filled him with dread and, by reminding him of his grandfather, forced him to face the terrifying fact that madness was not restricted to spectral figures behind bars but might be lying in wait for anyone. Sometimes an attendant took him down a long corridor past the dangerous lunatics' cells, and once, when the attendant had left him momentarily alone there, Hans Christian looked through a crack in the door and saw a naked woman crouched on a heap of straw. Clothed only by her long hair, she was singing in an eerily beautiful voice. Suddenly she stopped, leapt up, cried out and hurled herself against the door. The grating in the door flew open and, seeing the little boy, the madwoman thrust her arm out and managed to touch him with her fingertips. He screamed and fell down.

Equally but differently alarming to him was Odense prison, a long timbered building opposite the bishop's palace. Hans Christian supposed it to be full of desperadoes, and although many of the inmates could be heard placidly singing at their spinning-wheels, he could never look at it without shuddering, 'as children in Paris must have looked at the Bastille'. His horror of the place was magnified by a social outing made when he was still so small that he had to be carried part of the way. The jailer had invited the Andersens to a christening dinner to be held in his own quarters of the prison. To Hans Christian everything about this occasion seemed ominous, beginning with the great iron-bolted entrance door. While this was being locked behind them with one of a rattling bunch of keys, the little boy wondered if they would ever be allowed out. Usually Hans Christian had a hearty appetite, but on this occasion, with two prisoners waiting at table, he was too disturbed – like Stendhal's Julien Sorel on a different prison visit – to eat. His mother thought he was ill and put him to rest on a bed. There he fancied he could hear singing and the sound of spinning-wheels. Nearly half a century later he wrote in his autobiography: 'I was afraid and on edge all the time; and yet it was pleasant to lie there and imagine I had entered a castle full of robbers.' He also remembered that when he was carried home it was a rough night and rain dashed against his face. For the rest of his life prisons were to give him 'a nightmare of the spirit'.

The year that Hans Christian was six a great comet was

expected. His mother and most of their neighbours were as wild with fear as tethered horses in a burning stable since, according to word-of-mouth versions of a book entitled *The Sibyl's Prophecies*, this comet was to destroy the earth with a violence that would raise the dead and fling them, quick and dead together, into the implacable blaze of the Day of Judgment. The rational cobbler scoffed openly at the Sibyl and her prophecies, but this only added to Hans Christian's terrors, since he knew his father to be a good man but doubted if even the good would be saved if they greeted their Judge with laughter. Trembling, he accompanied his parents and neighbours to St Canute's and from the church-yard saw the comet fly past with its glittering dragon's tail. The Day of Judgment did not follow, but Hans Christian could not believe his father's scientific explanation for this and was still expecting the dreaded day when an event took place, without benefit of comet or prophetess, that put an end to the first part of his childhood.

About this time a shoemaker was wanted at one of Fyn's manor houses. The job carried with it a rent-free cottage with a small garden, pasture for a cow, and an opportunity for additional odd jobs. Hans Christian's father applied and was asked to make a pair of dancing slippers on approval. The silk for the uppers was provided but he had to furnish his own leather for the soles. While the father worked all three of them could talk of nothing but how wonderful it would be to live in the country and in security. The little boy prayed enthusiastically for a garden with flowers, sunlight and a cuckoo. Danish tradition had it that the cuckoo's call told its listeners how long they would live.

It was a solemn moment when the work was done. The middle-aged woman, the young man and the child believed – rightly, as it turned out – that their future as a family unit depended on these dancing slippers. The cobbler wrapped them in a kerchief and set out for the manor house, only to return pale, angry and defeated. Instead of trying on the shoes, his prospective employer had given them one quick look and said angrily that her silk had been wasted, whereupon Hans Andersen had whipped out his knife and cut the silk from the soles, saying, 'If you have wasted your silk I can waste my leather.' As he told this story all three wept over their lost cottage, garden and cow. For the first time Hans Christian had to struggle against resentment of God, who, since He was omnipotent, could easily have granted their harmless wish.

It was about then that Anne-Marie, still sturdy as a beast of burden, took the job of washerwoman for a prosperous official's family – and one day she came running home, distraught, explaining between sobs that the son of the house, just back from taking his degree as Master of Theology in Copenhagen, had tried to seduce her. 'I ran away as fast as I could,' she said to her outraged husband, 'our Lord Jesus Christ knows that I did. I ran straight home to you.' But she could not help adding bitterly, 'although it was an awful lot of money.' The child scarcely understood this incident; nevertheless he did not forget it, and used part of it in *She Was Good for Nothing*, the vindication of his mother's life that he wrote years after both his parents were dead.

Overwhelmed by a sense of total failure – such as his son with all his genius was often to experience – Andersen lost all faith in his future as cobbler, spent less and less time at his bench, and took to roaming the countryside as his own mad father did. He felt, as his son was one day to write: 'Just to keep alive is not enough, to live one must have sunshine and freedom and a little flower to love.' Starving for greater interests, wider scope for his mind than he could find in Odense, the cobbler became obsessed by his hero-worship of Napoleon. In this he was not alone. Beethoven composed his Third Symphony for Napoleon; Delacroix wrote that 'Napoleon's life is the epic of our century in all the arts'; and the historian and diplomat Guizot that 'The French Revolution and the Emperor Napoleon I have thrown a certain number of minds, including some of the most distinguished, into a feverish excitement which becomes a moral and, I would almost say, a mental disease. They yearn for events, immense, sudden and strange . . .' The self-educated Danish cobbler felt as strongly as some of these distinguished minds and soon talking of Napoleon was not enough for him. He decided to become a soldier. Denmark was at that time still allied with France, and by accepting a thousand thalers to take the place of a rich farmer's son he was able to provide simultaneously for his wife, his son and his own restlessness.

Anne-Marie wept and neighbours said 'like father, like son', pointing out that anyone who went for a soldier of his own free will must be mad. But the cobbler was adamant. He felt sure that he would return home an officer and was in high spirits until June 1, 1812, when the moment came to say goodbye to Hans Christian. The little boy was in bed with measles, and after his father had kissed him repeatedly and passionately, he lay in a fever listening to the receding drum-beats. Presently his grandmother arrived. With her dramatic imagination she already saw Hans Christian as an orphan and, bending over him, said that it would be a good thing if he were to die then and there, but that God's will was always best. The child did not answer, but as a man he was to recall this occasion as his first real sorrow.

This first parting did not prove as drastic as had been feared because Hans Andersen's regiment, the King's Own, remained in Fyn until the autumn of 1814 and he was able to keep in touch with his son's progress.

Hans Christian studied first with an old woman who kept an infant school and taught the rudiments of reading, writing and arithmetic. To her pupils, most of them girls, she was an alarming figure as she sat enthroned in her high-backed chair between her stout cane and a grandfather clock with little figures that moved jerkily when the hour struck. As Hans Christian was subject to convulsive seizures, Anne-Marie had stipulated that he was not to be caned. The old schoolmistress kept her promise until one day when her pupils made spelling aloud an excuse for rowdiness. Then she applied her cane indiscriminately. Hans Christian stood up and without a word left this school for good.

Anne-Marie's second choice was a school for poor Jewish boys founded by a Mr Fedder Carstens who had come to Odense originally to work at the post office. Anne-Marie told Mr Carstens of Hans Christian's nervous seizures and of his difficulties in getting along with other children. This was not due to any conscious reluctance on his part, for although, like his father, he spent much of his time in a dream world, he was then and always eager to be friends with everyone; but other children were inclined to tease and torment him, either because they instinctively felt he was different from themselves or because they knew that his grandfather was mad and his father eccentric. From the schoolmaster's point of view he was clearly a case of what would now be called a maladjusted child. Nevertheless, Carstens was so interested by the boy that he not only accepted him as a pupil but started him off with private lessons and saw to it that, as the youngest child there, Hans Christian was not knocked down in the rough and tumble of the playground. He often gave the boy sweetmeats and flowers and took him for walks with his own sons, pointing out details of the countryside that, according to Mr Carstens's granddaughter, bore fruit later in that miniature masterpiece of autobiography, *The Ugly Duckling*.

Even in this school there were pitfalls. Among Mr Carstens's pupils there was one little girl with whom Hans Christian became friendly. Slightly older than he was, she was a practical, well-organized child and told him that she wanted to learn to add up so as to become a dairy-maid in a manor house. He was busy drawing imaginary castles at the time and said, 'Then you must come to my castle when I become a nobleman.' Always ready to confide in people, he added that he had been kidnapped in infancy from noble parents, and that angels often came and spoke with him. Whether or not he entirely believed this, he certainly felt a compulsive need to create an imaginary world that was as real to him as the Gondal world was to be to the Brontë children in their isolated parsonage. The old women at the Grey Friars' Hospital had applauded his fantastic tales, but his new friend merely eyed him appraisingly and told the other boys, 'He's as mad as his grandfather.' He shuddered and never again felt at ease with her.

There was nothing, however, of Dotheboys Hall about this school. Mr Carstens soon noticed that Hans Christian was as nervous for others as for himself, and once, when one of the bigger boys was ordered to stand on a table as a punishment for neglecting his work, Hans Christian was so distressed that Mr Carstens let the culprit off. It is significant that Hans Christian should have found the instruction and sympathy he needed in a school for Jewish children. Later in life he was to find in cultured music-loving Jewish families in Copenhagen an immediate appreciation of his form of sensibility, and his poem 'Rabbi Meyer' shows his own understanding of orthodox Judaism. As an elderly man Mr Carstens became manager of the Taasinge telegraph service and used to tell visitors, 'You will probably not believe me when I tell you that I taught one of our most famous poets – Hans Christian Andersen was a pupil at my school.' It is agreeable to know that Andersen never forgot his old teacher's kindness, and as a well-known writer used to visit him and send him books. The letter he wrote to Mr Carstens for the latter's golden wedding can be seen today in the Hans Christian Andersen Museum at Odense.

Even more important to him than school was his first visit to the theatre, for which he was to have a life-long passion. Odense had possessed its own theatre since 1795, when one was built there for a local nobleman's private company of actors. The first time Hans Christian was taken there by his parents he looked around the packed auditorium and remarked, 'If we had as many casks of butter as there are people here, *what* a lot of butter I'd eat!' This prosaic reaction was quickly replaced by passionate enthusiasm for the performance, which was of a German vaudeville based on his father's favourite, Holberg's *The Political Tinker*. This satirical comedy, first produced in Copenhagen in 1722, is still in the Royal Theatre's repertory today. It tells the ludicrous tale of a Hamburg tinker so obsessed by politics that he neglects his work and his family to chat in cafés with like-minded cronies. The fun, the natural characters and lively dialogue enchanted the little boy, who was from then on to call the theatre his 'favourite place'. Half a century later he made one of his most disarming characters, Aunty, say: 'The theatre is my schoolroom, my fountain of knowledge. There I have brushed up on my old Biblical history. Take Moses, for instance, or Joseph and his brethren – they're operas now. It is from the theatre that I've gained my knowledge of world history, geography, and human nature. I've learned about Parisian life from French farces – it's naughty but very interesting. How I have cried over *The Rique-*

bourg Family – to think that the husband had to drink himself to death just so his wife could get her young sweetheart! Ah, yes, many's the tear I've shed in the fifty years I've been going to the theatre.'

His parents could not afford to take him to the play often, but he made friends with Peter Juncker, an old soldier who distributed the theatre posters, and in return for help with this task allowed the boy to keep some of the posters for himself. Hans Christian invented endless stories based on these posters' titles and names, and said later that this was his 'first unconscious literary work'. He spent more and more of his time playing with his toy theatre and showed such dexterity in dressmaking for his puppets that he made a character in his novel *Only a Fiddler* say, 'I am convinced that had I been born and educated in Paris, I should have been one of the first men-milliners.' As it was, the dressmaking he did for his puppets taught him to mend his own clothes and keep them neat, a great advantage later when he had only himself to rely on for this.

Like most children and many adults, he was leading a double life and the discrepancy between his daily routine and the world of his imagination was so great as to provoke an increasing number of the nervous seizures that alarmed his mother. In her husband's absence Anne-Marie consulted the local wise-woman, who advised taking him to be ducked in the spring at St Regisse, which had been considered holy in medieval times and even after the Reformation was still believed to possess magical properties. On St John's Eve people came from all over Fyn to the annual fair held there. This expedition did Hans Christian's nerves no good and possibly some harm, since while he and his mother spent the night sleeping out by the fateful spring, a thunderstorm broke over them and provoked a young lunatic near by into fits. Sane, let alone humane, treatment of the insane did not yet exist, and for a hypersensitive child who had been frightened once and for all by his grandfather's madness, every chance encounter with lunacy was a mental hazard.

In the autumn of 1812 Hans Andersen's regiment was moved south – but not across the frontier to join the Danish troops that helped defend Hamburg under the command of Marshal Davout.

After the French defeat at Leipzig in October 1813, the Danish expeditionary forces were pursued north by Bernadotte, who had changed allegiance since the French and Spaniards were at Fyn and was now at the head of 40,000 Swedish, Russian and German troops. The Danes were fatally involved in the French disaster and on January 1, 1814, King Frederik VI was forced to sign the Peace of Kiel, by which treaty Norway was taken from Denmark and given to Sweden. This dissolution of a four-hundred-year-old union reduced Denmark to one-seventh of its former size, and its population from two and a half to one and a half million. The formerly mighty empire became a small kingdom. When Hans Andersen was demobilized a week after the signing of the treaty, he was still a private who had seen no action save retreat, and at the cost of his health had gained only a smattering of German and a taste for travel.

There seemed nothing for him to do but return to his cobbler's last. Father and son resumed their readings and games and at first it seemed as if all was to be much as before in the Andersen household. When Hans Andersen heard his son use the German word *Besen* for broom in the 'kind of gibberish' he had invented for his plays, he laughed and said he was glad someone had benefited from his travels. He added, 'Goodness knows whether you will ever go so far afield, Hans Christian, but you *must*,' at which Anne-Marie asserted that as long as she had any say in the matter Hans Christian would stay at home and keep his health. A stay-at-home life was not what the cobbler dreamed of for his only child, and as the father's own health declined, his preoccupation with his son's future increased. Once he said to Anne-Marie, 'No matter what the boy wants to be, if it is the silliest thing in the world, let him have his own way.' He himself had seldom had his own way, and as he lay brooding over the past he became unable to distinguish between facts and fancies, history and legend. His hero-worship of Napoleon survived Waterloo and he was still talking of the Emperor in 1816, although by that time a Danish contingent was sharing in the Allied occupation of the new France of Louis XVIII.

When at last the cobbler became delirious and thought that he was receiving orders from Napoleon in person, Anne-Marie sent

Hans Christian running to consult the wise-woman who lived two miles outside Odense. The wise-woman questioned the boy, measured his arm, made occult signs over him and laid against his breast a green twig from 'a tree of the kind on which Christ was crucified'. She believed in *Doppelgängers* and told him to go home by way of the river: 'If your father is about to die you will meet his ghost.' The return journey was a nightmare for the emotional, superstitious child, and although he met no one, every creaking branch or shifting shadow seemed to presage a ghost. His father died three days later.

The night after Hans Andersen's death his body was laid out on the bed that still bore traces of mourning crape from Count Trampe's funeral. Mother and child lay on the floor beside it. Their vigil was shared by a cricket that chirped all night. Once Anne-Marie told it, 'You need not call him, he's dead, the Ice Maiden has taken him', and Hans Christian remembered a winter day when his father had shown him a pattern in the hoar frost on the window-pane. It suggested a girl with outstretched arms and the sick man had said jokingly, 'She must have come for me.' The Ice Maiden was very real to Hans Christian, who later described her as 'the slayer, the crusher . . . half the mighty ruler of the rivers, half a child of the air'.

Some of the neighbours who came to view the body noticed three scratches on it and declared that Satan must have made them in retaliation for the dead man's disbelief in him. This pious flummery only increased the grief with which Hans Christian followed his father's coffin to St Canute's and saw him buried just outside the left-hand door from the altar, a good position for seeing St Canute arise in majesty on the day of resurrection. Then he helped his grandmother to plant roses on her son's grave; but before long these flowers were choked by the growing grass.

Immediately after his father's death Hans Christian was left much to himself. Anne-Marie was by any standards a devoted mother and, although illiterate, had the wit to recognize something unusual in her son, but she did not understand him as his father had done. Apart from running errands and helping his mother, the boy had plenty of time to himself, and as he missed his father his inner life centred on the toy theatre his father had made for him, the plays he had read with his father. By this time he was familiar with all the books in his home and longed for more. These were presently lent to him by Mrs Bunkeflod, a parson's widow who lived across the street with her sister-in-law. Both these kindly, educated gentlewomen took a fancy to the odd little boy who would close his eyes when day-dreaming and tell endless stories in a voice that then, as later, had a particular charm in its soft slurred Fyn accents. They asked him to sing and read aloud and invited him to come and visit them whenever he liked, which soon came to mean every day.

It was in the Bunkeflods' little house that Hans Christian first heard poetry spoken of as something sacred. The late parson had written popular verse and the way his widow and sister cherished this work made the boy feel that to be a poet was 'a glorious and happy thing'. The Bunkeflods introduced him to Shakespeare, whom he found even more enthralling than Holberg. The melodramatic scenes were what first attracted him, the witches, ghosts and sword-thrusts. The three weird sisters chanting around their cauldron, the ghost in the sea-mists of Elsinore Castle, mad King Lear on the heath, were soon as real to him as his own dreams, and stimulated him to write a play of his own, a tremendous tragedy in which everyone died. The plot, like many used by Shakespeare, was not original but built around an ancient story, in this case the Babylonian story of the star-crossed lovers Pyramus and Thisbe. For good measure he added a garrulous hermit and his son who both loved Thisbe and killed themselves, in full view of the audience, on hearing of her death. Hans Christian called his tragedy *Abor and Elvira* and could scarcely wait to read it to friends and neighbours.

Some of them were disarmed by his he-that-hath-ears-to-hear-let-him-hear attitude, but one candid neighbour was so put out by the hermit's grandiloquence that she said, '*Abor and Elvira* – a perch and a cod (*Aborre og Torsk*) you mean.' This thoroughly annoyed Anne-Marie, who retaliated with 'She only says that because it's not her own son that has done it', but it distressed Hans Christian, who was always more easily cast down by censure than uplifted by praise. He did not, however, consider for a

41

moment stopping writing. Sixty years later a list of twenty-five titles for plays that he had planned as a child was found in his father's old military pay-book. These included *Zemire from Bagda, The Two Murderers* and *The Evening Promenade, or The Cook and the Count*. The play that he wrote immediately after *Abor and Elvira* concerned a king and a princess. This presented him with a technical problem. In Shakespeare's plays royalty spoke in much the same way as commoners, but Hans Christian could not believe they did so in fact. He questioned his mother and several other people about this, but their answers were tantalizingly vague. It was a long time, they said, since a king had come to Odense, and royalty probably spoke a foreign language. (The Court did in fact speak German.) With the help of a dictionary Hans Christian invented a personal Esperanto and soon had the princess greeting the king with '*Guten Morgen, mon père, har De godt sleeping?*' No sooner was it finished than he rushed forth to share his delight: 'It was a profound joy for me to read aloud and it never occurred to me that it could be anything but a pleasure for everyone to listen.'

Before long censorious neighbours complained that Hans Christian was idling his time away. The boy next door, they pointed out, had been put to work in a cloth mill and brought home weekly wages. Anne-Marie was persuaded to send Hans Christian to the mill, 'not for the sake of the money but so that I can know where he is', a remark that suggests that, like the boy's maternal grandmother, she did not consider him as ordinary working-class material. Her anxiety as to her son's future, and the probability of his indeed wanting to be 'the silliest thing in the world', may have been strengthened by a visit she received about this time from her illegitimate half-sister, Christiane Sørensen, a woman of suspiciously showy appearance who lived in Copenhagen. She gave Hans Christian a silver coin, but Anne-Marie was so irritated by her half-sister's blatant display of finery and its probable source that the two women quickly fell to quarrelling. This made Anne-Marie want more than ever to keep Hans Christian to herself, but she was not entirely successful in this, for his half-sister Karen Marie was later to play a disturbing part in his life.

The first time Hans Christian set out to work at the cloth mill his paternal grandmother accompanied him. She hated the idea of his having to 'mix with rough boys' and urged him to remember her noble ancestress in Kassel. At first, however, all went smoothly. Most of the workers were German, their obscene jokes made little impression on Hans Christian, and when they discovered that he had a beautiful voice they kept him singing while they worked and other boys performed his tasks. Spurred on by their enthusiasm, he told them that he could also act and proceeded to recite scenes from Holberg and Shakespeare. There was no music-while-you-work in those days, so the boy's performance was a godsend to men working long hours at monotonous tasks. One day when several of his mates were discussing the pitch and purity of his voice, someone said jeeringly that with a voice like that he must be a girl. Several of them held Hans Christian down while they investigated. The outraged boy raced home and his mother agreed that he must leave the mill.

His next job was in a small factory that turned out snuff and chewing-tobacco. Here he got on well with everyone, and again his singing was in great demand. When he had sung all the songs he knew he began improvising new ones. Several of his mates told him he was a born actor, thus encouraging his natural inclinations, for he could scarcely remember a time when plays and the theatre had not obsessed him. He was as hungry for art as his father had been for education. Presently he fell ill, and Anne-Marie concluded that the tobacco dust was damaging his lungs and took him away from the factory. As soon as he recovered he resumed his visits across the street, where Mrs Bunkeflod would read aloud while he sewed clothes for his puppets. In gratitude he made Mrs Bunkeflod a white satin pin-cushion for her birthday. She treasured this and today it can be seen, yellowed by time, in the Hans Christian Andersen Museum, between a picture of Mrs Bunkeflod's house and one of the school-teacher Mr Carstens and his wife.

About this time he made the acquaintance of a parson's wife who asked him to read aloud to her from her lending-library books. He was deeply impressed by her powers of literary judgment. Once, after he had read the opening sentence of a novel,

'It was a tempestuous night and rain was beating against the window panes', she said, 'This is a delightful book, I can tell right from the start.' Reading increased his longing to see more of the world. He remembered his father saying after his own ill-starred army venture, 'Goodness knows whether you will ever go so far afield, Hans Christian, but you *must*.' He was delighted, therefore, when harvest-time came and his mother took him on a trip to her birthplace, Bogense, on the north-west coast of Fyn, opposite Fredericia in Jutland. The two days' walk across their beautiful garden-like island was a treat for them both and developed Hans Christian's feeling for even the most common-place details of the countryside, from thistles, dandelions, the wild flowers of ditch and hedgerow and 'great burdock leaves . . . some so tall that little children stand upright beneath the biggest of them' to a hawthorn-tree seen in a field a mile from Bogense and described by him in detail twenty years later.

Anne-Marie was sorely in need of a holiday. She was a middle-aged woman and since her husband's death she had worked harder than ever. All weathers found her scrubbing other people's dirty linen in the river. She was tormented by rheumatism and caught one cold after another, for which she was advised to take juniper drops in brandy, a remedy that was to turn her eventually into a drunkard. Hans Christian was to say nothing of this in his autobiography, in many ways as secretive a book as it appears to be candid, but when asked, twenty years after his mother's death, what had inspired his story *She Was Good for Nothing*, he said: 'It has its origin in a few words that I heard my mother say when I was a child. One day when I had seen a boy hurrying down to the washing place at the Odense river, where his mother stood in the water and washed her linen, I heard a widow, noted for her frankness, call out from her window and scold the boy: "Are you going down again with liquor to your mother? That's disgraceful! Shame! Never let me see you become like your mother, she's good for nothing!" I came home and told what I had seen. They all said, "Yes, the old washerwoman drinks, she's good for nothing!" Only my mother took her part. "Don't judge her so harshly," she said, "the poor woman works and toils, stands in the cold water, and gets no hot meals for days at a time. She must have something to help her bear up. Of course it's not the best thing for her to take, but she has nothing better. She has gone through a great deal. She is honest, takes good care of her little boy, and keeps him looking neat." My mother's gentle speech made a deep impression on me since I, as well as others, thought ill of the washerwoman. Many years after, another incident led me to think how easily men judge harshly, where it would be just as easy to show kindness . . . My mother's words were fresh in my mind when I wrote the story *She Was Good for Nothing*.'

The trip across Fyn with her son was one of the rare happy interludes in Anne-Marie's middle years. Whether she visited her mother and her own illegitimate daughter is not recorded, but she had a standing invitation from the lady of a manor house near Bogense where she had once been in service, and all the way there she was pointing out landmarks to Hans Christian, who treasured every detail. They were made welcome at the manor, given delicious food, and while they helped pick the hops they listened to the peasants' stories of ghosts, omens and the Devil with his cloven hoof. Hans Christian was particularly struck by an old woman who said that God not only knew all that had ever happened in the past, but could foresee the future. He thought so much about this that in the evening he went by himself to a deep pond to test God's omniscience. God might have decided that Hans Christian was to live to be an old man, but what if he jumped into the pond now and drowned? He ran near to where the water was deepest, but at the last minute decided it was the Devil who was tempting him and rushed indoors, crying wildly but quite incapable of telling his mother or anyone else what was the matter. They concluded he must have seen a ghost and soon he almost believed them.

This was the last trip mother and son made alone together before Anne-Marie married again in 1818.

Anne-Marie's second husband, Niels Jørgensen Gundersen, was, like Hans Christian's father, a free master-cobbler much younger than herself. Little else is recorded of him except that he had brown eyes, a good temper, and came of a family of artisans who felt that he had married beneath him and therefore refused to meet his wife and stepson. The opposite of a Mr Murdstone, he showed no interest in Hans Christian's education, yet the marriage was a turning-point in the boy's life as the family then moved from the only home he could remember to a little house farther down Munkemøllestræde that possessed a narrow strip of garden with gooseberry- and red-currant-bushes and a path that led down to the Odense river and the water-mill, which were to be the scenes of his first successful exploits as a public entertainer.

By this time Hans Christian had collected a ragbag of scraps of cloth and silk and he loved to sit out between the bushes making clothes for his puppets. Anne-Marie encouraged this pastime as she thought it showed him to be a born tailor. She urged him to consider the enviable position of Mr Stegmann, the finest tailor in Odense, who owned a shop on Korsgade with big glass windows through which his apprentices could be seen sitting cross-legged on a table at their sewing. Hans Christian heartily disliked this picture and for the first time admitted that he wanted to be an actor. Anne-Marie, to whom the word actor meant tumblers, tight-rope walkers and poor strolling players, was horrified. She told her son that if he became an actor people would not only starve him to keep his weight down and force him to drink oil to make him supple but would also whip him. The boy's inner purpose nevertheless remained firm, and in the meantime he consoled himself with the thought that if he were forced to be a tailor's apprentice he would at least be able to pick up scraps of material for his toy theatre.

Now that he lived beside it, the river provided him with an eventful outdoor theatre. He would stand on the bank, poised among the alder-trees, waiting for the sluice-gates to close. As soon as the mill's three great wheels stopped turning the water would sink with dramatic effect, leaving pools full of agitated fish that were instantly surrounded by sleek water-rats rushing out of the mill for a quick drink. Immediately Hans Christian would leap down on to the river bed among the fish and water-rats, so interested by the spectacle that every now and again he was caught down there when the mill's wheels began to turn again. Then he would streak up the bank 'as frightened as amber gatherers on the North Sea coast when they are a long way out and the tide turns'. More important (for his future), he would stand in the evenings on one of the flat stones that Anne-Marie used as scrubbing-boards and sing improvised songs.

He sang out of the joy given him by his incandescent imagination, a joy so great that it had to find immediate expression; but he also sang to be heard. As with his plays, he longed for an audience, without which he instinctively felt that his joy was incomplete. An old washerwoman had told him that the Emperor of China lived under the Odense river and Hans Christian fully expected the Emperor to rise from the waters one moonlit night, and, in return for his songs, take him down to his palace beneath the water and load him with treasures with which, once back in Odense, he would build a castle. The Emperor's palace was as vividly real to him as the one he was to describe years later in *The Nightingale*: 'The Emperor's palace was the wonder of the world. It was made entirely of porcelain, extremely expensive but so delicate that you could touch it only with the greatest of care. In the garden the rarest flowers bloomed, and to the prettiest ones were tied little silver bells which tinkled so that no one could pass by them without noticing them.' To expedite matters Hans Christian made many drawings of his own future castle. The Emperor of China proved dilatory, however, and his role was temporarily assumed by the boy's next-door neighbours, by whom his own tinkling did not pass unnoticed.

The little garden of which Hans Christian was so fond was next to the large garden of a Privy Councillor, Mr Falbe, whose wife had been before her marriage a well-known actress at the Royal Theatre in Copenhagen. The Falbes often entertained artists from the capital and they were first amused, then charmed, by the beautiful voice of the washerwoman's son. They christened him 'the little nightingale', and presently local notabilities began to invite him to sing in their drawing-rooms. Hans Christian accepted his audience's admiration as innocently as the child Mozart had done, and though exuberantly grateful, was no more surprised than he would have been by a moonlit visit from the Emperor of China.

Enough is as good as a feast was never one of his mottoes and

before long he was offering his patrons readings and recitations as
well as songs. One evening, while performing at the Bishop's
palace, he aroused the interest of Colonel Högh-Guldberg, the
forty-year-old commander-in-chief of Fyn and Jutland, a well-
educated and imaginative man. The Colonel thought that, far
from benefiting from such experiences, Hans Christian was in
danger of being spoilt for the temporary amusement of adults.
He therefore invited the boy to his home, lent him books and
impressed upon him that no matter what he wanted to become, he
must first study seriously. When the Colonel thought his admonitions had made sufficient impression, he took Hans Christian to
see Prince Christian, the twenty-eight-year-old Governor of Fyn,
who was cousin to the reigning King Frederik VI. 'If the Prince
should ask you what you want to do,' the Colonel had told his
protégé, 'you must say that you long to attend the Odense
Grammar School.' Hans Christian obeyed, but without conviction. When it came to hiding his feelings he was a very bad actor
indeed, and on this occasion he was wildly excited by his first
meeting with a flesh-and-blood Prince (who spoke 'just like
anyone else' and not in *'Guten Morgen, mon père, har De godt
sleeping?'* language) and with his first sight of the inside of the
castle, of which he had heard from his mother who sometimes
went there to help with the washing. Whatever the reasons, the
Prince thought the boy impractical and, after pointing out that
his singing and reciting were very pleasant parlour-tricks but
certainly did not denote genius and that schooling required time
and money, offered to help him learn a trade such as cabinet-
making.

Hans Christian thought no better of this than of his mother's
suggestion that he should become a tailor, and could not even
give it his full attention, so busy was he storing up impressions of
the castle. He particularly noticed the royal housekeeper, who
was twenty-six years later to make a delightful appearance as the
crow in *The Snow Queen*. Despite the failure of this interview,
Colonel Högh-Guldberg and the local gentry continued to make
a fuss of him. His recitals earned him praise, sweetmeats, fruit,
and an occasional tip that went into his money-box, which, like
that of most Danish children, was an earthenware pig with a slit

in its back. There was clearly no chance of his going to the Grammar School.

Meanwhile he was growing fast and his unusual height was at variance not only with his youth but with the childish outlook that made him react immediately to whatever captured his imagination as if, for all the eager impatience that characterized him, there was no yesterday, no tomorrow, only an all-embracing here and now. Anne-Marie realized that he must stop wasting his time with his theatre, his songs and his almost perpetual day-dreaming – yet for all her poverty she sent him not to another wage-earning job but to the Workhouse Charity School. Here Hans Christian's spelling remained deplorable and unfortunately – since he would later have to spend a painful period correcting his faults – his excellent memory enabled him to dispense with homework. He learned his lessons while walking to school and cared only for the education he was giving himself through borrowed books. So great was his longing for books that he would ask strangers to lend them to him. He must have been extraordinarily persuasive, for no one ever refused him, and so careful was he with books that most of the lenders freely offered him more.

Although he continued to spend much of his time at school in day-dreaming, he would listen enraptured during Bible classes. The teacher, a Norwegian of violent disposition who was supposedly related to the poet Welhaven, told the sacred stories so vividly that the crude Biblical pictures on the classroom walls seemed to Hans Christian to be inspired works of art. Presently, stimulated by these lessons, he began to tell his schoolfellows stories of his own invention, in which he himself played a leading part. This, and the fact that he was reported to 'mix with the gentry', aroused jeers and jealousy among the boys. Once they chased him through the streets as they often chased his mad grandfather.

Anne-Marie was phenomenally tolerant of her son's odd ways, so long as they did not remind her of his grandfather's insanity or his father's senseless soldiering; but she had no idea what was in Hans Christian's mind and he scarcely knew himself. She still hoped to apprentice him to a tailor after his confirmation, and was troubled by the fact that while his gifts for singing, acting, poetry and drawing always aroused amused interest in the gentry, yet they seemed to her own friends to be merely symptoms of a mental disability likely to hamper him in the exercise of some rational job such as tailoring. She remembered her late husband's words, 'No matter what the boy wants to be, if it is the silliest thing in the world, let him have his own way,' but the neighbours quoted this as further proof of insanity on that side of the family.

Hans Christian listened good-temperedly to unsolicited advice without for an instant ceasing to think of the theatre as the world for which he was destined. No seventeenth-century French noble-man was more solicitous of *gloire* than this poor provincial Danish child who dreamed, as John was to do in his story *The Travelling Companion*, that: 'He saw the sun and the moon bow down to him. He saw his father well again and strong, and heard him laughing as he always laughed when he was happy.' The summer before his confirmation some actors and singers from the Royal Theatre, Copenhagen, came to perform in Odense. Anne-Marie had neither money nor desire for tickets, but thanks to his friend the poster-distributor Hans Christian was able to see the first per-formance from the wings of the stage. His overwhelming admira-tion for them and their calling amused the actors, who adopted him as a mascot and allowed him first to walk on as a shepherd, then to speak two lines as one of the red-clad pages in *Cinderella*. Beside himself with excitement, he was already dressed for his part long before the professional actors reached the theatre.

All over Odense the actors' visit was the chief topic of con-versation. Again and again Hans Christian heard people wish that they might go to the wonderful theatre in Copenhagen where, according to the envied minority that had been there, something even better than a play or an opera could be seen, something called a ballet. For the first time Hans Christian heard of a ballet-dancer, Madame Schall, who was, he was told, the 'idol of Copenhagen'. With his freedom from almost all sense of what was or was not possible, he began to dream that Madame Schall might help him to fame and fortune.

In the meantime he had to be confirmed. In the parish of

St Canute there were at that time two confirmation classes, one held by Dean Tetens for the gentry's children and one by the curate for the poor. The division was a matter of custom, not of law, and as he had often envied the Grammar School boys their many books and wide choice of professions, Hans Christian submitted his name for the Dean's class. It never occurred to him that he might be unwanted there and he was horrified when Dean Tetens, hearing that the boy had recited passages of Holberg at the apothecary's house, told him that as a confirmation candidate he had no business play-acting and would be expelled from the class if anything similar took place. He was plunged into misery until, after class, a fellow candidate, Miss Tønder-Lund, gave him a rose, whereupon he became as blissfully sure that he was surrounded by friends as he had a few minutes earlier felt himself a prey to enemies. The diary he kept intermittently for most of his life shows that what would be mere trifles to a person with an average nervous system – if such exists – were thunderbolts to him, with the result that he constantly oscillated between joy and anguish with almost no intermediate stages. The Dean's condemnation of his artistic exploits meant death, the young girl's rose meant life, and he responded to both with the same disquietingly whole-hearted emotion.

As the date for his confirmation drew near, his mother altered a brown coat of his father's for him and gave him his first pair of top-boots. To his delight the boots squeaked; no one could fail to notice that they were new. When confirmation Sunday came he tucked his trousers inside the tops of his precious boots and went to church squeaking with all his might and hoping that all the congregation would hear him. Then, aware of the solemnity of the occasion, he was dismayed to find himself thinking as much of his boots as of the promise he was about to make to renounce the Devil and all his works. He begged God to forgive him, but a minute later was again captivated by his boots. It was the memory of this struggle of conscience that, twenty-six years later, made him write the scene of Karen's confirmation in *The Red Shoes*: 'Every eye was turned towards her feet. When she walked up the aisle to the chancel of the church, it seemed to her as if even those portraits of bygone ministers and their wives, in starched ruffs and long black gowns – even they fixed their eyes upon her red shoes. She could think of nothing else, even when the pastor laid his hands upon her head and spoke of her holy baptism and her covenant with God, and her duty as a Christian. The solemn organ rolled, the children sang sweetly, and the old choir-leader sang too, but Karen thought of nothing except her red shoes.'

When Hans Christian's confirmation was over Anne-Marie began once more to insist he be apprenticed to a tailor. This prospect appalled him. He had never really taken it seriously. His sense of time was, and in many ways always remained, that of a child. So long as the threat of having to sit cross-legged in the tailor's window concerned only his distant future he had paid little heed to it. Confronted with this prospect in the present tense, he was panic-stricken. In his usual demonstrative way he wept and pleaded with his mother. When that proved useless, he took action. He smashed his earthenware pig money-box and discovered that he possessed what seemed to him a fortune, thirteen rigsdalers. With this he could seek fame in Copenhagen. He remembered that when the actors from the Royal Theatre were in Odense they often called on a local printer, Mr Iversen. Immediately he decided to ask Mr Iversen, whom he had never met, for an introduction to Madame Schall the ballet-dancer. Then, he thought, God would do the rest. Hans Christian never hesitated to make demands on God, but nor did he forget that God helps those who help themselves.

Iversen received the boy kindly and listened patiently before saying that in his opinion the proposed journey to Copenhagen would be nothing but a wild-goose chase. It would really be wiser, he assured the boy, for him to learn a trade. 'That would be a shame!' said Hans Christian, speaking with such extraordinary conviction that, according to Iversen's family, the printer wondered if the boy might not be right after all. Right or wrong, he obtained his letter of introduction to Madame Schall and was more convinced than ever that a new heaven and a new earth were to be found in Copenhagen.

Anne-Marie was distracted. What, she asked, would become of him in Copenhagen? But Hans Christian had ears only for stories of poor boys who left home to become famous. He remembered his father's stories of Napoleon, the little corporal, and told his mother, 'I shall become famous, that's the way it goes. First one has to endure terrible adversity, then one becomes famous.' He seemed so sure of himself that Anne-Marie began to yield. She consulted the wise-woman. 'Your son will become a great man,' the old woman prophesied; 'one day all Odense will be illuminated in his honour.' This, combined with her late husband's injunction to let the child do what he wished, no matter how silly, convinced Anne-Marie.

When neighbours protested against a boy of fourteen being allowed to venture so far from home, his mother said she had only consented because she felt sure that he would change his mind long before he reached the coast and saw the sea, the Great Belt between Fyn and the island of Zealand. Whether or not she had faith in his undertaking, she continued to make preparations for his journey. She did not understand him as his father had done but she was proud of him, and it was probably the robust quality inherited from her that gave Hans Christian, so dependent on affection, the strength of purpose required to leave home and face the unknown. Throughout his life there was a striking contrast between his extreme nervous dread of trifles and his fearlessness on great occasions.

The driver of the mail-coach to Nyborg agreed to pick the boy up outside the city gate of St Jørgen's. All the other Odense passengers would have taken their seats by then and Hans Christian could be slipped in as an extra passenger at the cut rate of three rigsdalers, on condition that he left the coach at Frederiksberg castle just outside Copenhagen. And so it was that on September 3, 1819, Hans Christian set out to seek his fortune armed with the money from his earthenware pig, his toy theatre, a bundle of clothes, bread for the journey, and above all, as strong a belief in his own destiny as Aladdin's in his magic lamp.

For Anne-Marie the walk to the mail-coach was the beginning of a tragic end. At fifty-two she was already an old woman. Her second husband could not earn enough for them to live without her going out to work, and she knew she could do nothing for Hans Christian in Odense beyond forcing him into an apprenticeship; yet without her son she would have nothing to look forward to but a life of drudgery, nothing but alcohol to keep out the many kinds of cold.

Hans Christian's grandmother was waiting for them at the city gate. She felt sure that her grandson would redeem the family honour by his achievements, and she looked forward to seeing him rise in the world, perhaps even to a clerkship. Her hair had turned grey and when at last, four years later, Hans Christian brought good news of himself to his home town, his grandmother was dead and buried in a pauper's grave. Like John in his own story *The Travelling Companion*, Hans Christian 'turned round for one more look at the old church where as a baby he had been baptized, and where he had gone with his father every Sunday to sing. High up, in one of the belfry windows, he saw the little church goblin with his pointed red cap raising one arm to keep the sun out of his eyes. John nodded goodbye to him and the little goblin raised his red cap to him . . .' The moment of parting was one of anguish and all three wept that autumn morning as the boy climbed into the mail-coach and waved goodbye to the town he was never to enter again except as a visitor. Hans Christian's first childhood was over. From now onwards Andersen was on his own.

2. *Adolescence in Copenhagen*

1819-22

. . . Look alive, and don't turn your toes in! A well-bred duckling turns its toes out, like father and mother . . . That's it! Now make a bow and say 'quack'!

Hans Christian Andersen, *The Ugly Duckling*

. . . there are a lot of halfway people in this world who help the winners win, and the failers fail. If a man stumbles, there's plenty of people to push him down. But if he's like 'the youth who bore', those same people are foreordained to help him along. They may hate to, worse than blazes, and they may do a lot of cussin' about it, but they have to help the winners and they can't dodge it. It's a natural law, like what keeps the big clock up there going, little wheels and big, and no mix up.

Willa Cather, *The Song of the Lark*

*

TODAY the trip from Odense to Copenhagen takes only four hours, but in 1819 the fourteen-year-old Andersen had a two-and-a-half days' journey ahead of him. Despite tears and loneliness, he still believed in 'all the splendid things he would see in the fine big world ahead of him' and when at last they reached the sea he did not, as his mother had expected, turn back. Nevertheless, he felt dreadfully lonely as he boarded the ship that was to carry him away from the island of his birth to a world as fabulous to him as his Emperor of China's porcelain palace. His spirits rose during the crossing, and when, early next morning, he saw the fifteenth-century fortifications of Korsør on the coast of Zealand his first impulse was to pray, and in his autobiography he writes, 'In fear and pain I cannot pray to God, but in joy, and when things go well with me, He is near me; then I can pray.'

From the port of Korsør he travelled by mail-coach across the island of Zealand, through forests and pastureland, past cities,

55

villages, castles and moated manor houses. A born traveller, he was as interested in people as in places and soon made friends with a fellow passenger, a Mrs Hermansen of Copenhagen, who was returning home after employment in Odense as a wet-nurse. Anne-Marie had spoken to her at St Jørgen's Gate and asked her to keep an eye on the boy during the journey. Always ready to like and confide in people at the slightest encouragement, Andersen had told Mrs Hermansen of all his plans, including his eventual castle, long before the mail-coach was within sight of the copper spires of Copenhagen. In return she gave him her address in case he should need help. In his autobiography he dwells only on the kindness of Mrs Hermansen, but as an old man he told a young friend about a Mrs Olsen, apparently another name for the same fellow passenger, who asked him to deliver a blackmailing letter for her in Copenhagen. There are traces of this episode, and of his first encounter with the underworld of the capital, in his fourth novel, *The Two Baronesses*.

Frederiksberg Park, where he left the mail-coach, was on the Sun Hill, so-called because for thousands of years sun-worshippers had annually assembled there. Even today people still go out to the Sun Hill on Whit Sunday to greet the sun as it appears three hours after midnight. To see this brings good luck, as the sun is popularly supposed to dance for joy on the horizon on this occasion. In the middle of the park was a seventeenth-century Renaissance castle built by King Christian IV, famous for his building and for his heroism and celebrated by the Danish lyric poet Ewald in a poem that became the Danish national anthem. Since 1660 all the kings of the House of Oldenburg, which had ruled Denmark since the fifteenth century, had been crowned at Frederiksberg. In a daze of excitement Andersen walked all round this palace before he set off down an avenue of linden trees towards Copenhagen.

Founded in the twelfth century on the site of a fishing village, Copenhagen (Købnhavn – Merchants' Haven) was then protected by five miles of massive stone ramparts planted with trees and windmills and surrounded by a deep moat where people skated in winter. Each of its four city gates was guarded by a sergeant who checked the mail-coach passenger lists. These were sent to King Frederik VI, as were the keys to the city after the gates were locked at midnight. The king was reputed to sleep with the keys under his pillow. Big cities, by today's standards, did not become a commonplace in Europe until after 1870, and in 1819 Copenhagen's population of 110,000 was small compared with that of Paris, which was 890,000, or London, already over a million. Nowhere was Copenhagen more than two miles long by one and a quarter miles broad, and as the harbour, docks, several islands and a web of waterways were an integral part of the city, its noblest palaces and churches rose in neighbourly fashion beside masts and sails. Grassy alleys, canalside walks and spacious public places were like so many open-air clubs, most of whose members knew each other at least by sight. Søren Kierkegaard, who was born in Copenhagen in 1812 and loved to walk and talk in its streets, later wrote that Copenhagen was singularly fortunate in being large enough for a real city yet small enough for the individual to retain an importance denied him in a conglomeration where 'it takes a dozen people to make one man'.

To Andersen, however, it was an immense city. Its lofty houses, some of them six storeys high, were skyscrapers to him. He handed over his passport, deposited his bundle at the Guards' Inn, a simple lodging-house near the western city gate that had been recommended to him by fellow passengers, and rushed out to see the Royal Theatre. No pilgrim ever drew near a sanctuary with more solemn rapture than that with which Andersen approached the Royal Theatre. Kongens Nytorv (the King's New Market-place) where the theatre stood was barely ten minutes' walk from the western city gate, and Andersen's joy was so intense and everything so strange to him that he supposed the rowdy crowds, the sounds of breaking glass and the presence of soldiers on horseback were merely normal manifestations of life in the capital.

Only later did he learn that what he had seen was a riot against the Jews. The disease of antisemitism had spread to Copenhagen from Germany, a not-yet-united Germany which at this time consisted of eighty-three loosely grouped sovereign states and free cities. The defeat of Napoleon, the withdrawal of French troops and the reactionary attitude of most of the returning German princelings had created a chaotic situation that had been exploited by Friedrich Ludwig Jahn, a hysterical Prussian peasant with a remarkable gift for inflammatory speeches. Jahn's patriotic resentment of the French had developed into a pathological hatred of all foreigners ('wild beasts') and he wanted Germany to revive the imaginary medieval glories of the Hohenstaufen. To prepare German youth for its mission, he founded a Gymnastic Association to develop healthy minds in healthy bodies. (Jahn was sometimes quaintly called the Father of Gymnastics.) A scapegoat is essential in such cases, and since Napoleon had given the German Jews the same rights as their fellow citizens, Jahn accused the Jews of 'cosmopolitanism', always a firebrand word to the illiterate. Jew-baiting, torchlight processions, book-burning and organized spying on fellow gymnasts were all part of the Association's character-building activities. When Jahn was imprisoned by the Prussian government in 1819, rioting followed and spread outside Germany. The quickly suppressed demonstration that Andersen saw in Copenhagen was mostly a matter of shop-windows being broken by rival tradesmen and hooligans; nevertheless, when told at the inn what had happened he was shocked and frightened. He had gone to school with Jewish children and could only too easily identify himself with the persecuted.

At the time, however, he walked through the noisy crowds thinking only of where he was going. When at last he reached the theatre he walked round it again and again and 'regarded the whole building as a home which was not yet open to me'. His reverence for the Royal Theatre, which was famous all over Europe for the excellence of its acting and the magnificence of its scenery, was an extreme form of a feeling common to the entire Danish nation. Unlike other small countries where playgoers had to rely mostly on translations and adaptations, Denmark possessed a truly national theatre. Drama, opera and ballet were performed there and the theatre's motto was '*Ej blot til Dyst* – Not for amusement only'. The actors, who were engaged for life after a rigorous apprenticeship in the theatre's own training-school and guaranteed a pension on retirement, were admired national figures and a directorship of the Royal Theatre was one of the most illustrious positions in Denmark.

The emotion with which Andersen walked around the theatre, hardly able to believe that he had arrived here at last and had only to stretch out his hands to touch the magical walls, was so excessive as to attract the attention of a street-corner vendor who sarcastically offered him a theatre ticket. Supposing this to be an instance of unsolicited generosity – just what he would have expected in this hallowed spot – Andersen burst into enthusiastic thanks, whereupon the vendor, thinking this hobbledehoy was trying to give him tit for tat, chased him away from the theatre with a stream of abuse.

After a night at the Guards' Inn, Andersen decided to use his letter of introduction to Madame Schall. Determined to look his best, he wore his confirmation suit and boots and his top-hat, which was so big that it almost covered his eyes. He asked the way to the ballerina's house, and before ringing the bell knelt down and prayed God to help him. A maidservant who was on her way out with her shopping-basket smiled at him and put a coin into his hand. This bewildered him. It did not occur to him that anyone so well dressed as he was could possibly be mistaken for a beggar. So he tried to return the coin, but the maid told him to keep it and tripped away. He rang the bell and, thanks to his letter, was admitted to see the beautiful Madame Schall herself.

The dancer was taken completely by surprise. She had no recollection of having ever met Iversen, and as she was over forty she knew far too much about hardship in the theatre to encourage false hopes in the stage-struck. Yet she found herself listening patiently to Andersen's excited story of his past, present and future hopes. Then, thinking that as she was a dancer she must want to see what he was worth in that line, he asked permission to take off his boots and, using his unwieldy top-hat as a tambourine, he proceeded to give a very personal rendering of one of the dances he had watched when he played the part of a page in *Cinderella*. Determined to give full value, he accompanied himself with a song:

> What do riches mean to me,
> What are pomp and pageantry?

The Wild Swan

It would have required an Edward Lear to discern any poetry in that prancing pelican and Madame Schall concluded, so she herself told Andersen later, that he must be out of his mind. Her discouragement reduced the boy to tears but he would not admit defeat. As he pulled on his boots he repeated how much he loved the theatre and offered to work for the dancer as an errand-boy. Madame Schall did not want an errand-boy, wanted indeed only to get rid of this oddly inspired scarecrow; instead she found herself telling him that he might eat at her house now and again, and that she would speak to the ballet-master about him. This was quite enough to make the child that Andersen still was believe himself already a member in good standing of the glorious world of the theatre.

In addition to giving Andersen a letter to Madame Schall, the printer Iversen had advised him to try to see Knud Lyne Rahbek, an influential poet, editor, critic and Professor of Aesthetics who was on the board of the Royal Theatre. Although only fifty-nine years old, Rahbek already ranked as one of the Grand Old Men of contemporary Danish letters. His wife Kamma was charming and popular too, so their house, Bakkehuset, overlooking the Sound out towards Frederiksberg, had become the rallying-point for most of the leading Danish writers. Andersen found his way there on foot. His long legs, so often jeeringly likened by his school-fellows to a stork's, were very useful now that he needed to walk even more than to sing for his supper.

That Rahbek did not refuse to see an unknown boy from the provinces who had no letter of introduction and merely wanted to become an actor, tells us a great deal not only about Andersen's tenacity of purpose but about the simplicity and good will of Danish social life and the esteem in which the theatre was held. Like Madame Schall, Rahbek listened patiently to the boy's story, then advised him to see Count Holstein, a director of the Royal Theatre.

Andersen strode back from Bakkehuset to Count Holstein, only to find the latter more categorically discouraging than Madame Schall or Professor Rahbek. The Count began by bluntly pointing out that no matter how talented the boy might be, he was far too thin to be an actor. Andersen quickly answered that he would soon put on weight if he could earn enough to buy nourishing food, but he could find no answer to the Count's objection that the Royal Theatre engaged only actors who had had some formal education. He had found something to encourage him in Madame Schall's offer of meals and a word to the ballet-master and in Professor Rahbek's suggestion that he should try to see Count Holstein, but the latter left him in despair. He could improvise songs, stories, puppets' clothes, he could draw and make beautiful cut-outs – in Odense Museum there is a tiny rocking-chair, scarcely big enough for a young mouse, that looks as if carved in ivory but is in fact one of the countless paper toys that his big hands and clumsy-looking scissors made so delicately – but for all his artistic gifts he could not improvise the kind of education now required.

Standing again outside the Royal Theatre, he was torn between thoughts of suicide and a desperate belief that God would take the matter in hand. This dilemma was temporarily solved by his suddenly noticing a playbill announcing that *Paul et Virginie* was to be given that very day at five o'clock. A queue for the cheapest seats had formed, but Andersen was just in time to get into the second row of the gallery, from which he gazed enraptured at the decorations, faded roses and smoky garlands, in the soft moving light of tall candles which were snuffed and trimmed by special attendants. The opera Andersen saw was based on the famous novel *Paul et Virginie*, published a year before the French Revolution by Bernardin de St Pierre, friend and disciple of Jean-Jacques Rousseau. As popular during the Revolution as in the last days of the old regime, *Paul et Virginie* extolled the beauties both of nature and of human nature in its pristine innocence. It had been translated all over Europe, been adapted for opera, pantomime, ballet, vaudeville and puppet-shows, and had also inspired fashions in love, clothes, jewellery and hair-styles. Hardened men and viragos who had survived war and revolution had shed tears over the sorrows of Paul and Virginia, so it was not surprising that Andersen should sob when he saw the lovers separated. Women sitting near by reminded him that it was 'only a play', and one of them gave him a sausage sandwich. Immediately convinced that he was among friends, Andersen had soon told them his life-story and explained that his tears were not only for Paul and Virginia but for himself, since the theatre itself was his Virginia and he could not bear to be separated from it. At this his new friends plied him with bread-and-butter, fruit and cake.

His situation was indeed critical. After paying his bill at the Guards' Inn he had only one rigsdaler left. Either he must return to Odense and become a tailor's apprentice and the butt of his neighbours, or else he must find work in Copenhagen, where he would be near even if not in the theatre. Of course he chose to remain, and set off with his bundle and his one remaining coin to find his travelling companion, Mrs Hermansen. She made him welcome, offered him a bed and food, and then accompanied him to a newspaper office where together they studied the offers of work. Here they noticed the name of a carpenter who was advertising for an apprentice. He lived in Boregade, a street only a few minutes' walk from the theatre, and Andersen hurried there immediately. The carpenter was forbidden by law to employ a boy who could not produce his baptism certificate and references, but he suggested that Andersen write home for these and in the meantime offered him board and lodging and a chance to find out how he liked the trade. Andersen accepted gratefully. Just then he would have welcomed any job that kept him near the Royal Theatre.

By six o'clock next morning he was in the workshop. His mates seemed cheerful and friendly, but they soon began cracking obscene jokes that Andersen understood far better than the jokes he had heard in the mill at Odense, and his obvious embarrassment incited them to turn on him. The thought of serving a nine-years' apprenticeship in that atmosphere was more than he could stand. So he went to the carpenter, thanked him for his kindness, but said he did not like the trade. His agitation was visible and although the carpenter tried to calm him, Andersen insisted on leaving then and there. Alone in the streets of Copenhagen he thought again of suicide. Indeed, considering his poor heredity, his dangerously emotional temperament and the adversity that he had to endure both before and after he became famous, it seems miraculous that he resisted his suicidal impulses. Andersen's childhood had much in common with that of his contemporary and future friend across the North Sea, Charles Dickens. Nervous and emotional, both were born to poverty and insecurity; both listened avidly to ghost stories and had a passion for the theatre; one saw his grandfather chased through the streets as a madman, the other saw his father imprisoned for bankruptcy; both at twelve years of age were given a brief foretaste of nineteenth-century factory life. Whether or not the blacking factory where Dickens worked for three months was as terrible as George Cruikshank's drawings of the London slums suggest, it is certain that Dickens felt like a little prince cast to the rabble and never forgave his parents for submitting him to an experience that marked him for the rest of his life. Andersen felt no such revolt against mill and factory as such, but his will-power was as strong as Dickens's, and because he had unconsciously decided that he was meant to be an artist, he instinctively proceeded to sing rather than spin for his supper.

Singing did indeed come to Andersen's rescue on this occasion just as it had done beside the Odense river, for as he stood thinking of ways to die he suddenly remembered having read in an Odense newspaper that an Italian, Giuseppe Siboni, had recently been made director of the Royal Singing Academy in Copenhagen. He also remembered how often his own voice had been praised by the gentry when he sang for the Emperor of China, so he decided to appeal to Siboni in person before admitting defeat. The Italian was so well known in Copenhagen that his address was easily come by, and at four o'clock that afternoon Andersen was ringing the bell of Siboni's house, No. 134 (today No. 5) Vingaardsstræde. The housekeeper told him that Siboni was at table with his guests. (Four o'clock was then the usual dinner-hour in Denmark.) In his desperation the boy poured out his story, adding that his only remaining hope was that Siboni would engage him as a singer. Gawky and grotesque though he looked, the strength and sincerity of his emotion communicated itself to the housekeeper. Accustomed to artists, she knew that oddity did not necessarily denote lack of ability, and instead of shutting the door on the suppliant, she repeated his story in the dining-room with such evident sympathy that Siboni and his guests came out to inspect the young visitor.

Giuseppe Siboni, at this time a genial man of forty, had been invited to Denmark by Prince Christian (the very prince to whom Andersen had been presented in Odense) after the Prince had heard him sing in Italy. The guests included the fifty-five-year-old Danish poet Jens Baggesen, an effervescent enthusiast who combined eighteenth-century elegance with the sensibility of the new Romantic movement. Another guest was Christoph Ernst Frederik Weyse, already a celebrated composer at the age of twenty-three. All three men had generous imaginations.

Siboni led the boy to the piano in the drawing-room and asked him to sing. This he immediately did. Everyone listened with the intentness particular to people with highly developed artistic standards. Next Andersen acted two scenes from Holberg and recited several poems. By this time he was so overwrought by contact with his first audience of sympathetic professionals – it was in fact the first time that he was judged by his peers – that at a tragic passage in his recital he burst into tears. Instead of laughter there was spontaneous applause, which drew from him more tears, of joy this time. This final result surpassed his day-dreams. Siboni promised to train his voice free of charge and said that Andersen would almost certainly find work at the Royal Theatre. Baggesen was so persuaded that the boy from Odense was going to be a great man that he begged him not to let his head be turned by his eventual success. Professor Weyse was so impressed that when Andersen left, almost incoherent with happiness, the housekeeper patted his cheek and told him to be sure to call on Weyse next day as she knew the Professor meant to do something for him.

Moved by Andersen's artless talent and vulnerability, and by recollections of his own early poverty, Weyse persuaded friends to join him in putting up some money to give the boy a chance. Seventy rigsdalers were contributed and Weyse arranged to give Andersen ten of these a month, while Siboni offered free meals at his house on top of singing lessons.

Andersen immediately sent his mother a rhapsodical letter announcing that 'all the good fortune in the world' had been granted him. Anne-Marie could scarcely believe it when the letter was read to her, then she rushed out, with a precipitancy as great as her son's, to relate this news to all who would listen. Some of her neighbours congratulated her, others wondered sceptically how it would end. This was something about which the boy himself had no doubts. Having lost his own kind and understanding father, he thought of God as essentially a Father who could produce not only theatres but miracles. Andersen's literal-minded belief in Christ's teaching, 'Ask, and it shall be given you; seek, and ye shall find; knock, and it shall be opened unto you,' had inspired him not only to take off his boots and dance for Madame Schall like David before the Ark, but to believe against all evidence to the contrary that, like little Kay in *The Snow Queen*, he was destined to be 'his own master and win the whole world and a new pair of skates'.

Mrs Hermansen helped Andersen to find cheap lodgings with a widow, Mrs Thorgesen, in Ulkegade (now Bremerholm), a narrow cobbled street of four-storey houses near the water. It was a forbidding place, especially at night when oil-lamps patterned it with flickering shadows, and was inhabited chiefly by women with faces painted as if to counteract the drabness of their surroundings. These prostitutes would greet Andersen with cheerful familiarity when he went to and from his lessons, but since he attributed this purely to friendliness on their part (and probably he was right), they did him no harm, which is more than can be said of the sordid, windowless larder off the kitchen where his landlady lodged him.

Later, back in Odense, a tutor named Krøyer spread the story that on arriving in Copenhagen Andersen had been accosted by a prostitute, who was so amused by his naïveté that she had invited him to stay in her house, which he did for several days. Whether or not there is any truth in this, it is certain that in his early days in Copenhagen he brushed shoulders with many a wolf in sheep's clothing, and several scenes in his novels show that, however naïve he was at the time, this period left him with an impression of having skirted the edge of a poisonous swamp. Indeed, in *The Book of My Life*, the manuscript of which was discovered by Hans Brix only in 1925, he uses the very word 'swamp' and reveals justified fears of being clutched and pulled down into the morass of poverty from which he only just escaped. It was probably during his first months in the capital that he looked up his mother's gaudy half-sister, Christiane Sørensen, but she would have nothing to do with him since he was for her purposes a useless nephew, not a potentially useful niece. She was reputed to be running a brothel, and had two girls living with her. Fortunately he did little but sleep in Ulkegade. Mrs Hermansen's son gave him some German lessons and he spent most of the day at Siboni's house. When he was not singing scales or listening to the opera singers – whose mistakes provoked Siboni to explosive outbursts that alarmed Andersen far more than they did the culprits – he passed hours with Siboni's Italian cook and the two gay Danish maids, one of whom spoke Italian. He ran errands for them and listened with delight to their stories. Then one day they asked him to carry a dish to the table, whereupon Siboni stormed out to the kitchen, saying that he had not invited the boy to his house to make a waiter of him. After this Andersen spent more time in the drawing-room with Siboni's niece, Marietta, who was just then painting a portrait of her uncle in his most famous part, that of Achilles in Paer's opera *Ferdinando*. As she needed a model, she called on Andersen, and very odd the thin overgrown boy must have looked dressed as a mighty Greek warrior.

Siboni was an excellent teacher who tried to develop his pupils' mastery not only of technique but of the thoughts and emotions required by their parts. Unluckily for him, he was too far ahead of the times for Copenhagen. His production of Bellini's gloriously melodious opera *La Straniera* was hissed off the stage as foreign and eccentric by people who twenty-five years later, when Siboni was dead, would have nothing but Italian opera. To Andersen, the Italian was much more than a singing teacher. Siboni gave him affection, time, food, warmth and his first contact with Italy, a country with which Andersen was to fall lastingly in love. Despite Siboni's inadequate supply of Danish words, which he eked out with Italian and German, teacher and pupil understood each other well and Siboni never stormed at Andersen as he did at his other pupils but would start his lessons by saying, 'You are not afraid,' and afterwards he sometimes gave him pocket-money, 'for a little fun'.

All went well until Andersen's weather-worn boots betrayed him. He was growing so fast that, despite the generosity of strangers, he had barely enough money for essentials. That winter and the following spring the weather was exactly as he described it in *The Two Baronesses*: 'Real Copenhagen November days with grey skies, dusk instead of day, and muddy streets, so that umbrellas and galoshes become a necessary part of the body, its limits above and below. Furthermore, the only variation is raw, dense fog, which can even be tasted. All the air is cold moisture which penetrates through the clothes into the pores of the body. It pours its clamminess over gates and doors, over the wooden banisters in the hall. One feels oneself in an element fit for frogs, not for warm-blooded animals.' Andersen possessed neither umbrella nor galoshes and his boots were beyond repair. Had he told Siboni he needed new boots he would certainly have been given them, but although innocently ruthless in his demands for an opportunity to be an artist, Andersen was always frugal where his personal comfort was concerned and scrupulous about earning kindness. So he endured frog's weather with sodden feet, and when his voice broke he lost his gift for singing. He was just fifteen and it seemed as if all his endeavours had been for nothing. Summer was approaching and the Royal Theatre would be closed from June 1 until September 1. Even Siboni advised his protégé to go home to Odense and learn a trade. Andersen seemed to be right back where he started.

He still, however, had the courage that had brought him to Copenhagen, the courage to try to find a new solution for his problems. Unable to imagine a life for himself outside the theatre, he hoped that even if he could no longer sing he might still become an actor. His friend Colonel Högh-Guldberg of Odense had a brother living in Copenhagen who was a poet. Andersen wrote him a letter, and after allowing time for its arrival, he followed this up with a personal visit. The Professor received him in a room packed with books and tobacco pipes. He had heard of the boy from his brother and was ready to help him. Andersen's misspelt letter had shown that no matter what his ambitions might be, he was in immediate need of education. Professor Guldberg offered to tutor him in Danish and German and to ask a friend, the well-known comedian Lindgreen, to coach him in acting. He also gave him some clothes and fifty rigsdalers, the proceeds of a pamphlet that the Professor had recently written in honour of King Frederik VI's birthday. This sum was supplemented by Weyse and several others.

Unfortunately Andersen was incapable of keeping his gratitude to himself, and as soon as his landlady heard of it she called him into her parlour and offered him full board as well as lodging. Knowing how credulous he was, she emphasized the care she would take of him, the good food and drink she would give him, and above all the protection she would furnish him against the wickedness he would be sure to encounter elsewhere. It was a perfect performance of 'Come into my parlour, said the spider to the fly'. There was no suggestion that he should move from his dark closet to a better room, but she invited him to sit in her kitchen whenever he liked – all this for only twenty rigsdalers a month. Andersen was horrified. To meet her demands would mean his spending, on lodgings alone, four rigsdalers a month more than his friends were giving him for all his expenses. The landlady told him that she would give him two days to make up his mind, after which he must either accept her offer or go elsewhere. Then, having said what she described as her last word on the subject, she went out for a tactical airing.

Alone in the unfamiliar parlour, crushed by the harpy's ultimatum, Andersen realized that on her terms the money so generously provided by his friends would last him only a few months and he certainly could not ask for more. He was still only a child who dreamed of building castles and had so little experience of lodging-houses that it did not occur to him that better as well as cheaper rooms could be found in Copenhagen. Nor did it occur to him to consult his friends. Over love and art he could not hide his feelings, but in other matters he could maintain a gently obstinate reserve. Now as he sat alone, tears pouring down his cheeks, he suddenly noticed a portrait of the landlady's late husband over the sofa. Moved by one of the folk-memories by which his gifts were nourished, and unaware that he was trying to enact a primitive form of magic, he wiped some of his tears on to the painted eyes of the portrait in order to communicate his distress to the dead man, who would then, thought Andersen, influence his widow.

When the landlady returned she calmly announced that she was willing to give him full board and lodging for sixteen rigs-dalers a month. This seemed to the boy a miracle. It was a miracle that left him with no spending money, but whenever the landlady sent him on errands, often far out to Frederiksberg, she gave him four skillings, always with the observation that she was not one to put on people. These skillings were spent on writing-paper, second-hand copies of plays or material for his toy theatre.

If Kierkegaard is right that 'it is a divine kind of madness lovingly not to be able to see the evil that lies just in front of one', Andersen was divinely mad. He had no idea what was going on under his nose in the lodging-house. For example, there was a young woman who rented a room overlooking the yard who often spoke to him kindly and was clearly unhappy. Her only visitor was her father, a shabby old man who came to take tea with her regularly, but always after dark. The landlady told Andersen to open the back door to the old man and to be sure never to go near the young lady's room during these visits, 'as her worthy father is abnormally shy'. Years later, as a guest in a fashionable house, Andersen was astonished to recognize in a 'distinguished-looking elderly gentleman wearing decorations' the shabby old 'father' who had in Andersen's Ulkegade days been distinguished only for his abnormal timidity.

The landlady often had visitors herself, particularly one man who would sit for hours in the kitchen and made the boy feel so much in the way that he took to having his meagre dinner in his room. Here as in Odense he lived in a world of make-believe. He searched the shops for left-over scraps of stuff with which to dress his puppets for performances of the plays he had started writing. And, as always, his most pressing problem was where to obtain more books to study.

He often thought of Mrs Bunkeflod who had been the first person to lend him books, and one day he remembered her telling him that Rasmus Nyerup, the librarian of Copenhagen University, was a peasant's son and had gone to school in Odense. Convinced that any book-hungry boy from Odense would therefore be sure of a welcome from him, Andersen set out for the students' quarter, which was near the Royal Theatre. Rasmus Nyerup discerned some quality in Andersen that made him immediately give him permission to read to his heart's content in the university library. This was housed in the seventeenth-century Round Tower, nine storeys high, that had been built by King Christian IV as an astronomical observatory and as a tower for the church beside it. The top was, and still is, reached by a spiral staircase up which Peter the Great of Russia is said to have ridden his horse when he visited Copenhagen in 1716. As soon as Nyerup saw that Andersen could be trusted to cherish books and return them, he gave him permission to take books home with him.

Professor Guldberg had kept his promises and the actor Lindgreen started coaching Andersen for the stage. Both teacher and pupil were full of good will, but unfortunately Andersen preferred drama to comedy, and when he attempted the famous soliloquy in the picture-gallery from Oehlenschläger's *Correggio*, his teacher patted him on the back and said, 'You have certainly got feeling, but you are not cut out to be an actor. Heaven knows what you are suited for, but have a talk with Guldberg and see about learning some Latin; that will help you become an undergraduate.' This was not such a blow to Andersen as it would have been had he not been virtually adopted by the ballet-master of the Royal Theatre School, Dahlén, and his wife, very much as he had been adopted by Siboni. As determined as ever to make a name for himself in the theatre, Andersen now thought that if he could not be a singer or an actor, he might still succeed as a dancer. He was admitted to the theatre's ballet school and attended classes which were held in Christiansborg's court theatre, where today a plaque beside the former stage-door commemorates his industrious hours there.

In the evenings he would make his puppets perform for the Dahlén family at their home in Badstuestræde, or else watch the performances at the Royal Theatre from the wings. He was very proud of this privilege, for great ladies and gentlemen would pay the stage-hands to let them stand in the wings during a performance.

One evening, just before the curtain went up on the opera *The Children of Savoy*, a fellow pupil told Andersen that everyone, including the stage-hands, was to walk on and swell the crowd in the market scene. Overjoyed, Andersen at last found himself on the stage of the Royal Theatre, seeing the footlights, prompter and audience from the actor's viewpoint, the magical other side of the curtain. His jubilation was soon spoilt by his feeling that he must be looking grotesque. His hat was still too big, his much-mended confirmation suit out at the elbows, his waistcoat so short that he dared not stand up straight, and the patched boots that had once creaked so splendidly were sodden, silent and inglorious. His odd posture drew the attention of one of the singers. A popular favourite, able to take liberties with an audience, he seized the boy's hand, dragged him to the footlights and said mockingly, 'Allow me to present you to the Danish public.' For the first and last time, Andersen fled from the stage.

But this humiliation was soon followed by a real triumph. Nineteen months after his arrival in Copenhagen he was given his first part at the Royal Theatre, that of a masked troll in Dahlén's new ballet *Armida*. After the performance the unmasked troll took the programme back with him and could scarcely bear to stop looking at it and blow out his candle. It was indeed a programme worth keeping, for near the name Andersen, Troll, was that of Hanne Petcher, a misprint for Johanne Luise Pätges, a nine-year-old girl who was to become the greatest actress Denmark had ever known.

Slender and aquiline, with immense dark eyes, this extraordinary child, the youngest but one of a family of nine, had been born, like Andersen, to poverty and hardship. Her Jewish mother had escaped at twelve years old from an intolerable home in Frankfurt and made her way by begging and domestic service to Copenhagen, where she married Christian Heinrich Pätges, who had himself fled from Cologne to avoid military service. Pätges became a tavern-keeper and took to drink, so that one of Johanne Luise's earliest recollections was of her father taunting her mother with her Jewish blood while he tried to smash open the drawer in which his wife kept her savings. It was Johanne Luise's mother who earned the family living by cooking German delicatessen, which in summer she sold from a booth in the Deer Park. When Johanne Luise was admitted to the Royal Theatre's ballet school at eight years old she was poorly dressed, unused to polite society and could not speak Danish properly. At first she was treated as a pariah by her fellow pupils, but within a few years her talent won her solo dances and small speaking parts. When she played in *Armida*, however, her career was only beginning, and when the troll blew out his candle and went to sleep with the programme under his pillow, he was far from dreaming that he and Johanne Luise would work together as adults. That night he dreamt only of his own name, seen in print for the first time – ANDERSEN.

When Andersen was sixteen the news of Napoleon's death reached Denmark. Its traumatic effect on the Romantic movement was equalled only by that of Byron's death three years later, of which the great French painter Delacroix wrote: 'Hatred dies; envy forgives, and the future will range him among those condemned to unhappiness just because their passions and overwhelming energy were those of genius.' Andersen was reminded of his father's death-bed ravings about Napoleon. He was old enough now to realize that his father had died young and frustrated, and he wondered if he himself would have as short a time in which to try to make his dreams come true.

It was difficult for him to keep in good heart. Most of the money given him was spent, and after two years in Copenhagen he was still in the anomalous position of living in poverty on the proceeds of generosity. Despite his powerful belief that 'it would all come right in the end', preoccupation with money was always a torment to him, as is shown by many of his fairy tales, such as *The Tinder Box*, which are more deeply and truly personal than is his autobiography.

By now he had moved into lodgings in Dybensgade kept by a seaman's wife, Mrs Henckel, who had a large family of children. She gave him a cup of coffee for breakfast and often this and a roll of bread were all the food he had for the day. He would eat his roll in a solitary corner of the park so that Mrs Henckel might think he had been invited out to a meal. His appearance, too, was a worry to him. Although from time to time friends gave him clothes, he was so unusually tall and thin that they seldom fitted him and so increased his natural awkwardness. Once he received a blue top-coat that was as good as new, but so much too large for him across the chest that he stuffed the front with old newspapers and dared not unbutton it in warm weather. He was saved from complete despair only by his trust in God and his profound belief in his own star.

One of his superstitious beliefs was that whatever one does on New Year's Day will decide the pattern of one's life during the coming year. So on January 1, 1822, he went to the Royal Theatre and, slipping past the half-blind porter at the stage-door, walked on to the dark stage. He believed that if he recited aloud in this (to him) sacred place he would be given a speaking part during the coming year. But when he stood alone on the empty stage he was so moved that all the many parts he had learnt fled his memory. Instead of declaiming in grand style, he knelt down and said the Lord's Prayer to the empty auditorium. Then he left in high spirits, sure of his immediate future as an actor.

City life had not lessened his love of the country. One spring he walked out to Frederiksberg to see the beech-woods with their new leaves. They seemed so beautiful to him that he flung his arms around one of the beeches and embraced it. A park-keeper who happened to pass by shouted at him, asking 'What's the matter, boy? Are you crazy?' This purely rhetorical question, so often provoked by emotional people, terrified Andersen. He remembered his grandfather running through the streets of Odense, remembered too his father's death-bed, and to these memories was now added a sense of the dangerous strength of his own emotions. These thoughts sent him flying back to the theatre, to the world in which it was not only safe but desirable to use all one's imagination and emotions. He had been transferred from the ballet school to the chorus and was playing walking-on parts regularly. The theatre and the reading and writing of plays took up so much of his time that he had begun to neglect the Latin lessons provided by Professor Guldberg. Believing that one could become a great actor without knowing Latin, he was amazed and appalled by the Professor's angry declaration that he would have no more to do with him. When he wept and begged for forgiveness Professor Guldberg coldly accused him of the added crime of play-acting. Andersen's distress was in fact totally sincere. The emotional equipment that made daily life so difficult for him would have made the fortune of an actor capable of dominating it with knowledge and discrimination.

Although Andersen clung tenaciously to the idea of himself as a dancer, he spent more and more of his time writing. At this period he wrote almost as instinctively as he breathed, so it did not occur to him that if he was to become a professional writer he must do what his friends urged him to do, namely, acquire an education. He had many friends in Copenhagen now, people of distinction whom he had met through Siboni, Weyse, Guldberg and the Rahbeks, and nearly all agreed that his most immediate need was for education. But for all his superficial malleability, they could not weaken his wild reluctance to let himself be trapped into work that was not, so he mistakenly thought, essential to the artist he instinctively felt himself to be.

Among the friends who encouraged his belief in his future as an artist was old Mrs Jürgensen, the widow of a royal watchmaker and mother of Jørgen Jürgensen, a wild and gifted man, notorious in 1809 as the self-appointed 'King of Iceland'. To his mother Jürgensen appeared entirely heroic, and she found in Andersen a responsive listener to her tales of her son's exploits. Born in 1780, Jørgen Jürgensen had gone to sea at fourteen years old aboard an English coaling ship. In four years he qualified as a merchant marine officer and as such was eligible for British citizenship. In 1798 he went by whaling ship to Cape Town, where he enlisted, under the name of John Johnson, in the Royal Navy. He pioneered the Tasmanian whaling industry and when he returned to Copenhagen in 1807 was given a hero's welcome as 'the first Dane to circumnavigate the globe'. When Denmark became involved in Napoleon's war with England, Jürgensen was made a captain in the Royal Danish Navy and in 1808 was taken to England as a prisoner of war. There he offered his services as a secret agent and in 1809 he organized a 'revolution' against Danish rule in Iceland, appointing himself Protector or King of the island. Nine weeks later he was deposed by the captain of a British warship and taken back to England, once again as a prisoner of war – and this time he was outlawed in Denmark as a traitor. He was a born gambler, not only with money, and in 1822 he was sentenced to transportation for life to Australia, where he did so well that although he began as a convict, he later won an honourable place in the new country's mythology as 'the Viking of Van Dieman's Land'. It was his heroic deeds rather than his ambivalent attitude that impressed his mother, and even a less credulous boy than Andersen would have seen the matter as she did in that age of individualistic rebels.

Mrs Jürgensen stimulated Andersen's imagination not only with tales of her son's exploits but with reminiscences of the great Holberg, who used to discuss politics with her father as the two men paced the floor at Antvorskov castle. She also translated for the boy her favourite dramatists, Racine and Corneille, showing him that violent emotions could gain power by being compressed into formal terms. He never forgot her and wrote in his autobiography: 'How attractive that old woman's company was to me. I listened to all she had seen, thought and read and I was in her house as a dear child whom she loved to have near her. I read her my first verses, and my tragedy *Skovkapellet* [The Chapel in the Wood], and she said one day with an earnestness that made me humble: "You are a poet, perhaps as good as Oehlenschläger! In ten years – yes, when I am no longer here – please do remember me!" I remember that tears rushed to my eyes, I was so solemnly and wonderfully touched by these words; but I know also that I thought it impossible for me to reach so high as to be an acknowledged poet, and far less to be named with Oehlenschläger. "What a good thing it would be for you to study," she said, "but many roads lead towards Rome . . ." '

Excited by her enthusiasm, he wrote a 'patriotic tragedy', *The Brigands of Vissenberg*, the subject that of an old legend, the style an imitation of Schiller's *The Robbers*. He decided to submit this to the Royal Theatre, but not under his own name. The pseudonym he chose was William Christian Walter – because: 'I loved William Shakespeare and Walter Scott, and then of course I love myself.' He confided this project to Miss Tønder-Lund, the girl who had given him a rose during his discomforting confirmation class days. She was now in Copenhagen, staying with an admiral's family, and willingly aroused her prosperous friends' interest in the poor boy from her home town. The admiral's sister-in-law, Mrs Colbjørnsen, was the widow of a statesman and jurist, and her daughter, Mrs van der Maase, was lady-in-waiting to Crown Princess Caroline. Thanks to this connection, Andersen was invited to Frederiksberg castle to sing and recite for the Princess, who gave him ten rigsdalers and loaded him with grapes, peaches and sweetmeats.

Miss Tønder-Lund offered to copy out the manuscript of *The Brigands of Vissenberg* so that Andersen's handwriting should not be recognized at the Royal Theatre, but despite this further aid to anonymity, William Christian Walter's manuscript was returned six weeks later with the pronouncement that the Royal Theatre could not consider the work of dramatists who clearly revealed 'a lack of the most elementary education'. (In August of this same year a scene from *The Brigands of Vissenberg* was published in a small magazine called *Harpen* [The Harp]. As the manuscript of the play was subsequently lost, the scene in *Harpen* is all that remains of it.)

On top of this came a blow that stunned him. In May 1822, at the end of the spring season, he lost even the little foothold he still had in the Royal Theatre. The management informed him that as it was felt he had no future there, he had better not return next season but rather 'get an education'. Still unable to believe that the theatre could utterly reject him, he hastily completed a new tragedy, *Alfsol* (The Elves' Sun), based on an old Scandinavian legend, and with the first act of this in his hand called on Admiral Wulff. He had never met this officer before, but knew of him as a translator of Shakespeare and supposed that his own adoration of the English poet would suffice as an introduction. Although easily intimidated, Andersen was not shy in the ordinary sense; nor can he have been in the very least brash since he was as lucky in friendship as he was unlucky in love. Admiral Wulff not only invited him to breakfast (a meal taken around eleven) and listened to *Alfsol*, but subsequently introduced him to the rest of the Wulff family, all of whom became the boy's friends but most particularly the Admiral's clever little hunchbacked daughter, Henriette, who was only a year older than Andersen.

Alfsol was refused by the Royal Theatre, but not in the same terms as *The Brigands of Vissenberg*. For all its incoherence and immaturity, it was considered to show talent – enough talent to change his way of life completely. On September 13 he was summoned to the Royal Theatre and told that the management intended to recommend him for a royal grant to enable him to continue his studies. Although he was not yet completely aware of this, singing, acting and dancing had been merely stepping-stones towards his becoming a writer. One of the four men present was Jonas Collin, and it was he, backed up by Rahbek and G. H. Olsen, who decided to speak to the King about the boy. Jonas Collin was at this time forty-six years old, a distinguished civil servant in whom King Frederik had particular confidence, a member of the Royal Theatre's administrative board and a director of the Treasury, so it was extremely unlikely that any recommendation of his would be ignored. Collin was not a sentimental man, and far from perceiving genius in Andersen, he gave most prosaic reasons for wishing to help him – namely that, since Andersen was entirely dependent on private charity, he might get into trouble if allowed to drift, and hence 'be lost to respectable society', whereas with education he might become a useful citizen.

There was truth in this, for alone in Copenhagen, Andersen might eventually have been dragged down by his disreputable relatives. His illegitimate half-sister, Karen Marie, had wanted to follow him to the capital, imagining that he might help her rise in the world, and although Anne-Marie had for a long time refused to give her his address for fear she might compromise him, the girl did eventually get herself to Copenhagen and was vainly seeking for her half-brother at the very moment when Jonas Collin was planning a respectable future for him.

Andersen's was only one of many cases that had come to Collin's notice, so although his interest was genuine, the Councillor would probably have been astonished had he been told that within a few years he and his entire family would consider Andersen as one of themselves. The boy himself would have been even more astonished to learn that he had found a second father in Collin, and that the fine old house in Bredgade where Collin lived with his wife and five children would become a home to him. Formerly the residence of the Spanish ambassador to the court of Christian II, this house, now vanished, was then half-timbered, with a massive overhanging roof, pointed gables, and a wooden gallery overlooking an inner courtyard shaded by an old linden tree. If it did not at first appear as a haven to Andersen, who was usually abnormally quick to respond to kindness, this was because his judgment was confused by the calm, reserved and businesslike manner in which Jonas Collin told him that King Frederik had decided to grant him a scholarship to Slagelse Grammar School, of which the recently appointed Rector was still young, a poet himself, as well as an authoritative teacher.

On Andersen's second visit to Collin the Councillor unbent and told the boy not to hesitate to write to him from Slagelse of his needs and progress. It was characteristic of Jonas Collin that he put needs first. By this time Andersen had accepted his temporary exile from the theatre with bewildered gratitude, and on October 26, 1822, just over three years after he set foot in Copenhagen for the first time, he left the capital to start his school life at seventeen years old.

3. *In Meisling's Classroom*

1822-30

We've recently made a little journey and already we want to make a longer one. Where? To Sparta or Mycenae or Delphi? There are hundreds of places whose names make the heart pound with the love of travel.

Hans Christian Andersen, *The Bond of Friendship*

In those blest days, when life was new,
And hope was false, but love was true.

Thomas Love Peacock, *Newark Abbey*

*

ANDERSEN SET OUT happily for Slagelse. His mercurial spirits rose and he looked forward to his new life, regretting only that his father could not see him 'elevated to a Grammar School'. Once as a child he had been present when an Odense schoolboy called at the Andersen cottage to be measured for a new pair of boots and lingered to chat with the cobbler about his studies and show him his books; after the schoolboy left the cobbler had kissed his son passionately and said, 'That was the path I ought to have taken.' Again and again, when life went well with him, Andersen remembered his father's frustrated aspirations.

Slagelse, fifty miles south-west of Copenhagen, near the west coast of Zealand, was a small town of two thousand inhabitants, most of whom knew one another's business. Two churches and a windmill showed above its red-roofed houses. It was near the forest of Antvorskov and, like Odense, full of legends and traditions. The abbey of Antvorskov, founded by Valdemar I in 1177, had sheltered Slagelse's patron saint, Holy Anders, who was in the habit of hanging his hat and gloves on a sunbeam while performing his devotions in the open air.

It was late in the evening when the mail-coach stopped outside the inn at Slagelse, but Andersen's first question there was what were the sights of the town. A new fire-engine, the innkeeper's wife told him, and Pastor Bastholm's library. He found excellent board and lodgings awaiting him with Mrs Henneberg, a civil servant's widow, who gave him a cheerful room with a window ot greenish glass framed by white curtains inside and grape vines outside that overlooked the garden and a view of fields. It seemed palatial after his Copenhagen lodgings and Andersen reached the Grammar School full of optimism. This was soon dashed by the Rector of the school: most ironically since the latter's youthfulness and literary ability had influenced Andersen's patrons in their choice of a school for him.

Simon Sørensen Meisling, who was at this time thirty-five years old and had taken up his post as headmaster at the Grammar School only three weeks before Andersen's arrival there, was a distinguished philologist and classical scholar. He was also a most unattractive man, with red hair, short arms and a chronically ill-kempt appearance, who was growing every day more embittered by lack of recognition as an author – he wrote verse and had translated several of the classics – and by the tedium of small-town life and a sluttish wife. He had excellent capacities as a teacher, but these did not include patience, and his favourite pedagogic weapon was sarcasm, which Andersen was particularly ill-equipped to meet. The sight of a nervous overgrown seventeen-year-old who was so behind in his studies that he had to be put in the same class as boys nearly half his age and size so exasperated Meisling that he soon made his charity pupil feel as if he were lost in a storm. Fumbling, stammering, answering at random, Andersen would wait, bewildered and submissive, for the irascible comment that inevitably followed. His talents for scripture, history and Danish composition seemed of no consequence to Meisling compared with his ignorance of the headmaster's favourite subjects, Latin and Greek; nor had his conscientious industry and desire to please any effect on a man who had decided once and for all that his new pupil was uncouth, uncivilized, and good for nothing but to serve as a scapegoat. It was a case of complete incompatibility. Meisling could sympathize with the problems of the ancient Greeks and Romans but not with those of a lanky charity boy who was struggling to adjust himself to an entirely new way of life, socially as well as intellectually.

In Odense Andersen had been a respectable working-class boy seemingly destined to be apprenticed to a trade and go no farther afield than his father had done; in Copenhagen he had been an innocent adventurer precariously balanced between the magic world of the theatre and the underworld of disreputable poverty; in Slagelse, where he was virtually entering the middle classes, of which he knew very little since it was artists and the gentry who had hitherto helped him, Meisling's taunts and threats filled him with a misery and confusion so great as to provoke nightmares that recurred even when he was an old and world-famous man. His visit as a small child to a prison had made prisons for ever afterwards a 'nightmare of the spirit' to him, and Meisling's persecutions undermined his confidence to such an extent that he often thought of his heredity and feared for his own sanity. The diary that he kept at Slagelse reveals another genuine 'nightmare of the spirit' and goes from childish terror or elation about examination results – 'Thou lookest into me and wilt be my help so that I can be promoted to the fourth class. Have answered well in Hebrew' – to suicidal longings since 'death cannot be more awful' and 'life without hope is hell'. Part of this hell was that Andersen, who dreaded insecurity because he had known so much of it, never knew exactly where he stood with Meisling, who would every now and again be cheerful and friendly outside the classroom, especially on Sundays when he would invite some of the pupils, including Andersen, to his home, produce tin soldiers and play with his children.

Given Meisling's attitude, Andersen's popularity with the other masters, and even his real gifts, were all against him. Once when the Bishop was due to visit the school, the singing master asked Andersen to write a song for the occasion. In his Copenhagen days he would have jumped at the opportunity; as it was he could take no pleasure in the task and fancied that, when the song was sung, Meisling looked at him with even more contempt than usual. During the service Andersen slipped out into the churchyard and had to be fetched from beside the neglected grave of a minor poet who had celebrated the ruins of Christiansborg castle. Andersen was peculiarly sensitive to the lingering presence of the dead, and that day he prayed there that he too might become a poet or else die young. His belief in his own star was offset by his defenceless readiness to believe whatever anyone said against him. Thus when Meisling stormed at him for being a dunce he immediately told Jonas Collin of this, saying that he feared he did not deserve all that was being done for him. Collin replied: 'Don't lose courage, my dear Andersen! Compose your mind and be quiet and reasonable; you will see that all will go well; the Rector bears goodwill towards you. He takes perhaps another way of showing it than others would, but still it leads to the same end. I may write more another time, today I am prevented. God bless you! Yours, Collin.'

The week-ends, when he could escape from Slagelse, became Andersen's happiest times. On Saturdays he would visit Antvorskov castle. His passion for Walter Scott had stimulated his interest in romantic ruins, and he approached these with thoughts of long-lost lovers, ghosts and brigands.

> Strange sounds along the chancel pass'd,
> The banners waved without a blast . . .
> Yet somewhat was he chilled with dread,
> And his hair did bristle on his head.

On Sundays he would walk the seven miles to Sorø, a beautiful little town set in a forest between two lakes. Here he made friends. The poet Ingemann, whom he had already met in Copenhagen, was now teaching at the famous Sorø Academy, the Danish equivalent of Eton. This academy occupied a twelfth-century Benedictine monastery built by Asser Rig, the warrior-builder, whose son, Bishop Absalom, had founded Copenhagen in 1167.

Ingemann, who was then thirty-three, had recently married and he and his young wife Lucie lived in one of the lakeside cottages allotted to the academy tutors. Their cottage was full of objects of art, including portraits of most of the leading European poets; their garden was full of flowers, wild and cultivated; and they had a sailing-boat with an Aeolian harp attached to the mast. The Aeolian harp played as important a part in the Romantic picture of nature as Gothic ruins, noblemen's follies, hermitages, obelisks, and Chinese pavilions. During Andersen's visits to the Ingemanns, which he described as 'blissful', he made friends not only with them but with two of the academy pupils, Petit, who later wrote a biographical sketch of Andersen, and Carl Bagger, the future poet, who was to appear as one of the characters in Andersen's own first novel. For the first time he had friends of his own age who showed him something of the Bohemia that Balzac describes as consisting of 'young people who are still unknown but who will one day be famous'.

Friends such as these, full of literary plans, undermined Andersen's resolve to follow the advice of his benefactors in Copenhagen and stop writing poetry and plays. Feeling guilty, but unable to resist the impulse, he showed some of his work to Mr Bastholm, editor of a West Zealand newspaper, who told him that at this stage in his development he ought to write only when he 'needed air for his feelings'. This was useless advice to give to an adolescent whose emotions were often so violent that he could scarcely bear them, and who in his desperate need to give and receive affection sometimes wrote as many as ten letters in one day in addition to his school work, his poems, his diary and a prodigious amount of reading. When one considers that all this was done by hand and much of it by candlelight, one is almost as astonished as by Balzac's physical capacity for writing – and not at all surprised at the state of nervous tension in which Andersen permanently lived.

There was no time here for his toy theatre, but he was able to visit Slagelse's small private theatre whenever free seats were distributed to the students. This theatre, which he described eighteen years later in his *Picture-book without Pictures*, was housed in converted stables, with the horses' stalls transformed into boxes and the woodwork covered with coloured paper. The auditorium was lit by a small iron chandelier that was hoisted up into an inverted iron tub when the prompter's bell rang for the performance to begin. No matter how crowded the house, no one wanted to sit under the chandelier as candle grease dropped from it. In warm weather the windows were left open and constables stood at the entrance to prevent people from looking in gratis from outside. The lowing of cows in the neighbouring meadows mingled with the actors' voices, and no matter what the play, street scenes were invariably performed against a painted backdrop showing Slagelse market-place. In that familiar setting even the most exotic historic characters seemed to the audience like old acquaintances.

Despite Meisling's bullying, Andersen began to make progress in his studies. His Danish compositions were so good that the other pupils used to ask him to write theirs – 'But don't make it so good that they'll find out' – and in return they helped him with his Latin. Altogether he did so well that at Christmas he was allowed to go to Copenhagen, where he was the guest of Jonathan Balling, a warehouse-keeper who lived at 18 Nyhavn, a house where Andersen was himself to have rooms during the last years of his life. In *The Story of My Life* he writes: 'When I came to town in the Christmas holidays, I had a wonderful time . . . I stayed with Balling, the warehouse-keeper. He was a lovable, charitable man who had often been kind to me before I went to Slagelse. In the few days when I stayed with him, I always accompanied him to the stalls; I was extremely happy. How much I still loved the theatre was proved by the fact that in order to see a play which was performed on Saturday evening, I preferred, instead of taking the stage-coach in the morning, thus missing the play, to walk the whole way to Slagelse.'

During this visit he was for the first time invited to a meal at the Collins' house, where he met the young people who were to be like brothers and sisters to him – eighteen-year-old Ingeborg Collin, sixteen-year-old Gottlieb, fourteen-year-old Edvard, nine-year-old Louise and seven-year-old Theodor.

In the summer, he was invited to Odense by Colonel – now General – Högh-Guldberg, who sent him money for the crossing. Andersen walked the eighteen miles from Nyborg to Odense and wept with excitement at the sight of the tower of St Canute's. For his mother this visit offered a rare occasion for triumph and rejoicing. She had told everyone that the King was paying for her son's education, and even her most sceptical neighbours admitted that 'Marie Shoemaker's Hans Christian had not done so badly after all.' The poor woman had little else to rejoice about. Early in 1821 she and her second husband had moved to live with her mad father-in-law in the little house for which they paid six rigsdalers a year, and here, on June 4, 1822, Niels Gundersen had died at the age of thirty-four, leaving her so nearly penniless that clothes and tools had to be sold to pay for the funeral. In August Andersen's paternal grandmother died and Anne-Marie planned to try to get his grandfather admitted to the Grey Friars' Hospital. Later, at his mother's request, Andersen wrote about this to the mayor and his letter is still in existence. A year later his grandfather was admitted to the hospital, where, despite attempts to escape, the poor demented old man remained until his death in 1827.

From all these sordid tragedies Andersen's visit gave his mother a respite. Everyone, she proudly told her tall son, wanted to see him – the grocer, the clerk, the bookseller, and of course the Guldbergs and 'all the fine folk'. She wept for joy to see him treated 'like a nobleman's son' by the Guldbergs and the Bishop's family, who took him sailing on the river past the gardens where as a child in wooden clogs he had sung for the Emperor of China; and she shared his ingenuous delight when the old bookseller, Søren Hempel, took him up the little observatory that he had built and, looking down over the town, showed Andersen a group of old women who had known his grandmother pointing up at him. This foretaste of admiration in his home town made his return to Meisling's bitter nagging hard to endure.

About this time he was submitted to the horrible experience of watching an execution. A rich farmer in that part of the country had opposed his daughter's marriage to the man she loved and in her despair the girl drove her lover to kill her father. Their accomplice was a servant who hoped to marry the farmer's widow. Now all three were to be beheaded at Skjelskør, and Meisling decided that the execution would provide an edifying sight for his senior pupils. For those days there was nothing abnormal about Meisling's attitude. In that Victorian best-seller for young people, *The Fairchild Family*, the eminently respectable Mr Fairchild takes his young children to see an abandoned house with a gibbet in the grounds on which the body of a man is hanging in chains, its clothes intact but the face 'so shocking' that the children long to run away but are forced to remain while Father improves the occasion by explaining: 'When people are found guilty of stealing they are hanged upon a gallows and taken down as soon as they are dead; but when a man commits a murder, he is hanged in iron chains upon a gibbet till his body falls to pieces, that all who pass by may take warning by the example.'

Andersen and his schoolfellows travelled by open coach all night in order to reach Skjelskør at sunrise, and they were in time to see the three criminals being driven in a cart to the scaffold. The girl, 'deathly pale', leaned against her lover's breast, but the squinting black-haired servant managed, though livid, to nod to friends who shouted goodbye to him. On the scaffold, where a parson was waiting, they stood beside their coffins and sang a hymn. The girl's voice could be heard above that of the men. Andersen said later that this singing had seemed even more terrible to him than the actual moment of death. After the execution two superstitious peasants made their son drink a bowlful of blood, believing that this would cure him of the effects of a stroke of apoplexy. Immediately after gulping down the blood their son fainted. Meanwhile an itinerant poet circulated among the crowd selling sheets of laments and dirges. Andersen never forgot this scene. It haunted his dreams, appeared in two of his novels, and when he described it in his autobiography it was still as horribly vivid to him as if it had just taken place.

Brief visits to friends provided moments of respite from Slagelse, but Meisling's oppressive influence had played upon Andersen's childlike credulity and his stifling consciousness of being financially dependent on strangers so that he felt that even among friends he existed only on sufferance and must expect affection only as a reward for work achieved. (Some of this feeling was to show in his first fairy tale, *The Tinder Box*, when riches bring the soldier crowds of admiring friends but once the riches vanish, 'None of his friends came to see him, because there were too many stairs to climb.') He was plagued by the constant obligation, as he saw it, to sing for his supper, and rare was the help he received unaccompanied by admonitions. Thus on March 7, 1823, Mrs Colbjørnsen sent him ten rigsdalers from the Crown Princess who had liked a little poem of his, but she could not refrain from adding: 'I wish, my dear Andersen, to make one request of you: do not let the thought of becoming what you call something great, yes, something very great, become all too deeply rooted in your soul, for in such a case it could perhaps do you a great deal of harm. Try instead to learn something thoroughly, so that you perhaps in time can acquire a minor office, the duties of which you can discharge efficiently. This is my advice, given in all friendliness.' It was also advice accompanied by the odiously complacent remark: 'You know that I always make a practice of speaking my mind.' Even motherly Mrs Wulff told him categorically not to dream of a career as a writer: 'You won't become a cabinet minister nor the leading poet of the land, and you won't become a tailor or a cobbler either, but aren't there a hundred jobs beside these?' It was easy for even a nature as generous as Andersen's to feel himself always a beneficiary and as such obliged to attend to advice that sapped his faith in himself.

On top of this, early in 1825 his mother's state gave him reason to despair. Poverty, loneliness, cold and painful rheumatism had driven her to drink, and despite the efforts of General Högh-Guldberg – one of the few friends from whom this tragedy could not be hidden – Andersen was finally obliged to ask for her to be admitted to the Doctors Boder, a charitable institution with beds for sixteen patients that later became part of the Grey Friars' Hospital. Andersen applied for her admission early in March 1825, and since one of the beds had just been vacated she was immediately taken in. The mother who had said 'My Hans Christian is a strange boy' and had yet found the strength of character to let him leave her and go out into the great world in which he might find fulfilment for the strangeness she herself could not understand, had been transformed into a crazed stranger for whom he could do no more than he had been able to do for his mad grandfather or his dying father. It was a time of anguished loneliness for him and the knowledge of his own heredity made it impossible for him to listen without a feeling of panic to Meisling's reiterated declarations that he himself would come to a bad end – this was, he felt, only too probable. So convinced of this was he that in September 1825 he wrote in his diary with a characteristic mixture of desperation and lucidity: 'Life without hope is hell –

seeing my comrades rise while I sink – tearing myself from the world of cultured people . . . What could I become – and what am I becoming? My strong imagination will lead me to the madhouse, my violent emotions will drive me to suicide – yet united these two things could transform me into a great poet.' Without his often ridiculed hope of becoming 'something great' he would not have survived.

To grief over his mother and anxiety about his studies were added lesser but painful worries, both social and material. In November 1825 the Meislings were expecting a maidservant from Copenhagen. Her name was Marie and, remembering what his mother had told him of his half-sister's attempts to pursue him, Andersen became obsessed by fear lest this servant should be Karen Marie. By this time he may have known how his aunt in Copenhagen earned her living and even if not, instinct told him that if Karen Marie came to work for the Meislings, revealing some of the most unsavoury elements of his family history, it would mean further humiliation for him and possibly even disgrace and expulsion. His chances of gratifying Jonas Collin by becoming a 'useful citizen' seemed to be vanishing. Even when the new maidservant turned out to be no relation of his, he could not relax. His big troubles did not lessen the small ones, and he wrote to Jonas Collin: 'I have three things to ask you for, two of them I did not dare mention until I had good news to give you; but now that the last examination has come out so well, I venture to do it, since I can turn to no one else – the first is a new pair of boots, because the pair I have is all in pieces; they have indeed been mended, still they let in water . . . I was silent as long as possible, it is hard for me to ask, I feel too much of that might weaken the noblest interest . . . The other thing I need very much indeed too, but it is the most expensive, I nearly blush to mention it, but you won't get angry – put yourself in my place, then you couldn't – but perhaps so many words will annoy you, so to come to the point – may I get a new coat? . . . I can't come to Copenhagen for Christmas unless I have one decent thing to wear, for no matter how careful I am of my only good coat, which I got last year, it won't last any longer . . . The third thing is about text-books . . .' It was indeed hard for him to ask since every time he was obliged to do so he feared losing some of the affection that was far more necessary to him than boots – yet without the new boots and text-books he could not earn the affection.

Collin immediately gave him what was required, and Andersen was invited to spend the Christmas of 1825 with the Wulffs, a holiday of which he later wrote: 'There was something very strange . . . something almost of a fairy tale in being moved from school to the family circle in Copenhagen, where everything was in absolute contrast. Admiral Wulff opened his home to me, his wife had taken a motherly fancy to me and his children were kind and friendly . . . His residence was in one of the royal palaces at Amalienborg, which at that time housed the Naval College, of which Wulff became principal. My room faced the Square, and I remember that on my first evening there, as I stood at the window looking down, I remembered Aladdin's words as he looks down at the square from his rich palace and says: "Down there I walked as a poor boy!" ' No wonder Andersen was dazzled as he looked down from one of the four Amalienborg rococo palaces that form one of the loveliest architectural unities in the world. For the first time in his life he slept in a luxurious bedroom, had a sitting-room of his own, and he received as a Christmas present the three volumes of Wulff's translations of Shakespeare.

This invitation from the Wulffs infuriated Meisling. He could not bear to see the object of his own ridicule petted by the gentry in houses to which he himself would never be invited, and a squalid form of envy made him forbid his pupil to take part in festivities, fancy-dress balls and all such 'pretexts for idleness'.

Andersen was unable to escape Meisling, for when, in the spring of 1826, the Rector was transferred from Slagelse to Elsinore Grammar School, he suggested that Andersen should not only accompany him there but join the Meisling household as a paying guest. The boy would be useful, he was always ready to mind the children, and now that Meisling was drinking heavily, he felt an increasing need to have a scapegoat at hand. As an incentive, he offered to give the boy extra tuition in Latin and Greek to help him pass his university entrance examination. Andersen accepted this proposition at its face value and wrote to

Collin: 'Of course I am delighted to have won the goodwill of a man who seemed to dislike me. Only last year he said, "It was the last straw to get him added to the blockheads who surround me!" Now he wants me in his family and I haven't really improved that much.'

The ancient city of Elsinore, twenty-eight miles north of Copenhagen, was not only a repository of poetry and tradition but, thanks to its strategic position as guardian of the Sound, a lively modern town. For the past four hundred years all foreign ships entering or leaving the Baltic had had to lower their flags and pay Sound dues at Elsinore and it had become a favourite port of call for sailors with money to spend. After the Napoleonic wars the maintenance of Sound dues had been guaranteed to Denmark by the Congress of Vienna. When Andersen came to Elsinore this was a matter of over 13,000 ships a year, so the three-mile strip of water between Denmark and Sweden presented an animated shipping scene. But to Andersen, with his passion for Shakespeare, even the ships and the busy life in the twisting cobbled streets of Elsinore meant less than his first sight of Hamlet's sixteenth-century fortress-castle of Kronborg, which stood just outside the town on a rocky eminence overlooking the Sound. The first performance of *Hamlet* at Kronborg castle had taken place as recently as 1816. This massive Renaissance castle, surrounded by a moat on which swans floated, was built of brick covered by sandstone, with octagonal towers at its corners and glittering roofs of green copper. Overlooking the sea were the battlements where the ghost of Hamlet's father stalked in the sea-mist. Elsinore was also the birthplace of Saxo Grammaticus, the chronicler who first recorded the story of the historic Amleth, the wild and bloodthirsty son of a Jutland chieftain, and many of its buildings, such as its two fifteenth-century churches and the apothecary's shop with its diamond-paned windows, were already in existence sixteen years before *Hamlet* was written, at which time a company of English actors had come to Elsinore to play for the court. Even if Shakespeare was not himself a member of this company, as one tradition has it, he was certainly given an eye-witness account of the visit by his friend William Kempe, the famous Elizabethan actor who first played several of Shakespeare's great comic parts.

To the Danes, Kronborg was associated not only with the poet's rather than the historian's Hamlet but also with Holger Danske, the legendary hero who has slept for so long in a deep dark cellar under the castle that his beard has grown right through the marble table on which his head rests. Nothing but a threat to Denmark can wake Holger Danske, who then rises in fury, wrenches his beard from the table and strikes mighty blows for his country. Many ancient legends had combined to produce Holger Danske – that of Ogier le Danois, the valiant liege of Charlemagne; that of Frederick Barbarossa, who sleeps in the mountains of Thuringia, whence he will emerge to succour Germany in her hour of need; that of the medieval Ogier who, after two hundred years spent in Avalon, the island of the dead, returned to France with a firebrand in his hand on which his life depended; that of the Danish Ogier the Terrible, the god of sea and death, who played the harp on the island where he lived with his nine daughters. To all these legends Andersen was nineteen years later to contribute his own story, *Holger Danske*.

Wildly excited by all he saw in this beautiful month of May, Andersen wrote to Jonas Collin: 'What activity! What a lot of excitement on the docks! Here some fat Dutchmen are speaking their hollow-sounding language, and there I hear the musical sounds of Italian, and farther along coal is being unloaded from an English brig, so that I think I smell London. The Sound is covered with vessels, they hover along the coasts like sea-gulls. Yesterday I visited Marienlyst with Meisling, oh, it's one of the most splendid things I've ever seen. It all seemed like Switzerland to me, and I felt so inexpressibly happy; oh, upon seeing that wonderful landscape one must become a poet or a painter. Oh, my benefactor, thanks for each happy moment! Life is wonderful, after all!' He wrote in this vein to several other friends, including Rasmus Nyerup, who thought his letter so remarkable that he had it published in *The Copenhagen Post*.

The Meislings too seemed exhilarated by the change of scene. During their first weeks in new surroundings Meisling refrained from tormenting his pupil and Mrs Meisling, gratified by social calls from the local ladies, ran her household in a less slovenly manner than usual. This improvement was only temporary, however. Once Meisling realized that the move to Elsinore did not signify professional advancement, his temper became savage. He had always been on bad terms with his pupils, now he fell out with the other teachers as well, several of whom were disposed to be friends and champions of Andersen. Before long the atmosphere of the Meislings' new home was that of 'a mental torture-chamber'.

As a middle-aged man, looking back on this period, Andersen was to write: 'The life I led during these days comes back to me in bad dreams. Once again I sit in a fever on the school bench, I cannot answer, I dare not, and angry eyes stare at me, laughter and gibes echo round me. Those were hard and bitter times: I lived in the Rector's house at Elsinore for fifteen months, and I had almost broken down under treatment which became ever crueller . . . Each morning I prayed God to let this cup pass from me, or that I should be spared the day to come. In school the Rector took pleasure in mocking me, making fun of my person, and discussing my lack of talent. And when school was over, I found myself in his house.'

A couple of months after his arrival in Elsinore he got up at three in the morning and walked the twenty-eight miles down the coast to Copenhagen for a breathing spell with the Wulffs. The beautiful walk between the beech-woods and the swan-fringed sea temporarily banished his troubles from his mind and next morning he wrote a poem, 'The Evening', which was to be accepted the following year by the exacting critic Heiberg for publication in his newspaper *The Flying Post*. But such escapes were rare and winter was a terrible time for Andersen. He was so ill-fed that he began to look like a scarecrow, and even in the deepest snows he was allowed only five pieces of wood a day for his stove. After lessons were over he would linger on in the schoolroom, where at least his fingers were not completely numbed and he could be free of the obstreperous Meisling children. Hardest of all to bear was his loneliness. In his comfortable Slagelse lodgings he had enjoyed the companionship of his fellow pupils; in Elsinore none of them wanted to visit him after school hours for fear of meeting the hated Meisling. In his isolation Andersen did not know which to dread most, Meisling's outbursts or Mrs Meisling's advances. Unable to leave any young man alone, she kept inventing excuses to visit Andersen's room – once she said she kept the butter there in order to hide it from the maids – and although he was too naïve to realize precisely what she wanted, her manœuvres disturbed him, as is shown by the description he gave of her nine years later in his first novel. Nevertheless, he was so restrained in his complaints that his friends in Copenhagen had no idea of what he was enduring at Elsinore. This enabled Meisling to equivocate successfully. In July 1826, at a time when he was actually treating Andersen as a loutish imbecile, Meisling reported to Jonas Collin:

'H. C. Andersen was at the close of the year 1822 admitted to Slagelse Grammar School and, being in want of the most necessary preliminary knowledge, was in spite of his advanced age put in the lowest class but one.

'Endowed by nature with a lively imagination and warm feelings, he attempted and acquired more or less completely the different branches of instruction, and in general made such progress that it entitled him to be promoted successively from the lower classes to the highest, to which he at present belongs, only with the difference that he has removed with the undersigned from Slagelse to Elsinore.

'The kindness of others has until now maintained him in his course of study, and I cannot refrain from saying that he is perfectly worthy. His talents are good, and in one direction even excellent; his constant diligence and his conduct, which springs from an affectionate disposition, are such that he might serve as a model for the pupils of any school . . . Not only the disposition of mind, but also his faithful assiduity and undoubted talent give sufficient warrant that what may be bestowed upon him for his welfare will never be lost.'

Reassured by this praise, Jonas Collin wrote to Andersen advising him to be patient and reasonable. The year 1826 was the darkest period of the young man's life and one day in September, as he was sitting alone in the schoolroom, thinking of his mother, he wrote a poem, 'The Dying Child'. Later he showed this to a Baltic German consular official, Schley, who had translated Tegnér's *Frithjof's Saga* and liked 'The Dying Child' enough to translate it and get it published anonymously in a Libau paper. Subsequently it was published in a Copenhagen paper and became so popular that it was even sold on separate sheets at fairs. But at the time when it was written it brought Andersen only abuse from Meisling, who called it 'idle rubbish' and forbade him, as a punishment for wasting time, to go out for walks, even to walk to church. The pathological quality of Meisling's hostility towards Andersen suggests that part of the schoolmaster's mind was aware of the young man's potential talents and felt them as a challenge to his own mediocrity. Andersen's spirit might have been irremediably broken had not Christian Werljin, an assistant master at Elsinore who was himself only a year older than Andersen, taken advantage of a trip to Copenhagen early in 1827 to call on Jonas Collin and tell him exactly how his protégé was being treated. Scandalized, Collin immediately arranged for Andersen to leave Elsinore and be given private tuition in Copenhagen.

For Meisling this was the last straw. When Andersen went to say goodbye and earnestly thanked him for all he had learnt there, Meisling told him that his examinations would bring him disgrace, his writings would 'rot as waste paper' and that he himself would finish up in a lunatic asylum. So ended, in anger and humiliation, Andersen's four and a half years with Meisling.

Eleven years later, when Andersen was beginning to be well-known as a writer, he chanced on his old teacher, shabby and out of work, in the streets of Copenhagen. Andersen described the encounter in a letter to his friend Ingemann, written on January 5, 1838: 'Meisling came up to me in the street and said he wanted to tell me that he knew he had been unkind to me at school but that he had been mistaken in me, and he was sorry, and I was far above him – as he put it. He asked me to forget his harshness and said "Honour is yours, shame is mine." Oh, how it touched me.' On another occasion he met Mrs Meisling, too, in the street and she insisted on telling him how unhappy she had been, married to a man she had 'long abhorred'. She was visiting Copenhagen and suggested that Andersen call on her at the

Three Mangles Hotel in Vestergade. These chance encounters were the last he ever saw of the lamentable pair, but their treatment of him had marked him so deeply that, as his diaries show, Meisling still figured in his nightmares even when Andersen was on his death-bed.

In Copenhagen, the Rahbeks had not lost sight of him, and it was as a guest at their house that he later met two men who were to be his lifelong friends and have a direct influence on his writing. These were the physicist and naturalist Hans Christian Ørsted and the poet Adam Gottlob Oehlenschläger.

An apothecary's son, born in 1777 in the island of Langeland, Ørsted had his first lessons from an old German wig-maker before starting to work in his father's laboratory at the age of eleven. At seventeen he went to Copenhagen University and won two gold medals before taking his degree as a doctor of philosophy. After travelling in Germany and Holland and spending a year in Paris studying the electrical discoveries of Galvani and Volta as well as the philosophy of Schelling, Ørsted was appointed Professor of Physics at Copenhagen University, and in 1815 was elected secretary of the Royal Danish Society of Sciences. His discovery of the relationship between magnetism and electricity (his name is used today as a term of measurement for electromagnetic units) helped to make possible the use of electric light, telephone and radio. Both the Society for the Promotion of the Study of Natural Sciences and the Copenhagen Polytechnic School were established through Ørsted's initiative. He was a man of exceptional charm, modesty and breadth of outlook and the first to appreciate Andersen's fairy tales at their true value.

The other future friend whom young Andersen met at the Rahbeks' house was Adam Oehlenschläger, at that time the most famous poet in Denmark. He had been born in Vesterbro, then a suburb of Copenhagen, in 1779. His father, a native of Slesvig, had been valet to a German count and at the time of Adam Oehlenschläger's birth had been given, thanks to the German count, the post of organist and beadle at the tiny chapel of Frederiksberg castle, of which he was later made steward. The child therefore grew up in dramatic surroundings. Summer brought him the

pageantry of court life and the stimulus of music, and in winter
when the court returned to the capital the boy was made free of
a vast snow-bound world of empty rooms and corridors that he
filled with his imagination. When at twelve years old he went to
school he was captivated by Scandinavian mythology and began
writing plays which he and his schoolfellows acted, encouraged
by their amiable Rector who said, 'My dear young friend, you
surpass even Molière, for he needed a week in which to write and
rehearse a comedy, and this was regarded as a prodigious performance, but you do the whole thing in a day.' Oehlenschläger's
scholastic studies were interrupted by the English attack on the
Danish fleet, which drove him to write a dramatic sketch, *April 2,
1801*, and to attempt – unsuccessfully – to become an actor. Just
as he had decided to resume his studies he attracted the interest
of Ørsted and his brother, who generously tutored him for the
university entrance examination. In 1802, when Oehlenschläger
already had an old Scandinavian romance and a book of poems
going to press, the young Norse philosopher Henrik Steffens
returned from visiting Schelling in Germany and gave some
lectures on Goethe and Schiller that made a sensation in Copenhagen. Oehlenschläger and Steffens met and, after they had
talked for sixteen hours, Oehlenschläger went home and wrote
his narrative 'The Golden Horns'. It became one of the seminal
books of the Danish Romantic movement and was translated into
English by George Borrow. His next success, the poetic drama
Aladdin – a favourite with Andersen, who identified himself with
the poor boy whose washerwoman-mother wanted to apprentice
him to a tailor and who was saved from this fate by his magic
lamp – won Oehlenschläger a royal travel grant. During the next
four years the poet worked with Steffens at Halle, with Tieck at
Dresden, spent several months with Goethe at Weimar, wrote
Axel and Valborg in Paris and *Correggio* in Rome, where he was
the guest of the famous Danish sculptor Thorvaldsen. Oehlenschläger was admired all over Europe while still a young man.
Goethe, Byron and Chateaubriand mention *Aladdin* in their
letters; as the guest of Madame de Staël he read *Axel and Valborg*
aloud to her brilliant circle at Le Coppet; and Louis-Philippe was
to call him the Corneille of Denmark.

Top, Andersen's departure from Odense; above, Odense in Andersen's time; below, Meisling in the classroom

Above left, Giuseppe Siboni

Above right, Christoph Friedrich Weyse

Left, Admiral Wulff

Right, Jonas Collin

Below, Edvard and Henriette Collin

*The old Theatre Royal,
Copenhagen*

*The Actors' Entrance as it
was in Andersen's time*

Hans Christian Ørsted

Bertel Thorvaldsen

Riborg Voigt

Louise Collin

*Bregentved and Glorup, two of the manor houses where
Andersen often stayed*

The screen Andersen made for Mrs. Melchior

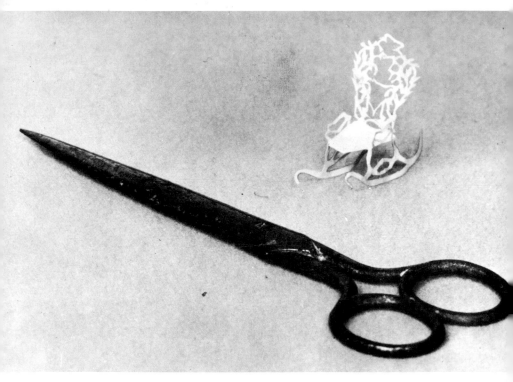

Andersen's scissors and a paper cut-out rocking-chair

In Meisling's Classroom

Back in Copenhagen, Andersen rediscovered the delights both of society and of solitude. He also discovered a new self: 'From a cowed creature of the classroom, I became a free and independent individual.' For the first time since going to live with the Meislings he had enough to eat. Friends such as the Collins, the Wulffs, the Ørsteds, observed the custom, widespread among prosperous Copenhagen families, of inviting a poor student to dinner once a week. Even more than the good food, Andersen valued the regularity of these invitations and their assurance that a given hour would find him with that best of all families, the family one has chosen for oneself. Now that he was removed from Meisling's influence his high spirits were infectious and he could give amusement and pleasure as readily as he received them.

At the Collins' house, where he was the family candle-snuffer because his height made it easy for him to reach all the candles on the table without leaving his place, even the fastidious and exacting Edvard found that no one could be so funny as Andersen. Looking back on their lifelong friendship, Edvard later wrote: 'I had of course often seen Andersen during his first stay in Copenhagen, but whatever image I had of him from those days is now rather thoroughly erased from my mind; I have only a dim memory of an overgrown boy with a long, oldish face, pale eyes and pale hair, dressed in a pair of yellow nankeen trousers which reached only half way down his shins. But at the time of his return to the city I quite naturally had a clear notion of his earlier appearance, and with astonishment I was forced to notice the change for the better which had taken place with respect to his physical development.' Of Andersen's mental development, Edvard reported: 'In conversations where there was a touch of irony and his humour could be brought into play, he could be incomparably amusing. I have never known anyone who in quite the same way could seize upon a simple and essentially unimportant detail and then, not troubling himself much about the correctness of the matter, could make it bear fruit with his humour. Almost every day he had a comical story to tell about something or other that had befallen him; and it is not surprising that, after one such story, Admiral Wulff threw up his hands and cried: "It's a lie, the Devil take me if it isn't, things like that don't happen to anyone else" – a scene of which Andersen himself then gave hilarious re-enactment.'

Jonas Collin had rented a room for Andersen high up under the eaves at 6 Vingaardsstræde, and the hours he spent there by his window, studying, writing or gazing over the moonlit roofs, laid the foundations for his *Picture-book without Pictures*. His studies were no longer drudgery. Collin had arranged for him to be tutored by Christian Müller, a candidate for holy orders who was later to distinguish himself as a linguist and historian. The two young men became friends – Andersen said later that Müller's nature was as peculiar as his own – and their only differences of opinion concerned religion. Although he was a follower of one of the most controversial churchmen of the day, Grundtvig, the theologian, poet, patriot and founder of the Folk High Schools to which much of Denmark's high standard of literacy is due, Müller held rigid views in matters of doctrine and often feared that his pupil might be in danger of eternal hell-fire. By this time, however, Andersen no more believed in hell-fire than his own father had done. The young men's discussions were free of acrimony and to Andersen, fresh from Meisling's tyranny, it was exhilarating to express his views freely and without fear of reprimand.

Müller lived at Christianshavn on the island of Amager, a part of the town crossed by canals, where classicism and baroque met in the shadow of the eighteenth-century tower of Our Saviour topped by a golden globe on which stood (and stands) a lifesize statue of Christ blessing the city. Heiberg also lived there in a house overlooking the beautiful garden of the sailors' hospital. The walks to and fro were an unending pleasure to Andersen. On the way there he concentrated on the work he had prepared, but on the way back he could observe the varied scenes of the city streets that, according to Kierkegaard, were better adapted to pedestrians than to traffic. These walks increased Andersen's desire to write. For as long as he could remember he had felt an immediate need to exteriorize his feelings, and neither the well-meant admonitions of his friends nor Meisling's contemptuous jeers had really convinced him that writing was, for a youth in his circumstances, a sinful waste of time. They did, however, produce a change in the viewpoint he now adopted. For the past four and a half years all his emotions had been systematically ridiculed by Meisling, so now, in unconscious self-defence, he began to write parodies and humorous verse that satirized emotions, including his own. But, as there was no changing his fundamental nature, he remained liable to be 'made wretched for a whole day if he met with a sour countenance where he expected a friendly one'; and he could not write a poem without immediately showing it to his friends, for without their approval he was uncertain of its value.

Accustomed to treating him as if he were still a child, his friends did not hesitate to tell him that he ought not to take time off from his studies to write verse. Jonas Collin warned him that if he failed to pass the university entrance examination he could expect no further grant from the King and would thus be debarred from a professional career. His tutor urged him to buckle down to Latin and remember the danger of hell-fire. Mrs Wulff accused him of overweening ambition and said that if she herself, for example, were seized by a longing to be the Empress of Brazil, she would soon pull herself together and remember her duties in her appointed station in life. Edvard Collin saw nothing but vanity in his friend's need to read his work aloud, and Andersen could not tell him, since he was himself still unaware of the fact, that, destined as he was to be the first Danish writer to use colloquial speech in his prose, the effect of the sound of what he wrote was of sovereign importance to him. Andersen was accustomed to pedagogic advice and seldom revolted against it, but there were times when, for all his good nature, he felt resentment and wrote in his autobiography: 'My dependent position and my ties of gratitude were often thoughtlessly or unconsciously strained to the utmost. Everybody tried to teach me. Everybody wanted to tell me the truth. As a result my faults were incessantly drummed into me. On a few occasions my temper flared up . . . I passionately exclaimed that I would become a poet who should be spoken about and honoured.'

While studying in Copenhagen for his university entrance examination, Andersen met at one of Ørsted's dinners the famous critic Johann Ludvig Heiberg, editor of *The Flying Post*. Heiberg was a handsome and witty writer of thirty-six, the son of two well-known writers. His father, Peter Andreas Heiberg, was absorbed by politics and displayed such aggressive sympathy for the French Revolution and hostility to the Danish monarchy and nobility that he was exiled in 1800. Since then he had lived in Paris and worked at the Foreign Office until his retirement in 1817. Young Heiberg was brought up partly by the Rahbeks at Bakkehuset, the house overlooking the Sound that had been one of the fourteen-year-old Andersen's first ports of call after his arrival in Copenhagen. In 1822 young Heiberg was appointed Professor of Danish at Kiel University, where he was joined by his mother, who had obtained a divorce from her exiled husband in 1801, married Baron Ehrensvärd-Gyllembourg and was now a widow, a brilliant woman with a writing career still ahead of her. After mother and son returned to Copenhagen in 1825 Heiberg began writing plays – it was he who introduced the French *vaudeville* (a comedy with music and songs) into Denmark. An astringent critic and newspaper editor, he was to become a literary dictator in Copenhagen. His standards were those of the French eighteenth century, the Age of Reason, and he disliked the new Romantic movement. Andersen stood in awe of him, but nevertheless showed him some of his poems, which Heiberg accepted for *The Flying Post* – much to the joy of Henriette Wulff. Andersen had so often been accused of abnormality himself that Henriette's deformity aroused a special protective chivalry in him. One day he was with her and the family when Admiral Wulff came in with a copy of *The Flying Post*. It contained two poems, signed only H., which Admiral Wulff insisted on reading aloud, declaring that they were so good they must be by Heiberg himself. When Henriette proclaimed triumphantly that they were by Andersen, the young author expected that everyone there would be as pleased as she was. Instead, to his astonishment and dismay, Admiral Wulff left the room with an air of vexation and not a word was spoken by anyone else present. Considering his past and future kindness to Andersen, it must have been only the fact that he had been left in the dark as to the authorship of the poems that had so strongly vexed the Admiral.

In October 1828, a few days before he was due to take his university entrance examination, Andersen dined at the Ørsteds' and there met a shy young man whose name he did not hear and who bore a strong likeness to Napoleon. He said that he too was going to the university for the examination. Wishing to put him at his ease, Andersen chatted away about the coming ordeal with a confidence he was so far from feeling that on the morning of the examination he fainted. When at last he dragged himself to the large lecture-room at Elers College, he discovered with consternation that the young man with whom he had joked at the Ørsteds' was the brilliant Professor von Schmidten who was to examine him in mathematics. In *The Story of My Life* he wrote of this occasion: 'I was examined in mathematics by von Schmidten, who knew me . . . He was very shy and bashful, so tender-hearted and still exceptionally brilliant. – We were both of us embarrassed, he wanted to encourage me and his first question was: "What do you intend to do when you have passed your examination? Then you will be on your own . . ." I answered, "Oh God, won't you begin the examination, so that I can leave, I'm so scared . . ." I did pass, but this was because I gesticulated so much with the pen that I sprinkled the Professor's face, and he out of the kindness of his heart did not say anything, but simply wiped off the ink.' Despite this dishevelling mathematical interlude, Andersen did well in all his other subjects and earned his matriculation certificate. This precious document was signed by Oehlenschläger, the Dean of that year, who made a point of shaking hands with Andersen and welcoming him as a new member of the university. For all Meisling's cruel prophecies of disaster, Andersen was at last triumphantly a student at the university. His struggles had made of him an unusually cultured as well as compassionate young man. Ingemann wrote: 'Every time your picture presents itself to me, it is as if I saw it grow from the pupil in Slagelse to the tall, good-natured, sincere poet so rich in fantasy, in whom one might make a knot or two without his becoming conspicuously short or fat.' He was as eager for life as the soldier in *The Tinder Box* returning from the wars 'with his knapsack on his back and his sword at his side'.

Although Andersen intended to continue his studies at the university and sit for a further examination in a year's time, he could no longer resist his passionate desire to write. All that he had seen in his daily walks across Copenhagen 'flew out like a swarm of bees' – out and into his first book, *A Walking Tour from Holmens Canal to the Eastern Point of Amager*. The resulting kaleidoscope of his thoughts, impressions, emotions and sheer high spirits owed more than a little to E. T. A. Hoffmann, one of the great figures of the German Romantic movement, who had died in 1822 at the age of forty-six. Andersen was at this time so enthralled by Hoffmann's books that he seldom went without a copy of *The Devil's Elixir* in his pocket.

Although Hoffmann is often thought of nowadays merely as the author of 'The Sandman', the story which was made into the libretto of Offenbach's famous *Tales of Hoffmann*, he was in fact a man of pyrotechnical gifts. Not only Hoffmann's writing, his painting and his music but his life-story fascinated many people, of whom young Andersen was one. He summed up in himself all the attractions of the Romantic movement, with his passion for music and the theatre and, above all, his ability to reveal the inner life of the artist, who was to be one of the nineteenth century's favourite types of hero.

Andersen offered his first book to Reitzel for a hundred rigsdalers, but the publisher refused to give more than seventy, so, on the advice of Heiberg who was enthusiastic about the manuscript and published extracts from it in *The Flying Post*, he decided to try to raise a subscription for a first edition. It was published in January 1829, five hundred copies were quickly sold, and Reitzel promptly offered him a hundred rigsdalers for a second edition. His 'fantastic arabesque', as he called it, was successful not only in Denmark but in Sweden also, and Andersen was able to ask Collin to open a bank account for him with money that he had at last earned by his writings. At the same time *Love on St Nicholas Tower*, a little vaudeville that he had written satirizing the high-flown foreign dramas that had dominated the Danish stage up to Holberg's time, was accepted by the Royal Theatre for production in April. Only seven years had passed since he knelt on the stage of that same theatre, an illiterate adolescent reciting the Lord's Prayer to empty seats in the hope of winning a speaking part. Now he was a university student, a poet, and a dramatist.

In Meisling's Classroom

After the first performance of *Love on St Nicholas Tower*, Andersen rushed, incoherent with excitement, to the Collins' house. Only Mrs Collin was at home, and as she shared the family's constant fear lest Andersen's emotions betray him into making a fool of himself, she gently reminded him that many famous dramatists, such as Oehlenschläger, had their plays hissed off the stage. When he could calm himself, Andersen told her that not only had his little satire been applauded but his fellow students had shouted 'Long live Andersen!' It was with ecstasy that he learnt that he had a free pass for the coming season as one of the Royal Theatre's dramatists.

That summer he made a sad secretive trip to Odense to see his mother and take her money. He never discussed Anne-Marie's condition if he could avoid it, and although the Collins knew that it oppressed him, not even they could enter into his particular darkness. In his mother's lucid moments she felt proud of her son's success, but more often than not she was full of alcoholic recriminations. As for him, she was far more than a tragic reminder of the poverty-stricken life from which he himself had just barely escaped. He thought of the care she had taken of him when he was a child, of the neatness of their small house, snug in the winter snows and fresh in summer with wild flowers and white curtains; above all, he thought of the exceptional understanding she had shown him. No other working-class mother of his acquaintance would have allowed her only son to escape with his savings to the perilous world of the capital. All that he had become he owed to that escape, yet not all his gratitude and compassion could bridge the gulf that now existed between him and this stranger who was as lost in alcoholic dreams as his father had been in dreams of military glory, and his grandfather in the wild poetry of the grotesque figures he carved. Face to face with Anne-Marie, Andersen felt utterly alone.

That same summer he was invited to stay at Nørager, the Zealand estate of Chamberlain Bang. Here began his timid participation in the life of the manor-house world that was to be an integral part of his future. From the first he fitted into this new and attractive world as easily as if born to it, ever a rewarding guest, natural, obliging, full of fun and a favourite with the children of the house. He liked people so easily and showed his liking so readily that almost everyone liked him in return, though often without suspecting the depth of his attachments. Cut off as he was from the world of his own childhood, friendship meant far more to him than to the average person whose affections are centred on a family circle. Friends were not a luxury to him but a necessity; he needed them and was puzzled when the happily married Ingemann warned him against the dangers of wasting time on people in social life.

Social life did not prevent him from studying hard for his next examination at the university, the Examen Philologicum et Philosophicum. This he passed with distinction. His friend Ørsted was one of the examiners, and as Andersen left the room he called him back to ask him one more question: what did he know about electro-magnetism? Andersen had read nothing on the subject and could not remember having even heard the word before. Ørsted smiled at his candour and said that that was a pity, as otherwise he would not only have passed but would have obtained an honourable mention in that subject.

Andersen was keenly interested in science, and ten years later when a magnetic telegraph was set up in the Polytechnic Academy in Copenhagen, it was Andersen who at Ørsted's request wrote an article in *The Copenhagen Post* popularizing the new discovery.

With this examination successfully behind him, Andersen decided not to go on with his academic studies but to try for a career as a writer. Even prudent Jonas Collin gave him his blessing, and with this Andersen left the schoolroom and had his first youthful experience of what was to become ever increasingly important to him – travel.

4. First Love

1830-3

Frontiers oppress me . . . I want to wander as much as I like . . . to talk, even
in broken language, with everybody.

Yevtushenko, 1958

*On trouve non loin de la Baltique les plus beaux établissements, les savants et les hommes
de lettres les plus distingués, et depuis Weimar jusqu'à Königsberg, depuis Königsberg
jusqu'à Copenhague, les brouillards et les frimas semblent l'élément naturel aux hommes
d'une imagination forte et profonde.*

Madame de Staël, *De l'Allemagne*

*

ANDERSEN'S FIRST VOLUME of poetry, published for the new
year 1830, was so enthusiastically noticed that he invested some
of his earnings in travel, which he was later to describe as his
'workshop'. Fyn and Zealand were all that he had seen of
Denmark and he longed to visit Jutland. Formerly covered by
dense forests from which the Vikings invaded England in the
eleventh century, Jutland was still the wildest part of Denmark,
and Andersen's interest in its graveyards where the stones were
arranged in the form of ships and its vast stretches of moors and
heaths over which the gipsies roamed had been aroused by the
writings of Steen Steensen Blicher, a poor Jutland parson who,
unhappily married and often in debt, was happiest when wandering about his native countryside and talking to the Tartars or
Kjæltringer (rascals), as the Jutland gipsies were called. In summer
the gipsies moved about in gangs, exotic interlopers who slept in
the heather and lived by tinkering, fortune-telling and thieving
from isolated farm-houses; in winter hunger sometimes forced
them to work for the peasants, who paid them parsimoniously and
despised them as aliens.

105

The Wild Swan

A steamboat service had been so recently established between Zealand and Jutland that when Andersen went aboard the *Dania* the twenty-four-hour crossing was an adventure in itself. For thousands of years men had travelled only on foot, or on the backs of animals, or in vehicles drawn by animals, or aboard ships dependent on tides and winds; so it was natural that most people should consider the revolution in transport that heralded the industrial age as dangerous and even impious. Although Andersen was himself as enthralled by the progress of science as Jules Verne was later to be, he could nevertheless understand the feelings of an old sailor, related to Ørsted, who said in his hearing: 'From the Creation until now people have been satisfied with reasonable ships driven by the wind; now they must go and meddle with things, they want something better – but whenever I see one of these "smoke caps" passing I cannot resist getting out my megaphone and scolding the ship for as long as it can hear me.'

The crossing to Aarhus was a rough one and the weather in Jutland so trying, with constant rain and sea-mists, that Andersen knew his clothes would not survive the trip he had planned. He had to make do with a mere glimpse of the moors and heaths before going on down the east coast to Kolding. This privation did not prevent him from writing excellent descriptions of the North Sea and the west coast, based upon his avid reading. His gift for vivid reportage would at a later period have made him a first-class journalist. In Aarhus and all the smaller towns of Jutland that he visited he had the unexpected satisfaction of discovering that both his book on Copenhagen and his poems were already popular. From Kolding fjord he crossed to Fyn, where he once again saw Bogense, where as a child he had helped with the hop-picking, listened to ghost stories and been tempted by the Devil to throw himself into a pond. While there he visited Vedel-Simonsen, an old historian, who lived near by and gave him material for an historical novel about the sixteenth century that Andersen was planning. Luckily only sixteen pages of this novel were ever written, for Andersen was still under the influence of Walter Scott and had yet to find his own unique form of expression. From there he went to Odense, where he had been invited to stay just outside the town at Mariehøj, the country house of the widow of his old friend Iversen the printer. Mariehøj overlooked the canal at the point where it flowed past the ruins of Næsbyhoved castle and had been an object of admiration to Andersen from his earliest childhood. Its quaint garden was scattered with inscriptions on wood or stone indicating the sentiment appropriate to each spot, and protected by a wooden soldier with a wooden cannon aimed at the ships that constantly passed along the canal.

In this house Andersen was for the first time in his life surrounded by a group of charming young girls, Mrs Iversen's granddaughters. They all made much of him, especially the eldest, Henriette Hanck, who was only two years younger than himself and crippled. She had a poetic nature and he thought of her as a swan born with only one wing. Although he did not fall in love with any of them – so far his passionate emotions had been singularly sexless – their youth and gaiety awakened in him a longing for a wife; he was so profoundly decorous by nature as well as by training that he always thought of love within the framework of marriage.

New emotions were, however, precipitated in him by this visit. One day early in August, while visiting Valdemars slot, a castle on the island of Taasinge, he was suddenly subjugated by the sight of an old portrait of a long-dead lady of the Iuel family. The painted face disturbed him as none of the girls with whom he saw it had done. He wrote to a friend: 'It is the first woman's face that has touched my heart, I felt sad at the thought of this beautiful form having turned to dust . . . my blood craves for love, as my heart is made for it.' Two days later, still spellbound by this portrait, he left for Faaborg, a small market town on the south-west coast of Fyn, where he was to visit a fellow student, Christian Voigt, the son of a prosperous merchant family.

He arrived so early in the morning that he had time to wander round the narrow streets and the wharves below wooded hills overlooking a bay full of islets before he presented himself at the Voigts' big timbered house. He was welcomed by Christian Voigt's sister Riborg, a gentle dark-eyed girl only a year younger than himself, who gave him coffee and talked discriminatingly and with frank admiration of his writing. Both the young people were shy with each other at their first meeting; and the room full of books, flowers and early morning light suggests one of Trollope's demure courting scenes. With Riborg's brother and Andersen's books as topics of mutual interest, they were soon talking as eagerly and easily as old friends. Riborg was witty, gentle, well read, and full of deference for Andersen as a poet. Accustomed to liking people warmly and readily, Andersen had at first no idea what was happening to him. Part of him was still overwhelmed by the portrait at Valdemars slot, yet even in his dazed state he realized that being in the same room as Riborg filled him with a totally unfamiliar joy, and that all he wanted was to please and protect her.

His few days at Faaborg were outwardly not very different from the days he had spent at Mariehøj. There were outings, picnics, sailing parties, and yet with all the gaiety, in which he joined wholeheartedly, he was aware that something grave was happening to him. Being happy, he was at his best and most spontaneous and therefore charmed the entire household. Everybody paid him compliments and every compliment seemed to him a gift for him to offer to Riborg, who showed timid but unmistakable signs of singling him out from the others. When they went sailing and landed in a wood, she made and offered him a wreath of oak leaves; at a dance where he remained an onlooker, she deliberately chose to sit talking with him rather than take part in the dancing she usually enjoyed; and always, when they were alone together, there was an unspoken sympathy between them that made conversation seem almost superfluous. A whole new world of joys and hopes seemed to be awaiting him. Then he learnt at the inn where he was staying that Riborg was unofficially engaged to her childhood sweetheart, Poul Bøving, an apothecary's son who was studying forestry. Her parents, however, were against the match. So chaotic were Andersen's feelings that although the Voigts asked him to prolong his visit and he longed to do so, he yet insisted on leaving.

On his way back to Copenhagen he stopped again at Mariehøj, where Mrs Iversen's granddaughters immediately noticed a change in him. He wrote poetry constantly, dragged the Voigts' name into every conversation, and appeared to be labouring under a violent obsession. Only when the girls teased him for being in love did he begin to associate his hallucinatory state of mind with Riborg. Immediately he became conscious of missing her, his imagination set to work on the experience, so curiously preceded by the emotion aroused by the portrait of the long-dead woman, and at last he realized what it meant to be in love with a living woman.

Back in Copenhagen, Andersen could no longer concentrate on his work. So distraught was he that for the first and last time in his life he thought of giving up writing in order to study for a steadier and more remunerative profession such as would enable him in time to support a wife. He even thought of becoming a parson. One moment wildly elated, the next moment wildly downcast, he could settle to nothing. In short, 'I had only one thought – her.' His friendship with Christian Voigt became more intense. Only with him could he reveal his passion without fear of being laughed at. The change in him was so apparent that all his friends commented on it, and his voluble denial of being in love carried no conviction. To Henriette Wulff he wrote: 'Some say it is the Elmquists' daughter at Aarhus, others that it is the Countess Moltke! . . . there are also those who think it is Miss Voigt. This last is really foolish as she is already engaged and I could almost swear that she means no more to me than I do to her. As a matter of fact we have spent only a few days together . . .'

Feeling more than ever obliged to justify his existence by writing, Andersen toiled at *The Raven*, a libretto for an opera to be given at the Royal Theatre, the story of which was based on a fairy-tale opera by the eighteenth-century Venetian dramatist Carlo Gozzi, to whom Andersen's attention had been directed by Hoffmann. Meanwhile he visited his friends and tried to take the same interest as before in his Copenhagen life, but in vain, for he ached for Riborg, wondered whether she really loved him, whether in that case it was still her duty to marry her childhood sweetheart. His thoughts raced round in circles; not only did he not know where he stood with her, but he did not know exactly where he wanted to stand, and it is possible that Riborg, who never failed to send greetings to Andersen in her letters to her brother, was equally confused. Then, that autumn, she accompanied a sick friend to Copenhagen. Andersen called on her at her brother's and read her *The Raven*. As he did so, it suddenly occurred to him that what he had written applied to their relationship. By this time she too was in a highly emotional state, and at the end of the reading she impulsively offered him her hand, which he fervently kissed. Since she was an unmarried girl his action seemed to both of them daringly significant. Only then did he realize how passionately he was in love with her – 'all my soul clung to God and I felt that I had the force and courage to do everything to win her.'

This mood of exaltation did not last long. On his way home after confiding in Christian Voigt, Andersen found himself weeping, shivering and dizzy with panic. He continued to feel so ill that for long afterwards he did not dare walk alone after dark. He was also strangely reluctant to see Riborg alone. Instead he wrote her an impassioned letter begging her to make sure before God that she really loved her fiancé, and in that case he prayed God to bless her union with Poul Bøving; if not, then there was nothing he himself would not do to make himself acceptable to her parents as a son-in-law. With her at his side he would be capable of anything. He could think only of her. The letter showed him to be under extreme nervous strain; it begged for love yet seemed to take a refusal for granted. On receiving this, the girl burst into tears and wrote him a letter of farewell which her brother delivered to Andersen. A week later, on November 8, her last day in Copenhagen, Riborg and her father went to the theatre. Beside himself with misery, Andersen waited outside. Her father gave him a cordial invitation to come to Faaborg the following summer, but Riborg, with tears in her eyes, whispered 'Farewell for ever.'

In his autobiography Andersen sums up this unhappy love in one decorous paragraph: 'I was filled with plans for my new life; I would put a stop to writing verse, for what could that lead to? I would study and become a parson; I had only one thought – her – but there was a disappointment in store for me; she loved someone else and she married him. Only many years later did I feel and confess that this, too, was the best thing that could happen, both for me and her. Perhaps she did not even have any idea how profound my feelings were and what an effect they had on me.' At the time, however, he could not accept his disappointment philosophically. In January 1831 he wrote to the Ingemanns: 'I met her for the first time last summer . . . I spent only three days at their house, and as I felt what I had never felt before and heard that she was engaged, I went away at once . . . but here in Copenhagen we met again . . . I shall never see her more . . . I ought not to, and I dare not. I have one consolation: her brother is for us, he knows all and feels for both of us . . . through him I shall hear of her, but never from her . . . she dares not, and will not, speak to me again, but will do her duty . . . She is so beautiful, so gentle and good, you would love her . . . I know she has the same feeling for me as I have for her . . . I wish I were dead, even if death means annihilation . . .' To Henriette Hanck he said: 'You mean that I only imagine myself to be unhappy. Certainly you have reason to believe it, and the world will agree with you; but remember that much passes, not in the heart alone, but in reality itself, which nobody knows and which I dare not reveal.'

No one knows exactly what passed between Riborg and Andersen, but that she gave him some encouragement that seemed to him in retrospect like a betrayal is probable. It is unlikely, too, that she did so entirely against the wishes of her parents, since so respectable and prosperous a merchant as her father would not have invited Andersen to visit the family again had he wished to put an end to the connection. It is clear, however, that Riborg felt acutely guilty towards Poul Bøving and could not have made up her mind to break her engagement without a show of masterfulness on Andersen's part, of which his respect for other people's feelings would have made him incapable even had the violence of first love not robbed him of all emotional initiative and left him humbly worshipping his idol. In addition, his lack of financial security put him at a disadvantage. It has been deduced by the extraordinary panic that seized him after his formal declaration of his love that he may have been moved by an unconscious instinct, powerful as that which drove Kierkegaard to break his engagement to Regine Olsen, to fear family life as inimical to his work. Yet his love for Riborg was such as to make its denial a desperate matter for him, and after she left Copenhagen he was wild with grief.

Karen Blixen, who felt in her last years that she had lived more courageously than she would have done had she not read Andersen throughout her life, once said that 'Grief is always bearable if one can write it', and as if he too knew this, Andersen drew out of his grief a book of poems, *Fantasies and Sketches*, which was published in the New Year of 1831. He also wrote a vaudeville, *To Meet and to Part*, in which he gave his love for Riborg a happy ending. But nothing really helped him, and though he genuinely longed to be free of his suffering, a part of him dreaded the loss of the heightened sense of living that even unhappy love bestows on people of his temperament. For neither himself nor Riborg was this a trivial matter. They cherished every memento of their brief encounter. Today visitors to Odense can see a letter from Riborg to Andersen in the little leather bag he was wearing around his neck when he died. Copies of his poems to her, and also the flowers he gave her at Faaborg, long since dried of colour, which she had always kept together with a piece of paper on which she had written 'From Andersen' remained, traces of a sad passion.

About this time a friend who knew German called Andersen's attention to the work of a young German poet—Heine, whose *Das Buch der Lieder* had been published only four years earlier. Both Heine's lyricism and his obsession with tragic love captivated Andersen, who was for a time completely under the influence of Heine as he had been under that of Hoffmann. His favourite authors could not, however, help him to forget his misery. To his consternation he found himself becoming irritable, seeing only the darkest and saddest aspect of everything, and writing too much because he needed money, though knowing all the while that what he wrote was too immature to deserve publication. All the hopes that had been aroused in him by the success of his first book vanished. He felt as lonely and insecure as in his schooldays, and this sense of insecurity made him passionately dread any adverse comment on either his work or himself.

He was thus in a particularly vulnerable state when, at the end of 1830, Henrik Hertz, a writer seven years his senior who had been one of Meisling's star pupils, published anonymously a book of literary criticism entitled *Letters from a Ghost.* Written in the style of Jens Baggesen, an earlier writer whom Hertz admired, this book praised Heiberg's ironic and sophisticated outlook at the expense of the Romantic Oehlenschläger and his followers. Andersen especially was penalized for his early success and became a butt for jeers and mockery. This attack on him was so unexpectedly wounding that he felt he had failed in every way.

The Collins, who, no matter how freely they might criticize him themselves, considered all Andersen's private and public troubles a matter for family concern, finally realized that something was seriously wrong with his state of mind, stopped making fun of his vulnerability, and advised him to spend his savings on a trip abroad to remove himself from all that reminded him of Riborg.

Riborg married Poul Bøving in April 1831, and a few days later Andersen sailed for Germany.

In Andersen's day European countries differed one from another to a far greater extent than in modern times. Transport and communication were limited by the capacity of the horse, stage-coach, river barge and sailing ship, with the steamship still a novelty. Four-fifths of the people of Europe lived in the country, and the skylines of the walled cities were still to be identified by their churches and castles. The Germany of independent states through which Andersen passed on his first visit abroad was to be transformed within his own lifetime. The Holy Roman Empire with its three hundred and ninety-six principalities, ecclesiastical states and free towns had been completely reorganized by Napoleon in 1806. After his defeat it was found impossible to restore the old order; the new Germany that emerged from the Congress of Vienna now consisted of thirty-nine sovereign states (the largest being Austria, Prussia and Bavaria) loosely grouped into a German confederation or *Bund.* Almost every state had its own separate tariffs and customs house, which caused disgruntled travellers to be delayed at every frontier for no matter how insignificant a reason. The obstacles to trade became more and more serious and some inland states had to pay as many as a dozen different transit duties on every article imported or exported.

Lübeck, Andersen's first foreign city, had been founded in the eleventh century by the German Emperor Konrad. Outwardly its massive city walls and feudal gates, its medieval houses, Gothic churches and Rathaus had changed very little since the fifteenth century; but the nineteenth century had left the scars of war on the city's landmarks. After Napoleon's victory at Jena in 1806, Bernadotte, Soult and Murat had pursued Blücher and the remnants of the Prussian army as far as Lübeck, which they sacked and then quartered 75,000 troops there. Besides the war damage, the sights pointed out to visitors in Andersen's day included the birthplace of Godfrey Kneller, who became court painter to George I of England.

There were as yet no railways in Germany – England, the pioneer where trains were concerned, had inaugurated its first railway service only five years earlier – so Andersen travelled by public coaches. An avid traveller, he said of himself: 'To be in a strange haste is really my chief characteristic. The more interesting a book is, the more do I hasten to read it through that I may at once get the full impression of it: even in my travels it is not that which is present that pleases me; I hasten after something new in order to come to something else. Every night when I lie down to rest I hanker after the next day, wish that it were here, and when it comes, it is still a distant future that occupies me. Death itself has in it something interesting to me. What can it be that my uneasy self hastens after?' For so emotional a young man he had come late to first love with its physical and mental torments, and it seemed to him as if life itself were being denied him.

From Lübeck he went to Hamburg, Germany's most important port. People had always interested him even more than monuments, and he was eager to notice foreign customs and costumes. In Hamburg maidservants out shopping wore lace caps, long kid gloves and handsome shawls that covered their baskets; the city's funerals were accompanied by hired mourners who carried swords and wore curled and powdered wigs, plaited ruffs and short Spanish cloaks.

Driving from Hamburg across Lüneburg Heath, which he

found exactly like the description of it given by Jens Baggesen in 1792, he listened attentively to his fellow passengers' talk. One of them said: 'Heine is a great man in poetry, and his brother a great man on 'change. But I don't like his verses – they are so short. You get a rap on the nose, and then the poem is gone!' This same man resented Heine's calling the Germans '*Kartoffel-Gesichter*' (potato-faces) and added: 'I would not for anything in the world travel with such a man, for before one knew a word about it there might be a whole book written about one.' At Lüneburg, a little town of medieval appearance which the travellers reached late in the evening, the night-watchman making his rounds of the dark and narrow streets stopped his singing to call a greeting to the travellers. Andersen was overwhelmed by excitement at his first sight of the power and purity of a mountain landscape, and from Goslar he walked over the Brocken to Halle, a town of salt springs with a monument outside the city walls commemorating the battle of Leipzig. Here he again took the coach to Leipzig, where he found two or three booksellers in every street. 'Everywhere were to be seen bookcases filled with volumes,' he wrote, 'and in the large bright glass windows, engravings and pictures were innumerable.' He visited the church of St Nicholas where Luther was said to have preached, the room in the Auerbach-Keller from which Doctor Faust supposedly flew out riding on a wine-cask, and the river Elster where Poniatowski was drowned covering the French retreat in 1813. From there he followed the route through Meissen to beautiful Dresden, the capital of Saxony. The old city was divided from the new by the river Elbe and had been a centre for scholars and artists ever since the days of king Wenceslaus of Bohemia, the fifteenth-century king who gave gifts and privileges to the Minnesingers.

It was the custom for writers travelling abroad to call on the writers of the country and Andersen called on Ludwig Tieck with a letter of introduction from Ingemann. Now fifty-eight, Tieck was one of the best-known men of letters in Germany and had been called the greatest poet of the German 'soul' after Goethe and Jean-Paul Richter. For a long time he had been pouring forth poetry, drama, romances, folk and fairy tales, and dramatizations of fairy tales such as *Puss in Boots* and *Bluebeard*; he had also translated Spanish and English literature and, when Andersen met him, was completing the translation of Shakespeare begun by Schlegel who had died in 1829.

This was Andersen's first friendship with one of the writers whose interest in Germany's past was revealing a world of myth and fantasy in which he himself felt completely at home. His impression of homecoming was encouraged by the warmth of Tieck's welcome. Round-faced, blue-eyed, with an amiable smile and placid manner, Tieck was like an easygoing landowner rather than a Romantic poet. Andersen was invited to hear him give a reading of the second part of Shakespeare's *Henry IV* – an original reading, for he did not constantly name the characters, but played every part so well that there was never any confusion in his listeners' minds as to who was speaking. When Andersen left Dresden, Tieck embraced him and wished him good fortune as a poet. The kindness in the German's eyes moved Andersen to pray that when next he saw Tieck he might have written something worthy of the older man's attention and praise.

One of Andersen's best qualities as a traveller was that he felt so much that it never occurred to him to fake the currently fashionable reactions. He knew almost nothing of the great visual arts of the past, and when, for example, he saw Raphael's Madonna, his first reaction, like that of the youthful Proust to Sarah Bernhardt, was one of intense disappointment until the after-effects made themselves felt: 'It appeared to me as a friendly face, but not more beautiful than many I had seen. Is this the world's most beautiful picture? I thought, and I wished to be astonished in seeing it, but it remained the same. It appeared to me that several paintings of the Madonna, several women's faces in the gallery, were far lovelier. I went to see them again, and then the veil fell from my eyes. They now appeared to me as painted faces, for I had seen the divine one . . . It now became intelligible to me how a rational Catholic can kneel to an image.'

From Dresden Andersen made an excursion to Saxon Switzerland, going almost to the Tyrolean frontier, so eager he was to smell the air of Italy. His longing for the south increased on his last afternoon in Dresden, for it poured with rain, the Elbe

turned the colour of coffee, and porters scurried through the
streets with sedan-chairs carrying ladies who peered out from
behind red curtains. Regretfully he turned his back on the south
and started for Berlin, the capital of Prussia.

Few traces of the past existed in its broad regular streets and
two-storey houses of brick and plaster. Feeling no admiration for
the appearance of the city, he concentrated on meeting the poet
Adalbert von Chamisso, to whom he presented his letter from
Ørsted. When Andersen went to call on him, Chamisso opened
the door himself, a tall serious man in a brown dressing-gown
with long grey curls hanging down to his shoulders and strikingly
honest eyes. The fifty-year-old Chamisso was of a highly complex
temperament, an aristocrat and a liberal, a poet and a naturalist,
in sympathy with the German Romantic movement and bitterly
opposed to the reactionary political atmosphere of post-war
Germany. He had been born in Champagne, the son of a French
nobleman, but when he was eight years old his family fled from
the Revolution and lived as émigrés in the Low Countries and
southern Germany before settling in Berlin. There Chamisso
became page to the Queen of Prussia and later an officer in the
Prussian army. When in 1806 he was allowed to visit France, he
made the distressing discovery that he felt German in France, just
as he felt French in Germany. While in Paris he fell in love
with Madame de Staël and later followed her to Switzerland, but
despite her own mixture of 'German seriousness, meridional fire
and French manners', nothing came of it and he returned to
Berlin. In 1814 he published *Peter Schlemihl*, a novel about a
man who sold his shadow, which was a dramatization of the
conflict within himself and anticipated the twentieth-century
world of the displaced person. *Peter Schlemihl* was read all over
Europe.

Despite their divergent backgrounds and Andersen's poor
German, the two writers instinctively understood each other.
Chamisso quickly discovered 'wit, fancy, humour and simplicity'
in Andersen and proposed to translate his poems and present his
work to the German public. An exhilarated Andersen set off
homeward bound in the company of a baker, who was so thirsty
and so fearful of cholera that he drank six bottles of wine and fell

to singing dirges of death, the Devil and the White Lady as they drove along.

This journey to Germany, the country where he was to find fame before he received it at home, enlarged Andersen's universe. Like most writers who belong to small nations and whose native language is not widely spoken abroad, he needed to draw on the riches of foreign literatures. His father had read him Holberg, Voltaire, and the *Arabian Nights*; as a schoolboy he had delighted in Hoffmann, Walter Scott and Byron; Mrs Jürgensen had introduced him to Racine and Corneille, and as a young man in love he had turned to Heine. Now Tieck's romanticism and Chamisso's man without a shadow became an important part of his private universe, like those first medieval towns with their mountain backgrounds and museums, like the unearthly and unforgettable singing of the choir of eunuchs in Dresden Cathedral. He was now reading Goethe and Schiller as avidly as he had read Shakespeare and Walter Scott, and – what was undoubtedly of even more importance to his future – he read for the first time some tales by the brothers Grimm, who had resuscitated Germany's ancient folklore.

As young law students, Jakob Grimm and his brother Wilhelm had been followers of the great jurist Friedrich Karl von Savigny, whose lectures on Roman law stimulated their study of antiquity. It was in the year 1806, when the brothers were living together in Kassel, that Napoleon's armies occupied the town. Of this period Wilhelm wrote: 'Those days of the collapse of all existing establishments will remain for ever before my eyes . . . The ardour with which the studies of Old German were pursued helped overcome the spiritual depression . . .' Surrounded by 'foreign persons, foreign manners and a foreign, loudly spoken language', while 'poor people staggered along the streets being led away to death', the brothers Grimm steadily resuscitated the folk beliefs and tales of old Germany. They were encouraged in their research by two friends, Clemens Brentano and Ludwig Achim von Arnim, who had made their own collection of folk songs.

The first volume of the Grimms' *Nursery and Household Tales* was published during Napoleon's retreat from Moscow and had an instantaneous success all over Germany; curiously enough, it was banned in Vienna as 'a work of superstition'. The second volume appeared in 1815 and was equally appreciated, as it is to this day. The Grimms' masterly compilation won readers from all over the world and created a love and appreciation of folklore and fantasy that was to contribute to the nineteenth century's becoming the great age of books for children, who were no longer treated as miniature adults but as young people with special needs of their own.

After six enriching weeks in a foreign world of friendly strangers and stimulating sights, Andersen reached home with a sense of anticlimax. Everything in Copenhagen seemed just as it had been when he left, everyone just as ready with the admonitions do and don't, and his unhappiness over Riborg was just as acute as when he had gone away. He was shaken by his friends' attitudes and realized that only in work would he find refuge. At once he began to write a book about his travels.

Andersen's *Rambles in the Romantic Regions of the Harz Mountains and Saxon Switzerland* was published in September 1831. To read it today is to see the bygone Germany that came into existence with Napoleon's downfall and was transformed by the rise to power of Bismarck. It is also to see an eager, awkward young Danish poet who never lost sight of the figures in a landscape. The book was as individual as Andersen's account of his walks across Copenhagen, but this time the critics pounced on his deficiencies, calling him a presumptuous fool for having written a book about Germany after spending only six weeks there; they also deplored his spelling and grammar, and found him wanting in intellect and high moral purpose. Once again, it seemed to him, everyone was trying to teach him better, this time in public. He was even scolded for having written puppy with a small p (in Danish all nouns begin with a capital letter) and his reply that 'it was only a little puppy' was repeated as proof of his unwillingness to learn from criticism. Particularly humiliating for him was an ill-tempered attack from the prominent critic Molbech, who had been one of the first to praise Andersen's poems, though this attack was far more in keeping with Molbech's pedantic and spiteful nature than his praise had been, particularly since the critic had in his youth written an ornate account of his own travels through Germany, France and Italy. Molbech disliked Andersen's personality, and in his capacity of play-reader for the Royal Theatre would have many a future opportunity to do him harm. It was this July that Johanne Luise Pätges, the girl whom Andersen had known as a child actress, married the critic Heiberg a few months before her nineteenth birthday.

During the two years that followed his trip to Germany Andersen undertook far more work than he could accomplish with justice to his talents. First he adapted two French plays for the Royal Theatre, then turned to libretti. One of these, *The Bride of Lammermoor*, was accepted for production in May 1832. This gave his old friend the composer Weyse the idea of asking him to write a libretto for *Kenilworth* – which was unfortunate, because as soon as the project was made public Andersen's self-appointed critics began complaining that he was ruining one masterpiece after another. Although proud to be asked to collaborate on terms of equality with a composer he admired, Andersen would have abandoned the project had it not been for the insistence of Weyse, to whom he could refuse nothing on account of the help the composer had given him when he first arrived in Copenhagen. It did not occur to him to stipulate that the general lines of what he – not to mention Walter Scott – had written were not to be altered. As a result Weyse, who could not bear unhappy endings, had Amy Robsart stay married to Leicester. ('Why make them unhappy when a few strokes of the pen can improve their fate?') When Andersen objected that this was contrary to history and asked what in that case was to be done with Queen Elizabeth, Weyse answered cheerfully, 'She can say "Proud England, I am thine!" '

It was Andersen who was blamed for these ineptitudes. As a result, there was truth in his remark that for his next book of poems, *Vignettes for Danish Poets*, he was 'not criticized but reprimanded'. At such times it was to the Collins that he turned for the particular comfort of family affection. Their undemonstrative ways often hurt his feelings – Edvard, for example, though devoted to him, refused to address him as 'thou' rather than 'you', as was the habit in Denmark between intimate friends –

but Andersen set such store by their affection that he never ceased hoping that one day the Collins' words would speak as loudly as their actions.

He loved them all, but the one in whom he found it easiest to confide just then was Edvard's eighteen-year-old sister, Louise. The gentlest of the Collin children, she had a gift for sympathy that made her an active rather than a passive listener. She seemed to understand his feeling for Riborg, which, since he had spent so little time with her, was as much of the imagination as of the heart and generated its own torment. Riborg's marriage had not checked in Andersen the process that had been described ten years earlier by Stendhal as *crystallization* – just as a bare branch thrown into a deserted salt-mine is in two or three months covered with diamond-bright crystals, so Andersen's first impression of Riborg had been enriched with every perfection by his imagination. Enslaved by what he had himself created, he felt a desperate need to write and talk about Riborg, yet in so doing he only gave his obsession more power over him. Louise was the first person whose sympathy refreshed him. Gradually his need to discuss Riborg became a longing to talk of her to Louise, and presently this in turn was transformed into a need to be with Louise for her own sake. Once again an intoxicating excitement took possession of him. He felt the need to explain himself to Louise, to draw her into the love-duet in which one is alternately performer and spectator. Yet he had known her for so long – ever since she was a child for whom, as a schoolboy, he had made up stories, cut out paper dolls and invented games – that even when he was moved to write a poem to her, it did not occur to him that he was in love with her.

In the summer of 1832 Andersen went to visit his mother. He had hoped to take her away from the hospital and put her into comfortable lodgings in the country, but her reputation had gone before her and no one was willing to take her in. That same summer Prince Christian, on an official visit to the hospital, asked to see Anne-Marie and said to her in the hearing of other patients that her son did her honour. Andersen did not mention all this directly in his letters, but told Edvard: 'I haven't felt really well here in Odense, it's a strange exhaustion, a tenseness in my nerves. I get tired at the least exertion and am in a bad humour. People do all they can to entertain me, the most distinguished families show me the greatest attentiveness imaginable, but it doesn't help.'

It was fortunate for him that for the moment he had Louise to occupy his mind. Before the Collin family moved for the summer to their house outside Copenhagen, Louise had asked Andersen to write to her. Eagerly, he wrote and wrote. And not only letters. Longing to offer himself completely, he wrote an autobiography and stitched the sheets into a little *Book of My Life*, in many respects a more candid account of his youth than his later official autobiography. (This is the one that was first discovered in 1925 by Hans Brix and published in 1926.) Louise was pleased with his letters, in which all the proprieties were observed although love was evident in every line.

When the family returned to Copenhagen obstacles were put in the way of his seeing Louise alone. She had realized belatedly that in listening so sympathetically to Andersen, who was as dear to her as a brother, she had aroused an emotion she could not return. She consulted her married sister, Ingeborg, who advised her to tell Andersen that she had to show all her letters to Ingeborg. This, being a normal procedure among unmarried girls of her class, should calm Andersen's style without hurting his feelings. Louise agreed. She was herself already in love with her future husband, a young lawyer, J. W. Lind.

By depressing him without removing all hope, this half-measure merely increased Andersen's nervous tension, and when Louise's engagement was announced on New Year's Day, 1833, he felt betrayed by the entire family. 'No matter how good people are to me,' he told Edvard, 'I continue to be an outsider.' He did not blame Louise; he had not blamed Riborg; but this second defeat seemed to him to destine him to unhappiness in love. He longed to escape from everything familiar, but how? His friends advised him to apply to Frederik VI for one of the royal travel grants. He had received permission to present his latest book of poems, *The Twelve Months of the Year*, to the King, to whom it was dedicated, and was also advised to collect testimonials from as many well-known authors as possible and to present these and his petition at the same time as his poems. He was shocked at the idea of offering his book and immediately afterwards asking for something, but was assured that this was the custom. He had no difficulty in obtaining the testimonials: Oehlenschläger praised his lyrical talent, Ingemann his understanding of the people, Heiberg singled out his humour, Ørsted wrote that he was a true poet, and another writer, J. M. Thiele, expressed his admiration for talent that could struggle against such adverse circumstances as Andersen's.

Although Andersen set out for the palace with trepidation, it seemed to him quite natural to appeal to the King as one human being to another. The relationship between the Danish Crown and its subjects was unusually democratic. In Andersen's lifetime Edmund Gosse wrote: 'I was struck by the extreme tenderness, rather than awe, with which the King and his family were spoken of in Denmark, whenever their names came up in a conversation. It was less as a "reigning house" that they were discussed, than as fellow-citizens whose losses all the nation had shared with them, but who had suffered most, and who must therefore be assured by every smile and gesticulation of the passionate sympathy of their friends.' Thinking therefore of the King as a fatherly figure, Andersen presented his poems—and, as he was about to be dismissed, blurted out that he 'had a lot more to say yet'. He told the King of his studies, of the books he had written and his longing to travel. When the King said he must supply a petition for this, Andersen's embarrassment got the better of him and he came out with 'Yes, Your Majesty, I have it with me already. And that is what I think is so dreadful, that I have to bring it along with the book, but I was told I had to and that that was the way to do it, but I think it is so horrible and I hate doing it.' The King laughed and accepted the petition.

The suspense that followed was hard for Andersen to bear. He knew that his petition was only one among many, and the Collins, as always, advised against too optimistic hopes. Yet his longing for travel grew as he more and more often met Lind calling on Louise. Copenhagen, which had once represented to him the great world, now seemed like a prison. He told Edvard: 'It is not a year of my life that I wish to escape from; it is my whole spiritual self I wish to save.'

When at last his petition was granted Andersen found that the King's generosity had exceeded his own best hopes. He was to have not one but two years abroad. At last he was to begin a new life. With an exultant heart he left Copenhagen on April 22, 1833. The great adventure of Germany, France, Switzerland and Italy lay before him.

5. First Travels

1833

The chief objects of my journey were these: to free myself from the physical and moral uneasiness which rendered me almost useless, and to still the feverish thirst I felt for true art.

Goethe, from Rome, to the Duke of Weimar, April 22, 1788

Foreign travel, even to unintelligent, uninquiring minds, is always of great influence, not merely by the presentation of new objects, but also, and mainly, by the withdrawal of the mind from all the intricate connections of habit and familiarity which mask the real relations of life. This withdrawal is important, because it gives a new standing-point from which we can judge ourselves and others, and it shows how much that we have been wont to regard as essential is, in reality, little more than routine.

George Henry Lewes, *The Life of Goethe*

*

NOT SINCE HE LEFT ODENSE as a child had Andersen set out on so important and exciting a journey. Furthermore, this time he was sent off with scores of good wishes, some of them recorded in the album he took with him, its first pages already filled by circumstantial verses in which his friends exhorted him to hasten o'er the Rhine, to taste of joy beneath the palm, to let his fancy flit around him like a busy bee, to forget not Denmark's pleasant land, and to remember that all he saw while away must be recorded another day. All the Collins gathered to see him off, and Louise wept. As he watched the skyline of Copenhagen grow small behind him, he prayed that he might either justify his existence by producing a work of art or else die far from Denmark without having further disappointed his friends.

As the ship approached the spectacular white cliffs of the island of Møn the captain handed Andersen a letter, saying jokingly that this had just arrived by air. It was from Edvard and had been written that morning: 'Dear Friend! Suddenly the idea struck me that it might please you to receive a letter from me before you reached Hamburg and before you could expect a letter. What have I to say? Nothing! I cannot collect my thoughts at this moment. Believe me, I deeply regret your departure, I shall miss you dreadfully, miss our frequent talks in my room, miss you at the dinner-table on Tuesdays, yet I know it will be harder for you, for you are alone. But if it is any comfort to know that one has friends at home who think of one, then that comfort is certainly yours, for we shall constantly remember you with love. Farewell, my dear, dear friend. God grant that we may meet again happily in two years' time.'

A letter from another friend was presented to him as they reached the island of Falster, a third one that evening and yet another early next morning when the ship was just off Travemünde at the mouth of the Elbe. Andersen was overwhelmed by these proofs of affection and his letters home from Hamburg were full of gratitude.

This time Germany was not his main objective and he hastened across it by stage-coach. In Hamburg he made the acquaintance of Lars Kruse, a Danish poet now forgotten but then well-known, a plump, good-natured man who contributed some patriotic lines to Andersen's album. In Kassel he met the composer Ludwig Spohr, who was the court *Kapellmeister*, and visited the gardens of Wilhelmshöhe, known as the German Versailles. Its artificial ruins, lime avenues, cascades and fountains, which were the highest in Europe except for those of Chatsworth, impressed him less than a sudden unexpected glimpse of Napoleon's name, painted over but visible, at a street corner in Kassel. He still saw Napoleon in primary colours as the hero of his childhood.

In Frankfurt-am-Main, a Free City and since 1815 the seat of the Diet of the German Bund, he was fascinated by the narrow twisting cobbled streets, medieval town hall, quaint wooden houses with overhanging gables and wrought-iron well-tops, by the gilded street signs, and shops full of furs and Bohemian glass. He visited the house where Goethe (who had died the previous year aged eighty-three) was born and where he had written *The Sorrows of Werther*, the tragic love-story that had made its twenty-five-year-old author famous all over Europe and even in America and China. For Andersen there was poetry of another kind in the Rothschilds' childhood home in the old ghetto quarter. The gate behind which the Jews used to be locked into the ghetto at night had been destroyed only in 1796 by a French bombardment, and even in 1833 no more than thirteen marriages a year were permitted within the ghetto; yet still the old mother of the rich and powerful Rothschild brothers lived on there, unwilling to leave the home where she had raised her children.

Andersen's first sight of the Rhineland disappointed him. Its ruined castles and vineyards seemed to him less striking than the figures that haunted them, the Emperors Charlemagne, Barbarossa and Napoleon, Götz von Berlichingen who gave the rebellious peasants a leader, Siegfried who slew the dragon that stood guard over the gold of the Nibelungs, and the siren Lorelei whose songs lured boatmen to their doom. From here he wrote to Louise: 'Now you are with me by the Rhine. My thoughts have called you here; I see you so clearly. You are here, you sit at the window looking across the river at the vineyard on the mountainside – I speak to you, picture to myself every feature, every mood, every expression. Oh, I have so much to tell you . . . Do not forget me even if we should never meet again . . . No brother can be more faithfully attached to you than I am.'

The journey through Saarbrücken and across the chalky plateau of Champagne to Paris took three days and nights. Andersen kept asking how soon they would arrive, but was taken by surprise when at last, on May 10, 'pickled in dust and boiled with heat', he found himself at the *barrière* surrounded by Frenchmen in green uniforms who searched the carriage in vain for a wanted man. Then the carriage rattled along the exterior boulevards, between surging crowds and iron-wheeled vehicles that filled the air with an urban roar. The Paris of Louis-Philippe, who had been brought to the throne as a 'citizen king' by the July Revolution of 1830, seemed to Andersen a maelstrom of a city with its gas-lit streets and horse-drawn omnibuses. So exhausted was he that he could scarcely take in all he saw and as soon as he had found himself lodgings at the Hôtel de Lille in the Rue des Filles de St Thomas, between the Palais

Royal and the recently completed Stock Exchange, he fell into bed, incapable of sorting out his impressions – 'just because the curtain has risen, the spectators do not necessarily understand what the play is about'. He had not been asleep long before a tremendous noise awoke him. He went to the window and saw across the street the façade of the recently built Théâtre de Vaudeville with its statues in niches set between Ionic and Corinthian columns. People were pouring out of the theatre with shouts and cries that suggested yet another revolution. Andersen rang the bell and a waiter and chambermaid explained with a profusion of gestures that the disturbance was due merely to a thunderstorm.

It did not take him long to make friends among the large Danish colony and he was soon writing home: 'Paris is the place! Berlin, Hamburg and Copenhagen, all of them are nothing. I have now been here five days and already feel at home, and can find my way about quite easily.' Like the Germany of his youth, the Paris that Andersen saw then was to be transformed within his own lifetime. It was then still the Paris of Balzac's *Comédie Humaine*, still full of narrow medieval streets, noisy with the cries of vendors of food, drink, lottery tickets and old clothes, the trumpet of the public crier announcing lost and found objects, and the haunting music of the barrel-organ. There were still booths down either side of the Pont Neuf and at many of the bridges toll charges were enforced by war veterans. The Arc de Triomphe was not yet completed and it was dangerous to adventure alone at night into the rural Champs-Elysées. Montmartre was still a village, with a row of windmills against the skyline.

Of course it was to the theatres that Andersen hurried first. At the Opéra he heard Adolphe Nourrit, a great singer who had shown outstanding courage at the barricades during the July Revolution yet was to commit suicide after being hissed in Naples; at the Théâtre Français he saw the great tragedienne Mademoiselle Mars, who was reputed to have been Napoleon's mistress and at fifty-four still looked twenty years younger and had not lost the beauty of her voice. He visited Notre Dame, taking with him a copy of Victor Hugo's *Notre Dame de Paris* which had been published two years earlier. He saw the post-Revolution museum in the Louvre, of which he wrote home: 'The Louvre is the finest gallery imaginable. The whole in one hall, but this is so long that it made one giddy. In length it looked just like the main road to Roskilde.' He walked in the Jardin des Plantes, through the lime alleys, labyrinth, laboratory, and among the natural history exhibits laid out by Buffon. The giraffe which had attracted vast crowds ever since its arrival there in 1827, was still the main attraction of the Zoo. He spent a day in beautiful Versailles, which had been saved from demolition by Louis-Philippe, who turned it into a museum '*à toutes les gloires de la France*'. He visited the Grand Trianon and Napoleon's bedroom – which had also been the bedroom of Madame de Maintenon and Madame de Pompadour – kept exactly as it had been the last time the Emperor slept there.

He wandered every day about the streets of Paris. The modern aspects of the city appealed to him too. He was amazed by the multiplicity and gaiety of the shops – 'shop after shop; copper-plates and woodcuts; butchers' shops with sausages hanging in festoons; confectioners' with artificial cakes like Gothic castles; glass window after glass window, so that you are constantly in danger of breaking them, as you have to press up against them whenever two carriages pass each other in the street.' He enjoyed going out to the edge of town to watch the masons at work on the Madeleine, which had been started as a church by Louis XV, continued as a temple to the glory of the Grand Army by Napoleon, and only narrowly escaped being turned into the first railway station in Paris before its final consecration as a church in 1842.

During his first month in Paris Andersen received not a single message from home, although he himself wrote twenty-one letters – and when at last he did receive one it proved to be merely a newspaper lampoon against himself. Since he did not know that this was meant as an answer to verses praising him that had recently been published in the same paper, he saw in this incident further proof of the poor opinion his own country-men had of him. He was therefore very grateful for the friendship of the group of Danes with whom he went to theatres, made excursions and chatted in cafés. Not all his new friends were zealous sightseers – one of them told him candidly, 'You've got to see the damned places! It would be a shame to go home and have to say you hadn't been there when your friends asked you. Now I have only a few places left, and when I've finished with them I'm really going to enjoy myself' – but there were some remarkable characters among them. Andersen's favourite, Lieutenant Dinesen of the artillery, whom he described to Christian Voigt as 'a brilliant fellow', was the grandfather of the Danish writer Karen Blixen, who was to love Andersen's work so deeply.

Notre Dame de Paris was the first French book Andersen had tried to read in the original and he called on its young author, who lived in the Place des Vosges. This beautiful square with its houses of pink brick and white stone, its blue-tiled roofs and street-level arcades, was originally known as the Place Royale. It was built in the seventeenth century by Henri IV, the first Bourbon King of France, and renamed Place des Vosges in 1800 because the Vosges had been the first Department to pay its taxes after the Revolution. Victor Hugo, who was at this time thirty-one and the acknowledged head of the French Romantic movement – his play *Hernani* had provoked riots three years earlier – lived in a corner house, No. 6. Like Chamisso, he opened the door to Andersen himself, wearing an elegant dressing-gown and slippers, and readily showed his visitor over his rooms, which were hung with prints, woodcuts and paintings of Notre Dame. Andersen was full of admiration for this handsome and successful young man. Only one incident marred the visit. When Andersen asked him to write his name on a piece of paper, Victor Hugo carefully wrote it at the extreme top of the sheet in order to prevent anything being written above his signature.

A visit more in the nature of a pilgrimage was the one Andersen paid to the Italian composer Cherubini, to whom Weyse had given him an introduction. Cherubini, who was seventy-three and had lived in Paris for the past forty-five years, had recently composed a new opera, *Ali Baba*. Andersen was charmed to find the old man, who looked exactly like his portraits, seated at his piano with a cat on either shoulder. Later he called on Heiberg's father. Now old and half blind, Peter Andreas Heiberg was living alone in a small hotel. The former revolutionary was distressed that his son should have married an actress and relieved to hear from Andersen that Johanne Luise Heiberg was as respectable as she was talented.

The only encounter that disappointed Andersen was the one with Heine, who had settled in Paris after the July Revolution and, coming upon Andersen in a club called the Europe Littéraire, held out his hand and said, 'I hear you are Danish. I am German. Danes and Germans are brothers, so I offer you my hand.' With unfeigned enthusiasm Andersen told Heine how much the latter's poetry meant to him, and added that there was no one he would rather have met. Next day Heine called at Andersen's hotel and after that they often met, and sometimes walked along the boulevards together; but despite Andersen's enthusiasm for his poetry, he was never completely at ease with the sophisticated Heine. There was something about Heine's complex and erotic personality that Andersen could not entirely trust and no real intimacy developed between them.

In July, towards the end of his stay in Paris, Andersen was present at a spectacular ceremony in the Place Vendôme. In honour of the victorious French campaign of 1805, Napoleon had raised a column there modelled on that of Trajan in Rome and encased in bronze melted down from the cannon captured by the French at Austerlitz. At the top had stood a statue of Napoleon in the character of Cæsar. In 1814 this statue had been replaced by one of Henri IV, which was itself removed during the Hundred Days. Next Louis XVIII installed the old royal emblem, the fleur-de-lis. Now Louis-Philippe had decided to replace a statue of Napoleon on the column. On the evening before the ceremony Andersen joined the crowd that was watching the men still at work on the column. As he stood there an old woman approached him and, with a crazy laugh, said: 'Now they've put him up there. Tomorrow they'll tear him down again! I know the French.' Next day Andersen returned to the Place Vendôme to watch the ceremony. He found a niche on some scaffolding, where he sat in the sun from eleven in the morning till five in the afternoon. He got a good view of Louis-Philippe, his sons and generals, and saw 100,000 National Guardsmen march past, with flowers in the barrels of their guns, to the music of brass bands. That evening, wearing gala dress with silk stockings, white gloves and curled hair, he went to a ball at the Hôtel de Ville, where he saw the handsome young Duc d'Orléans dance with a poorly dressed working-class girl. When the orchestra played the dance music from the scene in *Gustav III* in which that King is assassinated, Queen Amélie turned pale and clutched Louis-Philippe, who appeared completely unmoved. The festivities lasted for several days with fireworks, illuminations, tournaments of boats on the Seine, and dancing under the trees in the Champs-Elysées. Theatres opened at midday, free for all, and performances were often interrupted by the entire audience singing 'La Marseillaise' or 'La Parisienne'.

For all the time he spent on letter-writing and diary-keeping, Andersen had been intermittently at work in Paris on a long poetic drama, *Agnete*, planned before he left home. His play was based on an old Danish ballad about a young girl who throws herself into the sea for love of a merman, but after seven years wearies of the grandeur of her life in the caves of coral at the bottom of the sea and returns to earth, only to discover that, as seven years under the sea amount to fifty on earth, her abandoned fiancé is an old man and all her friends and kinsmen are dead. Andersen so loved this ballad, in which he saw 'the great image of life, the never-satisfied yearnings of the heart and its strange longing for a new and different form of existence', that it haunted him even in Paris, even 'on the gay boulevard and amid the treasures of the Louvre'. He responded eagerly to mountains, foreign landscapes and cities, but he came from a kingdom of islands and in his finest stories there is the sound of the sea, its melancholy long withdrawing roar.

At last he found Paris too distracting for regular work and thought of making a stay in Switzerland before going on to Italy. Friends in Copenhagen had given him a letter to a Swiss relative of theirs in Paris, who in turn sent him to a family called Houriet at Le Locle in the Jura mountains, in the canton of Neuchâtel, where he would be welcome and able to live cheaply.

First Travels

After the excitements of his life in Paris he suddenly longed to be back at work, and he set off happily on August 15, with his head full of sea-scapes, coral caves and love doomed by time.

The journey to Le Locle took several days, and by the time the dusty diligence reached the Jura mountains Andersen was its only passenger. On a Sunday morning, as the diligence was swaying along beside steep precipices, the mist suddenly cleared and Andersen saw Mont Blanc for the first time. Now that photography has made armchair travellers of us all, it is difficult to imagine the thrill aroused by unfamiliar scenes in those who saw them before the railway age, at that exciting transitional moment when travel was no longer primitive and not yet streamlined.

As the road wound downwards Andersen saw the great Lake of Geneva, with the city at its western extremity, and an alpine panorama, the glaciers shining in the sunlight, and the lower slopes of the mountains in a bluish haze. Soon they were driving past woods, vineyards, meadows and cornfields to the ramparts of Geneva. The most populous city in the Swiss Confederation and its intellectual metropolis, Geneva was divided into an upper town, with the large and handsome houses of the burgher aristocracy, the senators and magistrates, and a lower town, the business section. Andersen took advantage of his halt there to visit an old man called Puerari who had formerly taught French in Copenhagen. He kept open house for Danes and regaled Andersen with the story of how he had entertained Louis-Philippe to dinner during the latter's exile.

Farther along the lake Andersen stopped at Chillon to visit the castle. Drawbridge, trap-doors and dungeons complete with iron rings that had held the chains of long-dead prisoners impressed Andersen less than the sight of Byron's name carved there by the poet himself in 1816. The woman who showed Andersen round had been there at the time and, unaware of Byron's identity, had vainly remonstrated with him. Now, however, she told Andersen, all her visitors wanted to see that pillar because 'he was an unusual sort of person, that gentleman'. From there Andersen travelled back to Le Locle, a market town set just inside the Swiss border in a mountain valley that in prehistoric times had been a lake. Fossils of fishes were still to be found there, although Le Locle was now often above cloud-level. The intensely green grass was already dotted with autumn crocus and the peasants' immaculately white houses stood out against a background of spruce trees and red-berried mountain ash.

Andersen was astonished by the enthusiasm with which the Houriet family welcomed him. Jules Houriet was a watchmaker, like his brother-in-law, the late Urban Jürgensen, and neither he nor his wife would hear of the young Dane's paying for his board and lodging. They were eager for first-hand news of Jules Houriet's sister, whom they had not seen since she followed her husband to Denmark, and because of Andersen's connection with her they treated him as if he were one of the family, which consisted of themselves, their children and 'two magnificent old aunts', Jules Houriet's sisters, Rosalie and Lydia. The fact that the Houriets spoke only French made communication erratic, and since they could not read anything he had written, Andersen was forced to conclude, with surprise and pleasure, that they liked him independently of his work. They did. The children showed this liking by shouting at him in the belief that this would render their local dialect comprehensible, and the aunts insisted on mending and knitting for him.

Even in this peaceful eyrie there were echoes of political unrest. Although Neuchâtel had become a Swiss Canton in 1815 it was still claimed as a principality by the King of Prussia, and those of its inhabitants who favoured Prussia were constantly provoking those who favoured Switzerland and vice versa. As always in such cases, molehills were easily transformed into mountains and during Andersen's visit there was angry talk of a member of the pro-Prussian faction who had visited a pro-Swiss neighbour and 'accidentally-on-purpose' broken the glass over a picture of William Tell. As the very nature of Andersen's gifts made him apolitical, he listened to such stories with puzzled sadness, thinking of the individual rather than the mass psychology involved. Most of the time, however, his stay was deliciously peaceful. Although it was the month of August there were days when snow fell in the mountains and wintry clouds floated below the town. Andersen was given a fire in his room and the tranquillity peculiar to mountains helped him to work steadily at

Agnete. In the evenings he could hear church bells chiming from the French border across the river, and he would walk out of the little town to a deserted house from which he could see the water turning the wheels of a mill. So much of his early dreaming had been done beside the water-mill at Odense that he was irresistibly drawn to domesticated rivers. He worked so well here that he was able to send the completed manuscript of *Agnete* to Copenhagen on September 14.

The next day he left for Italy. The parting from his new friends was an emotional one. The Houriets shook his hand again and again, the children wept, the servants had tears in their eyes and the aunts presented him with knitted mittens to keep his hands warm when crossing the Simplon, the first transalpine route, opened to the public in 1807. He was sorry to leave them all, but now that *Agnete* was finished he could yield to his longing to see Italy. He felt himself about to embark on an extraordinary experience. '*Agnete* and Le Locle', he said later, 'closed one part of my life.'

6. Italian Journey

1833-5

At length they came to the warm countries. There the sun shone far more brightly than it ever does here, and the sky seemed twice as high. Along the ditches and hedgerows grew marvellous green and blue grapes. Lemons and oranges hung in the woods. The air smelt sweetly of myrtle and thyme. By the wayside the loveliest children ran hither and thither, playing with the brightly coloured butterflies. But the swallow kept flying on and on and the country became more and more beautiful.

Hans Christian Andersen, *Thumbelina*

Almost all that sets us above savages has come to us from the Mediterranean.

Dr Johnson

*

WINTRY CLOUDS floated now above, now below the diligence as it climbed the mountains, rumbling alongside precipices, through ravines and past glaciers. The road that 'by the command of Napoleon was blown out of the very backbone of the earth' had been completed only in 1806, and Andersen thought with shuddering admiration of the French army that had crossed the pass in 1800 burdened with stores, cannon and ammunition. The air was cutting as a northern winter, isolated inns kept fires roaring in their stoves, and shepherd boys went wrapped in cowhide. Andersen was dazzled by the contrast when later he found himself driving in brilliant sunshine past leafy chestnut trees into Domodossola, the little town's market-places offering gay miniatures of Italian street-life.

When Andersen entered Italy for the first time, he came, he saw, he was conquered. Here at last was the world of light for which he had longed. Like Goethe on his first visit to Italy forty-five years earlier, he suddenly felt 'at home in the wide world, no longer an exile'; and like his own swallow, he found the country more and more beautiful as he kept flying on and on, first along Lake Maggiore shining between its dark mountains, and then in Milan, where he stood gazing with wonder at the cathedral that rose in the moonlight like some mighty cliff, its marble population peering out from under little Gothic canopies. Although the cathedral had been planned in the fourteenth century by Gian Galeazzo Visconti, it was still not entirely completed. Napoleon had contributed Gothic windows, pinnacles and flying buttresses; now the Austrians were at work on both the cathedral and the Porta della Pace, as they called the triumphal arch that the Milanese persisted in calling the Porta Napoleone. Next day Andersen visited the Scala opera-house, so called because it had been built on the site of Santa Maria della Scala. He was awestruck by its size and splendour; it could seat three thousand spectators and each of its boxes had a small sitting-room behind it. Seventeen years later Stendhal described it as 'the focal point of the entire city . . . the universal salon. *Rendez-vous at the Scala* – such is the accepted convention of all manner of business. The first experience is literally intoxicating.'

From Milan Andersen crossed the fertile plains with their weeping willows and fields of maize to Genoa, where he attended one of the first performances of Donizetti's *L'Elisir d'Amore* at the Teatro Carlo Felice, the third largest opera-house in Italy. What impressed him most in Genoa, however, was neither art nor beauty but a visit to the arsenal, where he saw about six hundred galley-slaves at work amid scenes that recalled Piranesi's prison engravings. Experiencing again the 'nightmare of the spirit' that he had known as a child visiting Odense prison, Andersen felt the ignominy of being a tourist in such a place. At night the prisoners were chained to their plank beds: 'Even in the infirmary a few lay in chains. Three of them, with yellow-brown faces and glazed eyes, were on the point of death . . . one of the criminals there stared at me with an evil look in his eyes and burst into bestial laughter. I understood him, for I had come merely out of curiosity, to see them suffer . . .'

As he travelled farther south Andersen was for the first time even more bewitched by his surroundings than by the people in them. His visual capacities were roused to their utmost: oranges, lemons, pomegranates in their natural sunny surroundings, nut-brown fishermen in scarlet caps; grey-green olive groves turning silver when the wind tossed over the undersides of the leaves; the bay of Spezia, where Byron's friend Shelley had been drowned eleven years earlier; vines slung from tree to tree; black piglets frolicking like kids; Carrara decked with garlands for the Duke of Modena's birthday; soldiers with sprigs of myrtle in their caps; marble quarries in magic mountains full of figures waiting for a sculptor to liberate them; a Capuchin monk holding a grass-green umbrella over himself and his unruly ass; ancient bridges of ivy-clad stone; three old women, their silvery hair hanging over their golden-brown shoulders as they sat spinning under a tree at the foot of an old tower; and everywhere the patterns of art coincident with those of husbandry.

The beauty, interest and novelty of all he saw did not blind Andersen, however, to the fact that Italian travelling conditions were the worst he had yet encountered. Inns were fly-infested, innkeepers dishonest, stage-coaches dirty and bandits still active. At this period Italy's unity was merely geographical, since the country was divided into seven states. The Kingdom of Naples, Tuscany and Sardinia, and the Papal States had been restored by the Congress of Vienna to their pre-Napoleonic rulers; the duchy of Parma was ruled by Napoleon's widow Marie-Louise, now morganatically married to her lover, Count von Neipperg; Modena had an Austrian grand duke, and the Lombardy-Venetian kingdom had been restored to Austria, which therefore dominated Italy. After the revolutionary uprisings of 1830, in which the Duke of Modena and Marie-Louise had been temporarily driven from their thrones and provisional governments set up in the papal territories east of the Apennines, Austrian repression had been severe and at the time of Andersen's visit the Austrian police were much in evidence and travellers constantly badgered for their passports. Andersen, who had a particular dread of being separated from his passport, counted ten demands for it within his first few days in Italy. This disturbed him. He said of himself: 'I am one of those who get up in the middle of the night when they have to start early next morning,' and all too often his fears were justified. Near Pisa, for example, the coachman lost his way and they did not reach the town until the middle of the night, when the travellers had to search for their hotel through streets lit only by the flame of a torch provided at the city gate. And everywhere their lack of Italian made them a prey to garrulous guides, like the one in Leghorn who announced: 'There lives a Turkish merchant, but his shop is shut today. There is a church with a pretty painting in it, but it has been taken away. The man who just passed is one of the richest in town.'

None of these inconveniences seemed to Andersen of any importance, however, when he saw Florence. Until then the plastic arts had meant little to him. At home he had seen almost no sculpture, and in Paris he had looked at it with an untrained eye. Nor had painting moved him deeply. Now, in Florence, a revolution took place in his powers of perception. Faced with the Venus de Medici and especially with the Hall of Niobe, where he walked among the statues of the bereaved mother and her daughters feeling himself to be 'in the midst of the action', he became aware of tactile values. (Both these works of art were then intensely admired – Byron had celebrated the Venus de Medici in a stanza of 'Childe Harold' and Shelley called Niobe 'the most consummate personification of loveliness with regard to its countenance . . . that remains to us of Greek antiquity'.) To Raphael, too, Andersen responded with a spontaneity that had not been his in Dresden. Architecture, painting and sculpture never appealed to him as strongly as music and literature, but, thanks to Italy, they became integral parts of the world of his imagination. He was sufficiently aware of the change in himself to write to Henriette Wulff: 'If only I could be seventeen again, but with my present feelings and ideas, then I could become somebody. Now all I see is that I know nothing, can do nothing, and life is so short. How am I to learn so infinitely much? This is an emotion I never knew before, it makes me intensely sad . . . My heart grows too big for me here in Italy, and yet it cannot hold all the splendour.'

The journey from Florence to the Papal States—which had been restored and placed under Austrian protection by the Congress of Vienna—began inauspiciously. No sooner were Andersen and his two Danish fellow travellers seated in the coach than a fourth passenger arrived, who described himself as a Roman nobleman but was so filthy and evil-smelling that at the first stop the Danes insisted on his riding outside with the coachman. The inn that night was a particularly sordid one, and the alleged nobleman sat by the fire resentfully plucking the chickens that were to be cooked for dinner and calling down audible curses on the 'heretical Englishmen', all of whom were subsequently bitten by insects so severely that Andersen, for one, had a high fever. When at last they reached the frontier of the Papal States and had undergone the usual pettifogging customs examination, they were obliged to put up at an inn swarming with maimed beggars. The doors were hinged with string, bats flew about the ceiling, and the filthy landlady spat on the floor as she served watery soup flavoured with rancid oil, dubious eggs, roasted cockscombs and sour wine.

The rest of the journey to Rome was a matter of contrasts, a visit to Perugia with its Etruscan buildings and Gothic cathedral, its pictures by Perugino and his great pupil Raphael being followed by a dismal night in Folignano where, thanks to a recent earthquake, dilapidated houses were propped up by beams of wood and appeared likely to collapse at any minute. At the waterfalls of Terni, situated among laurels and rosemary above a sea of olives, Andersen became so absorbed by the sunset that he lost his party and found his way back with a young American traveller who talked to him of the Niagara falls, James Fenimore Cooper's novels and the great prairies of America.

After a night fit for entomologists at Nepi, they approached the Campagna, the wild and undulating plain around Rome where the yellow Tiber marks the ancient boundary between Latium and Etruria. When at last, on October 18, they reached the spot where many a pilgrim from the north fell on his knees in rapture as the postilion, pointing ahead, cried *'Ecco Roma!'*, they were so exhausted that all Andersen could say was: 'Thank goodness! Now we shall be able to have something to eat.'

The Rome Andersen saw, a medieval and Renaissance city, with the ruins of antiquity not yet completely excavated, was a mixture of the cosmopolitan and the provincial. Foreigners lived for the most part in the neighbourhood of the Piazza di Spagna, known locally as the English ghetto (the adjective English being applied impartially to all foreigners), and the piazza itself was full of foreign coaches, parked there because they were too big to go through the entrance archways into their owners' courtyards. Hotels were few and expensive and most travellers preferred to rent furnished rooms, which were plentiful. Foreign artists formed a group of their own, subdivided according to nationality, as in Goethe's day. Their headquarters, the Caffè Greco, just off the Piazza di Spagna, had been founded in 1760 and still flourishes today. The American sculptor William Wetmore Story, later to be a friend of Andersen's, described the Caffè Greco as 'a place where artists meet and discuss subjects of art, pictures and statues, read the French newspapers and *Galignani*, and fill the air of the crowded little room with tobacco smoke. There you may see every night representatives of art from all parts of the world, in all kinds of hats, from the conical black felt, with its velvet ribbon, to the stiff French stovepipe; and in every variety of coat, from the Polish and German nondescript, all befrogged and tagged, to the shabby American dress-coat, with crumpled tails; and with every cut of hair and beard, from that of Peter the Hermit, unkempt and uncut, to the moustache and pointed beard of Anthony Vandyck . . .'

Andersen chose rooms in the Via Sistina, and was soon invited by the Scandinavians and Germans, who were grouped together, to 'give a Ponte Molle', a ceremony which he describes in his novel *Only a Fiddler*: 'Formerly it was the custom among the artists, when a well-known countryman arrived, to go out to meet him as far as Ponte Molle, the bridge over the Tiber across which the Via Flaminia leads into Rome, and to drink to his welcome in the inn there. Now this takes place in Rome, in the hostel where the artists assemble of an evening. Every artist, be he of great or small repute, is a brother of the order as soon as he has given a Ponte Molle, that is to say has paid for everything the guests consume on his evening of induction. The writer sets one jug of wine after another on the table; several comical ceremonies are performed, and the new candidate is nominated knight of the Bajocco order, the decoration of which consists of a copper Bajocco [a small coin] attached to a riband and worn at every subsequent Ponte Molle. Horace Vernet [the painter of battle scenes who was director of the French school of art in Rome from 1828–34], Friedrich Overbeck [the leading German painter in Rome, who specialized in religious scenes] and Thorvaldsen [the Danish sculptor] are members of this order . . .'

Andersen arrived in Rome in time to see Raphael buried for the second time. Doubts having been cast on the authenticity of the skull exhibited as that of Raphael in the Accademia Santa Lucia, Pope Gregory XVI had given permission for the painter's body to be exhumed. The skeleton was found to be complete and was reburied in the Pantheon. Most of the artists in Rome attended the ceremony, at which the coffin, draped in gold cloth, stood on a black dais while an invisible choir sang the *Miserere*, and it was here that, for the second time in his life, Andersen saw Thorvaldsen.

A handsome genial giant of a man, then sixty-three and at the height of his fame, Bertel Thorvaldsen was the outstanding figure of the Danish colony and an object of hero-worship to Andersen, who had seen his statue of Christ above the altar in the Church of Our Lady in Copenhagen, his figures of the apostles down the aisles – with Judas replaced by St Paul – and the angel holding a mussel shell in which the children of Copenhagen are still baptized. Born in Copenhagen of a Danish mother and an Icelandic father who was a shipbuilder by trade and carved wooden figureheads for ships, Thorvaldsen showed a talent for sculpture and drawing so early that at eleven years old he was taken from the free school and sent to the Academy of Arts. There he won all the prizes, including the gold medal that carried a grant for study abroad, and, like Andersen, Thorvaldsen was given several years of scholastic studies as a foundation for his artistic career. In 1797 he went to Rome. There he worked hard and well but without selling anything, so that in 1803 he saw nothing for it but to return home. He was saved by a providential delay. At the last minute the German sculptor Hagemann, with whom Thorvaldsen was to travel, discovered that his passport was not in order. Even so, the carriage was already at the door, the luggage corded, when an English connoisseur, Thomas Hope, called to see Thorvaldsen's statue of Jason, which he had heard praised by the Italian sculptor Canova in whose studio Thorvaldsen had worked. Hope was so struck by this work that he asked Thorvaldsen to execute it for him in marble and offered 800 zechins instead of the 600 that the sculptor was asking. After this orders poured in from all sides and Thorvaldsen was able to remain in Rome, where he attained such a position that in 1823 he was chosen to design the tomb of Pius VI.

As a boy of fourteen, newly arrived in Copenhagen, Andersen had once seen Thorvaldsen, who was then visiting his native land. Recognizing him in the street from his pictures, Andersen had taken off his hat to him. Thorvaldsen walked on a few paces, then stopped, turned back and asked the boy, 'Where have I seen you before? I seem to think we two know each other.' When Andersen later reminded him of this incident, Thorvaldsen smiled, pressed his hand and said, 'Yes, I must have had a feeling then that we should be friends.' Thorvaldsen was a leonine character who was popularly supposed to have once told a rival, 'Tie my hands behind my back and I will bite the marble better than you can chisel it,' and he took an immediate liking to his young countryman and gave him excellent advice. He fully understood Andersen's dread of the pedagogic criticism to which he was subjected in Copenhagen and told him: 'Never let that sort of thing touch you. Feel your own strength. Don't be led by public opinion. Go quietly ahead. Peace of mind is essential to creative work. You are unfortunate in needing a public, but this is something the public must never be made aware of, otherwise one becomes a prey to its whims. I know what they are like at home. It would have been no better for me had I stayed there. I might have been prevented from working from the nude. Thank goodness I don't need them. If one needs them they know how to torment and irritate one.'

With his new friends Andersen made sorties into the Campagna, which in those days extended right into the city to where vines grew around St John Lateran, the chief of Rome's fifteen basilicas. Some of these excursions had a touch of danger, for brigands still roamed among the ruined towers and aqueducts, isolated farmhouses, herds of buffaloes and flocks of sheep. At Frascati, formerly the bishopric of the last of the Stuarts, Bonnie Prince Charlie's younger brother, Andersen lunched in a rustic *osteria*, full of priests and peasants. Hens cackled underfoot and ragged children led the travellers' donkeys to the fireside. Andersen rode past the ruins of Cicero's villa and of ancient Tusculum; visited the well at Monte Pozio, renowned for its liquid music; saw the Cenci castle by moonlight, its cypresses black against the sky; and the monastery at Grottaferrata where Domenichino found refuge after a murder and in gratitude painted four pictures for his pious hosts. He was dazzled by the topiary splendour and unique waterfalls of the Villa d'Este and by the mysterious aspect of lake Nemi, set in the crater of an extinct volcano. Here the cult of the Goddess Diana had been celebrated until well into the second century after Christ by a high priest known as the King of the Wood, who was a runaway slave and spent most of his time, sword in hand, guarding a tree in the sacred grove from which another runaway slave would one day pluck a bough prior to killing and succeeding him. The ancients thought this was the tree Aeneas visited before making his journey to the underworld. The year after Andersen's visit here Turner painted the scene in his famous picture 'The Golden Bough', and here Sir James Frazer was to find inspiration for his great study of magic and religion. To Andersen's delight these striking landscapes were peopled with picturesque figures: a gold-braided quack making extravagant claims for his medicines from the cart in which he travelled; bandits chained to a cart drawn by oxen and surrounded by a posse of gendarmes; a funeral procession with the setting sun giving a simulacrum of life to the dead man's pale face, and boys catching the wax from the monks' candles in paper cones; groups of young men playing *morra*, and of girls dancing the *saltarello* to the sound of tambourines.

Absorbed by his travels, Andersen would have been completely happy had it not been for the unsatisfactory matter of letters from home. Either his friends were dilatory – provoking him to write unwisely, 'This letter of mine is equal to four of yours; therefore please don't make them so short. The last one I got drove me to despair; it was as short as a sneeze, but still I would say "God bless you";' or else they lectured him. Edvard Collin, in particular, could find nothing good to say about *Agnete*, and, discerning in it reflections of Andersen's love for Louise, recommended more manliness, less exaggeration. Edvard also felt it his duty to point out that all but a handful of Andersen's friends were heartily sick of his writings, and no wonder, said Edvard, since he wrote too much and 'this furious, this deplorable productivity' was reducing the value of his work. He was horrified, too, at the thought that Andersen might be so foolish as to write a book about his travels: 'Who do you think will buy a book in several volumes dealing with your journey, a journey which a thousand others have made? . . . Fundamentally it is enormously egotistical of you to think that people are interested in you . . .' He also reminded Andersen that his *Collected Poems* had been spitefully reviewed by Molbech, and yet again urged him to stop writing and give himself up to study and enjoyment. This negative advice was useless to Andersen. His 'furious productivity' was due less to the need to earn money, to which he placatingly attributed it, than to the desperate vitality with which his talent was struggling to discover the form of expression best suited to it.

Andersen's diary shows that despite the good nature that made him instinctively forgive injuries, he had moments of bitter rebellion against his affective dependence on the Collins, moments when Edvard appeared to be an egotistical prig, and when even Louise's tears on parting from him seemed, in retrospect, merely hypocritical. Nothing good, he felt in these moods, would await him at home. For once he wrote Edvard an angry letter, but Jonas Collin wisely kept this from his son, destroyed it, and himself wrote to Andersen: 'You no more deserve his reproofs than he deserves your passionate anger. He really does care greatly for you, and is your warmest defender when need be. I shall say nothing about all the trouble he has taken to get *Agnete* published in the most handsome and economical form, and how untiringly he has himself packed and despatched copies for subscribers and booksellers. He takes every chance to prove his interest in you, without wanting it to be noticed. Like his father, he does not care to have his heart peered into . . . I do not approve of his admonishing tone with you, but, dear Andersen, bear with him; everyone has his weakness, that happens to be his . . . When next you get a friendly letter from him, tear up the bad one; those are not memories to cherish.'

Andersen's disappointment over *Agnete* was still fresh in December when he received a letter from Jonas Collin telling him that his mother was dead. He knew that Anne-Marie had had nothing ahead of her but suffering and degradation, yet at her death a dreadful loneliness seized him. In his diary he wrote: 'I cannot accustom myself to the idea of being absolutely alone, without a single person who *must* love me on account of ties of blood.' Memories of his happy childhood rose to the surface of his mind and he saw his mother as she had been then, upright and vigorous, a pillar of strength. He thought of the little room in Odense that she had kept so neat and snug, and of the window-box on the roof that was her garden. He saw again the best dress in which she used to accompany his father and himself to the woods to greet the spring; he heard again the susurration of the river which to him had meant the Emperor of China but to her only backbreaking work at her scrubbing-board. He thought of her belief in signs and portents, and of the way in which she had obeyed his father's plea that their child be allowed to choose his own path in life no matter how foolish a one it might seem. In her drinking, as in his father's surrender to dreams, he recognized a need for stronger sensations than daily life had provided, a need that in himself had found an outlet in writing. This reminder of the brevity and sadness of life made him painfully aware of his own immaturity, and he told Henriette Wulff: 'I was a child until I had passed beyond the years of youth. I have never known what youth really is.' There was some truth in this. Andersen retained the childlike immediacy of his reactions until old age.

On November 17 Henrik Hertz, the Danish writer who three years earlier had lampooned Andersen and other young poets in his *Letters from a Ghost*, had arrived in Rome. Jonas Collin, who seems to have understood Andersen far better than his son Edvard did, had written announcing Hertz's arrival and had added that personally he would be glad to hear that Hertz and Andersen had had a friendly meeting. One day soon afterwards, when Andersen was sitting in the Caffè Greco, Hertz came in, went up to him and offered him his hand and expressed his sympathy over Andersen's mother's death. A reconciliation took place then and there, and they agreed to travel to Naples together after the Roman Carnival, which began on New Year's Day and continued until Shrove Tuesday.

The Collins understood perfectly what his mother's death meant to him. Edvard wrote to him feelingly: 'I cannot console you, dear friend; the knowledge that you have been a good son, a son who did not forget his poor old mother on entering a new sphere, should offer you a great deal of consolation. If there is something among her effects – these have presumably become the hospital's property – which could have sentimental value for you, something from your childhood which could be of interest to you, then I shall be happy to acquire it for you.'

Thorvaldsen and his fellow artists were full of sympathy too, and saw to it that he played an active part in their Christmas celebrations. Christmas Eve merrymaking was forbidden within the walls of Papal Rome, so the Knights of Bajocco hired rooms outside the city in the Villa Borghese park. Together with two other artists, a painter and a medallist, Andersen was kept busy preparing wreaths and garlands. There were presents and prizes, and Andersen received a silver beaker inscribed 'Christmas Eve in Rome, 1833'. Returning to Rome after midnight, the revellers had to knock on the city gate. The night was warm and mild as Scandinavian summer, and the voices that broke the stillness with 'Who goes there? – Friends' reminded Andersen of times long past.

Despite Edvard's objections to his writing about Italy, Andersen noted down every detail of the Carnival, from the maskers pelting each other with comfits to the horse-racing in the Corso, for which prizes were provided by the Jews who had formerly been obliged to race there on foot for public amusement. The riderless horses were spurred on by balls or spikes suspended from their backs, and checked at the end of their headlong course by canvas stretched across the Piazza Venezia, which was then known as the Ripresa di Barberi on account of the Barbary horses who had formerly raced there. Andersen was shown at that end of the Corso the covered balcony of the Bonaparte palace where Napoleon's mother, now eighty-three years old, blind and bedridden, took the sun and listened to the life of Rome going on in the piazza below. He made an excellent drawing of this palace, one of many that he executed at this time as easily and instinctively as his cut-outs. He told Edvard: 'I am getting good at drawing and the artists in Rome all praise my sharp eye; in any case all my sketches (already over a hundred) are a treasure to me and will give me pleasure at home. If only I had learnt to draw!' From our viewpoint it is well that he did not learn to draw, since these simple, vivid sketches perfectly convey both the impression that Italy made on him and the rich variety of his artistic talents.

Without misgivings Andersen set out for Naples with Henrik Hertz. Being a person of extremes, he thoroughly believed in Hertz's new friendliness towards him. Indeed, since their reconciliation, Hertz had talked to him so constructively of his work, so confidently of his literary future, as to convince him that he now had in the older man 'a more lenient judge than before'. It is significant that Andersen should have employed the word lenient in this context. Years of struggling had not made him either sour or aggressive, but they had left their mark upon him, so that even after his fame had spread all over Europe and beyond, he still felt unsure of his status at home. Kings and queens might sing his praises, but behind the kings and queens he always saw his dear unemotional Collins deploring the exaggeration of the compliments paid him, and behind the Collins lurked the threatening shadow of Meisling.

The journey itself created a bond between the two Danes. Andersen felt a religious joy, as if with every mile south he was coming farther out of darkness into a great light. 'Only now', he wrote, 'do I know what Italy is.' At Terracina there were orange groves, prickly pears, palm trees and pomegranates, and, high on the cliff like an eagle's nest, the ruins of a castle built by Theodoric the Great. At Mola di Gaëta they spent the day visiting the Villa that had been the scene of Cicero's political conferences with Pompey and of his hours of leisure with Scipio.

Andersen was still not used to the sight of oranges growing on trees, and with a child's exuberance he hurled some of the glowing sun-warmed fruit into the tideless blue sea, so different from the sea at home. They reached Naples after dark, just in time to see Vesuvius in full eruption, the lava flowing down the mountainsides like roots of fire from a tree of smoke.

Wanting to see the eruption at closer quarters, Andersen and Hertz and a little party of Scandinavians climbed the mountainside, through vineyards, past isolated buildings, the vegetation becoming scarcer and scarcer until at last they felt ashes underfoot. Wildly exhilarated and singing one of Weyse's songs, Andersen was the first to reach the limit of safety. The moon, which appeared to be directly above the crater, was hidden from them by clouds of black smoke every time a shower of glowing stones rose and fell to join the gulfs of fire all around them. The air smelt strongly of sulphur, they could feel the mountain shaking beneath their feet, and from the crater came a sound like that of a huge flock of birds flying up in the woods. During the descent it was again the light that bewitched Andersen, the moonlight brighter than an autumnal midday at home. There was no one to be seen in Portici so it was impossible to hire a coach and they had to walk back to Naples. Not a soul did they see as they made their way past white houses with roofs shining in the moonlight, and Hertz said he felt as if they were traversing the deserted city in *The Arabian Nights*. Every now and again they stood still, spellbound by the scene, and looked from the silent town to the still fiery mountain. They talked of poetry, then of food, for all at once they felt ravenously hungry.

There seemed to be no end to the sights that beckoned to them. Pompeii, discovered in 1748 by a peasant who, while sinking a well, had found a painted chamber inhabited by statues, was still under excavation and full of mysteries that stirred the public imagination. Bulwer Lytton's *The Last Days of Pompeii* was published this year. Paestum, too, was still a wild and isolated place, inhabited mainly by birds and buffaloes. Although despoiled in the eleventh century by Robert Guiscard of Normandy, who built Salerno Cathedral with the pickings, it still retained its city walls, twelve feet high in places, and its Greek temples, set by the sea in fields of asphodel, were the finest to be seen outside Athens. In Andersen's day the violets of Paestum were as celebrated as its roses, of a kind now vanished that flowered twice a year, and he never forgot a beautiful blind girl dressed in rags whom he found sitting among wild fig trees on the steps of a temple and fastening some of these violets in her long black hair. From Salerno he sailed to Amalfi and Capri. The Blue Grotto, known first as the Witches' Hole, then as the Grotto of the Fairies, had been discovered only twelve years earlier, some said by two German travellers, others by two Englishmen, but in fact by a local fisherman, Ferrara, to whom the government had given a pension.

Andersen's aesthetic sensibilities were not the only part of him prodigiously affected by his Italian experiences. Although his capacity for love was as powerful as the capacity for writing, with which it was bound up, he had never thought of his physical need for love as existing in its own right, quite apart from the romantic emotions with which it was connected. Now at last his body, the strong healthy body of a highly-strung man nearly twenty-nine years old, exposed for the first time to the light, music and warmth of the Mediterranean world, asserted itself. In his diary he wrote: 'My blood is in a violent commotion, I feel a tremendous sensuality and I fight with myself. Is it really a sin to satisfy this powerful lust? Then may I fight it. So far I am innocent but my blood burns, when dreaming my whole being boils. The south claims its rights. I am almost ill with it. Lucky is he who is married, is engaged! Oh, were those strong ties on me! But I shall fight this weakness . . .' He did fight what he called his weakness, and what in fact was only his need to satisfy one of the most powerful human instincts. He had a passionately emotional rather than sensual temperament; nevertheless, he had normal sexual needs and his diary shows the anguish with which he struggled against the only satisfaction left to a man who idealized love, namely masturbation.

Towards the end of his stay in Naples he went to the opera to hear the great contralto Malibran, then twenty-six years old and at the height of her powers. He wrote to Mrs Signe Læssøe: 'This I class among my most sublime impressions in the world of art. Hers is not one of those brilliant voices that startle you, but rather a heart dissolved in melody . . . when I left the theatre,

Vesuvius was flinging fire in the sky, the sea reflected it, the moon shone as clear as day, and a great three-master flew into the harbour . . . here, here is my country . . . when I die I will haunt the lovely Neapolitan night. Now I am sitting in my room, it is near midnight. I have sent for a bottle of Lacrimae Christi, my first time, Vesuvius is in it . . . they are singing a serenade in the street! They are playing guitars! Oh no, it is too beautiful! My soul is so full of love, it is long since I have been so happy. My pain is crushing when I suffer, but my joy is indescribable when I am happy. The heat of the south is in my veins – yet I must die in the north.'

Travelling north by the ancient Appian Way, he saw newly fallen snow on the mountains, and the scene was wintry when he stopped to visit the royal palace at Caserta, where he saw pictures left there by Napoleon's brother-in-law Murat, when King of Naples. The excitement of seeing Italy for the first time was replaced by passionate regret at seeing it for perhaps the last time, and he did his final sight-seeing with leaden feet. He spent Easter in Rome, where he saw fireworks even more magnificent than those he had seen in Paris, and was nearly crushed to death in the crowd pressing across the St Angelo bridge to see the dome of St Peter's illuminated. The Danish artists gave him a farewell party and Thorvaldsen embraced him with assurances that they would meet again in Rome or in Denmark. The journey to Siena was a trying one, what with perilous mountain roads, stormy weather and the ever-present threat of bandits, but it was spring-time in Florence and the flowering laurels increased his regret for all he was leaving behind him. From there he wrote to Mrs Læssøe: 'I bid farewell to Italy, which, as you say, is four hundred years behind the times, but in many respects an eternity in advance.'

After his first trip abroad to Germany he had for a while felt himself a stranger at home, but that had been merely a matter of six weeks in a neighbouring country; this time he had been worlds away and the self that had left Denmark two years ago had, he believed, vanished. When the director of the Cabinet Littéraire in Florence talked to him of literary life in Copenhagen, Andersen found to his dismay that he could muster none of the enthusiasm for home that had made him so glad of Danish fellowship in Paris. A 'sorrowful feeling' possessed him, driving him to write: 'Northward, there where my dear ones live in snow and fog, lies the iron ring to be fastened on my foot.'

In Venice he felt as if he were 'in the wreck of a gigantic phantom ship', and the gondolas with their sable trappings suggested floating biers. It still had very much the appearance of an oriental city and the great piazza of St Mark was full of Turks and Greeks smoking their long pipes. He felt uneasy here and was still weak and feverish from a scorpion's bite when he reached Verona, which seemed yet another city of tombs. In Palladio's Vicenza he searched in vain for the grave of a Danish painter whom he had known by sight as a child in Odense. In the gloom that had settled on him he envied the dead man for being at peace in Italy.

At last he could no longer put off his departure. He travelled through the Tyrol with a young Scot who at one point had tears in his eyes, so vividly did the Alps remind him of his native highlands. Listening to his talk of Scotland, Andersen realized that he himself had never before known real homesickness. Scarcely had he crossed the frontier than he was writing: 'My longing for Italy becomes greater every day. I don't know what I wouldn't suffer to get there again. I think I would even go with Molbech if that were the only means of getting there! You see to what lengths a man can go . . .'

Hitherto Andersen had visited Germany with the exhilaration of one setting out on his travels. Now, with Italy behind him, he saw Germany with powers of appreciation impaired by the imminence of his return home to baffled affections, professional and financial problems, and the cold of the north. Molbech, he was reminded by letters from home, had written in the *Monthly Review of Literature* that he was finished as a poet, and he had been publicly advised to 'study more and scribble less'.

In Munich Andersen found rooms with a comb-maker in the Karlsplatz, near the Botanical Gardens. By living economically he tried to postpone his departure. Later he was to grow attached to Munich, but at this time he was not at ease there. 'Every city,' he was to write later, 'from Rome the eternal to our own silent Sorø, has its peculiar character with which one can be intimate, even attach oneself to; but Munich has something of all places: we know not if we are in the south or the north, I at least felt a disquiet here . . .' Ludwig I of Bavaria, King since 1825, had been spending lavishly on public buildings – so lavishly that in 1830 there had been riots against the taxes he levied – but the city seemed to Andersen to lack unity. The post office with its painted red walls imitated Pompeii, the new palace was a copy of the Duke of Tuscany's palace in Florence, the Au church suggested St Stephen's in Vienna, 'every handsome detail appeared to have been taken from its original home' for the benefit of Munich.

Homesick for Italy and dreading his return to Copenhagen, he left Munich for a month in Vienna. One of his companions in the coach was Vespermann, a well-known actor whom Andersen had admired in Goethe's *Götz von Berlichingen*, so the journey went merrily until they reached the Austrian frontier, where there were more than usually pettifogging formalities to be endured. John Murray's *Handbook for Travellers on the Continent* noted a few years later, that 'of all the penalties at the expense of which travelling abroad is purchased, the most disagreeable and most repugnant to English feelings is that of submitting to the strict regulations of the continental police', and the English were not the only ones who found the 'cruel, hard-hearted sort of civility which leaves nothing to complain of, and everything to lament' repugnant to their feelings. For some reason – perhaps because French was the language of diplomacy – Andersen's passport had been made out in French and when he gave his name as Hans Christian Andersen the frontier guard pointed at 'Jean Chrétien Andersen' in his passport and accused him of travelling under a false name. All his luggage was minutely examined, he was required to swear that his letters from home dealt exclusively with family matters, and even his top-hat aroused suspicion. When did he wear it? His reply that he wore it when going into society made them pounce – did he belong to a secret society? The officials looked suspiciously at the wreath of ivy that had been presented to him at Christmas by his fellow artists in

Rome, and they took exception to his having stayed in Paris, that hotbed of revolutions. The alarming futility of the occasion, which suggests the world of Kafka, terminated in Andersen's being given a lecture on the excellence of the Austrian way of life in general and of the Emperor Francis I in particular.

At Salzburg he stayed only a few doors away from the house where the famous Swiss physician, alchemist and chemist, Paracelsus, had settled in 1541. Andersen had long been interested in this enigmatic character, who seemed to him to have been a genius far ahead of his time, and he was glad to listen to an old servant's account of local stories about Paracelsus. Here too Andersen visited the famous salt-mines and made an excursion to the Benedictine monastery of Melk, where he was shown a black patch on the floor caused by Napoleon having flung down a dispatch that he was burning during his occupancy of the place in 1809. Next he went to Vienna. Although its suburbs were spreading fast, the old city within the fortifications – which were not to be blown up to make way for the boulevard known as the Ring until 1858 – was still no larger than it had been in the days when Richard Cœur de Lion was captured there on his return from the Crusades. Here Andersen visited the Burgtheater, as famous all over Europe as the Royal Theatre in Copenhagen, and went out to Hitzing in the neighbouring countryside, where he met Johanne von Weissenthurn, an actress who had played Phèdre before Napoleon at Schönbrunn in 1809 and was as famous for her play-writing as for her acting. Here too he saw Johann Strauss, father of the waltz-king who was to write 'The Blue Danube', 'standing in the midst of his orchestra like the heart in that great waltz organism. It was as though the melodies were flowing through him and out of all his limbs; his eyes were shining, and that he was the life and the leader here was quite plain.'

In the coach for Prague he made the acquaintance of a young woman, travelling with her husband, who boasted at length about her father's library and the esteem in which he was held by all the leading Bohemian writers. She deplored the fact that Andersen was spending only a day in Prague, as she would have liked him to visit her father's library. Next morning, having decided to spend two days in Prague, Andersen thought he would after all visit his new acquaintances. The door was opened by an old man in a dirty dressing-gown, and the splendours described by the young woman resolved themselves into an untidy attic and an old clothes basket of shabby books. Andersen was reminded of his own imaginary castles.

His thoughts were still completely occupied by Italy. He could think and write of nothing else. Already, in Rome, he had written two chapters of a novel with an Italian setting. Memories fused one with another and formed themselves into characters. When he thought, for example, of Malibran's voice he was suddenly reminded of a singer whom he had admired on his very first visit to the theatre in Odense. As a child, listening to the audience's joyous applause, he had thought this singer 'the happiest creature on earth'; years later, while he was visiting Odense hospital, a wrinkled little old woman had been pointed out to him in the indigent widows' quarters as the singer he had so admired. Using this memory as a point of departure, he created Annunziata, one of the leading characters in *The Improvisatore*, as he was to call his novel, after a nickname that had been half jokingly given to him by Heiberg. The critics' attitude had convinced him that publication would 'result in more sorrow than joy', but he could not resist his longing to put his love of Italy into words. When he reached Copenhagen on August 3, 1834, it was as if he had left a part of himself behind in Italy.

Andersen's arrival home coincided with Louise's birthday and the Collins celebrated the two events together. Jonas Collin had tears of pleasure in his eyes as he greeted the traveller and all the family welcomed him as if to his rightful place. Glad as he was to see them all, it felt strange to be back in a Copenhagen no longer the centre of his world. For the first time there was a certain detachment in his attitude. He could even accept with equanimity the disturbing experience of missing people more in their presence than in their absence, of realizing that the Edvard of whom he had thought so much in Italy was not the flesh-and-blood Edvard of Copenhagen, still ready with the old advice. He told Henriette Wulff: 'Now I don't make such great demands, and everything is splendid. Not for a long time have I felt so gay; I am aware of my rightful place, and I see better than before where other people belong. If any admonishing preacher comes along, of the kind who wants to educate me, I listen first to see if it is nonsense and if it is he gets it on the nose . . . I am wonderfully polite, listen to a lot of silly talk, pretend to be modest and give others a chance to let their ego shine. I am even praised for my virtuous modesty, though I really had more of it in the old days when I gabbled so much of myself than now when I act retiringly.'

His friends were aware of a change in him. Jonas Collin thought he had gained maturity; Mrs Læssøe said more subtly: 'He has learnt about human nature; he can act the confiding soul perfectly naturally, but he only tells what he wants to. I don't quite understand him.' Louise and Ingeborg were equally puzzled: 'He can be wild with joy, exuberant beyond words, but still so distracted, so queer, you really don't know how he feels.' One reason for the change in him was that his novel gave him a private world into which he could retreat. The story of Antonio, a poor child from the Campagna who is given an education by a nobleman and becomes a poet, was his own story transported to an Italy of romantic ruins and picturesque traditions, blue skies, orange trees, serenades and bandits. To it he gave the force of an emotion as authentic as that which had produced 'Kennst du das Land'.

Absorbed as he had never yet been by his writing, he did not linger in Copenhagen but went straight to the Ingemanns in 'silent Sorø'. There, in a little room under the roof with a view over lime trees, he finished the first part of his novel. Funds were running low and when he returned to Copenhagen he rented cheap rooms on the sunless side of Nyhavn. From his window he could see the pennants and sails of ships and a leafy poplar that, when it looked black in the moonlight, reminded him of the cypresses of Italy. To Henriette Wulff, who was herself in Italy just then, he wrote: 'I have dreamt so clearly that I was in Italy last year, so I must write my Italian story, exhale all that I dreamt and saw.' He was writing fast and well and early in 1835 dedicated the completed manuscript 'To State Councillor Collin and his noble wife, in whom I found parents, whose children were my brothers and sisters, whose house was my home, I present the best that I possess.'

For all his hard work, he was in urgent need of money. He had not even enough to pay next month's rent, and while the regular dinners at friends' houses kept him from starving, his clothes would soon be too shabby for social outings. He urged Edvard, who acted as his agent in dealings with publishers, to settle for whatever would be immediately forthcoming: 'Never mind when it comes out, but I must have money!' Obtaining money proved difficult. The manuscript of what was to be Andersen's first great popular success was considered not on its own merits but in the light of the damaging reviews of his previous volumes of poetry. Edvard was a good businessman, but all he could obtain from the publisher Reitzel was twenty pounds, payable in instalments. Advice to write less was useless to a young man who found himself obliged to write literally for dear life.

This time, however, Andersen was not unduly cast down by his financial difficulties. No sooner had he handed over the manuscript of *The Improvisatore* than he set to work on a two-act opera, *Little Christine*, which was immediately accepted for production at the Royal Theatre. Then, anxious not to waste time, but with all his literary hopes pinned to his novel, he wrote as a sideline four fairy tales for children, stories in which for the first time in the history of Danish literature the rhythms of colloquial speech could be heard.

In retrospect it seems extraordinary that Andersen should have had no idea that at last, at nearly thirty years old, he had found the right form of expression for the genius of which all his earlier work had given only faint intimations. But such was the case. In March 1835, on a day of 'rain, slush and fog', he told Henriette Wulff that he had written a novel, a little drama to be performed the next month and also 'some fairy tales for children of which Ørsted says that if *The Improvisatore* wins me fame, the tales will "bring immortality" as they are the most perfect I have ever written. But I do not believe this. He does not know Italy and so cannot rejoice at the familiar air the novel makes me breathe . . . you cannot imagine how I am longing for Italy.'

The first of these wonderful stories, published in May 1835, was

The Tinder Box: 'A soldier came marching down the high road – one, two! one, two! He had his knapsack on his back and his sword at his side as he came home from the wars. On the road he met a witch . . .' With these words Andersen himself, fully equipped at last, marched on to the high road of the world's literature.

7. The Ugly Duckling

1835-40

Already you could tell that he had turned poet. Not that there was anything you could put your finger on, for it is foolish to suppose that a poet differs greatly from other people, some of whom are far more poetic by nature than many a great and accepted poet. The chief difference is that a poet has a better memory for things of the spirit. He can hold fast to an emotion and an idea until they are firmly and clearly embodied in words, which is something that others cannot do.

Hans Christian Andersen, *The Galoshes of Fortune*

Then, quite suddenly, he lifted his wings. They swept through the air much more strongly than before, and their powerful strokes carried him far.

Hans Christian Andersen, *The Ugly Duckling*

*

WHEN THE FIRST BOOKLET of Andersen's *Eventyr, Fortalte for Børn* (Fairy Tales Told for Children) was published in May 1835, few people except Ørsted recognized its value. Yet these tales were unique. *Eventyr* comes from the German word *Abenteuer* (itself derived from the twelfth-century Romance word *adventura*); it was used, along with the indigenous German *Märchen*, for the folk tales which were collected by the brothers Grimm in the nineteenth century. But Andersen did more than collocate traditional material; he invented new folk and fairy tales, fresh, beautiful and full of humour, and so became the greatest myth-creator of his century. Nevertheless, he was earnestly advised not to waste his time by a critic on the *Dannora*, who explained that although he personally had nothing against fairy tales for adults, he did not think this type of literature suitable for children, who ought to be offered books with a 'higher purpose' than that of mere entertainment. 'No one', declared this perspicacious

159

man, 'will allege that a child's proper sense of dignity will be stimulated by reading of a Princess who, in her sleep, rides off on a dog's back to a soldier who kisses her . . .'

For once Andersen was unmoved by adverse criticism. All he cared about just then was his novel, *The Improvisatore*, into which he had put his passion for Italy and much of his own life-story. To his delight, the reviews of this novel were laudatory, and what was even more important to him, his friends praised the book; not only friends such as Ørsted, who had long believed in his gifts, but even those who had fallen into the habit of treating him as a child constantly in need of firm guidance. Henriette Wulff's father, for example, went round Copenhagen telling people that he had been unable to put the book down. The first edition was sold out within a few months, and even before the second edition appeared, the book was acclaimed in Germany. Within a few years it had also been translated into English, Swedish, Russian, Dutch, French, Polish and Bohemian. Walter Scott's son-in-law compared it favourably with Madame de Staël's celebrated *Corinne*; Elizabeth Barrett wrote to her future husband, Robert Browning: 'Have you read *The Improvisatore*? . . . The writer seems to feel just as I do, the good of the outward life; and he is a poet in his soul. It is a book full of beauty and had great charm to me.' Seventeen years after Andersen's death, an American journalist wrote: '*The Improvisatore*, though it is fifty-seven years since it was written, is yet exhibited in the booksellers' windows on the Piazza di Spagna side by side with the latest Parisian successes; it is found in the satchels of nearly every tourist who crosses the Alps; and it was republished a few years ago in a complete set of the author's works by a well-known Boston publishing house.'

For the first time Andersen enjoyed popular success. He was temporarily freed from financial worries and told Henriette Hanck: '*The Improvisatore* has procured for me esteem from the noblest and best . . . I have no anxiety for my daily bread, thank God, and lately I have been able to enjoy life thoroughly. The publishers send me newspapers, books and prints; then I sit down wearing gay-coloured slippers and a dressing-gown, with my feet on the sofa, the stove purrs, the tea-urn hums on the table, and the incense feels good. Then I think of the poor boy in Odense who wore wooden shoes . . .'

The poor boy from Odense thoroughly enjoyed the invitations to country houses that success brought him. He had managed to look neat even when poor and now he was able to indulge in a little dandyism. He had his hair curled by the barber who shaved him, chose high starched collars to hide his long neck and wide trousers to hide the thinness of his long legs. From the manor house of Lykkesholm, in Fyn, where his hostess treated him like a prince, he wrote to the Collins: 'I have been given a most interesting room in one of the towers; there is a wide, old-fashioned four-poster bed; all Olympus is woven in the curtains, and Kai-Lykke's coat-of-arms has been carved above the fire-place. Besides this, there are ghosts here; everyone in the place believes that, but I have not noticed anything yet, although especially on the first night I was on watch . . . The passage leading to my room has a lot of noble, stiff, rather mouldy-looking portraits hanging on the walls. The day before yesterday I got the idea of wetting a rag and washing the eyes of them all. You should have seen how they all stared! One of the maids, who knew nothing about it all, suddenly noticed them and became quite frightened. The ladies pamper me. I am given everything I happen to say I want. I am asked what I would like to eat, and whether I would like to go for a drive. It is the first time I have really felt the ease there can be in a poet's life.'

He particularly needed just then to be reminded of the satis-factions of writing, for Edvard's engagement to Henriette Thyberg was reminding him of delights that he himself might never know. 'My eyes fill with tears as I write this,' he told Edvard. 'Like Moses, I stand on the mountain and look into the promised land I shall never reach. God has given me much in this world, but what I am losing is perhaps the best, the happiest. One does not have a home until one has a faithful lovable wife, until one sees oneself reborn in dear children . . . All this happiness will now be yours . . . Friendship must be my all. In a vision I see my whole future, with all its deprivations; I shall and must stand alone. I hope I shall always understand this as clearly as I do now. But my feelings are as strong as yours; as you love your

Jette, I too have loved; but it was only self-deception. But surely he who deceives himself suffers most. I can never forget it, but even we two do not speak of it.'

Andersen had from the first admired Edvard's fiancée, of whom he once said, 'The three beauties of Denmark are the beech trees, Jette Thyberg and the clover fields,' and she was to be a lifelong friend, a sister-in-law as close to him as his adopted sisters Ingeborg and Louise Collin. His eagerness to discern fatherly, motherly, brotherly and sisterly qualities in his closest friends shows how necessary it was to his precarious emotional equilibrium to find in voluntarily created family ties compensation for the inescapable ones of blood that linked him to insanity, alcoholism and degradation. His second novel, *O.T.*, published in 1836, shows that he could not help brooding on the squalor and darkness from which he had fought so hard to escape.

O.T. is set in Denmark, which Andersen describes as vividly as he had previously described Italy, and is even more intimately if deviously autobiographical than his first novel. Its hero, Otto Thostrup, whose initials are also those of Odense prison (Odense Tugthus), goes in fear lest a malevolent and deformed character named Sidsel prove to be his sister. In addition, he is haunted by a blackmailer, Heinrich, who knows how dreadful Otto's childhood has been. Finally it is the poetic Eva who proves to be his sister, but only when Sidsel and Heinrich are dead is Otto liberated from the burden of his past. He told Henriette Hanck: '*O.T.* is a portrayal of our own age, of the years from 1829 to 1835, and the action is limited to Denmark. I think the fact that the author depicts those places he knows and the things among which he lives will be of value and give the book an interest all its own. So in years to come people will have a reliable picture of the present day, and if I have been successful in doing this, then the older the book becomes, the more interesting it will be.' *O.T.* is indeed still interesting for these reasons, but even more so for all that it unwittingly reveals of Andersen's inner life.

Despite the success of his novels, he longed for success as a dramatist. His need to exteriorize his emotions and have immediate contact with his public still gave the theatre an irresistible attraction for him. For his fairy tales, however, he had no extravagant hopes. He published three more, *Thumbelina*, *The Naughty Boy* and *The Travelling Companion*, for Christmas 1835, but not until 1837, when he wrote *The Little Mermaid* and *The Emperor's New Clothes*, did he begin to have an idea of the importance of these stories to himself. As usual, it was his own emotions that made him understand this. *The Little Mermaid* was his favourite and he told Ingemann: 'Except for the little Abbess's story in *The Improvisatore*, it is the only one of my works that has affected me while I was writing it.' This story was to become an integral part of the imaginative life of Denmark. It was made into a ballet, and in 1913, after seeing this danced by Ellen Price, a ballerina who was Jonas Collin's great-granddaughter, the brewer and art patron Carl Jacobsen decided to give Copenhagen a statue of Andersen's heroine. The Little Mermaid was sculpted by Edvard Eriksen and set on a rock at Langelinie, the harbour-mole promenade where in Andersen's youth the eastern defences of the city extended to the Sound. Today the statue is a beloved landmark, attracting among its many visitors crowds of Dutch and Brazilian sailors, who believe that to kiss the mermaid brings good luck. When on April 4, 1964, some hooligans sawed off the Little Mermaid's head, furious indignation was aroused abroad as well as in Denmark. A head was immediately recast and the statue restored on June 1, at the expense of the Copenhagen Municipality. Contributions were immediately offered, too, by foreign countries, in particular the United States.

After the appearance of *The Little Mermaid* and *The Emperor's New Clothes* all nine of Andersen's fairy tales were collected in one volume, of which he said in the preface: 'None of my writings has been so differently appraised as *Fairy Tales Told for Children*. While some people whose judgment I value very highly think they are the best I have written, others have found these Fairy Tales to be unimportant and have advised me not to continue them. Such different opinions, together with the unmistakable silence public criticism has passed upon them, have dampened my desire to continue this type of fiction. Therefore a year has passed before the third booklet has followed the two preceding . . . With this third pamphlet the Fairy Tales are now gathered in one little volume. It will depend on the impression it makes on the public if this is to be the only one. A poet is always a poor man in his own little country. Fame is therefore the golden bird he has to catch! Time will tell if I catch it by telling Fairy Tales.'

No sooner was *O.T.* finished than Andersen was impatiently searching for a theme for his third novel. This, *Only a Fiddler*, also had a Danish setting. Its hero, Christian, is a poor boy who becomes a famous violinist but ends in failure and a pauper's grave. Once again Andersen had an immediate success with Danish, German and Swedish readers – in one of the last letters Chamisso wrote before his death in August 1838 he told Andersen, 'You justly belong among Germany's favourite authors' – but the Danish critics were less enthusiastic than they had been about his earlier novels, and one of those who most objected to the book was Søren Kierkegaard, then twenty-four years old.

Both Andersen and Kierkegaard belonged at this time to a group of young writers who met regularly at a table d'hôte in Østergade, next door to the Pharmacy of the Swan. They included the future Dean of Aarhus, nicknamed themselves 'The Holy Alliance' and were to be described by Kierkegaard in the banquet scene of his *Stages on Life's Way*. Kierkegaard, who had not yet published anything, was admired for his wit and erudition but feared for the sharp remarks he constantly made in a harsh grating voice. He himself believed that his gift for sarcasm had been given him to compensate for his physical fragility, and since his intellectual gifts were backed by wealth, there was nothing except consideration for other people's feelings (of which he seems to have had little at this time) to prevent his indulging in sarcasm as freely as he pleased. Of his criticism of Andersen the latter writes in his autobiography: 'For a short time the novel *Only a Fiddler* occupied the thoughts of one of the most gifted young men in the country – Søren Kierkegaard. One day when we met in the street he told me that he would write a criticism of it that would satisfy me more than previous ones had done, for, he admitted, people misunderstood me. A long time passed; he read the book again, and the first good impression was erased. And I believe that the more seriously he considered the work, the more full of faults it became for him, and when the criticism finally came, it was not one which could please me; it appeared as a whole book; I think it was the first Kierkegaard wrote, rather difficult to read, with a certain Hegelian weightiness in the phrases; people said in fun, too, that only Kierkegaard and Andersen had read the book right through; it was called *From the Posthumous Papers of One Still Living*. I understood from it that I was no poet, but a poetical figure who had run away from my group, and that it was the task of some future poet to put me back in it or to use me as a character in some work in which he was creating my supplement. Later I was better to understand this author, who has met me with kindness and discretion in my progress.'

The full title of Kierkegaard's first book, published in September 1838, was *From the Posthumous Papers of One Still Living. Published against his will by S. Kierkegaard. Concerning Andersen as a novelist, with constant reference to his last book, 'Only a Fiddler'*. The first part of this curious title reflected Kierkegaard's dismay at having outlived his father, who had died in August, and his belief that he himself would not live to be thirty-five (in fact he died at the age of forty-two). All he could find to praise in *Only a Fiddler* was that its author did not meddle in politics, and that he personally had enjoyed the book. The two young writers had little in common but nationality, sex and genius, and to Kierkegaard with his powerful brain, financial independence, his readiness to walk scornfully alone, his relish for an intellectual fight and his constant painful preoccupation with an intensely personal conception of religion that brought him into conflict with the established church, Andersen's obvious dependence on affection, his longing for security in which to work, seemed nothing but unmanly expressions of weakness. As Andersen had the discernment to value Kierkegaard's mind, he was hurt by this book, but not so much as he would have been before the success of his two previous novels had shown him that 'however scornfully I am dismissed, I am read'.

In the summer of 1837 Andersen went to Sweden for the first time. The journey took over a week. He sailed north to Göteborg, the great port that gives Sweden access to the Atlantic, and from there went by canal to the east coast and Stockholm, a crossing of varied waterways. Seventy-four lock-gates linked the seven portions of the hundred-mile-long Gota Canal with two hundred and seventy miles of bays, lakes and rivers. While the ship stopped at the lock-gates the passengers walked in the pine forests and talked of the local legends. At Trollhätten (Troll's Cap) Andersen looked for the spot where the Rhine Gold was stolen by Alberich, King of the Nibelungs, and he was dazzled by the mighty waterfalls – the last of which vanished in 1942 when the water was harnessed to hydro-electric power.

As they approached Lake Vänern – the largest lake in Europe, except for Ladoga in Russia – Andersen questioned the captain and several fellow passengers about Swedish writers who lived in Stockholm. He particularly wanted to meet Fredrika Bremer, a famous novelist, traveller and partisan of women's rights, but was told that he would miss her as she was then away visiting Norway. Three hours later, at Venersborg, the western entry to the lake, she came aboard on her way back to Stockholm. When Andersen was told of this he assumed he was being made fun of and thought no more of the matter until three o'clock next morning, when he went on deck to see the sunrise over the lake and was joined by a passenger whom he had not seen before, a lady 'not young, not old' (Fredrika Bremer was at this time thirty-six), wrapped in a shawl and a cape. He started a conversation with her and found her polite but cold, and when he asked her if she were not the famous writer she answered evasively. Nevertheless, she asked him his own name and on hearing it said that she had heard of him, but had not yet read his books, had he one with him that he could lend her? He lent her *The Improvisatore*, with which she returned to her cabin. After reading it she greeted him with a radiant expression, saying that now she felt she really knew him. They spent most of the rest of the journey together and she pointed out landmarks, and as they entered the mysterious seascape of the Baltic, scattered with barren rocks, whirlpools and grassy islands set with isolated farmhouses, she told him some of the local legends that Selma Lagerlöf was to put to beautiful use half a century later in *Gosta Berling's Saga*. Feeling between Denmark and Sweden was not particularly friendly just then.

Danish books were widely read all over Norway and Sweden, but Norwegian and Swedish books were little read abroad – indeed, even at a later period, a writer of Ibsen's stature chose to be published first in Copenhagen, in Danish – and prosperous Sweden resented her cultural dependence on Denmark. Neither Fredrika Bremer nor Andersen, however, was chauvinistic and they quickly became friends.

Among the Swedes who welcomed Andersen in Stockholm were the pastor, poet and humorist Karl Fredrik Dahlgren, who composed a poem in honour of the Danish visitor, and the distinguished chemist Johan Jakob Berzelius, to whom Ørsted had given Andersen a letter and who warmly welcomed him in the old university town of Uppsala.

One of the Scanian castles he visited was Borringe Kloster, where he was charmed by his host's fifteen-year-old daughter, Countess Mathilda Barck, one of the most beautiful young girls he had ever seen. Despite all he had suffered over Riborg and Louise, he still possessed the inner strength that had carried him away from home to seek his fortune and this kept him looking youthfully ahead, hoping against hope that love was just round the corner. This time differences of age, rank and income prevented him, he said, from falling in love. He was to see more of her and be increasingly charmed, but thanks in part to a mislaid letter, his feelings for her remained a source of poetry, not of torment.

The same was true of his feeling for another young girl, his friend Ørsted's sixteen-year-old daughter Sophie. He had known her since she was a child who climbed on to his knees and begged for stories and paper cut-outs, and her affection for him had not lessened with the years. On the contrary, she never failed to make a fuss of him when he came to dinner, which he did once a week, and he and she always had a great deal to say to each other privately, enough to provoke comments from other people. But as Andersen had no money but what he earned he could not, he felt, ask Sophie to marry him. In December 1837 he wrote to Henriette Hanck: 'If I were rich I would fall in love! Here is a girl who is pretty, gifted, good and lovable; she belongs to the intellectual aristocracy of Copenhagen – but I am not rich and shall not fall in love! Besides, she is only about half as old as I am. She has no idea I am especially fond of her, and she treats me too as an elderly gentleman. She trusts me and is capable of saying one of these days: "Andersen, you must congratulate me, I am engaged." Yet no, she will hardly say that; she is too bashful. I don't know of a more modest girl . . .' A couple of days later he was at the Ørsteds congratulating Sophie and Dahlström, the lawyer to whom she had become engaged.

Money problems tormented him at this time. It was one thing to be dependent on strangers as a child, but quite another to be a successful young writer who nevertheless could not rely on earning enough for marriage. His dissatisfaction with himself was increased at Christmas 1837 by the last chance meeting with Meisling in the street, when the latter apologized for his treatment of Andersen at school. Glad as he was of this reconciliation, it did not dispel the expectation of failure that Meisling had implanted in him. What, he wondered, would become of him if he lost his capacity to write? He thought of trying to find a job as librarian or editor that would guarantee him a fixed income and he even applied to the Royal Library, where he was truthfully told that he had far too much talent for such a post. Help, however, was on the way. Not only Collin and Ørsted but a new admirer of his, Count Rantzau-Breitenburg, who was a cabinet minister, spoke to King Frederik VI of Andersen's needs.

There was nothing unusual about their turning to the Crown for help. William Hurton, a Scotsman who made a trip from Leith to Lapland in 1805, noted: 'Denmark is really an intellectual Kingdom. Education is so generally diffused by the State that it is a nation of readers and, as a natural consequence, these readers have mental pabulum supplied to them by a strong array of native writers . . . The remuneration generally given to even first-class Danish authors is very small – not one-fourth so much as English writers usually get for magazine papers. We need not marvel at this, when we consider the very limited public addressed. All Denmark Proper contains one million less inhabitants than London alone. But then, nearly every Danish author of repute has a pension from the State . . . The Crown of Denmark also frequently aids in bringing out valuable works which, from their abstruse nature, are not likely of themselves to command a remunerating sale, and consequently would remain unpublished ... Denmark enables young wielders of the chisel, pen and brush to wander in classical lands at the State's expense, and pensions all who extend the renown of their country's name. What is still more surprising, there breathes not a Dane who begrudges his mite towards the fund thus applied.'

Oehlenschläger, Thorvaldsen, Ingemann, Heiberg and Hertz had all received financial help from the Crown, and in May 1838 Andersen was granted a pension of 400 rigsdalers a year, the equivalent of forty English pounds and at that time enough to keep a single man. With this to fall back on should his earning powers falter, Andersen could consider himself free to marry. He was no longer, however, hopeful about this. Unhappiness and love were by then irrevocably connected in his mind, and after congratulating Sophie on her engagement, he wrote in his diary: 'Now I shall never marry. No young girl is growing up for me; day by day I become more of a bachelor. Yesterday I was among the young, today I am old ...'

Nevertheless, Andersen's pension gave him a novel sense of security – 'I was less dependent on the people around me.' In December 1838 he moved into the Hôtel du Nord in the Kongens Nytorv, near the Royal Theatre and also near to the Collins, who had just moved to the neighbouring street of Amaliegade. For a writer who is a bachelor with a passion for travel, hotel life is ideal and until May 1847 Andersen stayed at the Hôtel du Nord whenever he was in Copenhagen.

By the time he moved to the Hôtel du Nord he had a well-organized and satisfying social life, enriched in 1838 by Thorvaldsen's return to Denmark. This was an occasion of national rejoicing. The sculptor's parents were dead, but, writes William Hurton, 'Denmark composed one open-armed family to receive him.' For some time past Thorvaldsen had been sending home casts of his work, many of the originals, and an accumulation of curiosities and paintings which he had bought from young artists to encourage them, all of which he intended to present to the nation. The residue, accompanied by Thorvaldsen himself, was now being brought to Copenhagen by the frigate *Rota*, sent expressly for that purpose. A special museum was to be built for his work. The King gave a piece of land close to Christiansborg Palace for this purpose and the entire nation subscribed towards the building.

The day of Thorvaldsen's arrival was damp and foggy, but a huge crowd was waiting to welcome him. A painted frieze in the Thorvaldsen Museum shows a flotilla of boats hung with flowers and flags and in one of them, together with Oehlenschläger, Heiberg, Hertz and Grundtvig, stands the tall figure of Andersen, holding on to the mast and waving his hat. As Thorvaldsen came ashore to a salvo of cheers, the foggy air was suddenly lit up by a rainbow. The King had allotted Thorvaldsen apartments in the palace of Charlottenborg; Bournonville had composed a special ballet for the occasion, *La Fête à Albano*, with figures and groups based on Thorvaldsen's works; and there was a banquet at which Andersen was asked to make a speech. From then on Thorvaldsen and Andersen often attended the theatre together and spent happy weeks as the fellow guests of Baroness Stampe at her country house, Nysö, where they both found ideal conditions for their work – and to Andersen's delight, Thorvaldsen proved as appreciative as Ørsted of his fairy tales.

Four more of these tales were published this year, *The Galoshes of Fortune* (in which Kierkegaard appeared in the guise of a parrot), *The Daisy*, *The Steadfast Tin Soldier*, and *The Wild Swans*, but Andersen thought less of these than of the play he was writing. Because the theatre caused him so much heartache, it is often assumed that he had no talent whatever as a dramatist. This is untrue. His gifts as a dramatist were negligible compared with the genius revealed in his tales, but of the twenty-seven plays, vaudevilles, adaptations and libretti that he wrote, almost all were accepted for production at either the Royal Theatre or the Casino, and some have recently been adapted for television. The play he now wrote was *The Mulatto*, based on a French story, *Les Epaves*, by Madame Reybaud, wife of the radical journalist Louis Reybaud whose *Réformateurs ou Socialistes Modernes* was to popularize the word 'socialism'. The plot concerned a high-minded mulatto who, after many vicissitudes, marries a white countess with whom he has long been in love. In his desire to do justice to the background, Andersen devoured books about Africa and America until he felt, he said, quite at home amid blacks, ostriches and lions and dreamt nightly of slimy snakes in long wet grass.

One of the theatre's readers objected to the effect the play might have on Negroes in the Danish West Indies, and it was promptly refused by Molbech. In his disappointment Andersen felt that this was yet another proof of his being despised in his own country, though Edvard Collin pointed out that he and Denmark would have got on admirably had it not been for the theatre. By now, however, Andersen had sufficient literary reputation to obtain a second reading for his play. This time he was asked if *The Mulatto* contained any 'new theatrical effects'. It contained a ball, said Andersen. This, however, was no novelty. Next Andersen mentioned the slave-market scene. This was approved of as new, and Andersen always believed that he owed the final acceptance of his play to the slave-market.

On December 1, 1839, two evenings before the first performance of *The Mulatto* was to take place, Andersen was invited to read it to the King's cousin, Prince Christian, and his wife – the Prince who as Governor of Fyn had advised the cobbler's son to learn a trade. The graceful way in which he now acknowledged his mistake, the kindness he subsequently showed Andersen, were in the best fairy-tale tradition. A real friendship grew up between them, and often, on meeting Andersen by chance, the Prince would ask him where he was dining and, if the answer was at a restaurant, would say 'Then come and dine with me and my wife instead.' Kierkegaard, who also had dealings with this prince, called him 'a sort of spiritual and intellectual voluptuary' who became 'almost fantastic if he was impressed by a superior intelligence'.

The reading was applauded, and the night before the first performance Andersen was sleepless from excitement. The posters were already up and early next morning people began queueing for seats. Suddenly royal messengers came galloping through the streets. King Frederik VI had died that morning. Since the King had no son, it was Andersen's prince who succeeded him as King

The Wild Swan

Christian VIII. The army took the oath of allegiance, the city gates were closed – and so were the theatres.

Frederik VI was sincerely mourned. He had reigned for thirty-one years, and his bluff patriarchal ways had endeared him to all classes. Whenever there was a fire in the city he would be there on his white horse directing the firemen's operations, and on Sundays his people had enjoyed seeing him and his family sailing their boat in Frederiksberg park. His last words were a recommendation that the poor be given wood to keep them warm during the coldest weather. Peasants carried his coffin for the last part of the journey from Copenhagen to the Cathedral of Roskilde, the royal burial place. The capital was in mourning for two months.

When the Royal Theatre re-opened in February 1840, *The Mulatto* was the play chosen for the first performance of King Christian VIII's reign. Andersen's intimate knowledge of an outcast's feelings had given authentic emotion to *The Mulatto* and it was enthusiastically applauded by the audience; but not by all the critics. Andersen was particularly distressed when Heiberg's mother ridiculed the audience's enthusiasm. However, the new King presented Andersen with a jewelled tie-pin, Edvard gave a dinner in his honour, and soon afterwards *The Mulatto* was performed in Sweden at the Royal Theatre in Stockholm, in Malmö, and in several smaller towns. Andersen was very moved when, on his next visit to Sweden, he was serenaded by the students of Lund University, who told him, 'When your own native land and the nations of Europe do you homage, do not forget that the first to do so were the students of Lund.' This aroused some jealousy and sarcasm at home. Even an older man as gifted as Heiberg was not above saying to him, 'When I go to Sweden you will have to come with me so that I too may have a little homage paid me!' For once Andersen had a sharp retort ready: 'Take your wife with you, then it will be much easier.'

Despite his renewed preoccupation with the theatre, Andersen continued to write his tales. *The Garden of Paradise*, *The Flying Trunk*, *The Storks* and *The Rose Elf* were published in 1839, and in 1840 came the first edition of his *Picture-book without Pictures*, a collection of prose poems in which the moon describes its nightly visits to different countries. His own visit to Sweden had sharpened his appetite for travel. It was also responsible for one of the most important encounters in his life. For this same year, glancing through the guest-book at his hotel, he noticed among the visitors from Sweden the name of Jenny Lind. Although scarcely known abroad, she was already, at twenty years old, the leading singer in Sweden, where an Uppsala journalist had named her the Swedish Nightingale – and as Andersen's recent visit to her country had made him feel particularly friendly to everything Swedish he decided to pay his respects to her.

A very shy, dignified girl who was visiting Copenhagen as a tourist with her father, she received Andersen with rather cold courtesy. Tall and slender, with auburn hair, a fine forehead and grey eyes, she could appear radiantly beautiful when singing, but could also look decidedly plain in repose off stage, and although she had worked in the theatre since the age of nine she had none of the warm, easy manners of that world. On this occasion she made no particular impression on the impressionable Andersen, who saw in her merely a representative of a country where he had been happy.

He was so unsure of himself that although he had had yet another play, *A Rustic Comedy*, produced at the Royal Theatre, he was still smarting from the critics' attacks on *The Mulatto*. He could behave with poignant dignity over disappointed love, but when disappointed in the theatre he would try and try again, obstinate and avid. *The Mulatto* had been attacked for lack of originality, therefore he was determined to write a play ebulliently original. The result was *The Moorish Maid*, a melodrama with a Spanish setting that brought him only further disappointment. Heiberg, at that time director of the Royal Theatre, disliked the play; and his wife, for whom the leading part had been written, refused to play in it. She gave ill health as a reason for her refusal but Andersen was not deceived. Unfriendliness from the Heibergs was particularly painful because his beloved Collins greatly admired their talents and usually shared their views on art. Johanne Louise Heiberg was, too, the only person with a position in the Collin family circle similar to his own. When she was a poor child-actress it was Jonas Collin who, by finding her a home with the actress Anna Wexchall, had changed her life in her own words 'from darkness to light'; and now that she was a national idol Andersen felt that she had repaid her benefactor as he himself could never hope to do.

Disappointment of this kind was more than a matter of writer's vanity. It combined with his defeats as a lover to make him feel himself a total failure, and his despair revived his dread of becoming insane. Louise was to marry her lawyer on November 25 and Andersen could see nothing for himself at home but desolation. So once again he turned to travel. Friends gave a big farewell dinner for him, and in October 1840 he left Denmark for nearly a year.

8. The Flying Trunk

1840-3

. . . When a man is born a coward, and yet combats this of his own accord, then he has done what he ought to have done, and need not be ashamed of the weakness he has been born with.

Hans Christian Andersen

You have not done enough, you have never done enough, so long as it is still possible that you have something of value to contribute.

This is the answer when you are groaning under what you consider a burden and an uncertainty prolonged *ad infinitum*.

Do not seek death. Death will find you. But seek the road which makes death a fulfilment.

Dag Hammarskjöld, Markings

*

ON THE OUTWARD JOURNEY Andersen stopped in Holstein for the first of many happy visits to Count Rantzau-Breitenburg, who drove him over the heath and marshlands and showed him the grave of Müller von Itzehoe, an eighteenth-century German novelist who had been first widely read, then forgotten in his own lifetime. The sight moved Andersen. Often during his travels he visited the graves of obscure artists, as if he hoped by his attentive presence to stay momentarily the hand of oblivion.

In Hamburg he attended a concert by Liszt. All his life Andersen felt a particular and reciprocated sympathy with musicians, and he was fascinated by the twenty-nine-year-old Liszt, whose passionate looks and playing frequently aroused hysteria in his audience. Women would shriek and faint, and Heine attributed this to 'magnetism, galvanism and electricity . . . histrionic epilepsy, the phenomenon of tickling, musical cantharides, and other unmentionable matters'. On this occasion the

concert took place in rooms gleaming with lights, gold and
diamonds, and wealthy Hamburg merchants stood 'walled up
against each other as if it were an important matter on 'Change
that was to be discussed'. When Liszt entered the room, a slender
young man with long dark hair and a pale face, the effect was as
of an electric shock and most of the ladies rose. Andersen, who
was standing near him, was impressed by the 'strong passions in
his face' and reported later that he had heard politicians say that
by playing the Marseillaise Liszt could drive peaceful citizens to
'seize the musket, fly from hearth and home and fight for an
idea', while he himself had seen peaceful Danes 'with autumn's
mist in their blood' transformed into 'political Bacchantes' by
Liszt's playing, and mathematicians turn 'dizzy with figures of
tones and calculations of sound'.

Since one of Andersen's own strong passions was speed – he
once told Admiral Wulff's son, Christian, 'I want to travel faster
than you with your ship. I should like to ride upon a cannon-ball
through the spheres' – he was wildly excited by his first train
journey, which he made on the recently established line from
Magdeburg to Leipzig. Travel by rail was then as thrilling as
space travel is today, and in his detailed account of this trip
Andersen dwells with wonder and triumph on all the processes
that had contributed to it – the levelling of the ground, the setting
of the tracks, the safeguards of signal whistles and flag-waving.
He conveys, too, the nervous tension suffered by travellers with
their heads full of the warnings of those who deplored the new
invention – warnings that ranged from moans about the ruin of
the carriage trade, the waste of arable land, the terror of cattle,
to prophecies that blindness and death would surely result from
such ungodly speeding. 'I will not deny that I had beforehand a
feeling that I will call railway-fever, and this was at its height
when I entered the immense building from which the train
leaves. Here was a crowd of travellers, a running with port-
manteaux and carpet-bags, and a hissing and puffing of engines
out of which steam poured forth. At first we do not know where
we dare stand, fearing that a carriage or a baggage-chest might
come flying over us . . . the carriages we are to enter are drawn
up in a row, like gondolas by the side of a quay, but down in the

yard one rail crosses the other like magic ties invented by humans
. . . to these ties our magic carriage must confine itself, else life
and limb are at stake . . . Everything seemed to have legs; and
the steam and the noise, together with the crowding to get a place,
the smell of tallow, the regular movement of the machinery, and
the whistling, snorting and snuffing of the steam as it is blown off,
increases the impressiveness . . . when one is here for the first
time one thinks of accidents, of breaking arms and legs, of being
blown into the air or crushed to death by another train, but I
think it is only the first time that one thinks of all this. The train
was divided into three parts, the first two were comfortably
closed carriages, quite like our diligences, but much broader, the
third was open and incredibly cheap so that even the poorest
peasant can afford to travel by it: it is much cheaper for him
than if he were to walk all the distance and refresh himself at the
ale-house and lodge on the journey. The signal whistle sounds . . .
it resembles a pig's dying cry as its throat is cut . . . The first
sensation is that of a very gentle motion in the carriages, and
then the chains are attached which bind them together; the
steam whistle sounds again and we move forward, slowly at first
as if a child's hand were pulling a toy. The speed increases
imperceptibly, but you read your book, look at your map and as
yet do not rightly know at what speed you are going, for the
train glides on like a sledge over level snowfields. You look out of
the window and discover that you are rushing forward as fast as
galloping horses; the train goes still quicker, you seem to fly, but
there is no shaking, no suffocation, nothing of what you anticipated would be unpleasant! . . . This is just the way to travel
through flat countries! It is as if town lay close to town; now one
appears, now another. One can imagine how it is with birds of
passage . . . seventy miles in three hours! . . . I have often heard
it said that on a railway all the poetry of travel is lost, that we lose
sight of the beautiful and interesting. As to the last part of this
remark, I can only say that everyone is free to stay at whatever
station he chooses and look about him until the next train comes;
and as to all the poetry of travel being lost, I am quite of the
contrary opinion. It is in the narrow, close-packed diligences that
poetry vanishes: we become dull, we are plagued with heat and

dust in the best season of the year and in winter by bad roads . . . Oh, what a noble and great achievement of the mind is this invention! We feel ourselves as powerful as the sorcerers of old! We put our magic horse to the carriage and space disappears; we fly like the clouds in a storm . . . Mephistopheles could not fly faster with Faust on his cloak! We are, by natural means, as powerful today as only the Devil himself was supposed to be in medieval times! I can remember few times in my life when I was as affected as I was by this railway journey . . .'

Andersen reached Leipzig with a sense of triumph and immediately called on Mendelssohn. The composer had met Collin's daughter Ingeborg and her husband during their visit to Germany a year earlier and asked them if by chance they knew Andersen as he had loved the latter's novel *The Improvisatore*. When Mrs Drewsen said that she considered Andersen as a brother, Mendelssohn immediately begged them to tell Andersen to be sure to call on him should he ever be in Leipzig. When Andersen actually arrived Mendelssohn was rehearsing and resented being interrupted by a message that a gentleman who was passing through town wanted particularly to see him. He began to explain that he had no time for strangers; then, suddenly realizing who his visitor was, shouted 'Andersen!' embraced him and took him in to the rehearsal to listen to Beethoven's Seventh Symphony.

In Nuremberg a further wonder awaited Andersen. It was here that for the first time he saw daguerreotypes, the first photographs, made by the French scene-designer and inventor of the diorama Louis Jacques Mandé Daguerre, who took his pictures on silver plate sensitized by iodine and then developed by exposure to mercury vapour. Andersen was one of the first of the general public to understand the significance of Daguerre's work and to foresee the 'imaginary museum' that it would provide; in February 1839 he had written to Colonel Högh-Guldberg: 'What do you say to Daguerre's invention? I am delighted about it. How easy it will be now to get prints of the most famous statues, pictures of the loveliest parts of the country, won't it?' Nevertheless, it seemed to him almost incredible that pictures could be produced by this method, and he described daguerreotypes and railways as the 'two flowers of the age'.

The Flying Trunk

From Nuremberg he went to Munich, where he met the poet Holst with whom he was to continue to Italy. There was a colony of Danes in Munich, but this Bavarian version of artistic life in Rome did not appeal to Andersen. He was there on Louise Collin's wedding-day and after writing a poem to her he set off through the Tyrol, Innsbruck and the Brenner Pass to Italy, reaching Rome on December 17.

He booked rooms in the Via Purificazione, and once again found Rome the only city in which an unaccompanied stranger could feel at home. His apartment overlooked a little garden full of roses and orange trees where he could hear the chanting from the Capuchin monastery, the very place where he had set his hero's childhood in *The Improvisatore*. This was not, however, so happy a visit as his first one. The weather was wet and cold, with storms and earthquake tremors, the Tiber rose and flooded the streets, fever spread – the Prince Borghese lost his wife, the young daughter of the Earl of Shrewsbury, and his children in a few days – and Andersen sat in his draughty drawing-room, wrapped in his cape, suffering from toothache and thinking of his manifold failures. Nevertheless, he complied with local superstition by drinking from the Trevi fountain on his departure in order to be sure of returning to Rome.

There was nothing to cheer him in Naples, where it was cold, he had a fever, suffered from toothache and found the opera-house closed. He remembered the young singer Malibran, and wrote: 'In the city of the dead I thought of the dead, I thought of Malibran-Garcia, the bird of song, in whose tones I had found expression of all that my mind now felt for Italy's wonders and beauty. Italy and Malibran were in my mind related, like the words and melody of a cherished song; I could not separate them – and now she was dead – she, who in so much of what we admire was so like Byron, found *her* death in the land which gave *him* life.'

He dreaded going home and, thanks to another travelling grant, was able to go on to Greece. On March 15 he sailed on a French warship. As it weighed anchor the crowd on shore cried '*Evviva la Gioia!* – Long live Joy!' and suddenly Andersen felt young again and light of heart, as if a stream of forgetfulness flowed between him and his bitter memories. A new life was beginning for him.

Andersen had a gregarious side that made him enjoy the chance encounters of shipboard life. When he found an injured bird and nursed it until it could fly again (a portly Roman priest suggested cooking it), 'it was a great event for us all, yet we soon sought our several occupations again: one at the piano, another over a book; some played cards, others promenaded up and down. The bedouin sat on the coal sacks, silent as a ghost; the eyes sparkled in that brown face under the white burnous, and his naked brown legs stuck out; the Persian played with his large sabre, clapped his pistols, or turned the silver rings in his dark-brown ears; the captain copied a picture out of my album . . . I myself read German with one of the French officers . . .' As usual, he became sufficiently attached to his travelling companions to regret leaving them, which he did at the island of Syra, from which he sailed for Greece.

He spent a month in newly-liberated Greece, where the German and Danish colonies made much of him and 'champagne popped for Denmark and for me'. He was presented to the new King, Otto of Bavaria, and his Queen, an Oldenburg princess, whose beautiful black-haired lady-in-waiting was a daughter of one of the Byronic heroes who had defended Missolonghi. Andersen was given a banquet for his birthday, which he spent at the Acropolis, and he took riding lessons from the resident Austrian minister Prokesch von Osten, a diplomat of particular interest to Andersen since he had written two studies of Napoleon's campaigns, befriended Napoleon's unfortunate son in Vienna, and when in Rome on a diplomatic mission had called on Napoleon's mother, then eighty years old and blind, to give her news of her already dying grandson. The excitement Greece aroused in Andersen gave him the idea of writing *Ahasuerus*, a play about the Wandering Jew, a character with whom he could easily identify himself.

On April 21 he sailed for Constantinople in a storm that made him feel certain of being shipwrecked. He fell asleep amid

clattering and creaking, and woke to find himself in the bay of
Smyrna. He saw its red roofs and narrow streets – people would
step back into open doorways in order to let ostriches or camels
pass by – a swarm of veiled Turkish women, Jews, and Armenians
in black and white hats like inverted cauldrons. That evening a
new moon shone over the plains of Troy as Andersen sailed
between Europe and Asiatic Turkey, past Gallipoli, into the Sea
of Marmara, and so to Constantinople, of which he had his first
glimpse in the rain, mosque after mosque. It was in Turkey that
he at last received a real tribute from Edvard, who wrote to him:
'You are a devil of a chap for travelling; the way you have
managed on this trip is something in which not many will be able
to imitate you, and even if you are not brave you have a strong
will, and that is just as good. This testimonial is given you by the
undersigned, who is not in the habit of flattering you.'

Andersen spent eleven days in Constantinople, including May
4, the anniversary of Mohammed's birthday, when he saw the
nineteen-year-old Sultan drive to the Sophia Mosque through
streets packed with crowds in many-coloured costumes. All the
minarets were lighted up and he saw Mount Olympus glowing in
the setting sun. He had planned to return home via the Danube,
and refused to be deterred, as were most of his fellow travellers, by
the news that parts of the vast disintegrating Ottoman Empire were
in revolt and several thousand Christians had been massacred.
He thought the matter over and wrote perspicaciously: 'I have
often been told that I am not brave, and I believe it, but it is only
small dangers which really frighten me. When dangers are great,
and there is something to be gained, my will makes itself felt, a
will which has become stronger year by year. I tremble and am
terrified, but do what I consider right. And I imagine that when
a man is born a coward, and yet combats this of his own accord,
then he has done what he ought to have done, and need not be
ashamed of the weakness he has been born with.'

On the evening of May 4 he was aboard ship off the gardens of
the Seraglio, which for him represented the Arabian Nights
stories of his childhood. Next morning passengers were told that
the Austrian ship that was to have met them there had struck a
rock in the Black Sea in the previous night's fog. Finally their

ship set off into mist and heavy seas. They had to spend a whole day off the town of Kirstandje, beside which ran a rampart of earth known as Trajan's Wall, where they landed and drove in basket-work carriages drawn by white oxen across the desolate landscape inhabited only by wild dogs and overturned grave-stones that showed where the Russians had recently fought the Turks. The first object Andersen saw on the sea-shore was a dead stork – 'It lay with one wing stretched out, and the neck bent; I became quite melancholy on seeing it. The stork has always been the most interesting of birds to me; it has occupied my thoughts when a child; it haunts my novels and tales; and it was now the first thing I saw as I was wending homeward by sea . . .'

From there the travellers went to Czernavida, a packet-station on the Danube, where they went aboard an Austrian steamer. Andersen was fascinated by the wildness of the Danubian land-scape with isolated villages and decaying fortresses. The first signs of the violence against which he had been warned occurred at Rustchuk, where white chimneys, mosques and minarets rose amid forests of fruit trees. Crowds stood watching while two young men were flung into the river. One swam ashore, and the crowd started stoning the other, who was then taken aboard ship. Next day the travellers heard that an armed Tartar carrying letters and dispatches across country to Constantinople had been ambushed and killed. At Widdin, called by the Turks the Virgin Fort because it had never yet been captured, the passengers were allowed to land after being 'roughly fumigated' to prevent their carrying the plague from Constantinople. There Hussein Pasha sent them copies of the newspaper *Allgemeine Zeitung*, in which they read of what was happening in the country they had just crossed. Serbia appeared to be a 'primeval forest' and at Old Orsova they had to endure ten days of prison-like quarantine. Andersen shared a room with William Francis Ainsworth, an English physician, geologist and traveller, who was the younger brother of William Harrison Ainsworth, author of *The Tower of London*. The two young men got on well, and later, describing his time in quarantine in the *Literary Gazette*, Ainsworth said that Andersen was 'a tall pale delicate young man of prepossessing appearance, with brown hair and sharp features, a very slight slouch in his gait and the sidelong movement of an abstracted man'. He also mentioned Andersen's gift for cutting out paper figures, and illustrated his article with Andersen's drawings of the dancing dervishes.

When the quarantine was over, the travellers returned aboard ship and sailed past a landscape of magnificent chestnut trees and Roman ruins inhabited by Wallachian peasants, gipsies and Austrian soldiers. By this time the ship was packed to capacity, since local people were flocking to Pesth for the great Fair. During the journey Andersen was busily planning *A Poet's Bazaar*: 'When travelling I must bestir myself from morning to evening; I must see and see again. I cannot do otherwise than pack whole towns, tribes, mountains and seas into my mind; always taking in, always stowing away, there is not time to write a single poem. I am not even disposed to do so; but it will come, I know it. It seethes and ferments in me, and when I am in the good city of Copenhagen and get a bodily and spiritual cold fomentation, the flowers will shoot forth.'

In Prague Andersen visited a church where he discovered the tomb of the sixteenth-century Danish astronomer Tycho Brahe. In Leipzig he saw Mendelssohn again: 'How snug ar d comfortable it was in his home; a handsome and friendly wife and all so hospitable to the stranger. A little morning concert . . . was given in Mendelssohn's room. The gifted Frau Goethe from Weimar [Goethe's daughter-in-law] and I were the fortunate guests. In the church, and on the same organ that Sebastian Bach had himself played, Mendelssohn gave me one of Bach's Fugues and a few of his own compositions.'

As always, he had contradictory feelings about arriving home: 'It seemed typical to me that while my trunk had only been examined twice – at the Austrian and German frontiers – during the whole of my journey from Italy through Greece and Turkey to Hamburg, it was inspected no less than five times before I was again at home in Copenhagen. First it was examined when I entered Holstein, then at Arøsund, then again when I went ashore at Fyn, then when I left the diligence at Slagelse, and finally when I arrived by coach in Copenhagen; that was the custom of the times.'

Just outside Slagelse he chanced to meet Pastor Bastholm taking his evening walk with his wife. They were taking the same walk as they had taken when Andersen was himself a child – 'out of the back gate of their garden, along the path through the cornfields, and home along the main road'. He himself had travelled so far since those days that it gave him a strange feeling to see this domestic routine still going on. It was Pastor Bastholm who had told the eighteen-year-old Andersen that he had a lively imagination, a warm heart and lacked only a certain development of the mind. As he recognized his old friends, Andersen felt like Rip van Winkle, the character invented by Washington Irving twenty years earlier.

When he reached home Andersen found his countrymen very dissatisfied with the new King Christian VIII. The monarchy was still absolute in Denmark, but although the old King had been popular enough for the majority of his subjects not to object actively to his saying 'We alone know what is good for the people,' the people were in fact beginning to have their own ideas as to what would be good for them. The new King had a reputation for liberal views, thanks to his conduct as a young man when he was Viceroy of Norway; he was therefore expected to transform absolute into constitutional monarchy overnight. But the fifty-three-year-old prince who ascended the Danish throne differed considerably from the young prince who had given Norway a Constitution. He was by this time an exhausted man, subject to fits of melancholy, and had reached the conclusion that the art of government consisted of simultaneously moderating reformers and restraining their adversaries. This inevitably satisfied neither side.

One of the apparently unimportant results of this public restlessness was that Copenhagen was given an amusement park unique of its kind and famous to this day. Georg Carstensen, a Dane born in Algiers, returned to Copenhagen in 1843 after a journey in the Middle East, and seeing what was going on, persuaded Christian VIII to rent him a swampy military training field near the city ramparts where he set up a park 'to amuse the citizens, who are too preoccupied with military and political matters'. This was the origin of Copenhagen's popular Tivoli, with its Chinese Peacock Theatre where a Harlequin and Columbine pantomime has been given every year since 1843. It was to play a providential part in Andersen's life, and today Tivoli is bounded on one side by the broad H. C. Andersens Boulevard.

Andersen heard plenty of political discussions at the castles and manor houses where he was now a regular guest. But since citizens did not have the vote he continued to believe that he had 'neither the ability nor the obligation to interfere in such matters'. Nor could he even think of such matters when 'by the side of the silent lakes in the woods, in the green meadows where the game sprang past me and the stork strutted about on its red legs . . . nature both around and within me preached and showed my calling'. In these country houses he developed a new love of his own country. Of Bregentved Castle, with its slim spire rising above the tree-tops, he wrote: 'It is as though I were living in the very heart of Denmark in every respect; there are kind and gentle people about me, and a wooded countryside the like of which I have never seen elsewhere. I love especially those great sunny green meadows right in the middle of the woods, those green spaces where stag and roe almost seem to hover as they gallop along; then they stand and listen with their intelligent eyes shining; I can spend hours watching in silence, but I hope those hours are not wasted; they have the same effect as sunlight on the surface of a daguerreotype – the time-picture is absorbed and fixed there.'

This was the kind of life he shared with Thorvaldsen at Baroness Stampe's house, Nysö. All day he would write or walk, while Thorvaldsen worked in the studio that the Baroness had built for him beside the moat. After dinner there would be music and games of lotto. Although the stakes were only pieces of glass, Thorvaldsen, who played with complete absorption, 'just had to win', and Andersen, who was bored by lotto, would escape and walk in the woods. He wrote two fairy tales at Nysö, and Thorvaldsen, who loved Andersen's tales, would insist on having his favourites read to him again and again, taking a childlike pleasure in repetition. It was while they were at Nysö that Thorvaldsen told Andersen of his experience with Byron in Rome: 'He sat down in front of me, but immediately began to pull a different face from what he usually did. "No, will you please sit still," I asked, "you must not pull faces." "That is my usual expression," said Byron. "Very well then," I said, and I sculpted him as I wished. When I had finished everyone said it was extremely like him, but when Byron looked at it he said, "It is not at all like me, I look more unhappy." ' And Thorvaldsen concluded cheerfully, 'You see, he just had to look unhappy.'

Thorvaldsen was himself completely without affectation. While he was working on the bas-relief of 'The Path to Golgotha' he asked Andersen whether he thought he had given Pilate the right dress. Baroness Stampe, who was standing beside the artist watching him work, said, 'You mustn't say anything to him! It's quite right, it's excellent, away with you.' Thorvaldsen, however repeated his question and Andersen said, 'Well, since you ask me I must say that I do think your Pilate is dressed more like an Egyptian than a Roman.' Saying that that was just what he himself had thought, Thorvaldsen pulled the figure to pieces, to the horror of Baroness Stampe, who told Andersen that he had ruined a work of genius. Thorvaldsen said good-humouredly that it could easily be replaced – and proceeded to model the Pilate that is actually in the Church of Our Lady.

Some of Andersen's middle-class acquaintances resented his enjoyment of aristocratic life. On hearing that he had been invited to a ball at Christiansborg palace, Professor Hornemann told him that he 'did not belong there' and goaded Andersen into saying, 'My father was a craftsman, and it is through my own efforts and with God's help that I have won my position and I should have thought you would respect that.' It would have been better for Andersen could he have ignored such foolishness; as it was, his vulnerability provoked unkindness. He realized this and once said, 'When boys throw stones at a dog which is swimming against the current, it is not sheer cruelty, it is because it amuses them; and people derive the same sort of amusement out of me.'

His new friendships did not lessen his devotion to the Collins, who remained his chosen family, just as Ørsted remained the dear friend whom he always consulted about his work. Nor did dining out interfere with his theatre-going. He was now the proud possessor of one of the Court Stalls, seats reserved for dramatists who had had three plays produced at the Royal Theatre and for courtiers, diplomats and leading officials chosen by the King. Thorvaldsen, Oehlenschläger and Weyse were also Court Stall-holders, and at Thorvaldsen's request, Andersen always sat by him. Success never lost its miraculous quality for him, and he would experience moments of overwhelming gratitude when he saw himself, as if from the outside, seated in a privileged position, among men he revered, in the theatre of which he had dreamed as a boy in Odense.

It was in the theatre world that he was confronted for the first time by the death of one of his early friends, the composer Weyse. Weyse had helped Andersen to earn the right to travel, but had never himself wanted to go further afield than Roskilde, thirty-one miles from Copenhagen, where he used to improvise on the cathedral organ. He would tease Andersen, saying, 'If you *must* travel, then go to Roskilde, that's far enough. Just wait until people start travelling to moons and planets.' Andersen visited him on his death-bed and, finding the body still warm in the pit of the stomach, begged the doctor to sever the arteries. Oehlen-schläger objected to Weyse's 'being cut up', but Andersen said, 'Better that than that he should wake in his grave, and you will prefer that too when you die.' He was intensely aware of death and wrote to Ingemann of a funeral he had attended at Gisselfeld: 'It had a strange effect on me to walk behind the coffin in the beautiful summer weather. I felt affected by it, but also filled with a burning delight in life. It is terrible to me to think of lying in a wet grave with all that earth upon my coffin. I love life and life is to rove, to fly with the railway flight round the earth, one is soon enough under it.'

By January 1843 Andersen could afford to rove again and so set off for Paris, where he hoped to see the great tragedienne Rachel act. He left by way of Slesvig-Holstein – there was still no railway there and he commented sardonically on 'the poetry of bad highways'. While staying with Count Rantzau-Breitenburg, even he became aware of political tension in the air: 'I, who always lived without thinking about politics and political conditions, noticed for the first time in a few people here a sort of tension between the Duchies and the Kingdom; I had thought so little about the relationship between these countries that I had unhesitatingly dedicated *A Poet's Bazaar* to *"my fellow countryman* Professor Ross of Holstein", but as to our being fellow countrymen, I soon realized that all was not as I had imagined. *"Unser Herzog,"* I once heard a lady say, meaning the King. "Why do you not call him the King?" I asked in political ignorance. "He is not our King, he is our Duke," she replied. Small political differences occurred, but Count Rantzau, who loved the King, Denmark and the Danes, and was an extremely attentive host, smoothed over what was said with a kind word and a joke – *"Es sind närrische Leute* – crazy people," he whispered to me, and I thought it must be a couple of eccentrics I had met, and not the increasingly general opinion I was hearing.' This was Andersen's first personal contact with the complicated Slesvig-Holstein question which was to involve his country in two wars during his own lifetime.

The southern part of the Jutland peninsula, where Denmark's land frontier joined that of Germany, consisted of the duchies of Slesvig and Holstein, united legally and 'indivisible' since the Middle Ages, with the King of Denmark as their duke. Slesvig was ancient Danish territory, but Holstein was German and since 1815 had been a member of the German Confederation and, as such, entitled by the terms of the Congress of Vienna to an independent constitution. Slesvig was not a member of the German Confederation, yet if Holstein and Slesvig were to remain indivisible they must both have the same constitution. All over Slesvig-Holstein German was spoken by the nobility and civil servants, Danish by the peasants and shopkeepers, and the administration was controlled by the German Chancellery in Copenhagen. The duchies had their own money and customs and thus virtually constituted a state within a state. After the July Revolution of 1830, which had brought Louis-Philippe to the French throne and given an impetus to radical movements all over Europe, a young civil servant, Lornsen, had started agitation for Slesvig-Holstein to have one constitution and Denmark proper another, with 'only God and war' in common.

From Holstein Andersen went to Hamburg, which he found barely recognizable. It had been devastated the previous year by

a fire as terrible as the famous fire of London. After a few days as
the guest of the Danish postmaster, Count Holck, he took the
mail-coach across Lüneburg Heath to Düsseldorf, where he saw
the Carnival, and on through Cologne and Liège, partly by
coach and partly by the as yet unfinished railway, to Brussels, the
capital of Belgium which had become an independent kingdom in
1830 and was ruled by Queen Victoria's uncle, King Leopold I.
There Andersen heard Donizetti's new opera *La Favorita*, was
bored by Rubens's 'fat blonde women with their plain faces', and
delighted by the City Hall with its memories of Egmont.

Spring was in the air when at last he passed the new entrench-
ments outside Paris and drove to the Hôtel Valois in the Rue
Richelieu, opposite the Bibliothèque Nationale. This time, to his
surprise, he was given almost as warm a welcome in Paris as
in Germany. An article about him in the *Revue de Paris* by his
contemporary Xavier Marmier, the traveller, translator and
critic, who had spent two years on a scientific expedition to the
north, learning Danish, Swedish and Icelandic in the process,
had brought his name to the ears of literary circles 'like a sound
from afar'. Victor Hugo was extremely cordial this time and invited Andersen to see his controversial play *Les Burgraves* at the
Comédie Française. The play was a spectacular failure and Hugo
did not write for the theatre again. Andersen thought Hugo's wife
Adèle so beautiful that he wrote a poem about her. Jacques
Arsène Ancelot, the dramatist, librarian and Academician, and
his wife opened their house to Andersen, and there he met the
thirty-two-year-old historian and socialist Louis Blanc, who had
published his famous *Organisation du Travail* three years earlier;
the Spanish statesman and poet Martínez de la Rosa; and a
young diplomat who had gone to Denmark for Christian VIII's
coronation and appeared to think that gold and white silks and
trailing velvet robes were everyday wear in official circles in
Copenhagen. Andersen also met the handsome poet, historian and
statesman Lamartine, then fifty-three, who struck him as 'the
prince of them all'. Lamartine had known Christian VIII as Prince
Christian in Italy when he himself was there *en poste* as a diplomat immediately after the Restoration, at which time Lady
Blessington had remarked of Lamartine that he dressed so like

a gentleman that one would never suspect him of being a poet. Alfred de Vigny, whose noble *Servitude et Grandeur Militaire* had appeared eight years earlier, went out of his way to show Andersen kindness. His wife was English and Andersen said that at their house he met 'the best of both nations'. On Andersen's last evening in Paris, Alfred de Vigny arrived at his hotel carrying a complete edition of his works as a parting gift.

Towards the end of his stay Andersen met David d'Angers, too late unfortunately for the sculptor to make a medallion of him as he wished to do. Like Thorvaldsen, the French sculptor was the son of a woodcarver, and his frank, cordial manner reminded Andersen of Thorvaldsen. He was also invited to receptions given by the Comtesse de Bocarmé, a great friend of Balzac. It was in her salon that Andersen met a Polish countess who later introduced him to Balzac, then forty-four, one of the most famous men in Europe and the most chronically in debt. At one point the two strikingly dissimilar writers found themselves seated one on either side of a woman who wrote verse and said simperingly that she felt quite shamefaced at finding herself between the two most famous men in Europe. Just as Andersen was about to try to answer this he turned his head and saw Balzac, his bright eyes sparkling with malice, make a satirical grimace behind her back. Shortly after this Andersen was walking through the Louvre when he passed a man in dirty and ragged clothes who so resembled Balzac that Andersen turned back and said, 'You are not Monsieur Balzac, are you?' The man gave a radiant smile and said, 'Tomorrow Monsieur Balzac is going to St Petersburg.' A few days later Andersen was told by the Comtesse de Bocarmé that Balzac had left for St Petersburg (he was off to visit his epistolary love the Countess Hanska) and had sent him his best wishes. The romantic mystifier would have been gratified to know that Andersen described him in his diary as 'elegant and well-dressed', a striking instance of Andersen's endearing capacity for seeing people as they saw themselves.

This visit also brought Andersen another meeting with Heine, now married to a Paris *grisette* with whom he had lived for seven years before their marriage. He was already in poor health – in four years' time he would be bedridden by spinal paralysis – but this time he behaved with such unaffected cordiality that Andersen at last felt at ease with him. Another meeting of particular interest to Andersen was with the traveller and historian Ampère, son of the mathematician and physicist whose name, like that of Ørsted, is now employed as a unit of electrical measurement.

But of all his new acquaintances in the French world of letters none endeared himself to Andersen so immediately as Alexandre Dumas *père*, whose *The Three Musketeers* was to appear the following year. When Andersen met Dumas, then forty years old, he was living at an hotel near his own. His wife was in Italy, his nineteen-year-old son, the future author of *La Dame aux Camélias*, had an apartment of his own, and Dumas told Andersen, 'I live a completely bachelor life and you must take me as you find me.' No matter at what hour Andersen called on him, this human dynamo was invariably in bed 'writing at top speed in a clear beautiful hand, and shying each sheet as he finished it across the floor in all directions'. Andersen dared not move his large feet for fear of damaging some portion of the flying manuscript, but Dumas would shout cheerfully, 'Sit down, sit down, my muse is here on a visit, but she'll be gone in a minute' – and indeed, in a minute he would leap out of bed 'with a jerk as of an earthquake', crying '*Viva!*' On one occasion he stalked about the room, a blanket draped around him toga-fashion, declaiming at the top of his voice, and finally, seizing the lapels of Andersen's coat, shook him gently and said, 'Now isn't that magnificent, eh? Superb! Worthy of Racine! . . . It's my new play, I write an act, and often more, before breakfast. This is the third act I have just finished.' Andersen found Dumas's spontaneity, animal spirits and passion for the theatre irresistible and jumped at the opportunity when his new friend offered to take him backstage. At the Palais Royal Dumas introduced him to Déjazet, then forty-six years old, who had been acting since she was a child of five and was famous for her playing of *soubrettes* and boys' parts; then he and Dumas wandered down the boulevard to the Théâtre St Martin. They made an extraordinary picture, the grandson of a French general and a Haitian Negress and the son of a Danish cobbler and washerwoman, both among the great men of their period, strolling arm-in-arm along the Paris boulevards, enjoying the spectacle of worldliness with equal zest and naïvety. When they reached the Théâtre St Martin, Dumas said, 'They're just in their short skirts now. Shall we go up?' and he led Andersen into the crowded, noisy, candlelit world of make-believe that they both loved. Back on the boulevards they ran into Dumas's son, and the authors of *The Little Mermaid*, *The Three Musketeers*, and *Camille* stood for a while chatting together outside the theatre.

It was Alexandre Dumas, too, who introduced Andersen to Rachel. The great actress was at this time twenty-two years old and in full possession of her stormy powers. The daughter of a Jewish pedlar from Alsace, she had come to Paris as a child of nine accustomed to squalor and violence, from which she had emerged to dazzle the town when she was seventeen with her performance of Camille in Corneille's *Horace*. It was said of her that no one else had ever possessed such power to make living and suffering statues out of Racine's and Corneille's blocks of marble. In the other theatres Dumas had led Andersen backstage without ceremony, sure of his own sovereignty there, but at the Comédie Française he asked Andersen to wait while he requested permission to present the visitor to Rachel. As they went upstairs Andersen said, 'I feel almost ill, my heart is beating so fast now that I am to meet the lady who speaks the most beautiful French in France.'

Excessively thin, fragile and youthful-looking, with immense dark eyes and a deep powerful voice, she seemed to Andersen, who could see people as works of art, the very picture of melancholy. In many respects Rachel's beginnings resembled those of Johanne Heiberg, but whereas the latter, with her happy marriage, had become what Karen Blixen was to describe as 'a glorious martyr to respectability', Rachel's native savagery still clung to her, giving her a feral quality like that of a black panther. Despite his poor French, Andersen found himself able to talk to her, and Rachel told him that, since poets always understood each other, she would rather listen to his bad French than to many a foreigner who spoke French fluently. She added that if ever she went to play in Copenhagen and St Petersburg, he must be her protector, and meanwhile, since he had come to Paris partly to see her, they must get to know each other better – and she invited him to one of her Thursday receptions. Then she got herself ready for her next entrance, and Andersen noticed that as she went on to the stage she already seemed to be another person. Accustomed to the non-declamatory style of the Royal Theatre in Copenhagen, he was at first disconcerted by the stylized majesty of French classic acting, but realized that in Rachel's case it corresponded with an inner necessity – 'As a Scandinavian I cannot accustom myself to the French manner of acting tragedies; Rachel acts like all the others there, but it is as though this manner is natural to her and the rest were only trying to imitate her. She is the French tragic muse herself, and the others are only poor human beings. When we see Rachel perform we think all tragic action must be like hers. There is truth and reality in it, but revealed in a different way from what we know in the North.'

At her invitation, Andersen visited Rachel's home, a Balzac-like setting for her which he found magnificent, though too artificial for his taste. The outer room was blue and green with subdued lighting and statues of French authors; the salon, where crimson dominated, was filled with books in ornate glass-fronted cases. There was a painting of her on the stage in London, and under it, a little bookcase containing her favourite poets, Goethe, Schiller, Calderón and Shakespeare. Rachel questioned him searchingly about the theatre in Denmark and Germany, and whenever he stumbled in his French, said, 'Just carry on. You do not speak good French. I have heard foreigners who can speak my language better, but it has not often interested me as much as this. I completely understand the spirit of your words, and that is the main thing; that is what interests me in you.' When they parted she wrote in his album: '*L'art c'est le vrai. J'espère que cet aphorisme ne semblera pas paradoxal à un écrivain aussi distingué que Monsieur Andersen. Paris, le 28 avril, 1843.*'

The grave spontaneity with which Rachel had saluted him as a colleague, reaching out and drawing him through the sound-barrier of language, made him react violently to the news that *Agnete and the Merman*, which had at last been produced in Copenhagen, was a resounding failure. On the day after his visit to Rachel's house he wrote thunderously to Henriette Wulff: 'May I never again see that homeland which has eyes for my faults but no heart for the greatness God has deposited in me . . . As always, the icy blasts come from Denmark and turn me to stone in this foreign land . . . When I was young, I could weep; but now I cannot; I can only feel pride – hatred – contempt – I can only give my soul to evil powers, in order to find a moment's relief! In this great and foreign city, Europe's most famous and noblest spirits surround me with their friendly wishes, treat me as a kinsman, and at home the streetboys spit upon my heart's best creation . . . Of course I'm using the typical expressions of a poet whose works have been hissed . . . may I never again see a place where I am a foreigner, more foreign there than in any foreign land . . .'

The immediacy of this outburst was characteristic, as was its ambivalence, its tone of a rejected lover. Andersen was a great traveller but not a cosmopolitan spirit capable, like Heine, of adapting himself completely to a foreign country. Had he not been so profoundly Danish he would have craved less for recognition at home; had he had a more fortunate family background he would have been less ready to believe himself an outcast among his own people.

Nowhere at this stage in his life was the contrast between Andersen's reputation at home and abroad more marked than in his beloved Germany, where he lingered on his way home, welcomed by the old poet and liberal historian Moritz Arndt, the young poet Emanuel von Geibel, and by his contemporary Ferdinand Freiligrath, who greeted him with the most exuberant enthusiasm, flinging his arms around him and saying that Andersen was responsible for his happy marriage, since it was Andersen's novel *Only a Fiddler* that had drawn him and his future wife into correspondence with each other. Moments like these compensated Andersen for many a literary stricture; nevertheless, every kindly foreign word and gesture increased his nervous dread of going home to be considered a failure. Jonas Collin was constantly in his thoughts and he told Edvard Collin, 'I shall only be happy as a poet when your father can say "I am proud of him." '

9. The Nightingale

1843-4

And the nightingale sang so sweetly that tears came into the Emperor's eyes and rolled down his cheeks. Then the nightingale sang still more sweetly, and it was the Emperor's heart that melted. The Emperor was so touched that he wanted his own golden slipper hung around the nightingale's neck, but the nightingale declined it with thanks . . . The whole town talked about the marvellous bird, and if two people met, one could scarcely say 'night' before the other said 'gale', and then they would sigh in unison without words. Eleven pork-butchers' children were named 'Nightingale', but not one could sing.

Hans Christian Andersen, *The Nightingale*

*

ONCE HOME AND AMONG FRIENDS who were as delighted to see him as – suddenly – he was glad to be back, Andersen completely forgot his fury against his own people and began to learn from *Agnete*'s failure. For the first time he half-believed that Ørsted might be right about his fairy tales, and he told Ingemann, 'I believe – and I should be happy to be right – that the best thing I can do is to write these tales. The first ones were of course mostly some which I had heard in my childhood and retold, but then I found that those which I created myself, such as *The Little Mermaid*, got the most applause and that has given me a new start. Now I look into myself, find the idea for older people – and tell it as if to the children, but remembering that Father and Mother are listening! . . . I have masses of material, more than for any other kind of work; often it seems to me that every fence, every little flower says "Just look at me, then you'll know my story!" and if I so desire the story is mine.'

Soon after his return Andersen encountered his first love, Riborg, and her husband, a meeting that prompted him to write *The Top and the Ball*, a sadly comic little tale of the fruitless love of two nursery toys. Thirteen years had passed since he said goodbye to the young girl who now seemed a middle-aged matron; and remote as the toys of childhood must this love have seemed to him just then – for it was precisely then that he met for the second time the woman who was to be the great love of his life. She was not a pleasant young girl embellished by his imagination but a young woman of genius, of whom it was impossible for even him to think too highly.

When Jenny Lind came to Copenhagen in the autumn of 1843 Andersen was told of her arrival by his friend and contemporary, the ballet-master Bournonville, whose wife was one of Jenny Lind's closest friends. The Swedish Nightingale had asked Bournonville to give Andersen her kind regards and tell him that she would like to see him again, so Bournonville suggested that Andersen should go with him to call on her and help him persuade her to appear as a guest artist at the Royal Theatre. This time the singer received Andersen as if they were old friends. Since their previous meeting she had read his books and talked of him with her friend Fredrika Bremer, who later wrote to Andersen: 'We are in complete agreement about Jenny Lind as an artist; she is as great as any artist can be in our time, but you do not know her enough in all her greatness; speak of her art and you will understand her powers of understanding and see her eyes light up with enthusiasm; then talk to her of God and religion and you will see tears in her innocent eyes; she is great as an artist, but she is even greater as a woman.'

Jenny Lind seems indeed to have had a dynamic purity of personality as striking as the beauty of her voice. She was only at the beginning of her career when Mendelssohn said that a personality like hers had not been born in centuries, and three years after her death the American showman P. T. Barnum told a reporter: 'It is a mistake to say that the fame of Jenny Lind rests solely upon her ability to sing. She was a woman who would have been adored if she had had the voice of a crow.' At her second meeting with Andersen she told him how nervous she felt at the idea of singing in Copenhagen. She had never before sung abroad, and having always been enthusiastically received at home, did not know how she would stand up to failure. Andersen advised

her to risk it – he had as yet no idea of her talents as a performer,
so told her that, given the Copenhagen public's taste for novelty,
she was bound to succeed there provided she had a medium
voice and could act a little. She liked him for not flattering her
and decided to sing in Copenhagen. Her success was immediate
and immense. She was applauded as Alice in Meyerbeer's *Robert
le Diable* even more enthusiastically than she had been at home.

Andersen and Jenny Lind had much in common, including
early familiarity with poverty and the theatre. Jenny's mother,
Anne Marie Fellborg, the daughter of a Stockholm harbour-
master, had married at seventeen a gay, irresponsible officer,
Captain Erik Johan Radberg. Before she was twenty she discovered that he had been unfaithful to her, insisted on divorcing
him, and, to support herself and her child Amalia, opened a
school. After some years of struggling she met Nicolas Jonas Lind,
a young man five years younger than herself and as gay and
irresponsible as her husband had been. They set up house
together, but religious scruples prevented her marrying Lind
until Captain Radberg's death, which did not occur until Jenny,
her daughter by Lind, was fourteen. As a small child Jenny was
boarded out with Carl Ferndal, an organist and parish clerk, and
his wife, in a village fifteen miles north of Stockholm. In the
thirteenth-century church there she had her first experience of
music and ever afterwards she was to feel a need for music, the
country and solitude. After four years with her foster-parents the
child found it hard to adapt herself to a mother who was a
stranger to her and of an obstinate and morbidly arbitrary
temper. In her mother's company the little girl developed a terror
of being unwanted that was to make her, throughout her life,
need constant reassurance that her friends loved her. In this too
she resembled Andersen. When she was eight her mother had to
close her school and obtained a post as governess at Linköping, a
hundred and fifty miles south-west of Stockholm. She took
Amalia with her, but Jenny was left behind and again boarded
out, this time with a childless couple who were the caretakers of a
home for widows to which Jenny's grandmother had recently
been admitted. Like Andersen, Jenny adored her grandmother.
She spent a happy year in the home, regaining gaiety and vitality,

and it was here that something happened which decisively altered her life.

The child had a cat to which she was devoted and would sit singing to it in a window-seat overlooking a street that led to St Jakob's Church. Passers-by would often stop and listen to her, and one day the maidservant of Miss Lundberg, a dancer at the Royal Opera House, told her mistress that she had never heard such a beautiful voice as that of 'the little girl with the cat'. The dancer made enquiries and when Jenny's mother was in Stockholm arranged for her to bring the child to see her. On hearing Jenny sing, she declared that she was a genius and must be trained for the stage. At first the mother was reluctant to allow the child, about whose illegitimacy she was very sensitive, to enter the immoral world of the theatre – all the more so since she herself was about to reopen her school and feared gossip. Miss Lundberg persisted, however, and so impressed were the court officials to whom the dancer presented the child that they not only offered to accept Jenny right away as a pupil at the singing and dramatic school attached to the Royal Theatre, instead of waiting until she was fourteen, the usual age of admission, but also offered to pay for her maintenance, education and training, the money to be later deducted from her earnings. Jenny became an actress-pupil in September 1830 and made her debut at the Royal Theatre in Stockholm in Weber's *Der Freischütz* in 1838. On this occasion the management of the theatre presented her with a pair of silver lyre-shaped candlesticks inscribed 'In remembrance of March 7', which she treasured all her life. Like Andersen, she attached immense importance to anniversaries, and she ever afterwards considered March 7 as her 'true birthday': 'I got up that morning one person, and went to bed another, I had found where my real strength lay.' In 1840 she was appointed Court Singer, but meanwhile she had been straining her voice by overwork to such an extent that when in 1841 she went to Paris to study with Garcia, the father of the great singer Malibran and the inventor of the laryngoscope, he at first said that it would be useless for her to take lessons as she 'no longer had any voice left'. He changed his mind, however, when he discovered that she had been trained in a faulty method of breathing, and after he had rectified this she made such progress that on her return to Sweden her second début was an even greater triumph than her first.

Although Jenny Lind lived for her work and had written from Paris 'life on the stage has in it something so enthralling that I think that no one who has ever tasted it can ever be happy away from it', she never felt completely at home in the world of the theatre as Andersen did. Although it did not show so much in her youth as later, there was a strain of bigotry in her – in Paris she thought that the people hired by artists to applaud were 'a terrible manifestation of original sin'. There was a striking difference between her public and her private personality. Andersen wrote of her: 'On the stage she was a great artist who dazzled all those about her; at home, in her drawing-room, she was a modest young girl with the mind and piety of a child.' She was a devout Protestant, with a touch of puritanism that made her recoil from success when off stage and crave the seclusion of private life and a small circle of intimates. Off stage, too, she often found it difficult to handle her feelings – when, for example, Andersen introduced her to Thorvaldsen and the sculptor kissed her hand admiringly, she blushed deeply and was so overwhelmed by emotion that for a second Andersen feared she was going to kiss Thorvaldsen's hand in return. This was the kind of impulse he himself understood, but he had been told he was over-emotional too often not to wish to prevent Jenny from exposing herself to ridicule. He could not bear the thought of her being hurt. He understood not only her character and temperament but could appreciate every detail of her performances, just as she could appreciate all that he wrote. From childhood Andersen had been passionately fond of music, and his enthusiasm for Jenny's work was that of a trained art-lover who could be moved by music to agree with Schopenhauer that all art is the representation of the essence of things, and music the ultimate reality. In perfect sympathy with each other, he and Jenny met daily. He showered poems, flowers and presents on her, and on September 10, 1843, noted succinctly in his diary: 'In the evening with Jenny Lind at Bournonville's. Her health and mine were drunk. In love.'

At this time he had an encounter even more strangely coincidental than his recent one with Riborg. One afternoon he was to meet Jenny and Bournonville at the house of a dramatic instructor, Mr Nielsen. As Andersen was on his way there a woman stopped him and said with profuse apologies that she had a letter for him from Countess Mathilda Barck, who had asked her to forward it to Andersen when he was in Rome, three years earlier. He remembered the beautiful little Swedish countess well, but had supposed that she had long ago forgotten him. The letter was a shyly affectionate one. Had he received it when intended, he would have been overjoyed. Now the adolescent girl he remembered was grown up, engaged to the Belgian minister in Copenhagen, while he himself could think of nothing but Jenny Lind. He never saw Mathilda Barck again. Later he was to hear that her engagement had been broken off, and in January 1844 she died, still a young man's fancy; but on the afternoon when her letter to Rome belatedly reached him Andersen thrust it into his pocket and hurried on through the streets of Copenhagen so as not to miss a minute of Jenny Lind. At twilight torches appeared outside Mr Nielsen's house and there was the sound of singing. It was the Danish students serenading Jenny. She was the first woman singer to be honoured in this way in Copenhagen. Among the songs they sang was one by Andersen. Jenny went to the window and sang two songs in thanks, but afterwards Andersen found her in a dark corner weeping. She explained to him, 'I shall work, I shall strive with all my heart, I shall be much better next time I come to Copenhagen.' Andersen understood her completely. His own immediate reaction to success was always a grateful desire to do better next time. Once, after she had sung for the benefit of the Society for the Care of Neglected Children and Andersen told her how much she had earned for the children, her face lit up and with tears in her eyes she said, 'Oh, it is lovely to be able to sing like that.' The similarity of their feelings about their work created a special bond between them and Andersen was to say that no one ever influenced his artistic development as Jenny did. Through her, he said, he learned to 'forget himself and feel the sacredness of art'.

On September 10 Andersen had written 'in love' in his diary. Eight days later he wrote in it 'I love her'. Two days later Jenny Lind left Copenhagen. Andersen went to see her sail, and at the

last minute handed her a letter, of which he wrote in his diary that
'she must understand'. His hopes were more poignant than his
youthful ones had been. Life no longer seemed to stretch ahead
of him illimitably. At thirty-eight he was only eight years younger
than Jonas Collin had been when he first knew him, and, still a
child himself, had seen the Councillor as a middle-aged man.
Soon he himself would be on the other side of the hill that led to
old age and he could not bear the idea that he might never
experience the fulfilment of love. This time, however, he had
every reason to believe that his love would be returned.

10. *Kept Secret but not Forgotten*

1844-5

. . . Ni bonjour, ni bonsoir,
Le matin n'est plus; le soir pas encore,
Pourtant de nos yeux l'éclair a pâli,
Mais le soir qui vient ressemble à l'aurore
Et la nuit plus tard apporte l'oubli.

Gérard de Nerval

*

SOON AFTER Jenny Lind left Copenhagen Andersen lost one of his dearest friends. On March 24 he dined with the Stampe family at their town house in Copenhagen. The other guests were Thorvaldsen, Oehlenschläger, the botanist Schouw and Constantine Hansen, the young painter who was to do the frescoes for the Thorvaldsen Museum. Thorvaldsen, who was not usually talkative, was in a particularly lively mood, enjoying his food, telling stories and describing the trip to Italy that he was planning for the summer. That evening *Griseldis*, a tragedy by the German author Halm, was to be given for the first time at the Royal Theatre, and Thorvaldsen invited his friends to go with him. Oehlenschläger had arranged, however, to spend the evening with the Stampes, reading them some of his work, and Andersen had a seat for next day's performance. When Andersen left to go home, Thorvaldsen was dozing by the stove. As Andersen reached the door the old man opened his eyes, smiled and nodded.

Andersen spent the evening at home at the Hôtel du Nord. Next morning a waiter said to him, 'What a strange thing, Thorvaldsen dying suddenly yesterday.' At first Andersen could not believe it. Then Bournonville arrived with the news. Thorvaldsen had gone to the theatre as planned and during the overture had stood up to allow someone to pass. As he sat down he threw his head back. People around him thought he was faint and ran for water; but as he did not regain consciousness they carried him out. Doctors were sent for, but he was dead.

Horrified, Andersen rushed to Thorvaldsen's house. There he found his old friend's body laid out and Baroness Stampe sitting on the edge of the bed weeping. She was quite distraught, for not only had she been both a daughter and mother to Thorvaldsen but she had a few days earlier also lost her beloved sister. The room was already full of strangers and the snow from their boots melted into rivulets over the floor.

The funeral, which took place on March 30, was a national one. Flowers from the Queen and the princesses, together with Thorvaldsen's many decorations, were laid on the coffin, which was carried and escorted through the streets of Copenhagen by artists and students. The children of the city contributed a wreath of silver leaves, the procession was headed by a deputation from the navy, and when the coffin reached the Church of Our Lady, the King, the Prince and the notabilities left their seats and accompanied Thorvaldsen to the altar. During the service the students sang Andersen's 'Sleep well', set to music by Hartmann.

Andersen's writings contain many admiring references to Thorvaldsen, whom he considered a far more important man than himself, but none is as touching as that in *Aunty*, the story of an old spinster who 'could not imagine heaven without a theatre' and therefore thought Thorvaldsen's a 'blessed death'. Aunty left all her money to a 'deserving old spinster' on one condition: namely, that as the legatee sat in the theatre every Saturday, 'she was to think of Aunty in her grave'.

One of the results of Andersen's passion for Jenny Lind was his story *The Nightingale*, a miniature masterpiece full of memories of the Tivoli Garden's Chinese motifs, of a small boy's songs to the Emperor who lived beneath the Odense river, and most of all, full of Jenny Lind herself: 'From all the countries in the world travellers came to the city of the Emperor. They admired the city. They admired the palace and its garden, but when they heard the nightingale they said, "That is the best of all." ' This was published, together with *The Ugly Duckling, The Angel, The Top and the Ball* in *New Fairy Tales*, 1844, and Jenny Lind wrote to him: 'What a glorious gift to be able to clothe one's *light* thoughts in words, to show mankind on a scrap of paper how the *noblest* often lies hidden and covered with misery and rags, until the transformation comes and reveals the figure in a heavenly light. Thanks, sincere thanks, for so much that is moving and instructive. Now I long for the hour when I shall be able to tell my dear brother how proud I am of his friendship . . .' Despite the in-auspicious words 'brother' and 'friendship', Andersen continued to hope for Jenny's love. It was a period when a young woman's lack of immediate responsiveness might credibly be attributed to modest manners and delicacy of feeling.

Still uplifted by these hopes, Andersen went to Germany again in the summer of 1844. On the way he stayed as usual with Count Rantzau, at whose castle he was now treated as one of the family and could therefore retire to work whenever he pleased. The Count's health was failing and one day in the garden he pressed Andersen's hand and told him he believed this year would be his last. He showed him a grass-grown grave near the chapel and said, 'That is where you will find me next time you visit Breiten-burg' – a prophecy which was fulfilled, for the Count died the following winter at Wiesbaden.

On June 24 Andersen reached Weimar, the residence of the Grand Dukes of Saxe-Weimar, described by Voltaire, who knew it in its great days as a literary centre, as *'un grand château où l'on s'amuse, plutôt qu'une petite ville'*. Andersen never needed to be reminded to praise famous men and he entered Weimar full of reverent thoughts of Goethe, Schiller, Wieland and Herder. He was eager to see the house in which Goethe had died in 1832, the deal table at which both Goethe and Schiller had written, the park designed by Goethe, and above all, the theatre of which both Schiller and Goethe had been directors. The Court Chamberlain, Beaulieu de Marconnay, a charming man six years younger than himself whom he had met once before, insisted on his staying with him. So instead of sightseeing alone Andersen found himself seeing the life of the little court from the inside, a Biedermeier Ruritania that he immediately loved.

Kept Secret but not Forgotten

On this occasion the city was celebrating the twenty-sixth birthday of the Hereditary Grand Duke, Karl Alexander. The young heir and his wife, formerly a princess of the Netherlands, were staying at their hunting-lodge high up in the Thuringian forest with a view over the Harz mountains. Beaulieu and Eckermann, famous for his *Conversations with Goethe*, published seven years earlier, drove Andersen out into the forest. As they stopped near the lodge a young man with 'a frank face and magnificent gentle eyes' appeared and greeted them, asking eagerly, 'Have you brought Andersen with you?' He shook hands with Andersen and said, 'It is delightful to see you here, I will join you presently.' This was Andersen's first encounter with the Hereditary Grand Duke. He dined at the royal hunting-lodge and afterwards he and the other guests accompanied the royal couple to the village to watch the birthday celebrations. There was climbing of beribboned greasy poles and dancing to violins under the lime trees. Andersen was impressed by the tenderness the young Duke and Duchess showed each other and reflected that, 'If one is to be happy while spending a considerable time at Court, it is necessary to forget the star for the heart beating under it.'

Andersen and Karl Alexander took an instant liking to each other, and as a result Andersen was to find himself adopted by the Court with its cosy domestic atmosphere – homely was the word he used – which suggests that of Queen Victoria's diaries. There were readings aloud, and for the first time Andersen read in a foreign language, giving the young Duke *The Steadfast Tin Soldier* in German. Karl Alexander combined a strict attention to etiquette and militaristic leanings (his grandfather Karl August, who had governed Saxe-Weimar during its most brilliant period, had been strongly influenced by Frederick the Great) with a passion for literature and a desire to revive Weimar's former glories by attracting artists to it. He showed Andersen the tree in the park on which Goethe, Schiller and Wieland had carved their names, did everything he could to make his guest feel at home, and when Andersen left pressed him to return soon. This was the beginning of a lifelong friendship.

In Leipzig another delightful surprise awaited Andersen. His contemporary Robert Schumann had set four of Andersen's poems, translated by Chamisso, to music, and these were sung for him by the well-known singer Frau Frege, accompanied by Clara Schumann. In Dresden he met Johann Christian Dahl, the Norwegian landscape-painter who 'knew how to make waterfalls rush and trees grow on canvas'; the manager of the theatre put a seat in the director's box at his disposal every evening; and Beaulieu de Marconnay's brother August, an army officer, came over from Tharandt and invited Andersen to stay with him. He was also invited to the home on a vine-covered hill near Meissen of the Dresden-born painter and engraver Retzsch, famous for his etchings in outline of Goethe, Schiller, Fouqué and Shakespeare. Andersen spent a week with the von Serres at their estate in Saxon Switzerland, where he met the Countess Ida Hahn-Hahn, the famous one-eyed novelist and travel writer, who scandalized London society by going there with her lover. She entertained Andersen with stories of her father, whose passion for the theatre kept him away from home travelling with his personal company of actors. Love for the theatre runs like a leitmotive through the lives of nineteenth-century writers.

Andersen went home by way of Berlin. His friend and translator Chamisso had died six years earlier, but Andersen saw his children. The little boys with whom he had played were now Prussian officers and he noted, 'It is in the young people that I see around me that I realize I am becoming old; I do not feel it within myself.' One of the most stimulating invitations he received during this visit to Berlin was from Savigny, who had been the favourite teacher of the brothers Grimm. This led to a meeting with Savigny's sister-in-law, the famous Bettina von Arnim. She had been born Bettina Brentano, and began to write when she was a widow of nearly fifty with seven children. In 1835 she had created a sensation by publishing the ardent correspondence that as a girl of twenty-two she had had with the fifty-eight-year-old Goethe. George Eliot's husband, George Henry Lewes, described Bettina in his *Life of Goethe* as 'this strange figure who fills a larger space in the literary history of the nineteenth century than any other German woman . . . She is one of those phantasts to whom everything is permitted. More elf than woman, yet with flashes of genius which light up in splendour

whole chapters of nonsense, she defies criticism and puts every
verdict at fault. If you are grave with her, people shrug their
shoulders, and saying "She is a Brentano", consider all settled.
"At the point where the folly of others ceases, that of the Bren-
tanos begins," runs the proverb in Germany.' Still exuberant,
contrary, intensely feminine and quaintly domineering, Bettina
was quite unlike any woman Andersen had met before – as
different from Jenny Lind as the Emperor's artificial nightingale
'encrusted with diamonds, rubies and sapphires' was from the
'little grey bird' that brought tears to its listeners' eyes – but he
was dazzled by her 'firework display of ideas' and touched by her
intimate connection with the German Romantic movement. He
was always ready to meet people half way and could see in this
handsome elderly woman with her intellectual pyrotechnics the
ardent young girl who had worshipped Goethe, the wife of the
Ludwig Achim von Arnim whose story *Isabelle of Egypt* Andersen
particularly admired, the romantic friend of Madame de Staël
and of the poet Karoline von Günderode, and above all, the
woman who had tenderly understood and befriended the
irascible Beethoven in his deafness. After the party Andersen
walked home with Bettina, her beautiful daughters and the
Prince of Württemberg, and when they reached his hotel she
gave him a military salute and said 'Goodnight, Comrade! Sleep
well!' Later he visited her in her own home and found her less
superficially witty, but equally brilliant and enthusiastic.

He returned to Copenhagen by way of Stettin, and after a few
days spent seeing old friends, went over to Fyn to stay at Glorup
with Count Moltke-Huitfeldt. There he received a letter from
Count Rantzau who was taking the waters with the King and
Queen at Föhr, an island off the coast of Slesvig. They had been
delighted, he wrote, to hear of Andersen's reception at Weimar
and would be glad if he could come now and spend a few days as
their guest at Föhr.

This first invitation to stay with his King and Queen was of
immense significance to Andersen. In his day royal personages
were no longer divinities as in the past, but not yet condemned to
display democratic respectability; they still seemed to retain

magical properties – and in their eyes he, as an artist, had magical properties of his own. The courts he knew intimately were as cosily domestic as those in his fairy tales in which kings opened the front door of their palaces in their dressing-gowns and slippers, and his attitude towards them was a continuation of the artist's attitude in the eighteenth century when, as Georg Brandes said, 'authors did not live on their works but on their dedications'. Wieland had accepted payment for his dedications, Schiller accepted financial help from Denmark, and the great Goethe could, at seventy-one, write in his diary: 'I . . . had the unexpected happiness of being permitted to pay my homage to their Imperial Highnesses the Grand Duke Nicholas and his consort, in my own house and garden. The Grand Duchess graciously allowed me to write some lines of poetry in her elegantly splendid album . . .'

It was with joy, therefore, that Andersen accepted this invitation. From Fyn he went by boat to Flensburg, on the east coast of Slesvig, then crossed the duchy by coach. In all the vast landscape only the clouds seemed to move and the only sound was the occasional cheep of a bird in the heather. After the heath came marshland. The recent rains had made lakes in the cornfields and meadows, and the dykes were like quagmires. In several places the horses sank in the mud and peasants came to the rescue. At last they reached the west coast of Slesvig and saw the North Sea – a strange sea-scape, for all this part of the coast was a vast dyke, fortified for miles by straw thatch on which the waves broke. Across the water were islands formed by fragments broken off the mainland by the sea.

Andersen reached the coast at high tide and, thanks to a favourable wind, was at Föhr within an hour. When he reached Wyck, the largest town on the island, built in Dutch style, Danish flags were being flown and he could hear music. As sailors carried his luggage ashore greetings were called to him from a one-storey wooden house near the landing-stage where the royal family were staying, and he had no sooner sat down to dinner in his hotel than one of the royal servants came to invite him to dine with the King and Queen, with whom he took all his meals for the rest of his stay. Their evenings were happily domestic. After dinner they would play games, such as impromptu rhyming, and read aloud. The King particularly liked to hear Andersen read *The Nightingale* and *The Swineherd*.

There were outings to the Halligen, flat islets on which a few sheep grazed until high tide, when waves drove over the islets and the inhabitants had to take to the lofts of their houses. In the island of Öland, where the little houses were huddled together as if for protection against the wind, all the men were away sailing to Greenland and Holland, and the women spent most of their time spinning. Their chief amusement came from the few books – in Danish, German or Frisian – that each family possessed. The sea often washed around their houses and sometimes a ship would be driven aground among them. In 1825 houses and people had been washed away, yet such was the attachment of the islanders to their home that they could not tolerate life 'on the mainland'. Andersen visited the dunes of Amrum, deserted except for a vast population of rabbits, the descendants of two rabbits who had landed there from a grounded ship. Roses and heather bloomed among the dunes and the burning sunlight made Andersen think of Africa. While he was visiting Amrum the tide ebbed, leaving dry land between Amrum and Föhr. Ships lay on the sand like stranded fish and a procession of carriages crawled across the white sand and blue horizon. Describing life here, Andersen wrote: 'The most important piece of furniture in the house – the most important in every dwelling that is well arranged on these islands – even more important than Ovngrøden [a local dish of milk, flour and bacon] which with its slow-burning fire boils itself on Sundays while they are all at church – is the house's telescope, which has its special place by the door. A telescope becomes a strange means of awakening the spirit; it is the telegraph joining land and sea.'

One of the high-spots of his visit occurred on September 5. As they sat at dinner Andersen told the King that it was exactly twenty-five years ago to the day that he had arrived in Copenhagen, a poor boy of fourteen who knew no one and could scarcely write his own language. They drank his health and after dinner the King congratulated him on his achievements, questioned him about his pension, and said that it did not seem to him adequate. Andersen said that he did not need much and that his writing provided him with a small income. The King looked thoughtful and said, 'You ought to have an easier life than before. If at any time I can be of any help to you in your literary activities, then come to me.' Several of Andersen's friends blamed him for not having seized this opportunity to ask for more money, but he had felt incapable of taking advantage in that way of the King's hospitality.

Towards the end of Andersen's visit the Duchess of Augustenburg invited him to spend a fortnight at Augustenburg castle on his way home. Augustenburg was in Als, one of the prettiest islands in the Baltic. Its woods and apple-orchards, its fields of wheat and clover enclosed by hedges of hazel and wild roses, resembled the landscape of Fyn. The castle was beautifully situated, its gardens stretching down to a winding fjord. Here again, a happy domesticity marked the atmosphere. He was able to start work on *The Two Baronesses*, perhaps his best novel. Here by chance Andersen met the Bishop of Ärö and Als – who twenty-five years earlier, as Dean Tetens of Odense, had not wanted the cobbler's son in his confirmation class. It seemed very strange to Andersen to go as the Duke's guest to the Bishop's house, and to be asked to take the Duchess in to dinner.

In the evenings there would be music – the composer Kellermann, who was a fellow guest, played his fantasies, romances and alpine melodies – and the Duchess's birthday was celebrated by a torchlight procession and a ball. Almost all the German-speaking Holstein nobility attended the festivities and Andersen was moved when he heard the Duke, addressing them in an after-dinner speech, praise contemporary Danish literature at the expense of German – and propose Andersen's health. On the surface nothing indicated the political dissensions that were to lead to war and would destroy Andersen's friendship with the Augustenburgs.

But enjoyment of noble company never lessened Andersen's devotion to old friends, and in particular to the Collins. They might snub him for exuberance and refuse to be impressed by his success, but they always considered him one of the family – and of this they presently gave him a poignant proof. In recent years Mrs Collin had suffered from bad health. She was growing deaf and had to undergo an operation to prevent blindness. In the winter of 1844 she was able to read again and often expressed gratitude for this and a longing to see the spring once more. One Sunday night in the spring Andersen, who had been at the Collins' house the previous evening, was roused by a servant with a note from Jonas Collin telling him that Mrs Collin was extremely ill and 'all the children' were wanted. Never had Andersen been shown so clearly that he was part of this family. It was the first time since his childhood that he had seen anyone die and he was deeply grateful for the sense of kinship that sustained him, as it did the Collin children, at this moment of awe, terror and grief.

In September 1845 Andersen had a very unpleasant experience that revealed his best qualities. People had been asking him if he had read his friend Johannes Carsten Hauch's novel *The Castle on the Rhine; or, The Different Points of View*, which he had not. Presently he was told that this book contained a cruel caricature of himself. He refused to believe this, pointing out that Hauch was a loyal friend, but he was finally persuaded to read the book. In it he found the ludicrous figure of a poet, Eginhard, who, born in a small country where no one admires him, travels down the Rhine in search of admiration, thrusts himself on strangers, seizes every opportunity to read aloud, cannot accept adverse criticism and is so over-emotional that he goes mad and is last seen on his way to a lunatic asylum, surrounded by a crowd whose jeering he mistakes for applause. At one point Eginhard says: 'My songs shall be read beneath the planc-tree and in the tents of the nomads, the camel shall bear them through the desert, the Negro shall sing them in the shade of his palm, and my name shall be remembered thousands of years from now, when the last descendant of my persecutors has vanished from the earth.'

After reading this Andersen wrote to Ingemann: 'Just after I sent my last letter from Bregentved I received Hauch's novel . . . Yes, it is correct to say "That's Andersen!" All my weaknesses are collected here. I hope and believe that I have passed beyond this period, but I could have said and done everything this poet says and does; I felt unpleasantly moved by this harsh picture, which displays me in my misery. I think, of course, that a supplement is necessary if an accurate picture of me is to be given; I try to console myself with the thought that I also have a number of better qualities, by which in actual life I become more bearable or – I might almost say – less contemptible. I am perfectly convinced, though, that Hauch did not mean the likeness to be so great, that it did not occur to him that everyone would recognize me. I know he appreciates what is good in me; I have and shall continue to have the greatest confidence in him . . . That which shook me and burns in my memory is the poet's wretched fate. My own grandfather was insane, my father's mind was affected shortly before his death. So you can understand the effect that the dissolution of the unhappy wretch in Hauch's novel had upon me . . . It is unpleasant to receive sympathy from people who, even as they speak, are keenly aware of the striking truth in Hauch's depiction of my weaknesses. There is nothing to do or say, I must let this wave break over me . . .' In conclusion Andersen sent his regards to Hauch, who was bitterly ashamed when Ingemann showed him the letter but protested that Eginhard was merely a composite picture of several writers. That Andersen accepted this explanation was a sign not of weakness but of weakness overcome. Soon after this he read to several of his friends a bitter criticism of his work, and when they protested at its severity revealed that he himself had written it.

Far more important to him this autumn was Jenny Lind's return to Copenhagen. This time her arrival was a public event. As Andersen said, 'The halo of fame makes genius visible to everyone.' People camped outside the theatre all night to obtain tickets. She stayed with the Bournonvilles and Andersen saw her every day. On one occasion he and she stopped for milk and buns at the court baker's, at the back of Christiansborg palace, and since the baker, recognizing them, would not let them pay, Jenny sang for him. For all their intimacy, however, it was becoming clear to him that Jenny's feeling for him was not of the kind for which he longed. Yet he found it hard to relinquish hope and wrote in his diary: 'Jenny is very sweet to me; I am glad – hopeful – although I know . . .'

She stayed in Copenhagen nearly a month, and on the eve of her departure gave a farewell dinner at the Hôtel du Nord. It was in this same hotel that, fifteen years earlier, Andersen had called on Riborg Voigt. In Jenny Lind's speech she said that Bournonville had been a father to her in Denmark, her second country – to which Bournonville replied that all the Danes would wish to be his children in order to be her brothers. She laughed and said that as that would be too many she had better choose one – and, touching Andersen's glass of champagne with her own, she asked him to be her chosen brother. Although he still could not believe it, Andersen half knew that this was the end of his hopes of requited love.

Not even the outstanding success at the Royal Theatre of Andersen's new comedy *The New Lying-in Room*, brilliantly acted by Johanne Luise Heiberg and based, like Holberg's old play *The Lying-in Room*, on the Danish custom of mothers receiving visits of congratulation from their friends immediately after the birth of a child, could prevent him from thinking constantly of Jenny Lind. This time he did not discuss his unhappiness with his friends, perhaps because to do so would have been to admit its irrevocability, and this he was not yet prepared to do.

By now he could afford to leave Copenhagen when he found life there too much for him and he decided to travel until Christmas, when he hoped to see Jenny again. First he went to Glorup Castle. In November 1845 he wrote to Edvard: 'I have cosy rooms overlooking the deserted garden where all the water has been drained from the pond. Every morning I make a short dutiful visit to the old Count, and half an hour later he comes to my room in return; the only variation in all this is that sometimes he comes first. Then I see no one till four o'clock, and all that time I sit quietly, read and write, or stroll up and down the two old avenues in the garden. My days are as long and uneventful as the days in a monastery.'

The loss of Mrs Collin had made him think more than ever of death. 'In one year', he said, 'the hearse can go through the gate many times.' When he went to Odense it seemed to him that everyone he had known there in his childhood was dead and the streets full of unfamiliar faces. He was always saddened by the sight of a coffin followed by only one or two mourners, not merely because it reminded him of his own mortality but because he was sharply aware of the unique value of every individual and believed literally that not a sparrow could fall without God's knowledge of it. Sometimes sympathy drove him to join the little cortège and write a poem to the man or woman he had never known.

Now politics began to affect his personal life. The Duke and Duchess of Augustenburg invited him to their castle for their silver wedding celebrations, but relations between the duchies and Denmark proper were so strained that he 'preferred to avoid being witness to possible words or remarks which could offend my Danish sentiments', so he compromised by going to their hunting-lodge at Gravensteen, where there were to be no official demonstrations. Here there was no sign of anti-Danish feeling; on the contrary, the Duke and Duchess both went out of their way to assure him of their Danish sympathies. His ignorance of politics made him easy to convince, and while there his mind was full of one of his most famous stories, *The Little Match Girl*. The editor of the Danish *Folkekalender*, a popular almanac, had sent him three woodcuts, asking him to write a story to go with one of them, and he chose one showing a ragged child with her apron full of matches that reminded him of his mother begging as a child. As he was taking his leave he heard the young princesses of Augustenburg playing. One of them called out '*Lotte ist tot* – Lotte is dead', and the word 'death' lingered in his mind and seemed in retrospect to have had a sinister significance at variance with the childish game in which it had been used.

Next he went to Hamburg to visit Speckter, the painter who was illustrating the German edition of his fairy tales and who, one evening when they were on their way to the theatre, insisted on taking him into a luxurious-looking house where a band of children immediately clustered around Andersen, wanting a fairy tale. Speckter had promised the children to bring Andersen to see them, thinking that since his stories were already a part of their lives, this sudden brief visit from the storyteller himself would give them a precious memory.

His next stopping-place was the duchy of Oldenburg, where he again stayed with his friend, the Minister von Eisendecker. The little town had an excellent theatre and a gay social life. Winter had transformed the surrounding meadows into frozen lakes where friends met daily for skating parties, and the little world of Oldenburg with its demure court and evenings of music, play-acting, reading aloud and conversation suggests one of those tiny glass globes in which a miniature snowstorm merely enhances the glowing windows of the tiny house in the middle of it. Andersen's innate faculty for entering into other people's lives was such that by the time he left Oldenburg he felt as if a part of him belonged there. On the eve of his departure he went to say goodbye to the poet Mosen's little son Erik. The child burst into tears and later insisted on sending Andersen one of his two tin soldiers 'so that he shouldn't be so dreadfully alone'. This tin soldier was later to appear in Andersen's story *The Old House*, in which a child gives one of his two tin soldiers to an old man who lives just across the street from him, all alone in an old house full of memories: '. . . it was almost three hundred years old. Tulips and hopvines and also whole verses of poetry were cut into the wood, as people used to do in those days, and over every window a mocking face was cut into the beam.'

Jenny Lind was to spend Christmas in Berlin, so Andersen went there, taking the train from Hanover and exulting in its speed: a hundred and fifty-five miles in one day. He was almost happy in Germany and enjoyed the warm welcome given him by Christian Daniel Rauch, the sculptor, a remarkable man who had started working as an artist while still valet to Frederick William of Prussia, as well as by Tieck, Savigny, the historian von Raumer who held the chair of history at Berlin University and was later German ambassador in Paris, and the great scientist and botanist Alexander von Humboldt. Now, too, he at last made friends with the brothers Grimm. One evening in December he was reading aloud at the Countess Bismarck-Bohlen's: 'There was one person in particular who listened with evident fellowship of feeling . . . This was Jakob's brother, Wilhelm Grimm . . . I saw these two highly gifted and amiable brothers almost daily, the circles into which I was invited seemed also to be theirs, and it was my delight and pleasure that they should listen to my little stories, that they should participate in them, they whose names will always be spoken as long as the German *Volksmärchen* are read . . .' But no matter whom he met at this time, his thoughts quickly returned to Jenny Lind.

He had been so sure of spending Christmas Eve with her that he refused invitations until the day itself, when finally he went to a party at the Zimmermanns', and for all his hosts' kindness, he felt intensely alone. To a person who attached so much significance to anniversaries this was very painful. Sitting in his hotel room he wrote in his diary: 'I wonder what fills her thoughts . . . she takes so little notice of me, who came to Berlin chiefly for her sake.' It is indeed difficult to guess what filled Jenny Lind's thoughts at this time. At twenty-five she was at the height of her success, particularly in Germany. When, during the previous August, Frederick William of Prussia unveiled a statue of Beethoven, who had died eighteen years earlier, the guests of honour were Queen Victoria, making her first state visit to the Continent since her accession, her husband Prince Albert, her uncle King Leopold of Belgium, and Jenny Lind, who sang for them – yet already Jenny was thinking of giving up the stage. Like Andersen, she longed for marriage and children, yet seemed unable to find the love she needed and clung desperately to her friends, constantly begging them not to forget her. The Bishop of Norwich's wife, who knew her well, once said that her habitual expression was one of deep melancholy despite her saying again and again how happy she was, all of which might equally well have been said of Andersen. When Andersen told her of this lost evening, she said teasingly that she had supposed him engaged with princes and princesses, but she also stroked his forehead, called him 'child', and added that they must make up for it by celebrating Christmas all over again, together, on New Year's Eve. On this occasion she arranged to be alone with him and her companion-chaperon and they were childishly gay. Knowing that trifles meant as much to him as to herself, she had prepared a Christmas tree laden with small presents for him, and she sang an aria and two Swedish songs that aroused in them both the pleasant nostalgia of the born traveller. They planned to see each other again in Weimar, so, despite her constant use of the word 'brother', Andersen's hopes not unreasonably revived.

On January 6, 1846, the King of Prussia decorated Andersen with the Order of the Red Eagle, Third Class. It was Jonas Collin's birthday and Andersen saw in this honour a proof that he had not betrayed Collin's confidence in him. Next day Andersen left for Weimar, where Jenny was to appear. He was welcomed by his old friend Beaulieu and made much of in court circles, particularly by an elderly woman, Frau von Schwendler, who had befriended the great romantic poet Jean-Paul and gave Andersen, in whom she saw a likeness to him, one of the poet's letters. She was full of stories not only of Jean-Paul but of Herder, Wieland, Goethe and Schiller. Andersen loved Weimar for its own sake and would have agreed with Thackeray, who told George Eliot's husband, 'with a five-and-twenty years' experience since those happy days of which I write, and an acquaintance with an immense variety of human kind, I think I have never seen a society more simple, charitable, courteous, gentlemanlike than that of the dear little Saxon city where the good Schiller and the great Goethe lived and lie buried.' But even here, among affections old and true, Andersen was obsessed by Jenny. In his autobiography he mentions merely that Jenny Lind came to Weimar and that he heard her sing there, but his diary tells another story:

January 22, 1846 Jenny arrived last night. Called upon her. She was glad to see me and gave me her portrait. Dinner at the Grand Duke's, conveyed there in a *poste-chaise*, it is the first time in my life that I have been carried in this way.

January 23 Called on Jenny. In the evening concert at court. I wore a sword and a cocked hat. Jenny looked at me and I was presented to the Duke of Gotha, a brother of Prince Albert of England. . . . Spoke to her. All were enraptured by her . . . . The Grand Duchess and all said they had spoken to Jenny about me.

January 24 Walked an hour and a half with Jenny in the park. She told me she would probably take up residence at Altona [near Hamburg].

January 25 Was with Chancellor Müller and Beaulieu and Jenny whom we took to Goethe's, Wieland's and Schiller's rooms. She was enchanted by the inscription beneath Schiller's bust.

January 26 The Hereditary Grand Duke took me to Countess

Radern's, where we found Jenny. She, the Duke and Duchess, Countess Beust and our hostess dined together. Jenny sang six songs and in conclusion a hymn which moved us all deeply. 'I cannot speak to her, I feel quite overcome,' said the young Duchess. She put her arm round Jenny's neck and kissed her. Jenny burst into tears. Jenny appeared in *La Sonnambula* in the evening, it was wonderful. Next to me sat a Frenchman with a sour face, he never moved a hand and when I asked him, 'Is it not beautiful?' he said only 'Oh yes.' Suddenly at the end he warmed up, there was a single clap from him and 'Good!' and I felt friendly towards him. Beaulieu was beside himself with admiration for Jenny.

January 27   Drove with Chancellor Müller and Jenny to Fürstengruft. We stood by the coffins of Schiller and Goethe. In the evening a party at Chamberlain Plötz's – all the princely personages. I read three sketches. Jenny wept over *Polichinel*. A little before twelve we drove home. I felt ill. Beaulieu said I was about to fall in love with Jenny. I told him that would not happen. He told me the story of his heart. I thought of my own and wept.

January 28   Called on Jenny with Beaulieu. Went to the Library. Saw Schiller's skull. Accompanied Jenny to the theatre. Called on Countess Radern. The lackey said there was someone with her and I found the Hereditary Grand Duke and Duchess and Jenny. The Grand Duke drank my health and put his arm round me, the Grand Duchess kissed Jenny and the Grand Duke seized her hand and kissed it. Jenny changed her mind about going to Erfurt; she leaves early tomorrow for Leipzig and from there to Berlin. Went with Beaulieu to call on Jenny. There was a crowd at the gate. She asked us to stay and have tea. Chancellor Müller came, I did not want him. The crowd in the street serenaded Jenny. We persuaded her to say thank you in German from the window. I was very moved. When all had gone, we four sat around the tea-table. She was good and lovable. 'God knows when we shall meet again', she said, 'but between us it is for life, I hope.' I had a cramp in my throat. Beaulieu embraced me. As we left Jenny said to him 'Thank you for being so good to Andersen . . .'

Jenny did indeed care for him, as she might have cared for a brother. She recognized in him qualities akin to her own, with imaginative humour and fantasy added, but her very anxiety that others should 'be good to him' indicated that she knew herself incapable of returning his love. Like herself, he had an unusual capacity for arousing friendship, devotion and loyalty but, unlike Jenny, he had no capacity for arousing sexual passion in those he loved. After leaving Weimar she wrote to Andersen,

> My dear good brother,
> Thank you for the time we spent together. Do you not agree that we have hardly ever before spent such a delightful time together? Yes, yes, Germany is a glorious country, I certainly long for no other, except of course, the best of all, the last one. Oh, how I wept at your story of the Grand Duchess and her little sweep . . .
> Dear Andersen, if you should write to our noble friends, tell them, if you should mention me, that I shall remember those few days I spent at Weimar as long as I live . . . I have never found such peace of mind and utter happiness, although I have everywhere and always been kindly received. I like these noble personages, not, as you say, brother, for the jewels and decorations they wear but for their genuine and honest hearts and souls. I get quite carried away when I think of them . . .

There was all too clearly no reason for Andersen to be carried away by this letter.

His failure in love has been ascribed by some writers to impotence or latent homosexuality. There is not, however, the slightest proof of this – Albert Hansen, the German journalist who wrote an article on Andersen as a homosexual, proved merely that some homosexuals are animated by a trades-union spirit: 'one more for our side'. Had there been any truth in this, so transparent a person as Andersen could not have hidden it from the Collins; and Edvard, for example, would never have permitted his teenage son to travel with Andersen on trips which, since gossip-mongers are determined to have it both ways, gave rise to rumours that Andersen had an illegitimate son, just as his friend Thorvaldsen had really had an illegitimate daughter. In an excellent psychiatric study of Andersen by Hjalmar Helweg, head of the hospital for the insane at Oringe, the author dismisses as absurd the suggestion that Andersen was a homosexual, and Andersen's own diary, which is now in the Royal Library at Copenhagen and not all of which has yet been published, makes it clear that although his passions were far more emotional than sensual, he had normal desires and suffered intensely because he would have considered it sinful to make love to a woman who was not his wife. Dr Emil Hornemann, a well-known doctor who was Andersen's friend and only five years his junior, was convinced that Andersen lived an ascetic life sexually. Thus frustration and an innately fragile nervous system kept him in a constant state of emotional tension that enriched his work at the expense of his peace of mind in daily life. Similarly, Søren Kierkegaard made a creative use of what in a lesser man would have been the mental handicap of maniacal depression. Neither Andersen nor Kierkegaard, the two most remarkable Danes of the nineteenth century, was what is conventionally called a normal man. It is not normal to be a genius. In Andersen's case early poverty, insecurity, a sense of being awkward and unattractive and an idealization of women that was far more genuine than that often attributed to Dickens's heroes, made him exaggeratedly humble in love. He idolized, suffered and failed to assert himself as a man. This same idealization, and native fastidiousness, made him recoil with distaste from women attracted by his fame; once, after a young and beautiful woman had declared herself infatuated by him, he was so distressed by her immodesty that he felt positively relieved to learn that she was mentally unbalanced. Only the common sense and robust physique that he inherited from his mother, together with his capacity for self-criticism and the wonderful humour that Ørsted was the first to recognize in Andersen's fairy tales, enabled him to maintain his precarious emotional equilibrium and, eventually, resign himself to his celibacy and put all his energy into loving his many true friends and winning the fame for which he had left home at fourteen years old.

Months after he had parted from Jenny Lind in Weimar, he wrote to Louise Collin Lind, whose marriage had not weakened their friendship: 'You ask me about Jenny. I hear from her frequently. She is like a sister to me, but nothing more . . . She is not likely to marry if I understand rightly. I know, to a certain extent, her intentions, but I have no right to speak of them. So far as I myself am concerned I know enough to be able to resign myself; I build no castles in the air but accept what God may ordain for me. I feel at peace as never before. I realize that everything which has happened to me has been for the best, and I am filled with gratitude and joy. God knows whether I could have been happier as a married man.'

After Jenny had left Weimar Andersen's friends did all they could to persuade him to prolong his visit there and he stayed until he had only just time to reach Rome for Easter as he had planned to do. Beaulieu accompanied him as far as Jena, where he stayed with Frommann, a publisher whose sister Andersen had met in Berlin. While he was there the Hereditary Grand Duke visited Jena and he and Andersen saw each other at the house of Schiller's sister-in-law. Although Andersen was famous in Germany, he had received no money for the German editions of his books. The Berne Convention protecting authors' rights did not come into effect until eleven years after his death. However, some German friends of his had taken the matter in hand, and while in Leipzig he received four offers of payment for his work from publishers, including one from the famous firm of Brockhaus and one from a fellow countryman, Carl B. Lorck, whose offer he accepted – a choice that his friends the Brockhauses took in good part. It was Carl B. Lorck who had the idea of collecting Andersen's fairy tales in one illustrated volume, for which Andersen chose as illustrator a young Danish naval lieutenant, Vilhelm Pedersen, whose drawings are for Andersen what John Tenniel's are for Lewis Carroll.

During this visit to Leipzig he spent a gay evening with the Mendelssohns and Niels Gade, a young Danish composer whom they treated as one of their family. Mendelssohn was now thoroughly familiar with Andersen's work and teased him about the frequency with which he wrote about storks, urging him to write a song about a stork. This was Andersen's last meeting with Mendelssohn, who died the following year aged thirty-eight.

The Wild Swan

In Dresden he was made much of by the King and Queen of Saxony and their family – the youngest princess, who knew his story of *The Fir Tree*, insisted on telling him about her own Christmas tree, and, after curtseying goodnight to him, turned at the door to kiss her hand to him because for her, said her parents, he was the *Märchenprinz* – the prince of story-tellers. From Dresden he went by coach (since there was as yet no railway) to Prague, where he was welcomed by the Archduke Stephen, to whom Karl Alexander of Weimar had written about him. Here he visited the Hradschin – the vast palace of the Kings, Queens and Emperors of Bohemia, begun by Ferdinand I in 1541 and completed two centuries later by Maria Theresa – and the palace of Wallenstein, where the only relics of Wallenstein were a bad portrait and a stuffed charger. He was appalled by the squalor of the Jewish quarter, a labyrinth of narrow filthy streets on the low banks of the Moldau river. According to tradition, there had been a Jewish colony here since before the destruction of Jerusalem. He visited the old Synagogue, erected after the fire of 1316, and saw the flag that had been given to the Jews for their bravery during the siege of 1648, when they had held out for fourteen weeks against the besieging Swedes. The Jewish cemetery seemed to him particularly disturbing, its headstones lying at all angles under a forest of stunted elderberry trees draped with spiders' webs, as savagely beautiful as Jacob van Ruisdael's picture of a Jewish cemetery with moonlit tombs among storm-twisted trees.

Andersen left Prague at the same time as some troops being transferred to Poland. (The Austrian Empire, that had in 1804 replaced the Holy Roman Empire, comprised eleven nationalities and there was usually political unrest in some part of it.) All the town seemed to have come to the station to say goodbye to the soldiers and Andersen had never before seen such dramatic mass scenes. All night long, as the train crossed Bohemia, he saw crowds gathered at every station and the effect of the brown faces, tattered clothes, strange language and flickering torchlight was heightened by the train's passage through tunnels and over viaducts, engine puffing, whistle blowing, windows rattling in an ecstasy of speed.

Kept Secret but not Forgotten

In Vienna, where Liszt invited him to a concert, Andersen had what in retrospect appears to be one of the strangest encounters in his life. The Queen of Saxony had given him a letter to her sister, the Archduchess Sophie of Austria, thanks to which he was invited to tea at the palace. Among those present were the dowager Empress (widow of Francis I), the Archduchess Sophie, often described as 'the only man of the family' and supposed to have been in love in her youth with Napoleon's son, and her sons, sixteen-year-old Francis Joseph and fourteen-year-old Maximilian. Almost all those who listened to Andersen reading fairy tales in his awkward German at that demure tea-party at the Hofburg would have been appalled could they have foreseen their futures. Francis Joseph became Emperor only two years later, and married his beautiful cousin Elisabeth, who was assassinated by an anarchist in 1898, nine years after their son Rudolf had committed suicide at Mayerling, leaving as heir to the throne Francis Joseph's nephew, Ferdinand, whose assassination at Sarajevo in 1914 led to the First World War. Francis Joseph himself lived on until 1916, 'the last monarch of the old school' as he described himself to Theodore Roosevelt, and two years after his death Austria became a republic. His young brother Maximilian was induced to accept the crown of the Catholic Empire that Napoleon III was trying to establish in Mexico, and was shot at Querétaro at the age of thirty-five, leaving his wife Carlotta to survive him by sixty years and die insane two years after the thirty-six-year-old Hitler had been released from the prison where he had written *Mein Kampf*.

As it was, there were unforced smiles over the tea-cups and the atmosphere seemed to Andersen to have the cosiness he had come to associate with courts. After the reading the Archduchess Sophie presented him with a 'tasteful breast-pin'. Andersen's life contains many fantastic pictures but none more so than this of the doomed Habsburgs listening over the tea-cups to *The Ugly Duckling*. 'He thought about how he had been persecuted and scorned, and now he heard them all call him the most beautiful of all beautiful birds. The lilacs dipped their clusters into the stream before him, and the sun shone so warm and so heartening. He rustled his feathers and held his slender neck high, as he cried out with a full heart: "I never dreamed there could be so much happiness, when I was the ugly duckling." '

From Vienna Andersen went by train to Graz, but had to complete the journey to Trieste by coach – 'How dreadful it was after a day in a train to have to crawl forward at snail's pace for a night and day and yet another night before reaching Trieste.' In Trieste, then the most prosperous sea-port in the Austrian dominions and a very cosmopolitan place, he made the acquaintance of a Count Waldstein, who interested him as being descended from that tragic seventeenth-century figure Eleonora Christina of Denmark, about whom Andersen had wanted to write a play. Her story and heroic pride during her unjust imprisonment had made her a legendary figure in Denmark; and not only a legendary figure but an inflammatory one – while doing research about her Andersen was told that Frederik VI thought the subject still too close to present times for representation on the stage. Later, Christian VIII encouraged Andersen to resume work on the subject, but by that time Oehlenschläger had written a play about Eleonora Christina.

From Trieste Andersen crossed the Adriatic to Ancona in the Papal States. He was beside himself with joy at being in Italy again. The blossoming fruit trees, the sunlit cornfields, the trees entwined with vines, the snow-topped mountains glittering against a blue sky filled him with exhilaration and he did his best to banish the fears of his fellow traveller, Count Wenceslaus Paar, a Hungarian who was visiting Italy for the first time, and, as provision against bandits, had loaded pistols ready in a bag under the seat. The only bandits they encountered, however, were chained and under military escort. They visited Loreto and saw pilgrims kneeling before the Holy House brought there by the angels from Palestine, and at last, on March 31, 1846, Andersen saw Rome again.

11. Amour de Voyage

1846-7

Is it illusion? or does there a spirit from perfecter ages,
Here, even yet, amid loss, change, and corruption abide?
Does there a spirit we know not, though seek, though we find,
    comprehend not,
Here to entice and confuse, tempt and evade us, abide?
Lives in the exquisite grace of the column disjointed and single,
Haunts the rude masses of brick garlanded gaily with vine,
E'en in the turret fantastic surviving that springs from the ruins,
E'en in the people itself? is it illusion or not?
Is it illusion or not that attracteth the pilgrim transalpine,
Brings him a dullard and dunce hither to pry and to stare?
Is it illusion or not that allures the barbarian stranger,
Brings him with gold to the shrine, brings him in arms to the gate?
            Arthur Hugh Clough, *Amours de Voyage*, Canto II

*

IT WAS THIRTEEN YEARS since Andersen had seen Rome for
the first time and he found the city very much changed: 'It is as
though everything is modernized, even the ruins; grass and
bushes have been taken up, and everything has been made tidier.
The popular life seems to have disappeared; I no longer hear the
tambourine rattling in the streets or see the young girls dancing
their *saltarellos* . . . during the Easter festivities I saw crowds of
people standing in front of St Peter's, standing, just like foreign
Protestants, when the Pope gave them his blessing . . . In ten
years' time, when railways bring the towns even closer together,
Rome will be even more changed . . .' His own sense of the wonder
of Rome had not, however, changed at all.

Sculpture meant far more to him than on his previous visit and
he remembered Thorvaldsen saying that 'the snow had thawed

from his eyes'. During his repeated wanderings in the Vatican it struck him that a love of nature might be taught by the love of art, rather than the other way round. The Danish, Swedish, Norwegian and German artists made much of him, and Frau Goethe, who was living in the house on the corner of the Via Felice and the Piazza Barberini that had been chosen by Andersen as the birthplace of the hero of his first novel, sent him a bouquet with the message 'From the Improvisatore's garden'. Immediately after Easter he went to Naples with Count Paar and took rooms at 28 Via Sta Lucia. Here, unaware of the power of the southern sun, he went sightseeing at midday and fainted in the street. From there he moved to Sorrento, where he and an English family shared a house overlooking the sea, which rolled into the caves under their garden. Most of his time there was spent writing the autobiography for which his German publisher had asked him. The first part of this gives as masterly a picture of childhood as *David Copperfield*, for, as he himself noted, 'It is far easier to write of one's youth than of later years; just as with age everyone becomes long-sighted and sees most easily that which is distant, so it is with the mind's eye and its vision;' but in the latter part he was hampered both by the need for discretion about people still living and by his personal form of whistling in the dark, which consisted of constantly assuring the reader of his happiness and belief that 'all is for the best'. He could not bring himself to write about his strongest emotions as an adult, and since frustration in love had made him yield completely to the belief that he was no one and nothing if not valued as a writer, he took refuge in exterior details of his professional and social life. Nevertheless, Edmund Gosse said of his autobiography, and of his 'chatty, egotistical books of travel', that they revealed his character 'coloured as richly as if Titian had survived to paint his features . . . The passion for hoarding up little treasures of every kind – pebbles that friends had picked up, leaves that had been plucked on a certain day, odd mementoes of travel and incident, was always strong in Andersen. He hated to destroy anything, and he dragged around with him, from one lodging to another, a constantly increasing store of what irritable friends were apt to consider rubbish. In like manner, he could not endure to tear up paper with writing upon it, even if that writing were derogatory to his dignity . . . Most people are glad to destroy any letter in which their own conduct is criticized . . . But it was part of the crystal innocence of Andersen's character, than whom a simpler or a purer character never breathed, to preserve with the utmost impartiality the good and the evil . . . In his writings we can trace every change of temperament, every turn and whim of this guileless and transparent mind.'

The Neapolitan festival of the Madonna del Arco, on which Bournonville had drawn for his ballet *Napoli*, attracted Andersen back to Naples, where he took rooms in a hotel in the centre of the town and was promptly overwhelmed by the heat. 'The burning sunlight filled every corner of the narrow streets and seemed to get the better even of tightly closed doors and shutters, and to the stifling atmosphere was added the merry chatter of ubiquitous workmen, the rumble of carriages, and the din made by town criers, church bells and a neighbour who never stopped playing scales.' From this Neapolitan cauldron he got the idea for his fiftieth story, *The Shadow*, but he had to wait until he got home to write it – 'I, who had believed myself to be a child of the sun because my heart longed so for the South, had to admit that there was the snow of the North in my body and that the snow was melting, and I became more and more miserable.'

Enervated by the heat, Andersen worried incessantly about his passport, visas and mail. He expected letters to go astray and his fears were justified. Despite the heat, he was obliged to prolong his stay in Naples for lack of a letter of credit that had, he felt sure, been dispatched from home as promised. At the bank in Naples 'the mighty Rothschild' (Karl, the fifth of the famous Rothschild brothers) became so tired of telling Andersen that nothing had come for him that, opening and shutting a drawer with a bang to prove his point, he dislodged the letter of credit – stuck to the back of the drawer by its wax seal which had been melted by the heat that Andersen found so trying.

Thankfully Andersen embarked for Marseille. The steamer was so crowded that several of the passengers, including himself, could find nowhere to sleep except under the carriages that occupied the whole of the deck. It took them three days and nights to reach Genoa and by that time most of the passengers were determined to quit the ship and finish their journeys by land. Andersen would gladly have followed their example, but, his letter of credit being made out for Marseille and some Spanish ports, he had to remain with the ship. In Marseille, however, the weather was so lovely that his desire to see Spain revived.

While seated at the table d'hôte at the Hôtel des Empereurs in Marseille he and another traveller recognized each other with shouts of pleasure. This was Ole Bull, the Norwegian violinist who had made his name in Paris and been applauded in Italy, England, Scotland, Ireland, Russia, Germany, and finally in his own country. Their travels were as much a bond between the two men as the fact that they were both artists and Scandinavians, and Ole Bull surprised and gratified Andersen by assuring him that he had enthusiastic readers in America.

Next day Andersen drove through Provence by coach, delighting in the pomegranate trees, the beauty of the women of Arles, the Roman amphitheatre at Nîmes and the original character of Reboul, the baker-poet of Nîmes, described by Lamartine in his *Souvenirs d'Orient*. From Montpellier there was a train to Cette, and the speed of the French train made him think of the street in Basle, where, just above the place on the wall where once the Dance of Death had been painted, was written 'To the Railway Station'. By this time the heat was so great that there were constant reports of people dying of it. At last Andersen saw the Pyrenees, crossed the Etang de Thau by steamer, and at the Languedoc canal changed to a larger vessel, towed by three or four horses, that was so loaded with freight that the passengers were like flies in a sugar basin. Half an hour from Béziers they were put ashore. The stage-coach that was to pick them up had not yet arrived and the burning sunlight had banished shadows. When at last the stage-coach arrived, Andersen found himself sharing it with a drunken sailor, two filthy farm-labourers who reeked of onions and took off their boots, and a fat woman who hung her yard-long head-dress in front of him. The travellers were repeatedly pestered for their passports, an annoyance attributed to the proximity of the Spanish frontier and the fact that there had recently been several murders in the district. In

Amour de Voyage

Perpignan, which at first seemed deserted, he was drawn to the balcony by the shouts of what he took to be revolutionaries but proved to be admirers of a man on a neighbouring balcony, Arago, the French astronomer and physicist, who had been born at near-by Estagel in 1786 and had played a vigorous part in the July Revolution.

By this time Andersen was so ill from heat and exhaustion that he had to give up the idea of going on to Spain. Instead he went for a rest to Vernet, a neighbouring spa that was so quiet it struck him as possessing 'a sort of state of innocence among spas' and only wanted 'minarets to look like a Turkish town'. Ibrahim Pasha had visited Vernet the previous winter and his name 'was still the halo of the establishment'. The only distractions were outings, on foot or on donkeys, to the Pyrenees. Andersen was excited by the relics of Moorish civilization and visited Ville-franche with Dumas's friend Dauzat, a well-known painter, but most of his time was spent finishing his autobiography. He was determined to be in Denmark for Christmas, 'when the white bees swarm'. So he returned to Nîmes by train, then, as the line ended there, took a stage-coach to Avignon, where the Palace of the Popes looked to him like a fortress transformed into barracks. It was so hot that he could eat nothing but a few figs and almonds and he was overjoyed to reach Lyons and longed to see Mont Blanc again. But the vexations of this trip were not over – 'I am always the one traveller in a thousand who encounters the worst nonsense with a passport. Sometimes it is because people cannot read, sometimes a minor clerk writes the wrong number on it, so that it cannot be found, sometimes an Italian frontier guard takes exception to the name Christian and thinks it is some religious sect . . .' In Lyons his troubles suggest Kafka. An oppressively hot day was entirely occupied by repeated trips to the Préfecture de Police to convince robot-officials that there was no reason why a Dane on his way from Marseille to Switzerland should have sent his passport to Paris for a visa. He was frantic with exasperation when at last he found an official with some common sense and culture who allowed him to continue his journey as planned. It was with intense relief that he found himself once more in Switzerland, a country where he always found rest for his heart.

The Wild Swan

While in Vevey he revisited Chillon castle and noticed that beside Byron's name two new names had been carved, those of Victor Hugo and Robert Peel. At the hill town of Fribourg he admired not only the ancient towers and battlements but the magnificent suspension bridge, then the longest in the world, which had been completed in 1834. At Berne he visited the famous bear-pit outside the Aarberg gate and heard of the strange lawsuit in which the animals had been involved. Bears had been the emblem of Berne ever since the twelfth century and at the beginning of the eighteenth century an old lady without near relatives had left her fortune for the bears' upkeep. Her will was contested by distant relatives, but according to contemporary accounts, 'the cause of the brutes was so ably pleaded by one of the most distinguished members of the bar of Berne that the plaintiff was non-suited'. The bears were made wards in chancery and the Supreme Council of the city administered their estate.

From Berne Andersen went to Interlaken and Basle, where he took the train to Strasbourg and embarked on one of the Rhine steamers. Here he met with anti-Danish feeling, provoked by the Open Letter in which Christian VIII had proclaimed the rules of succession for Slesvig and Holstein to be the same as those of Denmark proper. This was resented not only in the duchies themselves but also in the German Confederation, to which Holstein had appealed – and which raised the cry about oppressed minorities that was to echo with bellicose effects through the rest of the nineteenth and well into the twentieth century.

From Frankfurt Andersen went to Weimar, where he visited the Hereditary Grand Duke; in Jena he worked with Professor Wolff on a translation of some of his lyrical poems; and in Hamburg he received the news that Christian VIII had awarded him the Order of the Dannebrog. Two days later he reached Kiel, where the Landgrave and his party, which included Prince Christian, invited him to travel to Copenhagen aboard the royal steamship. He was scarcely home before he was planning his forthcoming journey to England. On December 10, 1846, he wrote to his English publisher, Richard Bentley: 'In a few days I begin to learn English and when I next year visit England, I hope to express to you in English my thanks and affections.'

Andersen's first visit to England was excellently timed. His first three novels had already been published and admired in English, as had his travel book *A Poet's Bazaar*, and in 1846 the first translation of his fairy tales appeared in both London and New York. The success of the latter was extraordinary, considering how deplorable many of the earliest English versions were – often translated not from the original Danish but from the German translations, bowdlerized or bogged down with 'happy endings'. It was not until 1942 – sixty-seven years after Andersen's death – that the first complete edition of his tales appeared in America, admirably translated and annotated by the Danish-American actor Jean Hersholt, who left his collection of Anderseniana to the Library of Congress in Washington. From 1950–60 a four-volume edition of eighty-four of Andersen's fairy tales was published at Odense in a fine English translation by R. P. Keigwin, winner of the Hans Christian Andersen prize for 1964. English-speaking readers of Andersen owe an incalculable debt to both translators.

On his way to England Andersen stopped at Odense, where he was horribly impressed by the sight of a half-insane yokel outside his windows: 'His face had some noble lines, and his eyes shone, but there was something crazed about him, and the boys chased and teased him. It made me think of myself and my childhood, my weak-minded grandfather, and wonder whether, if I had stayed in Odense and been apprenticed there, time and the conditions under which I lived would not have dulled the power of my imagination which now filled me with such might.' From there he continued via Hamburg to Amsterdam, 'where they live half in the water like amphibians', and so by train to Haarlem. 'We passed over a kind of bank between the open North Sea and the sea of Haarlem and I wondered at the grand enterprise of pumping out a sea.' (Between 1815 and 1875 the Dutch reclaimed 143,318 acres of land from the sea.) Everywhere he found admirers, including, in The Hague, Mendelssohn's brother-in-law who had just lost his wife, the beloved sister whose death was to hasten Mendelssohn's own. At Rotterdam, the liveliest of all the Dutch cities, he took a Dutch steamer, 'a true snail of a ship', its deck crowded with emigrants to America and baskets of cherries. Next morning he caught his first sight of the Thames, which was just as described in Dickens's novels – hosts of ships flying out like relay-racers, pleasure yachts, the smoke of steamers, chimneys and trains. As Andersen sailed up the Thames the river became more and more crowded until he could not imagine how the various boats could move without colliding. As the ebb-tide revealed the slimy river-bed Andersen thought of Quilp in *The Old Curiosity Shop*.

At the Customs House he took a cab which drove him into a sunset, red-gold as if it was shining through the glass of a beer-bottle. 'The throngs in the street became denser and denser, there was carriage after carriage in two directions; there were omni-buses filled both inside and on top, great carts which were only huge packing cases with posters of the latest news stuck on them; there were men with large signboards on a stick which they lifted high above the crowds and on which one could read of something or other that was to be seen or bought. Everyone was in motion, as though half London were streaming to one side of the town and the other half to the other side. Where the streets cross each other there are raised stone sections in the middle of them; thither folk darted from one pavement, in and out of the nearest stream of traffic; and then they waited there in safety until they could see their opportunity to dodge between the traffic and on to the footpath on the other side. London, the city of cities. Yes, that is what I immediately felt . . . It is Paris in a higher power; there is the life of Naples, but not the same noise. Everything hurries and rushes past, half silently, omnibus after omnibus – I am told there are four thousand of them – wagons, vans, cabs, hackney coaches and elegant coaches roll, jolt, rumble and dash along, as though there were some great event in each end of the city which they must all witness.'

On Ørsted's advice Andersen went to the Hôtel de la Sablon-ière in Leicester Square, where Hogarth had once lived. He had come without letters of introduction but the Danish Ambassador, Count Reventlow, on whom he called next morning, said that he did not need them and himself wrote to tell Lady Palmerston that

Andersen was in London. He immediately received an invitation
from her. At her house he found a big reception that included the
Hereditary Grand Duke of Weimar and his wife, and Count
Reventlow told him that he had obtained overnight a position
that most foreigners could not obtain in years. He and Jenny
Lind, who was there at the same time as he was, were the lions
of the London season. Their portraits appeared side by side
in shop windows and people talked of a Jenny Lind Crush, or
a Jenny Lind Fever, her picture appeared on chocolate-boxes,
cigar-boxes, soaps and toilet waters, and in August the young
Queen Victoria, who was as taken by Jenny Lind's character as
by her voice, which she called 'extraordinary and almost stun-
ning', invited the singer to Osborne and presented her with a
bracelet, saying, 'I must again express not only my admiration
but my respect for you.'

When Count Reventlow told Andersen he must leave Leicester
Square, the latter was puzzled. It had been good enough for
Ørsted, and there was 'a marble statue of Count Leicester standing
amid green trees outside my window'. Count Reventlow explained
that while the hotel had been fashionable eight years ago, it no
longer was, and fashion was all-powerful in England – 'in the
land of freedom one can be stifled by etiquette.'

Like Jenny Lind, Andersen thought the English very religious,
full of respect for morals and manners, and London seemed to
him a 'city of politeness', especially in the case of policemen and
shop assistants. He wrote immediately to Jenny Lind, who
invited him to visit her at the cottage she had rented near what is
now Gloucester Road but was then the country outside London.
After examining a map Andersen set off on a bus. A helpful
conductor told him where to get off for 'the Swedish Nightingale's
house' – and when a few days later he met the same conductor
again, the man questioned Andersen eagerly about Jenny Lind.
A crowd was standing, hoping for a glimpse of her, outside the
hedge that separated her cottage from the street – a crowd that
was rewarded when Andersen rang the bell and she opened the
door herself and rushed to him with outstretched hands. They
talked eagerly of their common friends and she showed him a
copy of his *True Story of My Life*, which had been given her by his

English translator, Mary Howitt. She insisted on giving him a ticket for the opera, saying that it was ridiculously expensive and he must let her sing for him and, in return, read his fairy tales to her. On July 3 Andersen heard her in Bellini's *La Sonnambula*. Queen Victoria and Prince Albert were present, also the Hereditary Grand Duke of Weimar, and the applause was as wild as any Andersen had heard in Naples. It seemed to him very strange to hear her singing in Italian, as she did in *I Masnadieri*, an opera based on Schiller's *The Robbers*, which Verdi, then thirty-four years old, had written specially for her.

Throughout his visit Andersen was deluged with invitations to breakfasts, luncheons, teas, dinners and receptions. His natural gregariousness and his wish to be a credit to his country, of which Count Reventlow appeared to consider him an official representative, made it impossible for him to refuse invitations categorically as Jenny did. Intent on protecting her voice and her solitude, she even refused to dine with old Baron Hambro, the distinguished Anglo-Danish banker, who offered to leave the choice of guests to her, or to invite only herself and Andersen. Jenny Lind was far more uncompromising than Andersen. They both believed implicitly that God was guiding them, but Jenny was inclined to give God instructions, a characteristic which was one of the bonds between her and Queen Victoria. A young sculptor, Durham, made busts of both Jenny and Andersen – and, considering Andersen's disappointed hopes, the way in which Londoners grouped him and Jenny together must have been very painful to him.

One of the most stimulating invitations he received in London was from Lady Morgan. The daughter of a Dublin theatrical manager, this remarkable woman had, when her father fell into financial difficulties, supported her family by working as a governess and had subsequently become the successful author o novels, verse, and travel books before marrying, at thirty-six, Sir Thomas Charles Morgan. When Andersen met her she was seventy-one, full of vitality and gaiety and, like her house with its small many-coloured rococo rooms, very 'painted and French in taste'. She quoted from Andersen's book, and although she had obviously learned the quotations for the occasion, he appreciated the courtesy. She also introduced him to Lady Duff Gordon, who had translated *The Little Mermaid*.

Equally interesting was his visit to Lady Blessington at Gore House in Kensington. A vivid character, Lady Blessington had been born into an impoverished Irish family and forced, at fourteen, to marry Captain Farmer, from whom she fled in three months. After Captain Farmer's death she had married the Earl of Blessington and the couple was transformed into a trio by the constant presence of the youthful Count d'Orsay, 'the last of the dandies', whose constant attendance on her was held to put her into an 'equivocal position' socially. After her husband's death in 1829 she had established a little court at Gore House with the Count d'Orsay, who had in 1827 married Lady Harriet Gardiner, Lord Blessington's daughter by a previous marriage. Now fifty-eight, Lady Blessington was 'a flourishing, rather corpulent lady, extremely elegantly dressed with glistening rings on her fingers'. She welcomed Andersen as if he were an old friend, an attitude to which he always responded, praised his *Poet's Bazaar*, and remarked that he and Jenny Lind were alike in being 'both fervent and natural'. She took him on to a balcony surrounded by vines and ivy and inhabited by two parrots and a large bird from Van Dieman's Land, from which he had a charming view of her garden with its roses, weeping willows and a cow grazing on the lawn 'for the sake of appearances'. Afterwards she told William Jerdan, editor of the *Literary Gazette*: 'I have seldom felt so strong an interest in a person of whom I saw so little; for he interested me as being quite as good as he is clever, and of how few authors could we say this!' Lady Blessington was the first Englishwoman he understood easily, for she spoke slowly, holding him tightly by the wrist and looking into his eyes to be sure he knew her meaning. She showed him Count d'Orsay's studio and an oil-painting of Jenny Lind in *Norma*. In most of her rooms there was either a bust or a portrait of Napoleon, whom she admired extravagantly, and she had first-hand impressions of his mother to whom she had been presented in Rome in 1825. She had also seen much of Byron in Italy just before he set out to fight for Greek independence. She invited Andersen to come again to meet Bulwer, the diplomat and author, and Charles Dickens.

The Wild Swan

This was a real joy for Andersen. He found the house full of festivity, with servants in knee-breeches, silk stockings and powdered hair. Bulwer had not come after all as Parliament had been dissolved in June, and, according to Lady Blessington, he was 'living for nothing but the elections and was out gathering votes'. She did not, however, seem very concerned by his absence and Andersen did not care in the least as he was wild with pleasure at meeting his favourite English author. Dickens had written that he would come to London specially to see Andersen. Andersen was writing in Lady Blessington's copy of *The True Story of My Life* when Dickens came into the room. He looked strikingly young (he was thirty-five years old at the time) and 'handsome, with an intelligent and kind expression and a mass of beautiful hair which fell to both sides. We shook hands with each other, looked deep into each other's eyes, talked to each other and understood each other. We went out on the veranda, and I was so moved and delighted to see and speak to the one living English author I loved more than any other that tears came to my eyes.' At dinner, which was taken at a table overlooked by an illuminated lifesize portrait of Napoleon, Andersen was toasted by the Duke of Wellington's son, the Marquis of Douro. There too he met the poet Richard Monckton Milnes, then thirty-eight years old, a spectacular character who went up in a balloon, down in a diving bell, was one of the first Englishmen to obtain access to Eastern harems, and was the devoted partisan of other poets. Andersen, however, had eyes only for Dickens.

Count Reventlow impressed upon Andersen the necessity for not mentioning in the 'great salons' that he had visited Lady Blessington, for her reputation was bad owing to the fact that her son-in-law obviously preferred her company to that of his young wife. Andersen was far too grateful to Lady Blessington for introducing him to Dickens to heed these admonitions, but he noticed that whenever he mentioned her there was a pause, and if he persisted in asking why one should not visit her, he was told peremptorily that she was 'not nice to know'. Even her tears over Jenny Lind's performance in *La Sonnambula*, which impressed him, were dismissed in the great world as 'play-acting'.

He also visited the translator of *The Improvisatore*, the Quaker

236

Amour de Voyage

Mary Howitt. This erudite and dogmatic person was full of admiration for Andersen at this date; but since she was also very possessive, she changed her tune and became spiteful about him when, on the advice of Joseph Hambro, he allowed some of his books to be translated by other people.

During this season the poet William Allingham noted in his diary: 'Wednesday, July 7 . . . I met Andersen the other day at dinner and we were mutually unintelligible. I had the pleasure of feeling his arm, his arm in mine, on the way to dinner; it was the thinnest arm I ever felt. He looks like a man in the last stage of consumption . . . He looks like a large child, a sort of half angel. There were many people of rank present, yet no one in the room looked more *distingué* than Andersen, the shoemaker's son.'

In August, Lady Eastlake wrote in her diary: 'Andersen dined with us. He had one stream of interesting talk – perhaps rather too much of himself, but to me that was novel and entertaining. His descriptions of Rachel and Jenny Lind most characteristic, each the symbol of Art and Nature. Spoke of the King of Denmark in the highest terms, and was hopeful about the Crown Prince. He said he had written to the King since he had been in England, just as he would have written to any other person. Altogether he left a most agreeable impression both on mind and heart, especially on the latter for his own seemed so affectionate. No wonder he finds people kind; all stiffness is useless with him, as he is evidently a simple child himself. He is struck with the religion in England, and says that Hegel's philosophy is doing harm in Denmark.'

Other notabilities he met were Leigh Hunt; Walter Scott's devoted son-in-law and biographer J. G. Lockhart; Mrs Caroline Norton, the beautiful novelist who was the granddaughter of Sheridan and whose husband tried in vain to divorce her for her friendship with Lord Melbourne; John Wilson, who wrote under the name Christopher North; Lord Jeffrey, the great lawyer who had been Lord Advocate in Earl Grey's ministry; the novelist Catherine Crowe; and George Webbe Dasent, the assistant editor of *The Times* who was particularly interested in Scandinavian literature. Andersen also met his contemporary Disraeli, then a novelist and member of Parliament, between whom and

237

Andersen a certain physical resemblance was noticed. They shared too a romantic belief in 'the Throne, the Altar and the Cottage'. His London experiences included a glimpse of electioneering – 'Hodges for ever! Rothschild the poor man's friend!' – bands and rabble, and a senile old man taken in a wheelbarrow to vote – that closely resembled the Eatanswill. elections in *Pickwick*. It was all exciting, exhilarating and exhausting. There were no meaningless encounters for Andersen, he threw himself wholeheartedly into each one; so much so that when, towards the end of his stay in London, Queen Victoria and Prince Albert invited him to visit them in the Isle of Wight, he was not well enough to accept. Count Reventlow advised him to tell them so quite plainly and, since he was due to go to Scotland when they would be there, to ask if he might visit them then. He was told he would be welcome at Loch Laggan.

Baron Hambro's son had rented a house outside Edinburgh for the summer and begged his father to bring Andersen to stay there, saying that he would find many friends in Scotland. Ties between Scotland and Denmark had for centuries been close and Andersen was stirred by the prospect of seeing Walter Scott's country.

In company with Baron Hambro he took the express train that 'dashed along without pause or rest'. (Railway travel was at this time more dangerous in England than on the Continent, fatal accidents being more than fifteen times as frequent as in Germany.) The journey took two days, with a night's stop at York, where Andersen stayed at the Black Swan and admired the picturesque old houses with their carved gable-ends and balconies, and the flocks of swallows. He even had the pleasure of seeing 'his own bird', the stork. From York they went to Newcastle, 'enveloped in dense smoke and steam'. The viaduct and bridge outside the town were unfinished, so they had to cross the town by omnibus and had luggage trouble, since in England 'one does not receive a ticket for one's luggage as is the case in other countries, it is a matter of looking after it oneself'. This trip was in some respects as adventurous as his travels in the East, since 'the track was not finished over some of the deep valleys, but was just fit to travel on'.

Amour de Voyage

Old Edinburgh immediately captivated him by its murky magnificence. Baron Hambro's son was waiting at the station to drive them out to his house and Andersen was swept up into the happy domestic life, complete with family prayers, that he and Jenny Lind both found so particularly satisfying. Rest was impossible with so much to visit. From the new town of Edinburgh, with its view over the old city that reminded him of Constantinople, he could see the hill called Arthur's Seat that appears in Scott's *The Heart of Midlothian*, and one of his first visits was to Scott's monument, which had been completed only three years earlier and was then considered to be one of the finest works of art in Edinburgh. Andersen saw what had once been the only hotel in Edinburgh, where Doctor Johnson had stayed; also the house of John Knox and the house formerly occupied by Burke, the murderer who supplied bodies for dissection to Doctor Robert Knox and was hanged 'amidst the execrations of the crowd' in 1829. As he was fascinated by Mary, Queen of Scots, he went to Holyrood and saw her rooms in which her own furniture still stood, including the boudoir in which Mary and a small party were at supper when her husband, Lord Darnley, and a band of conspirators burst in to murder Rizzio. At the time of Andersen's visit 'blood stains' were still carefully maintained on the stairs. In describing all this, Andersen wrote, 'People may call these pictures bits of travel description, but they are real parts of the story of my life.'

The Scots being highly literate, Andersen was already famous in Edinburgh. When he signed the visitors' book at the George Heriot Hospital, the oldest and richest charitable institution for poor boys in Edinburgh, the old porter looked at him with astonishment and said, 'So young! I have read him, and the boys have read him. It is strange to see such a man; they are usually all old or dead before one hears of them.' On leaving, Andersen bought a Bible 'to remember Edinburgh by'; his memory was unusually retentive, but material souvenirs meant as much to him as statues and pictures do to religious people who need outward signs to represent their inner life.

Hambro was taking his family to the west coast of Scotland and urged Andersen to travel with them as far as Dumbarton through the Highlands – the setting of *The Lady of the Lake* and *Rob Roy*. They crossed the Firth of Forth to Kirkcaldy, birthplace of the economist Adam Smith, with its romantic ruins, and sailed up the Firth by steamer, a violinist singing Scottish ballads as they approached the cliffs of the Highlands that seemed to appear, vanish and reappear according to the movements of the mist. As Andersen watched this he thought of Ossian. Like many nineteenth-century Romantics, Andersen was fascinated by this legendary Gaelic poet whose work had been 'adapted from oral traditions' in the eighteenth century by James Macpherson.

Andersen visited Stirling Castle, and near Darnley's house met a cobbler who was full of stories of Scottish history. He saw the plains where Edward I and Robert Bruce fought, the mound at Bannockburn where Edward planted his standard, the smithy where James IV sought refuge and was murdered by the priest to whom he wished to make his confession. He saw Loch Katrine, the place where James Fitzjames and Ellen met on Ellen's Isle in Scott's *The Lady of the Lake*, and Ben Lomond where Rob Roy kept his prisoners. He visited Smollett's monument at Balloch, and reached Dumbarton the second evening. There he experienced the rigours of a Scottish sabbath, even worse than an English one: 'Everything rests there, even the trains are not allowed to go, only the one from London to Edinburgh does not stop, to the annoyance of the religious Scots. All the houses are shut, and people sit at home, either reading the Bible or getting themselves drunk – that is what I have generally been told.' Andersen was himself prevented from taking a short sight-seeing walk on the grounds that it 'just would not do, people would be annoyed'. Even a short walk in the evening drew people to their windows to gaze in censure, and a young Frenchman told Andersen that he had been accused of 'ungodliness' for having gone fishing with two English friends on a Sunday. Not even Andersen's piety could reconcile him to this.

At Dumbarton he said a regretful goodbye to his hosts and took a steamer up the Clyde to Glasgow. He was still very tired and nervous of going to meet the Queen, since he had heard that there was no decent inn within miles of the spot and that he would have to appear with his own servants, which meant spending more than he could afford unless he asked the King of Denmark for extra money, which he was determined not to do. So he decided to forgo visits both to Queen Victoria and to Abbotsford. By this time, too, he was longing for home.

On his return journey he was invited to spend several days with his English publisher, Richard Bentley, founder of *Bentley's Miscellany*, whose firm was to be absorbed by Macmillan's in 1898. Bentley lived in the little town of Sevenoaks, twenty-two miles from London, near Knole with its famous thousand-acre park which enchanted Andersen, as did a little shop which he found in the village, exactly like Dickens's Old Curiosity Shop. Before leaving, Andersen wrote a little poem for his host's guestbook:

> With a mixture of longing and fear
> I went to the land of Shakespeare,
> My childhood's dream.
> Its Danish-looking fields and forests
> Make me feel at home immediately
> And though my lips were not able to
> speak the language,
> My heart understands it through my eyes,
> A rich and sunny day I saw in England
> As if every day's life was touched
> Into bloom by Aaron's rod.

What Andersen longed for most before leaving England was to see Dickens again. After their meeting at Lady Blessington's, Dickens had called on Andersen and left him a beautiful illustrated edition of his work, each volume inscribed 'Hans Christian Andersen from his friend and admirer Charles Dickens'. Now, at the last moment, Andersen heard that Dickens and his family were staying somewhere near by on the coast, so he wrote telling him that he was sailing from Ramsgate. His rough draft of this letter, full of corrections, is now in the Royal Library at Copenhagen:

August, 29, 1847

My dear dear Dickens!
to morrow I shall kome to Ramsgate, I hope will giw yours

Adresse in the Royal Oak Hotel, where I shall remane till the next morning, when I shall go by the stamboat to Ostende. I must see you, and thank you; that is the last flower for me in the dear England!

your Admirer and true Friend for ever,

HANS CHRISTIAN ANDERSEN

At the Royal Oak Andersen found a letter from Dickens saying that he was only five miles away, at Broadstairs, and expected him to dinner. He drove over and found the Dickens family in a charming little house facing the Channel, the sea coming almost right up to it. At dinner they could see the lighthouse and, when the tide receded, a massive sandbank. They talked of Danish and German literature. Dickens wanted to learn German. Five of Dickens's six children were there, all of whom kissed Andersen enthusiastically, including the youngest who kissed his own hand and gave it to Andersen. Mrs Dickens was a great admirer of Jenny Lind and longed for her signature, which was, she said, difficult to obtain, so Andersen immediately gave her the note in which Jenny had welcomed him to London. They parted with promises of future meetings, and to Andersen's astonishment and delight he found Dickens on the jetty at Ramsgate next morning: 'I had to come and say a final farewell to you,' said Dickens. He stayed until the ship's bell rang and, as the ship left England, he was the last person Andersen saw, waving his hat beside the lighthouse.

After a journey full of friendly encounters, Andersen's arrival home had the usual element of anticlimax. His resounding success in England had aroused jealousy that was painful to him. Jenny Lind, with less reason, had felt the same: 'What a pity it is that we Swedes cannot get on in our own country! No fame! Nothing! Nothing! In only seven months I have succeeded in making my reputation here [in Germany]; while at home not a soul knows of me.' This was certainly not true, but she, like Andersen, had great success outside her own country and she often said that she felt homesick everywhere, since Germany was her musical home, Sweden her natural home and England her spiritual one. For his part, Andersen had scarcely been a few hours in Denmark before, standing by his window, he heard two dandies say as they passed by, 'Just see, there is our famous orang-outang!' Scarcely better was the young author who told him 'frankly' that he had not read him before but would do so 'now that he had been so well received in England'.

Above all, this autumn Andersen was saddened by the death of Mendelssohn. Andersen was distressed not only for the bereaved family but for Jenny Lind, who had adored Mendelssohn and was prostrated by grief. It was Mendelssohn who, when she told him of her desire to leave the stage, had persuaded her to sing oratorios, and so launched her on her second career. Jenny proved tireless in raising funds for a Mendelssohn Foundation, and in 1856 the first Mendelssohn scholarship was awarded to Arthur Sullivan.

By now Andersen's fairy tales were appearing regularly at Christmas, and the volume that appeared for Christmas 1847 contained *The Old Street Lamp*, inspired by the fact that oil-lamps made way for gas-light in the streets of Copenhagen that year. In Andersen's story a shooting star grants the old lamp, who is the narrator, 'that everything I remember as clearly as if it stood before me shall also be seen by all I love! And in that lies true happiness; for if we cannot share happiness with others, it can only be half enjoyed.' This observation explains the particularly personal hold that Andersen has over his readers: everything he remembered as clearly as if it stood before him can indeed still be seen by all who love him.

With this story were printed *The Neighbouring Families*, a story in which birds and flowers talk with the unselfconscious individuality of Beatrix Potter's immortal animals, and in which his friend Thorvaldsen is commemorated; *Little Tuck*, which contains memories of his mother; and *The Shadow*, conceived in the torrid heat of Naples and possibly influenced by Chamisso's *Peter Schlemihl*. These and earlier ones he dedicated to Dickens, to whom he wrote: 'You were the last person to shake hands with me on the English coast, you were the last person to shout goodbye to me, and so it is quite natural that my first greeting from Denmark should be to you, and I send it with as sincere feeling as a devoted heart can do.'

Dickens's answer to this gave him more pleasure than any favourable review had ever done:

A thousand thanks, my dear Andersen, for your kind and dearly-prized remembrance of me in your Christmas book. I am very fond of it and feel deeply honoured by it, and I cannot tell you how much I esteem so generous a mark of recollection from a man of such genius as you possess.

Your book made my Christmas fireside happier. We were all charmed with it. The little boy, the old man, the pewter soldier, are my particular favourites. I have read that story [*The Old House*] over and over with the most unspeakable delight.

I was in Edinburgh a few weeks ago where I saw some of your friends who talked much about you. Come over to England again soon! But whatever you do, don't leave off writing, for we cannot afford to lose any of your thoughts. They are too purely and simply beautiful to be kept in your heart.

We have long since come back from that seashore where I said adieu to you, and we are in our own house again. Mrs Dickens says I am to give you her love. So says her sister. So say all my children. And as we are all in the same mind, I beg you to receive mine into the bargain as the love of your true and admiring friend,

CHARLES DICKENS

12. The Emperor's New Clothes

1848-9

... if we cannot share happiness with others, it can only be half enjoyed.
Hans Christian Andersen, *The Old Street Lamp*, 1847

The Emperor shivered, for he suspected they were right, but he thought,
"This procession has got to go on.'
Hans Christian Andersen, *The Emperor's New Clothes*

A spectre is wandering over Europe today – the spectre of communism.
Karl Marx, *The Communist Manifesto*, 1848

＊

EVEN THE APOLITICAL Andersen was aware of the violence in
the atmosphere of 1848, which began with revolts in Sicily against
the misrule of Ferdinand II of Naples, followed by revolts in all
the larger Italian cities. Barricades went up in Paris, Louis-
Philippe was dethroned, and a second Republic proclaimed in
France with Napoleon's nephew as President. Disturbances in the
Rhineland were followed by uprisings throughout the German
states, all bent on overthrowing Austrian domination and unifying
Germany. In Hungary Kossuth led a revolt against Austria, and
even in Switzerland – the only country in which liberals won what
was to prove a lasting victory for democracy – there were twenty
days of civil war. Since reaction had triumphed in 1815, there
had been an increase in the population of Europe such as had
never occurred before – an increase of eighty-six million between
1800 and 1850 that constituted a demographic revolution and
made political revolution inevitable. Karl Marx's *Communist Manifesto* – in which Russia was referred to as the 'bulwark of reaction'
– was published in London, and Matthew Arnold wrote: 'The
hour of the hereditary peerage and eldest sonship and immense

245

property has, I am convinced, as Lamartine would say, struck. Carlyle gives our institutions, as they are called, aristocracy, Church, etc., five years I heard last night.'

Early in January 1848 Christian VIII fell ill, though not, it was supposed, gravely. Just before Christmas he had invited Andersen to tea and asked him to bring something with him to read. Andersen found the King lying down, in the company of the Queen and a lady-in-waiting. He read him two chapters of his novel in progress, *The Two Baronesses*, and a few fairy tales, and the King seemed better and talked with animation. As Andersen was leaving the King said, 'We shall see each other again soon.' The King's condition worsened, however. Like many others, Andersen went daily to Amalienborg for news. When at last it seemed certain that the King was dying, Andersen took the news to Oehlenschläger, who had not realized the King's life was in danger and burst into tears. On the evening of January 20, Andersen was among the crowd standing in the snow looking up at the window behind which the King died at 10.15 p.m. At the moment of his death a wild swan flew into the spire of Roskilde Cathedral and crushed its breast, an event commemorated by Oehlenschläger.

The King's son, Frederik VII, was not popular at first. He was considered unreliable, and after two unsuccessful marriages, one with a Danish princess, the other with a German, he had contracted a morganatic marriage with a Danish commoner. Revolution was in the air and the form it took in Denmark was that a number of dissatisfied citizens put on top-hats and frock-coats and went to the new King to demand a constitution. Frederik VII received the polite rebels with the suave reply, 'Delighted we are in agreement', after which a constitution was drawn up.

At this point revolt broke out in Holstein and the Prince of Noer, brother of the Duke of Augustenburg whom Christian VIII had made Lieutenant-General of the Duchies, seized power by taking the Danish fortress of Rendsborg. In Copenhagen indignant crowds paraded the streets singing patriotic songs. Andersen, who was one of the committee called on to keep order – 'All that was necessary was for one single person to cry "Straight Ahead!"

whenever the mob called the name of some place where they might have run wild, and then the whole crowd of them went straight ahead' – said it was as if a completely new generation had emerged. What aroused the Danes' fury was not the desire of Holstein to join the German Confederation, but its determination to involve Slesvig.

Behind local interests were international ones. The expansion of the great powers had created two points of tension in Europe: the Baltic duchies of Slesvig and Holstein, and the straits of the Dardanelles and the Bosphorus. International agreements concerning Slesvig-Holstein dated back to the eighteenth century, and so long as the Russians exported and the British imported timber via the Baltic, both of them wanted the entrance to that sea controlled by a non-rival power. Now, however, the situation was altered. Britain had steam power and overseas interests, while Russia had a big trade in wheat which turned her attention to the Ukraine and the straits of the Dardanelles. Neither power, therefore, had any objection to German expansion at Denmark's expense.

On March 18 a deputation from Holstein came to Copenhagen to express its views on a common constitution for the duchies and Slesvig's entry into the German Bund. Three days later the Danish liberals outlined a programme, with which the conservatives agreed, which stated that 'to give Slesvig-Holstein a separate constitution would be virtually giving up the claims of the Danish Crown. Denmark and Slesvig must have a common free constitution and the King must choose a government that has the people's confidence.' The King agreed to this and absolute monarchy, which had lasted in Denmark since 1665, was peacefully replaced by constitutional monarchy. The King insisted, however, that Slesvig was to remain a part of Denmark, though with its own assembly to deal with local matters, while Holstein was to have its own constitution. On April 9 the duchies' insurgents were defeated at Flensburg and the Danes occupied Slesvig down to the river Eider.

Some Danish intellectuals stood aside from this struggle – Kierkegaard's only references to it in his diary are complaints that his servant was called up for military service, that his finances were affected and he himself prevented from travelling – but Andersen was officially asked to state the Danish case in the English press, a very important matter since Queen Victoria inclined to the German side. Andersen's long letter to Jerdan, published in the *Literary Gazette* and several foreign papers, was excellent propaganda because of its simplicity and sincerity. The situation was very painful to Andersen, who felt for his own country with a deep childlike piety but could not help also grieving for his many friends in Germany. Ørsted understood his mixed feelings completely and himself wrote a poem, 'Deeply we feel that the enemy is our brother and has been linked to us throughout the centuries.'

The war might have stopped after the Danes quelled the insurgents had not Frederick William of Prussia intervened. This complex character – Georg Brandes called him a 'romantic mystic' – had come to the throne of Prussia in 1840, aged forty-five, and began by suggesting reforms that were not often carried out. He also befriended artists and believed in the divine right of kings. After convening parliament in April 1847, he announced that no power on earth would make him consent to 'the exchange of the natural relation between the king and his people for a conventional constitutional relationship'; it was therefore a wish to gain sympathy from his people that made him join in the struggle for German unity. At the demand of the Duke of Augustenburg, Frederick William IV contributed troops to the German army of 30,000 that on April 23 encountered the Danish army of 12,000 at the Dannevirke (the ancient lines of fortifications built by Queen Thyra in the tenth century), occupied Slesvig and entered Jutland. Denmark appealed to the powers that had guaranteed Slesvig-Holstein, but France and Austria had their own problems and England favoured Germany. Only Russia disapproved of German intervention and insisted on Prussia's retiring from Jutland. Meanwhile 15,000 Swedish and Norwegian volunteers came to the help of Denmark in a wave of 'Scandinavianism'.

In the middle of May Andersen went to Glorup, writing from there to Richard Bentley about the Prussian occupation of Jutland and the German demand for four million dollars to be paid before May 28: 'Jutland cannot pay even half of this amount, and therefore Prussia will plunder and burn the towns. How can such things happen among civilized nations? England has guaranteed to help. Also Norway and Sweden are offering help . . . Disraeli's speech in favour of the Danish cause has been translated into Danish . . .' Troops were quartered at Odense, and Glorup had forty soldiers and several officers. The old Count Moltke-Huitfeldt made no distinction between soldiers and officers, all of whom he invited to his table. When the Swedish and Norwegian volunteers arrived at Nyborg they were given a tremendous welcome. By this time all the bedrooms at Glorup were occupied and only the barn was left to accommodate the volunteers, but the old housekeeper decided that all who had come to help should have beds and ordered wood to be sawed for beds which she made up with immaculate white linen. Sympathy immediately sprang up between the local peasants and the volunteers. The peasants would stand with folded hands at army prayers, and after drill was over, the volunteers would help bring in the harvest; in the evenings everyone danced to the music of the Swedes' violins.

In August 1848 Prussia and Denmark signed the Truce of Malmö, according to which Prussian and Danish troops were withdrawn from the duchies and both were to be administered by a joint Prussian-Danish commission – a solution equally unpopular in both countries. Most of this time Andersen was at Glorup, although it was at Sorø that he finished his novel *The Two Baronesses*, the best and most Danish of his five novels.

This was published in England, translated by Charles Beckwith Lohmeyer, in September 1848, shortly before the publication of the Danish edition, and it shows that though he was ignorant politically he responded instinctively to the political atmosphere. Like his short story, *Everything in its Proper Place*, written five years later, *The Two Baronesses* shows up the brutality of the 'good old days'. The old Baroness who is the chief character is a peasant's child who once saw her father tortured for being unable to pay the rent of the hovel in which his family lived. Thanks to her intelligence and beauty, she eventually became a member of the class that enslaved her father, but even so cannot stop brooding on social injustice. She is so interesting that one sympathizes with a character in the book who says, 'Long may she live! The eccentrics must not die out, for they create as good an effect in the world as uniforms in a theatre.' This book also offers an unusual picture of Danish country life.

That Andersen felt painfully involved in the war is shown by a letter he wrote to a German friend, Frau von Eisendecker, in October, 1848:

'After roaming about the islands of Fünen [Fyn] and Zealand, I am quietly sitting in a corner of Copenhagen, but a corner in which I can look over the sea to the Swedish coast, and see the ships go to and fro; and here at last I have received a letter from you. I was rejoiced at the sight of the handwriting, for I recognized the hand of a dear friend in a hostile country, a peaceful friend whom I have not seen for a long time. We *will* not talk of politics . . . One point I must touch upon. In speaking of the Slesvig-Holstein prisoners of war, you say that the manner in which they are treated by us is shocking, and contrary to the spirit of our times. I am delighted to be able to refer you to the last July number of a German journal, the *Leipziger Illustrierte Zeitung*. There you will find a faithful account by a German of the treatment of the prisoners, and I beg you to read it. Promise me you will. I place it before you as a duty! The prison ships lie in the shelter of the harbour, looking on to the Sound. The steamers pass every day, and thus there is life and change. I could choose no more beautiful spot for myself. The prisoners have several hours every day in which they can walk by the sea or bathe. They were also allowed to go into the town and visit pleasure resorts; but they abused their liberty: and some of them, for example, sang *"Slesvig-Holstein meerumschlungen"* in public places, which is, to speak mildly, unwise, and cannot be permitted just now on account of the necessity of maintaining peace and order. But most German papers publish false statements about Denmark, and represent matters in a false and bad light – a policy which must anger every noble German who is acquainted with the true circumstances.

'Germany has shown me *so* much kindness, so many people live there to whom I cling with love and gratitude, that my heart

suffers during the war, and I suffer as a Dane when I see the
shoals of lies that are circulated about us in the world. I am
convinced that Germany will see this herself before very long, for
truth will conquer.'

Soon after his return to Copenhagen Andersen received an
invitation from Heiberg, who, together with a group of friends,
wanted to congratulate him on *The Two Baronesses*. Always ready
to let bygones be bygones, Andersen immediately accepted this
friendly offer, as readily as he accepted that of Heiberg and
Collin to write a prologue for the centenary of the Royal Theatre
on December 18. In October 1848 Andersen had moved into
67 Nyhavn, by the harbour – rooms he liked so well that, except
for a few short breaks, he kept them until 1865.

This Christmas Fredrika Bremer paid her first visit to Copenhagen and Andersen had the pleasure of welcoming her and
showing her the city. She stayed in Denmark until well into the
summer, visited Andersen's friends the Ingemanns in Sorø, and
conceived a great love for Denmark, as is shown by her book
Life in the North, which was published in Swedish, Danish,
German and English. Denmark needed friends at this time, for in
April 1849 the success of the revolutionary movements in Prussia,
Austria and Hungary had inaugurated a new phase in the struggle
for German unity and in March a provisional general assembly
met in Frankfurt and sent 46,000 troops to attack the Danes.
Once again the Germans invaded Jutland, but finally had to
withdraw and leave the insurgents to fight alone, and be defeated
by the Danes at Fredericia on July 6, 1849.

Fredrika Bremer had urged Andersen to come to Sweden, and
on Ascension Day he sailed across the Sound to Helsingborg. *In
Sweden*, which he wrote about this trip, was his most carefully
planned travel book and its descriptions of land- and water-scapes,
people and legends, provide a fascinating picture of midsummer
in the far north. Scandinavianism being at its height, all the old
Nordic legends aroused passionate interest. That very year
Wagner, condemned to death for his part in the revolutionary
movement in Dresden, had taken refuge in Switzerland and was
working on *The Ring of the Nibelungs*.

The Wild Swan

At Trollhätten Andersen wrote to the Hereditary Grand Duke of Weimar: 'From the extreme north, on the boundary of Lapland, I have just reached here. I left Denmark in the spring, where I was useless in the struggle for victory, and have travelled through Sweden, have been up at Dalecarlia where no thunder of cannon resounds. Happy, politically-defined Sweden, with its secure boundaries! Three years ago I dreamt of undertaking the journey to Stockholm with you, but what a change has now come over everything! I travelled alone but you were in my thoughts – yes, I may say daily in my thoughts – with melancholy and sadness, oh, you scarcely know how highly I rate you, how firmly you have grown into my heart! I have only rightly understood that this summer. I have received no answer to my last letter which I wrote you in the spring. I heard afterwards that a contingent of Weimar troops had marched to the north, and finally I read that your Royal Highness had yourself gone to the seat of war. I understood the circumstances, and sorrowed deeply on account of them, but could write no more. But now the proclamations of peace are ringing in my ears, I may follow the wishes of my heart and send this letter to my friend. In the far north of Sweden I received the news so late, and am only now listening to the sound of the joy-bells. I can see you again, and look into your honest, affectionate eyes. You have certainly experienced sad days this summer, my noble friend.'

In Stockholm Andersen met Lindblad, whose songs Jenny had made famous, and he was presented to the King, Bernadotte's son Oscar I, whom he had once seen in Odense when they were both children. Andersen thanked the King for the Order of the North Star, they talked of the war – King Oscar had mediated the Truce of Malmö – and of their common friend, the Hereditary Grand Duke of Weimar. The King also invited Andersen to dine on his return from the north with him and the Queen, who was the Empress Joséphine's granddaughter. From Uppsala Andersen made a trip that he thought 'not unlike journeys in parts of America not covered by railways'. At Lekstand, on the shore of Lake Siljan, which is level with the toe of Iceland, he found everyone busy decorating maypoles for the midsummer festivities. Each lakeside village had its own distinctive peasant costumes, and crowds arrived by boat for Midsummer's Night, when there was maypole dancing to the sound of fiddles in the brilliant white light.

While he was at the inn at Lekstand Andersen made one of the paper cut-outs for which he was so gifted, a little Turkish minaret for his hostess's granddaughter. Presently he heard chattering in the yard, and saw the child showing the paper minaret to an admiring crowd. Next the grandmother came to his room with a plate of gingerbread and told him that although she baked the best gingerbread in all Dalecarlia, she knew only the old shapes that she learnt from her grandmother, so would be very grateful if he would cut her out some new models. Always obliging, Andersen spent most of that white night cutting out nutcrackers, ballet-dancers, windmills complete with millers – probably with scissors like the ones that can still be seen in Odense Museum, such big clumsy-looking scissors for the delicate intricate work he made them do.

The history and legends of this countryside attracted him as much as its mysterious beauty. In the vast forests, with their silent lakes and wild swans' nests, he felt as if he were back in the time of the sagas, when 'mighty fairies transformed into swans flew north to the Hyperborean Land, east of the north wind, where in the deep still lakes they bathed and recovered their original form'. In the copper-mining town of Falun that had for centuries provided so much of Sweden's wealth, Andersen was reminded of Hoffmann's story of a young miner's body found in a disused mineshaft in 1719, still fresh and youthful-looking although his fiancée was by then an old woman. In one mine a corpse found in 1635 had carried copper coins that proved it to have been there two hundred years.

Back in Stockholm, Andersen was twice invited to the palace and a cordial relationship sprang up between him and all the Swedish royal family. During one of his visits he was introduced to a striking elderly man, Count Salza, of whom he remembered reading in Oehlenschläger's memoirs. The Count at once invited Andersen to visit him at one of his estates on his way home. Andersen took this as an expression of courtesy rather than a genuine invitation, so thought no more of it, but when the steamer by which he was returning home anchored near Säby, the composer Josephson, with whom Andersen had stayed in Sorrento and Capri and whom he had recently seen in Uppsala, came aboard and said that he was himself Count Salza's guest at Säby and had been sent with a carriage to fetch Andersen as they had felt sure he would be aboard this steamer. The Count welcomed Andersen as if he had been an old friend, saying that he had felt from the first that there was an affinity between them. The old man, who was reputed to have second sight and was a living treasure-house of history, told Andersen many strange stories about his family. His ancestors had been Norwegian fishermen and peasants who had settled in Venice, where they had saved the lives of some Christian prisoners and been created Princes of Salza by Charlemagne. The little fishing village that was the site of St Petersburg had belonged to his great-grandfather, who believed Catherine I (who had shown great favour to his family) to have been of Swedish origin.

During the old man's birthday celebrations, in which everyone in the district took part, newspapers arrived with the first complete reports of the Danish victory at Fredericia. The Danish flag was immediately hoisted and the victory toasted in champagne. It was characteristic of Andersen that, for all his own delight, he noticed a German governess weeping at Count Salza's anti-German remarks, and in offering his thanks for the toast he took her hand and said that now the Danes and the Germans would again be friends. Again and again during his journey home he was congratulated on his country's victory. At Linköping a group of students gathered to greet him and sing the Danish national anthem and as they did so a rainbow appeared; at Motala he was serenaded by the factory workers; and when he went aboard ship at Göteborg a crowd gathered and sang the Danish national anthem repeatedly. Soon after this Andersen wrote the poem 'In Denmark I was born', which was to become a second national anthem.

13. The Phoenix Bird

1850-6

... the phoenix is not a bird of Arabia alone. In the glimmer of the northern lights he flies over the plains of Lapland and hops amid the yellow flowers in the short Greenland summer. Deep beneath the copper-mines of Falun, and in England's coal-mines, he flies in the form of a powdered moth.

Hans Christian Andersen, *The Phoenix Bird*

... a broken heart does not annihilate routine necessities, but merely makes them considerably more difficult to contend with.

Robert Aickman, *The Late Breakfasters*

*

1850 BEGAN SADLY for Andersen. In January he wrote to the Hereditary Grand Duke: 'Oehlenschläger died on January 20, the same date as that on which King Christian VIII died two years earlier, at almost the same hour. Late in the evening I twice passed the palace to visit Oehlenschläger, for I knew from the doctors that death was near; and it was strange to look up and see the palace windows dark at Amalienborg and think that two years ago I was walking about there full of anxiety for my beloved King and that I was once more experiencing the same thing for a King among poets. His death was without suffering, he had his children round him and asked them to read a scene from his *Socrates* to him, the scene where Socrates speaks of immortality and the certainty of an eternal life. He was so calm, and he prayed that his death-struggle might not be a hard one. I saw his body; jaundice had made him look like a bronze statue ... On January 26 he was followed to his grave by the people in the true meaning of the word, for there were officials, students, sailors, soldiers, all classes, who of their own accord took it in turn to bear his coffin on the long road out to Frederiksberg, where he was born and wished to be laid to rest.' Andersen and old Bishop Grundtvig were asked by the funeral committee to write a cantata, and a memorial performance was given at the Royal Theatre, with the audience in mourning and Oehlenschläger's seat occupied by a laurel wreath with black ribbons.

The dissatisfaction that Andersen had sometimes felt in his dealings with the Royal Theatre was lessened at this time by his finding another market for his plays at the Casino, a theatre recently established by the enterprising founder of Tivoli to provide popular entertainment at a low price. The Casino could seat 2,500 people and was at that time the only theatre in the country except the Royal Theatre to pay its dramatists. At first few well-known authors cared to write for the Casino, but its reputation rose, thanks to a dynamic actor-manager, Lange, and when the latter turned to Andersen he gladly provided two fairy-tale plays, one, *More than Pearls and Gold* (1849), based on an Arabian Nights story of which a version had been written by Count Carlo Gozzi, the eighteenth-century Italian author of *commedia dell'arte* fairy tales, and *Ole Lukøie* (1850), both of which were immensely popular and continued to be performed long after Andersen's death. He described these in a letter to Dickens written at Glorup on July 16, 1850:

My dear and beloved Dickens!

You are so vividly in my thoughts that I often think I live in the same house with you, and therefore put off writing. This is a strange explanation, but such is the case. I was far up in Sweden last autumn when I received your letter, which I keep with every dear line from you, amongst my best remembrances. I have been in Dalecarlia, where no sound of roaring cannon was heard in that happy, politically sound Sweden.

The Dale-river or as it is called Dal-Elv is more glorious than the Rhine, it is a transparent sea that glides through endless woody deserts. The rosiest hues of eve at Midsummer blend together with those of morning, and the wild swans live here in the winter.

I have however been diligent since I returned to Copenhagen, as I have written two romantic-comedies for our popular theatre, the one entitled *More than Pearls and Gold*, which is naturally a dear beloved wife. The other *Ole Lukøie*, where the idea is that *not money*, but health and good humour are the best gifts in life. These two pieces have gained immense applause and filled that very large theatre; the one was performed twenty-three times. I am now writing my pictorial sketches from Sweden, which I will transmit to you in English. Many thanks for your matchless *David Copperfield*. Your heart is in your pen! In another world I think that I shall be better able than in this, to express to you my admiration and affection.

In May I left Copenhagen and lived for some time in quiet woodland solitude with the old Danish poet Ingemann; I then visited the most picturesque part of Jutland, and am now for the fifth week on a visit to the old Count Moltke at Glorup.

My best regards to Mrs Dickens and children! I long incredibly to see and speak with you! Now farewell and may God bless you all – for with my whole heart I remain

Yours friend and admirer

HANS CHRISTIAN ANDERSEN

A week later, however, fighting was resumed, and on July 25 the Danish and Slesvig-Holstein forces clashed at Idsted Heath. The front was three miles long and the battle, which started at 3 a.m., lasted all day and ended in a Danish victory. After a few minor skirmishes the war was over. The duchies remained Danish and on August 2, 1850, the London Protocol, signed by Denmark, the Swedo-Norwegian union, England, France, and Russia, guaranteed 'the integrity of the Danish monarchy'. A second treaty, signed in London in May 1852 by England, France, Russia, Austria, Prussia and the Swedo-Norwegian union, included the clause that should Frederik VII die without male issue, the heir to the Danish throne would be Christian of Glücksburg, who belonged to a lateral branch of the Oldenburg family and was married to Christian VIII's niece, Louise Charlotte. The Duke of Augustenburg consented in his own name and that of his family to accept this, and to abandon his claims on Slesvig in exchange for payment for land that belonged to him there.

Andersen was at Glorup when the victorious soldiers returned home and he helped enthusiastically to organize the celebrations. A tent with a floor of planks was set up in one of the lime avenues by the large pond and he was indefatigable in planning decorations, drawing on the knowledge of stagecraft that he had acquired from Bournonville and Carstensen. On July 7, 1851, he wrote: 'On either side of a big ornamental pool in the park, there were 2 long avenues of lime trees. In one of these I had a tent erected 100 ft long, 30 ft broad and 20 ft high. The trees served as columns and were entwined with red damask that had been used before for decorating walls and had been lying about somewhere in a corner; to form the capitals of the columns there were coloured shields and large bunches of flowers. A canvas sail was used for the roof, but below this there was a ceiling formed of garlands of Dannebrog flags hanging from the middle to all sides . . . and right at the top of the room, amid flowering forget-me-nots, two vases with mourning crape and blazing lights; small black shields bore the names of the first and the last of the fallen, Hegermann-Lindencrone and Dalgas; two others bore the inscription "The Danish Soldier". "It's like a paradise," said an old peasant who had had to be carried to the festivities, "all those lovely things and all that music; and what a lot of things to eat." ' Andersen's own pleasure in the victory was marred by grief over the death of Colonel Læssøe, killed at Idsted. Andersen published a poem for him in *Fædrelandet* on July 31, 1850, and said 'Colonel Læssøe, as you know, was a friend of mine [he was the son of Mrs Signe Læssøe]; I knew him from the time he was a young cadet, and always felt that he would be something great; he had an exceedingly clear brain, his will was so firm, and in addition he had knowledge and a good education.'

The desire so manifest in Andersen's autobiography to express a rosy view of life came in part from his need to control his terrible fits of melancholy. Unaware that these were partly due to the starvation of his deepest emotions, he attributed his unhappiness to his failure as a writer. Even when, in October 1851, his pension from the Crown was raised and he was given the honorary title of professor – which seems incongruous now, but was then often bestowed on distinguished men of letters – he still felt, as he had told Mathilde Ørsted, that he had not yet accomplished anything of merit and never would.

In March 1851 the gloom into which Andersen had been plunged by the war was increased by the death of Emma Hartmann, wife of the composer who had been his friend, and often his collaborator, since their youth. Andersen had been strongly attached to Emma Hartmann. 'The humour and joy of living which were in this unusually gifted woman were revealed in the form of a natural grace which knew no wrinkles or shadows . . . It is impossible to describe the great store of joy and fun and fervour which streamed from her.' He also loved her little daughter, Maria, who to his horror died the evening after her mother's funeral. It was Maria whom he had put into *The Old House*, along with little Erik who had given him a tin soldier. Even at two years old Maria had instinctively danced whenever she heard music or singing, and once, when she was going to have her bath and Andersen asked if he might come with her, she said, 'No, because I am so little, but when I grow up you may.'

Then on March 9 a far worse blow befell him. Ørsted died. At first Andersen could not believe in his old friend's death. Although Ørsted was seventy-three and had the previous autumn celebrated his jubilee at Copenhagen University – the students had organized a torchlight procession and the city had given him for life the country house last inhabited by Oehlenschläger and to which Ørsted had looked forward to going in the spring – he had never seemed like an old man. At the funeral the march that Hartmann had written for Thorvaldsen's funeral was played. The last time Andersen had heard this he had been in Ørsted's company, at a party given by Fredrika Bremer on the eve of her departure for Sweden. Little Maria Hartmann had been there too, and had presented Andersen with Fredrika Bremer's parting gift to him of a silver beaker.

As always he sought refuge in travel. In May he went to Præstø Bay in Christinelund, once the home of Thorvaldsen and now that of Andersen's young friends, Edvard Collin's daughter

Jonna and her husband Henrik Stampe. They longed to have a
stork build its nest on their house, since this brings good luck, and
they had placed a wheel on a gable to provide a foundation.
'Just wait till I come,' wrote Andersen, 'then the stork will come.'
Sure enough a pair of storks arrived the morning of the day he was
expected, and as his carriage drove into the courtyard they were
at work on their nest. Such omens still seemed as mysteriously
significant to him as they had done in his childhood, and he
recorded many of them. Once, when fresh wreaths were to be
laid on Oehlenschläger's grave, a song-bird's nest was found
among the withered flowers; once at Bregentved he wrote in the
snow over the stones by the obelisk in the garden 'Immortality is
like the snow; tomorrow it is not to be seen', and when he passed
the spot a few days later, after a thaw followed by frost, he found
only the word 'immortality' in the remaining patch of snow.

For his first trip abroad after the war he invited Ingeborg
Collin Drewsen's son Viggo to join him. Ever since he had started
earning money he had revelled in providing treats for the Collin
children. He never forgot their birthdays, nor any occasion that
he could transform into an anniversary. Now that the children
were too old for toys he sought ingeniously for new ways of
pleasing them.

Andersen and Viggo sailed from Svendborg in the south of Fyn
to the island of Als, which they found disfigured by trenches and
makeshift huts from the recent war. In Flensburg fjord there
were more traces of fighting and in Flensburg itself they visited
the war graves and Andersen plucked a leaf from Læssøe's grave
for his mother. The city of Slesvig was still under martial law and
the commanding officer, Helgesen, a hero of Frederiksstad, went
out of his way to be helpful to Andersen and detached an officer
to show him over the Dannevirke fortifications. Helgesen had
read Andersen's stories and, most appropriately, loved *The
Steadfast Tin Soldier*.

The lingering atmosphere of war, useless deaths and suffering,
made Andersen glad to leave Holstein and Hamburg behind and
it was with immense relief that, on meeting old friends in Leipzig
and Dresden, he found that in most cases the war had not raised
barriers between them. Nevertheless, even in 1852, he could not

bring himself to accept an invitation from the Augustenburgs and told the Oldenburg Minister who was to have driven him to them, 'How can I go to the Augustenburgs? It is altogether contrary to my feelings to call upon a family that has brought misfortune upon my country. Even to meet them in the street would be painful to me. I *cannot* do it . . . let the Duchess say what she pleases . . .' For the first time in seven years he revisited the von Serres at Maxen, near Dresden. On his previous visit he had planted a tiny larch that he had found uprooted in their garden; it had prospered and been known as 'the Danish poet's tree' and when, one day during the war, lightning struck a birch tree that overshadowed it, the larch had survived. The superstitious strain Andersen had inherited from his mother, which was still strong in him despite education and religion, made him attach great importance to this.

In the train between Leipzig and Dresden Andersen and Viggo shared a compartment with an old French lady accompanied by a twelve-year-old boy called Henry and a lively young girl, Antoinette, who chattered about books, art, and music. The girl said that she had spent several years in England. This odd trio roused the other passengers' curiosity, and one of them whispered to Andersen that the old lady was a 'Demoiselle Bourbon'. Andersen made enquiries about the Demoiselle Bourbon in Dresden and was told that the two young people were the children of the famous watchmaker in Geneva who claimed to be the lost Dauphin, son of Louis XVI and Marie Antoinette.

As none of his friends was at Weimar just then, Andersen decided to postpone his visit there until the spring of 1853, when his long-awaited visit was a happy one. The barriers of war had vanished and he was enthusiastically welcomed by the Hereditary Grand Duke and by Beaulieu, now Lord Marshal and director of the theatre, and he renewed his friendship with Liszt, who was then *Kapellmeister* and Director of Court Music at Weimar, and was living with Princess Caroline de Sayn-Wittgenstein, having broken with the Countess Marie d'Agoult, by whom he had had the daughter, Cosima, who was twenty years later to marry Wagner. This was a particularly brilliant period in Liszt's professional life and he used his official position to help composers who could not get a hearing elsewhere. The long-neglected French composer Berlioz was given a Berlioz week at Weimar, and Liszt fought with all his might for Wagner's music. Andersen found Wagner curiously disturbing. When Liszt came to him, exultant, and asked how he had liked *Lohengrin*, all Andersen could say was, 'I am half dead.' Later he wrote: '*Lohengrin* seems to me a strange tree without blossom or fruit, through which the wind rushes . . . my judgment of music is of little significance, but in this art as in poetry I demand three qualities, understanding, imagination and feeling, and the last of the three is revealed in the melody. In Wagner I see a contemporary intellectual composer; he is great on account of his understanding and his will; he is a mighty innovator, rejecting everything which is old, but I feel he lacks that divine quality which was granted to Mozart and Beethoven.'

From Weimar Andersen went to Nuremberg and was delighted to hear a fellow passenger explaining to his small son that the electro-magnetic wire used by the railway had been invented by a Dane named Ørsted. His friends meant more and more to him now that he had relinquished all his hope of marriage, for in February 1852 Jenny Lind married Otto Goldschmidt, a Jewish pianist nine years younger than herself, who had been devoted to her since his student days, long before he knew her personally. The sight of Nuremberg moved Andersen to write *Under the Willow Tree*, a story based on his own love for Jenny: '. . . that evening Knud went to the theatre for the first time in his life. And what did he see? He saw Johanne, looking more charming and beautiful than he could have believed possible. To be sure, she was married to a stranger, but that was just in the play; it was only make-believe, as Knud understood very well. If it had been true, he thought, she would never have had the heart to send him a ticket . . .' Later: 'Her tenderness loosened his tongue. He told her how much he loved her and begged her to become his wife. Then he saw Johanne turn pale as she dropped his hand and said seriously and sadly, "Dear Knud, don't make us both unhappy. I shall always be a loving sister to you, one in whom you may trust, but I shall never be anything more."' In this same story he described the old Nuremberg that no longer exists, 'a strange old city, looking as if it had been cut out of an old-fashioned picture-book. The streets seem to wander along just as they please. The houses do not like to stand in regular rows. Gables with little towers, arabesques, and pillars lean out over the walls, and from the queer peaked roofs waterspouts, shaped like dragons or long, slim dogs, push out far over the streets ... The old moat around the town of Nuremberg has been converted into little kitchen gardens, but the high walls with their heavy towers are standing yet. The ropemaker twists his cords on a wooden gallery along the inside of the city wall, there elder-bushes grow out of the cracks and clefts, spreading their green branches over the small, lowly houses below.'

From there Andersen went on to Munich, which he found very much changed since he had last been there ten years earlier, in the reign of Ludwig I, the eccentric and art-loving King whose expenditure on pictures, buildings and favourites, including Lola Montez, had made him so unpopular that he had had to abdicate in 1848 in favour of his son, Maximilian II. Andersen was welcomed by Franz von Dingelstedt, the poet and novelist, who was then director of the magnificently organized Munich Court Theatre. Dingelstedt paid yearly visits to all the most important German theatres in search of new talent, and also went regularly to Paris, with the result that the Munich theatre had a vast and varied repertory. Neither trouble nor expense was grudged in matters of production and scenery. Dingelstedt put one of the best boxes in the theatre at Andersen's disposal and announced his arrival to the King, who immediately invited him to dinner at the royal hunting-lodge at Berg by Lake Starnberg, south of Munich.

The lodge faced a lake thirteen miles long and an alpine view, and Andersen found that although King Max was an uneccentric, kindly, duty-loving man whose happily respectable married life resembled that of Queen Victoria and Prince Albert, he had inherited some of his father's interest in the arts. On Andersen's first visit the King spoke enthusiastically of Oehlenschläger, Ørsted and of Andersen himself. After dinner King Max took Andersen sailing on the lake and asked him to read some of his work to him. Andersen read *The Ugly Duckling*. Thirty-four years later Maximilian's son Ludwig II, the passionate patron of Wagner, was to drown himself and his physician in this same lake a few days after he had been declared insane.

From Germany Andersen went through Switzerland, past Lake Como, to Milan. The city was still under martial law and when he was due to leave, the Austrian police, of whom Stendhal had so often complained, could not find his passport. Thanks to an open letter from the Austrian Ambassador in Copenhagen recommending Andersen to the civil and military authorities, the officials consented to search for his passport and eventually found it tucked away under the wrong classification.

At a station between Freiburg and Heidelberg Andersen was moved by the spectacle of a large party of emigrants leaving for America and parting from their friends and relatives with despair. One old woman had to be dragged from the carriage to which she clung. At Heidelberg he visited the remains of the castle, and while wandering among the cherry trees and elderberries that grew in the ruined halls, heard someone calling him. It turned out, most appropriately in that setting, to be Kestner, the Hanoverian ambassador to Rome, who was the son of Charlotte Buff, with whom Goethe had as a young man been unhappily in love and whom he had described as Lotte in *The Sorrows of Werther*. Instead of committing suicide like his hero, Goethe had become the author of a book that won him fame all over Europe and it was not until forty-three years later that he saw Charlotte Buff Kestner again, a meeting that was later to inspire Thomas Mann's *Lotte in Weimar*.

Andersen reached Copenhagen in July and the Queen Mother, Caroline Amalie, invited him to Sorgenfri, where he spent several happy days and thought often of his childhood and of the contrast, which never ceased to astonish him, between his past and his present life.

The nine tales that Andersen published in 1852 included the lyrical *The Swan's Nest* and the prophetic *In a Thousand Years' Time*, in which he wrote: 'It's a fact – a thousand years from now people will cross the ocean through the air on wings of steam! America's young settlers will visit old Europe. They will come over to see our monuments and our vanishing cities, just as we in our day go touring among the crumbling splendours of Southern Asia . . . "To Europe!" is the cry of the young sons of America. "To the land of our fathers, the wonderful land of memories and dreams – Europe!" . . . The airship comes. It is crowded with passengers, for the crossing is quicker than by sea. The electro-magnetic cable under the sea has already telegraphed how many the air caravan is bringing. Now Europe is in sight . . .' He goes on to describe brief visits to each country and concludes: ' "There's a lot to look at in Europe," says one young American, "and we've done it in a week. Yes, it's quite possible, as the great traveller [and here he names one of his contemporaries] has shown in his famous book *How To See Europe In A Week*." ' In addition, Andersen had written *The Elder Brother* for the Casino and *The Nix*, which was performed at the Royal Theatre in February 1853.

For Whitsun he went to stay with the Ingemanns at their lakeside cottage in Sorø. Scarcely a year went by without his visiting this couple whom he had nicknamed Philemon and Baucis, and although Ingemann was now sixty-four, the parlour with its portraits of European poets was as unchanged as the view of lime trees and lake from the days when the schoolboy Andersen first visited the young poet and his bride. Since those days Ingemann had at Grundtvig's suggestion written the series of historical novels exalting medieval chivalry and national pride that were as popular with his contemporaries as those of Walter Scott and were to be required reading in schools for several generations. From there Andersen went to Glorup, where Count Moltke-Huitfeldt was celebrating his silver wedding. About sixteen hundred peasants from the estate took part in the dancing and merrymaking, and Andersen was completely absorbed by the festivities when he received a letter telling him that two of his friends in Copenhagen had died of cholera.

Cholera, tuberculosis and typhus were the deadliest diseases of the period. Cholera had reached Europe early in the nineteenth century as a result of the Russian campaigns in Armenia and the first Turkish-Egyptian conflict. By 1825 the cholera had not spread beyond Astrakhan, but in 1830 it reached Europe and remained there for seven years, killing 100,000 people in France alone; in 1847 and 1851 there were fresh outbreaks. When the cholera reached Copenhagen in 1853 even the Collins, who never showed panic, wrote that they had had to move out of their house and 'God knows what will happen in another twenty-four hours.' Everyone advised Andersen not to return home and he spent the summer with Michael Drewsen in Silkeborg in the heart of Jutland. But despite the beautiful scenery of Jutland and the black storks – a landscape that he particularly loved, and described in *Ib and Little Christine*, *The Marsh King's Daughter*, *Valdemar Daae and His Daughters*, and *A Story from the Sand Dunes* – he could not relax there. Racked by anxiety, he would jump every time he heard the post-horn and run for letters and newspapers, and as soon as the epidemic lessened he returned to Copenhagen.

That November he published a book of stories and worked on bringing his autobiography up to date. One of the last decisions of his Danish publisher and friend Reitzel, who died in June 1853, had been to produce a cheap edition of Andersen's collected works, as had been done seven years earlier in Germany, and he had wanted this to include the autobiography which had been extremely successful in Germany, where it was compared with that of Rousseau. Andersen had therefore decided to revise and complete the 'earlier sketch' and he wanted this new autobiography to be ready for his fiftieth birthday.

In the spring of 1854 Andersen went to Vienna, where for the first time in seven years he met Jenny Lind, now Jenny Goldschmidt. Her husband, whom she described as an example of virtue, industry and domesticity, greeted Andersen with unaffected friendliness and her little son stared at him with large eyes. He heard her sing again and was overcome by the beauty of her voice and the way that, in his opinion, she was denying her gifts – 'It is her dramatic presentation, the dramatic truth, which is her strength and greatness, and only in the arias and songs she sings in the concert hall does she let us hear this – she has left the stage; it is a sin against the spirit, it is renouncing the gift which God has given her.'

Feeling 'distressed and yet glad, strangely thoughtful', he left for Illyria and from there by steamer for Venice. He loved Venice by night, with the gondolas silently gliding between palaces reflected in the moonlit water, but was repelled by its day-time aspect, the garbage-laden canals, the water-rats and the ovenlike heat, and he soon fled to Verona, where he was bitten by a scorpion in the neck and cheek. By the time he reached Munich he was in need of medical attention and was given it by the King's charming old physician, Gietl, who looked after him for two weeks, after which Andersen was able to accept the King and Queen's invitation to Hohenschwangau, where they were spending the summer. This was a small squat castle set in wild mountain scenery overlooking a valley between two lakes and the green Alp See, and surrounded by forests of fir and larch. It had been restored by the King in 1832, when he was still Crown Prince, and it made a particular appeal to Andersen because it was the centre of the Swan country. Here, according to a thirteenth-century German epic, Lohengrin, Knight of the Grail and son of Parsifal, was led by a swan to rescue Princess Elsa of Brabant. There were swans on the lake, swans in the frescoes on the castle walls, and every kind of swan ornament in the royal apartments – stuffed, embroidered, painted, jewelled and even swan-shaped inkpots. The King's nine-year-old son and heir Ludwig had a passion for Hohenschwangau with its swans and legends, and one of his earliest drawings shows a swan almost as large as the fairy-tale castle behind it. The background might have been specially designed to develop in the child the qualities that were to make the man a slave to the operas of Wagner. It was also a curiously inappropriate place for Andersen to find himself listening to Ludwig's father's common-sense talk of scientists such as Ørsted, Robert Fulton and Salomon de Caus.

From there Andersen went to Weimar. Karl Alexander, who had succeeded his father as reigning Grand Duke, was at Wilhelmsthal castle and Andersen spent entranced days in the Minnesingers' country. While there he was invited to dinner by the widowed Duchesse d'Orléans, who lived at near-by Eisenach with her two sons, the Duc de Paris and the Duc de Chartres, both of whom were enthusiastic readers of Andersen. Tears came into the Duchess's eyes when Andersen looked at a portrait of her husband, whom he had seen in Paris twenty years earlier, young and handsome, dancing at the ball at the Hôtel de Ville that followed the ceremony of replacing Napoleon's statue on the column in the Place Vendôme.

As always, Andersen's travels renewed his creative powers and in October 1854 he wrote to Henriette Wulff: 'I have a strange way of working in fits and starts, as people say. I can waste months at a time. That is a rest, or a sleep if you will, during which the same thing happens to mental offspring as to physical ones – they grow in their sleep; then suddenly I start to work as though it were a matter of life and death, as though I had only a few hours left at the end of which everything must be finished, and then I can almost wreck myself physically. That is how I have been for the past six or eight weeks. I don't think I have done so much work for years, and all that time my mind has been heavy, sometimes unhealthy. Now, as I begin to see the end of the work, new ideas and thoughts gush forth and the current carries me away with it.'

14. *A Visit to Dickens*

1857

We are in an age when, if brides sometimes swooned at the altar, Ministers sometimes wept at the Table; when the sight of an infant school could reduce a civil servant to a passion of tears; and one undergraduate has to prepare another undergraduate for the news that a third undergraduate has doubts about the Blessed Trinity – an age of flashing eyes and curling lips, more easily touched, more easily shocked, more ready to spurn, to flaunt, to admire and, above all, to preach.

G. M. Young, *Victorian England*

*

IN APRIL 1857 Andersen received a letter from Dickens saying that he had just finished *Little Dorrit* so was 'a free man'. He invited Andersen to stay with him at his new country house at Gad's Hill in June. Andersen arranged to go by way of Sorø, so as to be there for Ingemann's sixty-eighth birthday on May 28, and then travelled to Calais, where on June 11 he took a boat to Dover. The crossing was a rough one and as the steamer had to wait for the turn of the tide he almost missed the first morning train to London. 'Post haste we went through tunnel after tunnel, and soon we saw the great Crystal Palace glittering in full sunshine, and London, swathed in smoke, looming on the horizon. At London Bridge, on the other side of the terminus, the first bell was already ringing for a train on the North Kent Line that runs by Higham Station, near Dickens's country house. In hot haste I got a seat; and we flew away past towns and villages, ever close to the Thames, that glittered on our left, filled with sails and steamers.'

At Higham Andersen was greeted by a porter, who asked if he was the foreign gentleman for Mr Dickens and offered to accompany him to Gad's Hill and carry his luggage. After a two-mile

269

walk between hedges of wild rose and honeysuckle, they saw the weather-vane of Dickens's house glittering above the tree-tops. It was a fine new house with red walls, four balconied windows and a portico resting on small pillars, overlooking a lawn, a hedge of cherry-laurel and two handsome cedars of Lebanon.

Andersen found Dickens looking a little older than the last time they met, but thought this was largely because he had let his beard grow, and 'otherwise his eyes were bright as ever; the smile on his lips was just as friendly . . . He was now in the prime of manhood in his forty-fifth year; full of youth and life and eloquence and rich in a rare humour that glowed with kindness.' Andersen wrote to Henriette Wulff: 'My reception was very warm, Dickens took me in his arms. Later his wife and children came. I was given a charming room and can from my window look down over Higham to the Thames, which swarms with ships . . . Mrs Dickens I find this time beautiful, and the eldest daughter Mary takes after her, the second, Kate, has on the other hand quite Dickens's face, as you know it in his portrait; there are three sons over in Boulogne and four in this house; the youngest, Edward Lytton Bulwer Dickens, appears to be five years old. All the children are named after writers. The eldest is called Charles Dickens, the second, Walter Landor (he is leaving in four weeks for Calcutta where he will become an officer and stay away seven years); then come the sons in Boulogne, Francis Jeffrey, Alfred Tennyson, Sydney Smith, and here at home the two youngest, Henry Fielding and Edward Bulwer . . . The family life seems so harmonious, and a young Miss Hogarth [Dickens's sister-in-law], who has been living in this house for many years, pours tea and coffee, plays with the young Misses Dickens and seems to be a most kind and cultured lady.'

Other visitors included Miss Angela Burdett-Coutts, the philanthropist to whom Dickens had dedicated *Martin Chuzzlewit* in 1844, the novelist Wilkie Collins, and Andersen's English publisher Richard Bentley. It was Henry Fielding who wrote in his memoirs of Andersen: 'He had one really beautiful accomplishment, which was the cutting out in paper, with an ordinary pair of scissors, of lovely little figures of sprites and elves, gnomes, fairies and animals of all kinds which might well have stepped out of the pages of his books. These figures turned out to be quite delightful in their refinement and delicacy in design and touch.'

Dickens and his family had been only a fortnight in their new house, so the expeditions they made with Andersen were ones of discovery for them as well as for him. The weather was beautiful and the Kent that Andersen saw justified its claim to be the garden of England. They climbed to the highest part of Gad's Hill and saw the inn with a weather-beaten signboard painted with Falstaff and Prince Hal on one side and the Merry Wives of Windsor putting Falstaff into the clothes-basket on the other, in commemoration of Shakespeare's references to Gadshill in *Henry IV*. They found traces of Roman fortifications and of the ancient Danes; they watched the sun set over the river, turning the water gold and the ships to mysterious black vessels; they visited Lord Darnley's park and the busy streets of Gravesend, and on fine days they could just see the North Sea; they visited Rochester Cathedral and its ruined castle and saw scenes like those described in *Pickwick*; they met an old Scotsman in a shrunken kilt playing bagpipes with three children who tumbled and danced to the melancholy music; and one evening they came on a gipsy encampment, all the gipsies crowded around a cauldron in which their supper was cooking. When Dickens went up to London Andersen would often accompany him as far as Rochester. 'It was then that we had lively and jovial conversations. Dew-besprinkled spider webs spread over the fields and plains like veils . . . Often as we arrived at Rochester we would find the city enveloped in fog; as this lifted the artistic ruins of the old castle and the sublime cathedral came into view. We drew near to the new bridge and the ruins of the old, close by. Generally it was at ebb-tide. The boats lay on their sides like dead fish on a clean ground. Then I would wander around Rochester.'

There were language difficulties, of course, but as Andersen wrote later: 'Though I had not had much previous practice in speaking English, or hearing it spoken, yet from the very first I could understand nearly all that Dickens said to me. Whatever puzzled me he repeated in a new form; and nobody caught my meaning quicker than he. Danish and English are so much alike that we were often surprised at the likeness, and so, if a word happened to fail me, Dickens made me repeat it in Danish, and it often sounded to him just like English.

' *"Der er en Græshoppe i den høstak"* I wanted to tell him one day, and said it in Danish; his translation came fast enough – "grasshopper in the haystack". I saw a mass of green growing on a cottage roof, and asked what they called it here. In my own country the name is *"husløg"*; and the cottager's wife answered, "house-leek"; and so on without end. We once met a little girl on the road, who made us a low curtsy; and when I remarked that we called this *"at stóbe lys"* (to dip a candle), Dickens said that the English word dip was used in the same way both for a curtsy and a candle. In France, Italy, and Spain, the Dane feels himself among foreign races; such is not the case in England; here one feels that the blood is of our blood, and the language of the same root as our own. The mouth of the Thames, and Rochester too, knew the daring Danes of old with terror; they came hither, pushed far inland, and did many dreadful deeds. But there was a bond of kinship between the two races that was strengthened when King Canute reigned over England and the three northern kingdoms, with England for his headquarters, his royal seat. Some traces of this union still linger here. Worsaae, in his interesting work on England, has fully shown us the many Danish memories, still preserved in the names of places, and even in songs and sayings. When the evening wind rises, and sounds over the heath its melancholy drone, that, says the peasant, is "the Danish boy's song"; the Danish lad is singing his lament. The saying went to my heart; for I thought of what my fatherland, the oldest kingdom in Europe, once had been; now it is only by art and science, by song and sculptor's chisel, that its name is borne over the sea that parts this rich land from West Jutland.

'It is impossible to feel at home in a country till one becomes intimate with its daily speech. One soon learns enough to read the language, and make one's own meaning pretty clear; but not enough to understand other people. We can find words for expressing our own thoughts – words that we have worked up: but those around us have quite an endless store of them. The whole language, with all its riches, and all its shades of meaning, stands at their disposal; and we acquire a variety of expressions new and strange to us.

'I soon understood any single speaker who addressed me; but when the whole circle kept up a lively talk, the words ran too fast into each other, and I sat like a deaf man among the talkers. But gradually the ear grows familiar with various sounds and tones; and just as in a fog, one's eye catches a hill-top here, another there, and presently the lesser outlines of the landscape, so, after a while, my ear learnt to catch up stray words and phrases, till the general conversation became clear to me in parts, and at last in its entirety.

'The more ease I acquired in expressing myself, the stronger grew my desire to talk of something better than mere commonplace. I longed to exchange ideas – to be myself in my own proper person, and to find expressions in the foreign speech that would come to me naturally, like those of my mother tongue. Meanwhile, I felt more and more at home. Soon the younger children began to understand me; Baby, the youngest of all, who, the first day I asked him whether he liked me, had said bluntly, "I will put you out of the window", at length declared with a laughing face, that now he would put me "in of the window".'

On June 15 Dickens took Andersen to visit the Crystal Palace, which had just been reconstructed in Sydenham Park, mainly with the original material of which it had been built in Hyde Park for the Great Exhibition of 1851. In his diary Andersen wrote, 'It was the Handel Festival, really in the nature of a rehearsal for the forthcoming Centenary celebrations. *The Messiah* was performed, two thousand singers with music, over 10,000 audience [in fact there were 2,500 performers and the audience numbered 12,000]. Clara Novello sang solo, and began with "God Save the Queen". One of the directors, in whose house we left our cloaks, led us to a capital place in the gallery immediately opposite the Queen's box. The Crystal Palace is like a fairy city with wide, floating paths; a great marble basin was there with red, white and blue Lotus, creepers wound their way up from the earth around pillars; statues and flowering trees everywhere; figures of Natives under their natural trees; I saw too an enormous tree-trunk; there were rooms from Pompeii, French galleries, the whole ensemble fantastic like an arabesque. The sun was shining on the glass roof; an awning was stretched out within against the sun's rays. The wind whispered outside, and when the singing and the music rolled it vibrated in my heart; I was near to tears. When we came out later, fountains were playing; it was as if we were walking in Undine's garden; rainbows played, there must have been over a hundred fountains. Only the Blue Grotto has exerted such a magic power over me.'

In the evening they went to the Lyceum to see the Italian actress Ristori in Montanelli's *Camma*, written specially for her. By the end of the performance Andersen was too exhausted – the concert at the Crystal Palace had lasted four hours – to note down his opinion of Ristori, but later he wrote: 'Signora Ristori has an excellent appearance for the stage – noble features, lively eyes, and expressive action; the latter, indeed, too strong for my taste, and such as, I think, is only permissible in ballet, where mimic gestures have to take the place of words.' A month later he saw Ristori in *Macbeth* and this time was far more impressed by her: 'Her entire performance was pervaded by a deep psychological truth, terrible, yet never transgressing the limits of the beautiful. The sleep-walking scene was the highlight of the evening: no more faithful or moving picture of a woman utterly wrecked in body and mind has ever been, or can be, portrayed. Never shall I forget the strange, dry, deep voice in which the words were breathed, as if they were not utterances, but as if the thoughts from the depth within were revealed in these painful sighs, subdued, but so pitiful and heart-rending that they thrilled every nerve . . . It was as if the last remains of human nature waited under the curse of blood; you held your breath involuntarily – it was as if a despairing human soul cast out to annihilation passed by; its body seemed a mere husk. Something similar, akin in truth and genius, was brought to my mind by the very force of contrast – Jenny Lind's pure, innocent, womanly representation of the Sonnambula in the opera of that name.'

Next day Mrs Dickens and her daughters returned to Gad's Hill and Andersen and Walter Landor Dickens were invited to spend the night at Miss Burdett-Coutts's house. Andersen told

A Visit to Dickens

Henriette Wulff: 'Miss Burdett-Coutts is said to be one of the richest women in England. At any rate she is most benevolent, builds churches, gives rich alms, does unending good. Here I was last night and had a bedroom as never before, with a bathroom close by, a fire in the grate, priceless carpets, a view over the garden and Piccadilly. The whole of the large house was more than regal . . . I was told that many had courted this rich lady, but she refused every suitor, for she supposed it to be her money that pleased them. [At the age of sixty-seven she married William Ashmead-Bartlett, a man thirty-seven years younger than herself, who took her name and in 1885 was elected Conservative member of parliament for Westminster.] She is very straightforward, most kind and good-natured, and I could much better approach her than her all-too-grand servants.'

Andersen's visit was divided between domesticity at Gad's Hill and social life and sight-seeing in London. It was the year of the Indian Mutiny – full news of which had not reached England during Andersen's visit; of the first Pre-Raphaelite exhibition, of *Coral Island*, *Barchester Towers* and *Tom Brown's School Days*. 'It was also', said Disraeli, 'the age of statistical imposture.' Dickens's friend, the author and dramatist Douglas Jerrold, had died on June 8 and Dickens organized a performance of Wilkie Collins's *The Frozen Deep* for the benefit of Jerrold's widow. The cast included the author Thackeray, the actor Macready, Bulwer, Mark Lemon, the editor of *Punch*, Dickens himself, who was a born actor, his two daughters and eldest son, both his sisters and his brother Alfred. This was given on July 4 at the Gallery of Illustration in Regent Street. In his diary Andersen noted: 'She [the Queen] had wished to see it, said Dickens, but here in England it was not customary for the Queen to go to a private house; therefore she could not come to him, and his daughters, who had not been presented at Court, could not therefore play at Buckingham Palace, so this was a compromise . . .' The Queen, who was thirty-eight years old at this time, arrived at 9 p.m. accompanied by Prince Albert, the King of the Belgians, the Princess Royal, Princess Alice, Princess Charlotte of Belgium, the Prince of Wales, Prince Alfred, Prince Frederick William of Prussia, the Count of Flanders and the Prince of Hohenzollern-

Sigmaringen. According to Andersen: 'The piece was well played, the author performing the part of the happy lover, Dickens that of the unhappy one, which is the main part. He showed himself to be a quite remarkable actor, so free from all those mannerisms one finds in England and France just in tragic parts. It was so true, so natural, as we at home might see Wiehe [a leading actor at the Royal Theatre] play the part. The death-scene so moving that I burst into tears at it. Following was a farce after the French . . . Dickens here was so rich in humour and fun that it was a fresh revelation. Mark Lemon, editor of *Punch*, played the second rôle with so much liveliness and truth that it was a joy. After the performance I drove over to the *Household Words* office, where the actors, actresses and the whole company gathered for a lively, cheerful supper – we drank champagne.'

While Andersen was at Gad's Hill he found that his latest novel, *To Be or Not to Be*, had received a bad review in *The Athenaeum*. He fled to the garden, where Mrs Dickens found him in tears and immediately concluded that some terrible disaster had occurred. Dickens was sympathetic, but urged him to pull himself together and consider that even if he had written a bad book this meant nothing; the greatest writers had done that – and his work would not be admired all over the world if he were not a great writer. The whole-hearted intensity of Andersen's reaction astonished Dickens, who was not only a far more robust and fulfilled character than Andersen but had never known such prolonged humiliations as had come Andersen's way. Their earning powers too, in those days when publication abroad brought the author merely reputation, were very different. Once Dickens asked Andersen what royalties he had received for *The Improvisatore*, and when the latter replied 'Nineteen pounds', Dickens asked 'Per sheet?' and was at first unable to believe that Andersen had meant for the whole book. Dickens's earnings enabled him, despite the size of his family, to live luxuriously, but Andersen's genius and industry scarcely earned him a living and a natural result was the development of a rumbustious independence in Dickens and of a deep-seated lack of self-confidence in Andersen, which made for misunderstanding between them in daily life. Though Dickens was sincere in his

A Visit to Dickens

expressions of admiration for Andersen's work, he certainly did not care for him personally to anything like the degree to which the emotional Andersen cared for him. Andersen did not realize that Dickens was exasperated by his despair over a bad notice, nor could he do so, since what impressed him about the incident was Dickens's kindness – 'Dickens discovered what was the matter, and now he displayed his most dazzling powers of conversation, of wit and humour; and when these failed to irradiate the darkest corners of my mind, came earnestness beaming with true kindness, and such cordial recognition, that I felt myself inspired with new strength, and full of desire and craving to deserve it. I looked at my friend's mild beaming eyes, and felt myself indebted to my unkind critic for having procured me one of the happiest moments of my life – the rich amber of sympathy cast up by the sea of sorrow . . . Presently I regained my spirits, saw the world in sunshine – and this must be the effect of living with Dickens.'

At last, however, in his own words: 'The morning of separation came: I was to leave the celebrated living author, and before reaching Denmark was to behold the apotheosis of Germany's poetical greatness; I was invited to the festivities on the occasion of the unveiling of the statues of Goethe, Schiller, and Wieland. From the land of Shakespeare, from the home of Dickens, I went to the land of the Minnesingers, to the town of the poets – to Weimar.

'Dickens had the horses put to his little carriage, and himself drove me to Maidstone, whence I went by rail to Folkestone, where the steamers depart for the Continent. Dickens and I had thus the opportunity of being together yet a few hours in the loveliest part of Kent, amid rich fields and splendid woodland. Dickens was bright and cheerful, but I could not overcome my dejection; I felt that the parting moment drew nigh. At the railway station we embraced each other. I looked into the true eyes of him in whom I admire the poet and love the man. Once more we pressed each other's hands, and he drove away. I rushed off with the train. Past – past – and so will all stories be!'

The difference between their respective attitudes towards each other is perceptible in the letters they exchanged immediately after Andersen had returned to the Continent. From Maxen, Andersen wrote on August 1:

My dear good friend,

At last I can write. It has been long, indeed, far too long! But every day, nearly every hour, you have been in my thoughts. You and your home have almost become a part of my spiritual life, and how could it be otherwise? For many years I loved and admired you; that was through your writings; but now I know you yourself. None of your friends can be more closely attached to you than I. My visit to England, my sojourn with you, is a highlight in my life; therefore I stayed so long; therefore it was so hard for me to say goodbye. Indeed, when we journeyed together from Gadshill to Maidstone I was so heavy of heart that it was all but impossible for me to carry on a conversation; I was on the verge of tears. Since then, when I think of our parting, I feel intensely how hard it must have been for you, a few days later, to take leave of your son Walter on board the ship, and to know that you would not see him again for seven years. Even were I to write my letter in Danish I would not have the words with which to tell you how happy I was with you and how grateful I am. I realized every minute that you were good to me, that you were pleased to see me and were my friend. You may be sure that I appreciate what that means. Your good wife, too, received me so warmly, me the stranger. I realize that it cannot have been at all easy for the whole circle to have in its midst for weeks such a one as spoke English as badly as I, one who might seem to have fallen from the clouds. Yet how little was I allowed to feel it. Give them all my thanks. Baby said to me on the first day, when I arrived: 'I will put you out of the window'; but later he said that he would put me 'in of the window', and I attach his last words to the whole circle.

After having stayed in such a home and been so happy and occupied with it as I was, naturally Paris could be no resting-place for me. I felt myself to be in a hot beehive where no honey was to be found. The heat was oppressive; I had to leave, but made only short day journeys. Five whole days elapsed before I reached Frankfurt; not until the 27th was I in Dresden, where I was expected by the Serre family. The following day was the birthday of the Master of the house, and that was to be celebrated in the house of one of his friends, the famous pianist and composer Henselt who lives for the greater part of the year in Petersburg, but resides in summer on his estate in Silesia. There we came to gaiety and festivity. Only yesterday did we return here to Serre's property in Maxen.

I am writing this letter in the early morning. It is to me as if I were delivering it myself. I am standing in your parlour in Gadshill, seeing, as I did on the day I first arrived there, roses in bloom round the windows, and the green fields stretching out towards Rochester. I am aware of the smell of apples from the hedge, of wild roses out towards the field, where your sons are playing cricket. Oh, how much may lie between now and the time I shall feel and see it in reality again, if indeed it will ever happen! But whatever time may unfold, my heart will, faithfully, lovingly and gratefully, cling to you, my great, noble friend. Make me happy soon with a letter, and then tell me, when you have read *To Be or Not to Be*, what you think of it. Forget in friendship the dark side which proximity may have shown you in me. I would so much like to live in good remembrance by one whom I love as a friend and brother.

Your faithful

HANS CHRISTIAN ANDERSEN

The reference to his own dark side shows that, despite his happiness as Dickens's guest, Andersen felt that all had not been between them as he would have wished.

On September 2 Dickens wrote from Gad's Hill:

My dear Andersen,

I have been away from here – at Manchester – which is the cause of this slow and late reply to your two welcome letters.

You are in your own home again by this time, happy to see its familiar face, I do not doubt, and happy in being received with open arms by all good Danish men, women and children.

Everything here goes on as usual. Baby (too large for his name, this long while!) calls 'auntie' all over the house, and the dogs come dancing about us and go running down the green lanes before us, as they used to do, when you were here. But the days are shorter and the evenings darker; and when we go up to the Monument to see the sunset, we are obliged to go directly after dinner, and it gets dark while we are up there, and as we pass the grim dog, who rattles with his chain, we can hardly see his dim old eyes, as we feed him with biscuit. The workmen, who have been digging in that well in the stableyard so long, have found a great spring of clear, bright water, and they got rather drunk, when they found it (not with the water, but with some Gin I gave them), and then they packed up their tools and went away, and now the big dog and the Raven have all that place to themselves. The corn-fields that were golden, when you were here, are ploughed up brown; the hops are being picked; the leaves on the trees are just beginning to turn; and the rain is falling, as I write, very sadly – very steadily.

We have just closed our labour in remembrance of poor Jerrold, and we have raised for his widow two thousand pounds. On Monday I am going away (with Collins) for a fortnight or so, into odd corners of England, to write some descriptions for *Household Words*. When I come back, I shall find them dining here by lamplight. And when I come back, I will write to you again.

I never meet any of the friends, whom you saw here, but they always say: 'How's Andersen – where's Andersen' – and I draw imaginary pictures of where you are, and declare, that you desired to be heartily remembered to them. They are always pleased to be told this. I told old Jerdan so, the other day, when he wrote to me asking when he has to come and see you!

All the house send you their kind regards. Baby says, you shall not be put out of the window, when you come back.

A Visit to Dickens

I have read *To Be or Not to Be* and think it is a very fine book – full of good purpose admirably wrought out – a book in every way worthy of its great author.

Good by, dear Andersen,

Affectionately your friend

CHARLES DICKENS

This was the last letter Andersen ever received from Dickens. Too sensitive to be unaware that something had gone wrong, he had written in his diary for June 30, 1857: 'I feel a desire to leave England, really happy I am not'; but what had occurred he never knew. In his masterly account of the Andersen-Dickens correspondence, Elias Bredsdorff says: 'Of that which they had in common, poverty and hardship in which they both grew up, they did not speak; and the friendship which developed between them was unequal; for the one gave himself entirely and without reserve to it, whereas the other, impulsively and for short periods, might give a strong impression by word and deed, of an affection and admiration which did not in fact go very deep.' Andersen was an exacting friend who could not help illogically hoping for as much emotion as he himself could give – and possibly Dickens felt that in this case his Danish colleague had wept by the waters of Babylon once too often. At any rate, Andersen had been right when, after sadly bidding Dickens farewell at Maidstone, he had told himself, 'Past – past – and so will all stories be.'

15. *Morning to Evening without an Afternoon*

1857-64

Human relations are a question of nerves.

> F. F. Roget, *Vaussore, A Son of Rousseau*, 1898

*

IN WEIMAR Andersen stayed with Beaulieu for the festivities in honour of the unveiling of statues of Goethe, Schiller and Wieland. Scenes were acted from Part II of Goethe's *Faust*, which had been finished only in 1831, twenty-three years after the completion of the first part. Liszt had composed music for the occasion but Andersen did not care for its 'waves of dissonance', so when Liszt invited him to dinner next day Andersen resolved to leave Weimar earlier than he had intended rather than offer Liszt insincere compliments or be embarrassingly silent on the subject. He did not guess that this was to be his last visit to Weimar, the demurely gay little court where he had known so much happiness ever since the days when he was still only an ugly duckling, a travelling apprentice.

At Kiel he heard that there was again cholera in Denmark, and after a few days in Copenhagen, where he found many changes – it was this year that the ramparts around Copenhagen were dismantled and that a law introducing internal free trade transformed Denmark into a liberal democracy – he went to stay with the Ingemanns at Sorø and then at the Scavenius family estate at Basnæs, where he worked on the first draft of *The Will-o'-the-Wisps Are in Town*, a story rewritten in another form eight years later.

Among the novelties of 1857 was the formation in Copenhagen

of a Mechanics' Institute, one of the associations for the diffusion of culture among the working classes that were a distinctive feature of nineteenth-century life in Western Europe and North America. Andersen was invited to read some of his stories to them, and although he was so nervous that he could not sleep the night before – 'it was no single important person as a hearer who disturbed my mind; no, it is the many, the multitude that make a mist as it were about me and depress me' – his reading was as successful as one of Dickens's readings. In his introductory speech Andersen said: 'In England, in the Royal Navy, through all the rigging, small and great ropes, there runs a red thread, signifying that it belongs to the Crown; through all men's lives there runs also a thread, invisible indeed, that shows we belong to God. To find this thread in small and great, in our own life and in all about us, the poet's art helps us, and it comes in many shapes.' His success with this audience had a particular emotional significance for him, for among these working-class men with their thirst for knowledge, their response to poetry, he felt himself his father's son and tried to give them a little of the kind of help for which his father had longed.

That June he went to Maxen and Bremen, but this trip was ruined for him by terrible news from home. Since the deaths of Admiral Wulff and of his wife, Andersen's friend, their daughter Henriette Wulff, had made her home with her brother Christian, a naval lieutenant. Out of devotion to her brother, and for the good of her health, she often accompanied him on his voyages, and in this way had visited Italy, the West Indies and America. On the latter trip they travelled on a ship infected with yellow fever, which Christian caught and of which, despite Henriette's nursing, he died. Grief-stricken, she found a home at Englewood, New Jersey, with Fredrika Bremer's friends, kindly Marcus and Rebecca Spring. Marcus Spring was a prosperous trader in textiles and his wife Rebecca was a rich Quaker; both were keenly interested in intellectual and social problems. It was they who in 1846 had taken the brilliant and eccentric Margaret Fuller to Europe. When, the following year, Henriette returned to Europe, she and Andersen saw each other nearly every day. Andersen found her obsessed by her brother's death and by her own possible return to America, where he was buried. All summer she thought restlessly of America, and in September she sailed on the *Austria*. Once aboard, her feelings changed and from England she wrote to her sister that she did not feel drawn to anyone on board and longed to give up the journey, yet would be ashamed to do so. Soon afterwards news reached Denmark that the *Austria* had caught fire in the Atlantic and sunk. There was no immediate news of the survivors and Henriette was not among them. Her eldest brother Peter, a naval captain, wrote to a surviving officer, who told him that while the ship was being fumigated by burning tar, the tar-barrel was upset and its smoke and flames quickly spread all over the ship. Henriette, who had been seen at breakfast, was thought to have been suffocated in her state-room.

For a long time the loss of Henriette and the manner of her death obsessed Andersen. He would pray that if communication were possible between the living and the dead he might have a sign from her, if only in dreams; he reproached himself with having neglected old friends lately, and one day he was so perturbed that while walking in the street, he had a visual hallucination that the houses on either side were bearing down on him like the giant waves of some monstrous sea. His imagination conjured up picture after picture of shipwrecks as terrible as Géricault's *Le Radeau de la Méduse*, and his grief and horror combined to increase the dread of sea travel that prevented him from ever accepting the many invitations he received to visit America.

Some of Andersen's finest stories were written at this time, including *The Marsh King's Daughter*, of which he himself said: 'This belongs to one of those stories on which I have worked hardest, and perhaps some people may be interested to see, as through a microscope, how it has grown and takes its form. The substance of it comes suddenly, like all my fairy tales, just as a well-known melody or song can come to one. I immediately told the entire fairy tale to one of my friends; then it was written down and rewritten; but even for the third time it stood upon the paper, I would realize that entire parts did not work out as clearly and distinctly as they could and must. I read some of the

Icelandic sagas and through these was carried back in time and inspired by them. I came closer to the truth. I read a few of the current sketches of travel from Africa; the tropical profusion and strange novelty took possession of me; I saw the country and was able to talk about it with more authority. A few books on the flight of birds were also of value. They suggested new ideas and gave characteristic expression of the life of birds, such as I have used in this fairy tale. So, in a short time I had rewritten it five or six times, until I was finally quite certain that I could do no better with it.'

His new stories were awaited by his international public as eagerly as Dickens's novels, and in the spring of 1859 – the year that Darwin published his concept of evolution in *The Origin of Species* – Andersen was invited by King Frederik VII to spend two days at Frederiksberg and read him *The Wind Tells about Valdemar Daae and His Daughters*. This was based on old legends substantiated by historical records at Borreby Manor near Skjelskør. Andersen had rewritten it again and again so as to 'give the language something of the effect of the shining, moving wind'. Throughout Andersen's stay at Frederiksberg the weather was beautiful, meals were eaten out of doors, they sailed on the lake, and before Andersen left the King gave him a ring bearing his monogram in diamonds.

That summer he went to Jutland and found himself made as much of in his own country as if he had been abroad. It was in this still wild countryside that for the first time he saw pitch-black storks strutting on the moors and eagles sweeping down to seize fish from the lakes. A visit to Skagen and the west coast gave him material for *A Story from the Sand Dunes*, a long story, what would now be called a novella, which gives an extraordinarily clear and haunting picture of Jutland as it was in those days and its legends, almost all concerning the sea and shipwrecks: '. . . the peasants found a corpse on the shore and buried it in the churchyard; then the sand began to fly about, and the sea broke in with violence. A wise man of the parish advised that the grave be opened, for if the stranger was found sucking his thumb, they could then be sure that he whom they had buried was a merman, and that the sea would not rest until it had fetched him back. So they opened the grave, and sure enough, the dead man lay with his thumb between his lips. He was quickly laid on a cart drawn by two oxen, and as though stung by hornets they rushed with him over heath and moor to the sea. That stopped the shower of flying sand, but the dunes that formed it are still there.'

In his notes to the collected edition of his stories in 1858 Andersen wrote of Jutland and this story: 'I found here the beauty of nature and the mode of living that I could use as the foundation for the thoughts I wanted to incorporate into my writing, thoughts which had long possessed me, and had as their origin a conversation with Adam Oehlenschläger, the Danish poet. His words made a deep impression on my young mind, but at that time I thought only of the words and did not clearly understand them as I do now. We talked about eternity, and Oehlenschläger remarked, "Why are you so sure that there is a life after this?" I assured him that I was thoroughly convinced and based it on God's righteousness, but in telling him I used the ill-chosen words, "Man can demand it". Then he continued, "Is it not a lot of vanity for you to dare ask for an everlasting life? Has God not given you infinitely much in this world? I know", he continued, "what wonderful blessings God has granted me; when in death I close my eyes, I will thankfully pray and bless him; and should he grant me still an everlasting life, then I would receive it as a new and infinite grace." "It is easy for you to say so," I said. "God has given you so much on this earth; and I, too, must say that; but think how many live in this world who cannot say that – people born with sick bodies, diseased minds, living their lives under the most heartbreaking conditions, full of sorrow and want. Why should they suffer so, why is our allotment so unequal? That is wrong, and God can do no wrong. Therefore God will give compensation. He will do what we cannot do. He will give us eternal life!" This conversation gave me the idea for *A Story from the Sand Dunes*.'

In November he received a letter from King Max of Bavaria bestowing the Order of the Knights of Maximilian upon him. Only one other foreigner, the French astronomer and physicist Arago whom Andersen had seen cheered at Perpignan, had previously been honoured with this. He was also informed that

the Danish Parliament had raised his pension from six hundred
to a thousand rigsdalers a year. From Sorø he went to the Scavenius
family at Basnæs, spent Christmas amid snow, sleigh-bells and
wild swans singing at the sea's edge, and was back in Copenhagen
for Jonas Collin's eighty-fourth birthday. In August he had a disturbing dream that he paid a flying visit to his home. 'I went to
old Collin, found him on the stairs in his old blue coat. I said I had
come to see him once more. He burst into tears, embraced me
with a loud cry, so that I awoke and the thought trickled through,
icy cold: "He died at this minute." Old Jonas Collin did not in
fact die until the following year.' Now that Thorvaldsen,
Oehlenschläger, Ørsted and Henriette Wulff were dead he was
beginning to have that feeling of being a survivor that often marks
the second half of the life of those without children. It was as if
his life had gone from morning to evening without an afternoon.
He was glad when the spring of 1860 arrived 'and with it travel
time'.

After another visit to Sorø he went to a Captain Lönborg and
his wife, J. M. Thiele's youngest daughter, in Slesvig, where he
was asked to prolong his stay and give a reading for the Danish
soldiers stationed there. At midnight, after the reading, he and
his hosts were aroused by noise outside and imagined that this
might be a demonstration on the part of pro-German elements in
the town – instead it proved to be a crowd of admirers come to
sing 'Sleep well'! In the morning a military band played outside
the house, and the soldiers to whom he had read came to the
station to cheer him as his train left.

Planning to spend the winter in Italy, he crossed Germany via
Eisenach and Nuremberg, stopped to visit Regensburg, an ancient
city famous during the crusades for its boatmen who conveyed
pilgrims and warriors down the Danube on their way to the
Holy Land, and also the near-by Valhalla built by King Max's
father. From Munich he made an excursion to Oberammergau
to see the Passion Play. Andersen had read an account of the
1850 performance by Edward Devrient, one of a famous family
of German actors. This year, 1860 – the play was only performed
every ten years – performances began on May 28 and were to
continue once a week until September 16. The village was

crowded with visitors. Andersen wrote: 'There was life and stir in the houses and without; the townsfolk and peasants bustled about, the bells rang; cannon were fired, the pilgrims came singing on their winding way. The whole night long there was song and music, plenty of excitement but no rioting. The next morning Pastor Daisenberger took me to the theatre that had been built of beams and boards on the green plain outside the town. At eight o'clock the miracle play was to begin, and would continue, with only an hour's intermission, until five in the afternoon. We sat under the open sky; the wind sighed above us, the birds came and flew out again. I thought of the old Indian play in the open air where the *Sakuntala* was given and of the ancient Greek theatre . . . I saw before me the stage for the chorus, and the chorus-leaders who entered singing. Recitative and speech gave connection to the action. The whole story of the Passion, illustrated by parallel pictures from the Old Testament, was given by living pictures . . . There was an ease and beauty about it that must impress everyone. It is said that the persons whom the community unanimously appoint to the sacred rôles must be of spotless life, and that the one who represents Christ always, before the beginning of the Passion, partakes of the sacrament at the altar.'

In Munich Hanfstængl took one of the earliest photographs of Andersen, who was 'completely surprised, amazed that the sunlight should have made such a figure of beauty out of my face. I am incredibly flattered, and yet it is only photography.' From Munich he went on to Le Locle, the little town in the Jura mountains where in 1833 he had written *Agnete and the Merman*. In those earlier days the ascent had been a laborious one made by diligence; now he was able to go by train and was impressed by the long tunnels through which it passed. Andersen had his old room in the Houriets' house, which now belonged to their nephew, Jules Jürgensen, who was busy exporting watches to America. One hundred and eighty years ago there had not been a watchmaker in the district, now the industry supported 20,000 men.

While in Geneva he heard of Heiberg's death at the age of sixty-nine. Although there had been differences between them,

Hans Christian Andersen in 1860

Jenny Lind

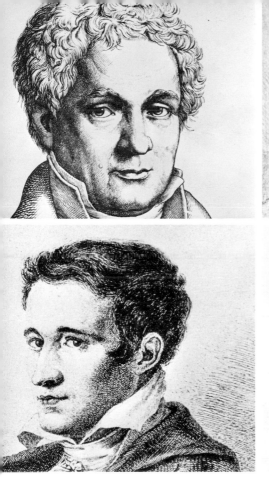

Johann Ludwig Tieck
Jakob Grimm
Bettina von Arnim

Wilhelm Grimm
Felix Mendelssohn
Heinrich Heine

Alexandre Dumas père
Victor Hugo
Richard Wagner

Alphonse de Lamartine
Ludwig II of Bavaria
Franz Liszt

Charles Dickens   *Richard Bentley*

Gad's Hill, Dickens's home

Andersen at Frijsenborg in 1865

Andersen on the steps of Rolighed in 1867, with the artist Carl Bloch and Moritz Melchior

Mary Livingstone

Andersen reading aloud to children

Above, Andersen's travelling bags, presented to him by the King of Denmark. Below, Andersen taking leave of the servants at Rolighed. His personal servant Jens is on the left

Andersen remembered chiefly all the kindnesses Heiberg had done him during his early years in Copenhagen. Andersen's feeling for the past was exceptionally acute. As a man of fifty-five he wrote in his diary: 'Again tonight I dreamed that I was with Meisling, could say nothing, knew nothing, felt terribly dependent on old Collin; also on Edvard in whom I tried to confide . . .' After Heiberg's death he noted: 'I am sometimes overcome by a diabolical weakness . . . I felt in Geneva as if something compelled me to throw myself in the Rhône . . .' He gave up his plan to visit Italy and Spain, where there was again cholera, and went home and to Basnæs, where he wrote *The Beetle*, a story prompted by Dickens. 'In a number of *Household Words*, Charles Dickens collected numerous Arabian proverbs and sayings. Among them was this: "When the Emperor's horse got his golden shoes, the beetle also stretched his leg out." "We recommend", said Dickens in a note, "that Hans Christian Andersen write a story about this." I did have a desire to do so, but no story came. Not until nine years after, during a visit to the homelike manor of Basnæs, when I accidentally read Dickens's words again, did the story of *The Beetle* suddenly develop.'

In the spring of 1861 – the year of the American Civil War – Andersen took Edvard's son Jonas abroad with him. Twenty-one-year-old Jonas was dedicated to science and zoology and convinced that literature was a waste of time, so he proved a bracing companion, who frequently lectured Andersen for his own good. To old Collin, Andersen had been a poor boy deserving help; to Edvard an over-emotional brother to be admonished; to young Jonas he was a nice old uncle who must be brought up to date.

They went via Geneva and Lyons to Nice, which had just been ceded by Italy to France. It was already a fashionable resort and the Promenade des Anglais, built by subscriptions from wealthy visitors, was nearly twenty years old. From there they drove along the Corniche, stopping to look at the 'rocky little kingdom of Monaco lying in the sunshine like a toy'. The journey from Nice to Genoa took a day and a half, and at Genoa, which Andersen had not seen since 1846, they went by steamer to Civita Vecchia.

This was the Italy of Garibaldi and his Thousand, whose exploits resulted in the unification of Italy this year under the rule of the House of Piedmont. So far no one had bothered Andersen and young Jonas for their passports, but once they reached the Papal States – Rome did not become part of United Italy until 1870 – they encountered the usual official fussiness, were woken at midnight to show their passports, obliged to obtain permits to travel by rail to Rome and to ask the Danish consul for residence cards. On this, his fourth visit to Rome, Andersen took rooms for Jonas and himself over the Caffè Greco near his friend Bravo, Consul for Denmark, Sweden and Norway. Then he set about showing Jonas the sights.

It was during this visit that Andersen first met Björnstjerne Björnson, the great Norwegian dramatist, twenty-seven years his junior. Björnson was only just beginning to be famous and was known to have a volcanic temperament. Old friends of Andersen, presuming as old friends will on opinions formed long ago, had assured him that he would dislike Björnson's work. In fact Andersen appreciated it readily and when the two men met in Rome they took an immediate liking to each other. Björnson, who was fascinated by Nordic legends, Walter Scott and Ingemann, said that no one could help liking Andersen for his originality and the love that shone through his words, and he soon added that although there was no Dane about whom so many jokes could be told, none since Holberg had told so many against himself. He also liked young Jonas – who was only eight years younger than himself – for his strength of character, and said, 'Stormy as my life is bound to be, I may need such people.'

The Scandinavian artists gave a party for Bravo and Andersen at a tavern described by Andersen in his story *Psyche*: 'On the outskirts of Rome there was a tavern frequented by artists. It was built in the ruins of an old Roman bath chamber. Large yellow lemons hung down among dark, shining leaves, partly covering the old red-yellow walls. The tavern was in the form of a deep vault, almost like a cave in the ruins. A lamp burned inside before a picture of the Madonna. A large fire blazed in the fireplace, and food was being fried, cooked and roasted. Outside, under the lemon and laurel trees, stood two tables, all prepared.'

While in Rome Andersen made the acquaintance of William Wetmore Story, the American sculptor, then aged forty-two, who lived in Rome with his wife and children and was writing that unparalleled guide to Rome, *Roba di Roma*. It was Story who generously helped Robert Browning look after Walter Savage Landor in the latter's unhappy old age. He took Andersen to his studio and showed him a statue of Beethoven and an allegorical representation of America, and invited him to his apartments where Andersen read *The Ugly Duckling* to a party of children. Describing the Storys' life in Rome at this time in *William Wetmore Story and His Friends*, Henry James writes: '. . . a pleasant legend of kind distinguished visitors still survives, one of them incomparably benevolent to a languid little girl who needed amusement and was to be for ever grateful. Hans Andersen, whose private interest in children and whose ability to charm them were not less marked than his public, knew his way well to the house, as later to Palazzo Barberini (to the neighbourhood of which *The Improvisatore* was able even to add a charm); where the small people with whom he played enjoyed, under his spell, the luxury of believing that he kept and treasured – in every case and as a rule – the old tin soldiers and broken toys received by him, in acknowledgment of favours, from impulsive infant hands. Beautiful the queer image of the great benefactor moving about Europe with his accumulations of these relics. Wonderful too our echo of a certain occasion – that of a children's party, later on – when, after he had read out to his young friends *The Ugly Duckling*, Browning struck up with *The Pied Piper*; which led to the formation of a grand march through the spacious Barberini apartment, with Story doing his best on a flute in default of bagpipes.'

On May 17 Story took Andersen to see Elizabeth Barrett Browning. Aged fifty-five, and within seven weeks of her death, she looked shockingly fragile, gazed at Andersen with lustrous gentle eyes, pressed his hand and thanked him for his writings. She told Thackeray, 'Hans Christian Andersen is here, charming to us all, and not least to the children'; and to another friend she wrote, 'Andersen (the Dane) came to see me yesterday – kissed my hand, and seemed in a general *verve* for embracing. He is very earnest, very simple, very childlike. I like him. Pen [her twelve-year-old son] says of him, "He is not really pretty. He is rather like his own ugly duck, but his mind has developed into a swan." – That wasn't bad of Pen, was it?' Her last poem, written that same month and published posthumously, was for Andersen and ended:

'Yet O, for the skies that are softer and higher,'
    Sighed the North to the South;
'For the flowers that blaze and the trees that aspire,
And the insects made of a song or a fire!'
    Sighed the North to the South.

'And O, for a seer to discern the same!'
    Sighed the South to the North;
'For a poet's tongue of baptismal flame
To call the tree or the flower by its name!'
    Sighed the South to the North.

The North sent therefore a man of men
    As a grace to the South;
And thus to Rome came Andersen:
'Alas! but must you take him again?'
    Said the South to the North.

As it grew hotter and those who could afford to do so left Rome for the hills, Andersen and Jonas started for home, going through Florence to Leghorn, where they sailed for Genoa. Here they heard cannon volleys. These announced the death of Count Cavour, the aristocratic liberal who had helped found the newspaper *Il Risorgimento* in 1847 and had advocated a constitution which the King had granted in 1848. It was on Cavour's advice that Italy had taken part in the Crimean War and thus been in a position to raise the Italian question at the Congress of Paris in 1856. In 1858 he had planned to drive the Austrians out of Italy and had obtained Napoleon III's support by giving Nice and Savoy to France. He had just lived to see Victor Emmanuel II proclaimed King of all Italy except Rome and Venetia. Andersen and Jonas spent a few days at Isola Bella before returning to Switzerland. In Montreux the story of a bridal couple drowned during their honeymoon off a little island near Villeneuve gave Andersen the idea for his story *The Ice Maiden*.

At Brunnen they met a Father Gall-Mosel, librarian of the Abbey of Einsiedeln, the birthplace of Paracelsus. This beautiful abbey, near Zürich, one of the finest examples of baroque art, was celebrating its thousandth anniversary. Andersen and Jonas were shown the treasures of Einsiedeln library, including an old Danish Bible. The latter was very worn, and as the librarian wanted a new one, Andersen subsequently sent one which can be seen today at Einsiedeln.

Immediately after his arrival in Denmark, Andersen heard that Jonas Collin was dead. He had been eighty-five years old and during his last days had recognized no one. For the second time Andersen had lost a father, and the second time was even more painful than the first. He hurried to Copenhagen. 'All the old friends are going and the new ones are never like the old . . . it is strange to see the ranks marching off like this, one after the other. The rank in which I am is coming to the front now, so I suppose that will march off next.'

The train to Copenhagen was crowded and Andersen shared a compartment with two ladies. The younger of them, a beautiful dark-eyed young woman – 'her black eyes shone and carried on an entire conversation before she began to speak' – was lying full length on the seat enjoying her fruit and refreshments. She told him in French that she believed she knew him. Andersen asked her name, and when she said Pepita he recognized her as a Spanish dancer who had been almost submerged by flowers at the Casino the previous year. She told him that she had been in a play of his, *Ole Lukøie*, in which she had played the part of the Spanish dancer with whom the young chimney-sweep falls in love in a dream. Too absorbed by grief for Collin to want to talk to strangers, Andersen changed carriages at the next stop and so cut short this personal encounter with the famous Pepita Oliva, whose liaison with a young English diplomat, Lionel Sackville-West, was to contribute gipsy blood to one of the great English families.

It was a terrible shock to Andersen to see old Collin in his coffin. As a child he had always looked forward, now he could only look back. In a letter to Ingemann at Christmas, which he spent at Holsteinborg surrounded by presents and affection, he wrote: 'I had many thoughts yesterday of my Christmas times in childhood, the richest in memory I have ever spent, even though the room was small and I had no Christmas tree. But grits, goose and apple-pie were never lacking, and in the evening there were two candles on the table. I have half a century of Christmas memories. How miraculous my fate has been.' That Christmas's book of fairy stories brought him an appreciative note from King Frederik and a long letter from Björnson, to whom he had dedicated them, ending: 'Dear, dear Andersen, how much I have loved you, yet I was sure you neither rightly understood me nor cared for me, although with your good heart you would gladly do both; but now I see clearly what a happy mistake I made, and so I have been deceived into doubling my affection for you.'

Early in the New Year Andersen received a letter from Ingemann in which the latter mentioned Ørsted. Ingemann and Ørsted had never met, but with his characteristic desire that his friends should appreciate each other, Andersen had often repeated the sayings of one to the other, thus creating a friendship by proxy. In this letter Ingemann wrote: 'This morning I was at the railway station and as I sat under the telegraph wires they began to hum . . . What does Ørsted want? The wires buzzed and talked. What in the world is going on up there? Then I felt it run through me – Ørsted knows I am going to write to Andersen today and so he is saying "Greet him for me!" '

This was the last letter Andersen ever received from Ingemann. In February 1862 he opened a newspaper and read that his old friend was dead. His thoughts returned to the days when the young poet had discerned promise in the uncouth schoolboy from Odense and he wrote to Mrs Ingemann: '. . . it must be for you like a tragic dream, from which you wake up and long to see him by you . . . we were both of us so young and yet now, all at once after all these years, old enough to go with him. I long for him . . . Do not be at pains to answer this letter, you have no mind for that now . . .' At the beginning of March he went to see Mrs Ingemann, and was shaken to find himself once more in the house where 'from my school days in Slagelse until now an old man, I had spent such happy hours, where our talk had gone on in earnest and in jest'.

With him Andersen took a four-leaved clover that had been sent him for Christmas by a Danish student, who wrote to him that as a child he had loved Andersen's stories and when told by his mother that Andersen had as a boy known hard times, had been so saddened that he had gone out into the fields and searched until he found a four-leaved clover which he asked his mother to send to Andersen. Now the boy's mother was dead, and, going through her belongings, he had found the four-leaved clover in her prayer-book. He told Andersen: 'I have just been reading your new story *The Ice Maiden*, and I read it with the same pleasure as when I read your stories in my childhood. Fortune has favoured you, and you do not need the four-leaved clover, but I send it to you and tell you this little incident.' Another letter of admiration reached him at this time from Horace E. Scudder, a twenty-four-year-old American writer who had contributed an article on Andersen to the *National Quarterly Review of Literature* for September 1861. As a result the young American and the elderly Dane became friends by correspondence, and in 1868, 1869 and 1870 Andersen gave eleven stories to *The Riverside Magazine for Young People*, of which Scudder was then editor. After this magazine ceased publication Scudder joined *Scribner's Monthly*, which serialized Andersen's short novel *Lucky Peer* and published three of his last stories.

After spending the spring in familiar haunts – Basnæs, Holsteinborg, Lerchenborg – Andersen decided to go abroad again. He was an assiduous buyer of lottery-tickets and had told Jonas Collin that if he won the lottery he would take him to Spain, perhaps even as far as Africa. As usual the lottery failed him, but at this point his Danish publisher told him that his collected works were sold out and offered him 3,000 rigsdalers for a new edition with additional stories. As he had received only 300 rigsdalers for the first and expensively illustrated edition, this seemed to him a windfall and he told Jonas to start packing.

After visiting Mrs Ingemann at Sorø, where he found Ingemann's room unchanged, 'as if he had gone out for a walk and might come home again any minute', and discussed the forth-coming edition of Ingemann's writings and the account of his life that Andersen had helped prepare, he and Jonas went to Flens-burg in time for the unveiling of the war memorial, a lion designed by Bissen that was transferred to Copenhagen in 1945. They were to meet Jonas's parents and sister, who were on their way to Italy, at Brunnen, and accompany them to Interlaken, Berne and Montreux, which last was reputed to be the place with the 'lowest rate in the world of deaths and imprudent marriages'. There the party separated, the Collins going to Italy and Andersen and Jonas across France to Spain. The railway stopped at Perpignan, where they took 'that tortoise-like torture box mis-named a diligence' to Spain, which they entered on the forty-third anniversary of Andersen's first arrival in Copenhagen.

From Gerona they went by slow train to Barcelona. Its glittering cafés seemed to Andersen to outdo those of Paris and he was shudderingly impressed by the Palace of the Inquisition. Here for the first time he attended a bullfight. Originally an exhibition of horsemanship, courage and dexterity in which the bull was attacked by gentlemen armed only with a lance modelled on the Iberian spears shown on old Roman-Iberian coins, the bullfight had been transformed by the conquering Moors into a game for professionals and stripped of its chivalrous character. In much the same way the tournaments of chivalry developed into today's boxing-matches. Having expected to loathe this spectacle un-reservedly, Andersen was astonished by its equivocal effect on him – 'was very near fainting, and yet I could not prevail on myself to quit the bullfight which I was now seeing for the first, and possibly for the last, time. There was something so interesting and attractive in the suppleness and strength, the alertness and dexterity . . . it is just like a stylized game, like a dance on the stage.' He would have agreed with John Murray's guide-book that 'the interest of the awful tragedy is undeniable, irresistible and all-absorbing. The display of manly courage, nerve and agility, and all on the verge of death, is most exciting . . . We must pause before we condemn the bull in Spain, while we wink at the fox at Melton or the pheasant in Norfolk. In Spain the animals are killed outright, not left to linger . . .'

While in Barcelona they saw a flood, torrents from the mountains rushing down the main street and into houses and churches where priests said mass while up to their waists in water. From there they sailed to Valencia, a city of spires and blue-and-white-tiled domes that had been captured by El Cid in 1094. They visited Alicante and Elche, with its great palm trees and cave-dwelling gipsies, and at the end of September they sailed from Cartagena, 'where nature and mankind were beautiful indeed – and red hot' to Málaga. Andersen was stirred by the Andalusian women, 'royally moving daughters of beauty, their eyes shining beneath long black eyelashes, their delicate hands playing gracefully with the fan'.

Granada was the high-spot of their Spanish journey. They left Málaga in a diligence drawn by ten mules with jingling bells, and as they reached the heights and took a last look back at the lights of Málaga a thunderstorm broke and a couple of guards arrived to escort them over a dangerous stretch of road. They reached Granada next day and immediately made for the Alhambra, which Andersen had longed to see ever since reading Washington Irving's *Alhambra*, published thirty years earlier. They found the Alhambra cluttered up with inept decorations for Queen Isabella's first visit to Andalusia, due to take place on October 9. For a week no one in Granada seemed to think of anything but the Queen's visit. Flags waved, church bells pealed, dancing-girls with castanets whirled through the streets, bands blared, and when at last the thirty-two-year-old Queen appeared, wearing a golden crown, she was showered with rose petals.

Once the Queen's visit was over Andersen and Jonas moved to an inn close by the walled-up gate of the Alhambra through which Boabdil, or Abu-Abdallah, the last Moorish King of Granada, had in 1491 ridden out of the city to be defeated by Ferdinand and Isabella. The place from which he had looked back at Granada for the last time after yielding the keys of the city to Ferdinand was still known as *el ultimo sospiro del Moro* (the Moor's last sigh). Andersen paid daily visits to the Sultan's rose-scented court, where great cypresses stood sentinel by crystalline fountains.

Next they sailed from Málaga to Tangier, stopping on the way at Gibraltar and reaching Tangier on November 2. All the consuls and Foreign Ministers to the Court of Morocco were stationed in Tangier, and Andersen and Jonas were welcomed by the British Minister, Sir Drummond Hay, whose Danish wife was the sister of the Carstensen who founded Copenhagen's Tivoli. He presented them to the Pasha, who invited them to tea in the paved courtyard of his palace, which reminded them of the Alhambra. Above the bustle of the city they could hear the voice of the Muezzin calling the faithful to prayer, and in the narrow lanes of the bazaar they heard the barbaric music of the snake-charmers and the voices of gesticulating story-tellers who would mark the pauses in their stories by beating a little drum. Most of the foreign officials had villas on a hill outside the city where there was boar-hunting and pig-sticking, and on the way there the travellers had their first sight of an encampment of Bedouins with their camels. From Algiers, which had been annexed by the French in 1842, they were to sail on a French vessel for Cádiz. They went aboard at sunset and when later, in the bay of Trafalgar, they stopped to measure the water's depth Andersen imagined they had struck a sandbank.

In Seville, still enclosed by Moorish walls of mud and lime, Andersen was captivated by Murillo's pictures. The church of La Caridad, where they went to see Murillo's 'Moses in the Bulrushes', had been turned into a hospital, but before that it had been a monastery founded by Miguel de Manara, who had ended his days as a monk there and written his own rather boastful epitaph, 'Here lies the worst man in the world.'

From Seville they went to Cordova, a quiet, deserted town 'where the spirit of desolation seemed to have spread a wide robe of forgetfulness over so much grandeur.' The great mosque was a plantation of pillars with a richly gilded Christian church in its midst. Hymns to Jesus and Mary resounded among Arabic inscriptions – 'There is only one God and Mohammed is his prophet.' Snow was falling in Madrid, and, except for the great picture-gallery, Andersen found it a disappointment after towns full of traces of the Moors. They made an excursion to Toledo, where they visited two synagogues that had been renamed Nuestra Señora del Transito and Santa Maria la Blanca, though on the walls remained the Hebrew inscription, 'Solomon's temples stand here still, but Israel's people are departed – the people that keep the law. There is only one true God.' The countryside was bleak and lonely. The only sounds to be heard were those of church bells, the hammering of Damascus blades, and an occasional passing train.

A Spanish writer, Don Sanibaldo di Mas, formerly Spanish ambassador to China, gave a reception so that Andersen could meet some Spanish writers, but rain, cold and bitter winds soon drove him from Madrid. They set out for France by rail, but at the Escorial a snowstorm was too much for the train and they were crowded into diligences and arrived frozen at San Childrian, where they had to wait several hours for another train. At Burgos they stopped to see the monastery where El Cid and his wife were buried, but they could not see El Cid's grave owing to the snow, so they took a train to Olazagutia, where they were again condemned to a diligence, in which they crossed the Pyrenees.

At the French frontier they found the sun shining, trees in bud and violets already out. They spent Christmas in Bayonne, with a candle stuck into a champagne bottle as a Christmas tree, and several days in Biarritz, which had been made fashionable by the Empress Eugénie. They met French and Danish friends in Bordeaux, where they heard Gounod's *Faust* for the first time. Andersen was enthusiastic about this opera, but his stage training made him object when Marguerite, returning from church and sitting down to spin, tossed her prayer-book into the wings.

Andersen found the Paris of Napoleon III very different from that of Louis-Philippe. Haussmann was at work widening streets, laying out boulevards and parks and building bridges. Björnson was in Paris, on his way home from Italy, and at his suggestion a group of prominent Scandinavians gave a reception for Andersen at a restaurant in the Palais Royal. He and Jonas lingered in Paris until late March, but were back in Copenhagen for his fifty-eighth birthday, after which he paid his usual spring and summer visits to Christinelund, Basnæs and Glorup, working all the time on a book about Spain.

In August Andersen returned to Copenhagen and his old routine of working and dining out. His *Elder Mother* was performed at the Casino, for which he now wrote a new play, and he adapted a play of Kotzebue's for the Royal Theatre and looked forward to a busy and contented winter. Soon, however, Denmark was to be again at war.

The southern duchies were still causing trouble. The German Confederation, to which Holstein now belonged, was constantly interfering in the internal affairs of Slesvig and trying to manœuvre it too into the Confederation. In order to check this, Denmark decided to give Holstein independent status and incorporate Slesvig into Denmark proper, thus at last separating the two duchies. An act to this effect was passed in the Danish parliament on November 13, 1863. Two days later, however, before he had had time to sign the act, Frederik VII died at Glücksburg castle in Slesvig.

When the news reached Copenhagen by telegraph, coastal guns thundered a salute to the last of the direct Oldenburg line and hundreds of people, Andersen among them, went to Christiansborg palace to hear Christian IX proclaimed King. The new King, who was forty-five, took three days deciding to endorse the new act, which was known as the November Constitution. Immediately the Duke of Augustenburg, whose father had renounced all his rights, proclaimed himself Duke not only of Slesvig but of a united Slesvig-Holstein – and he was backed by Prussia, thanks to Bismarck, who had become Chancellor of Prussia a year earlier at the age of forty-seven.

When the Duke of Augustenburg claimed the duchies, Bismarck decided to help 'liberate' them. As he was not yet ready to attack Austria, he made an alliance with her and offered the Duke of Augustenburg their joint support. A demand was then made that Denmark repeal the November Constitution in so short a time that, even had Denmark been willing, compliance would have been impossible from an administrative point of view. Bismarck had no intention of allowing Denmark to comply, since not only did he desire a war in which to try out his modernized army, but he wanted to control the bridge between the Baltic and the North Sea.

In Denmark a new government was formed. The army withdrew from Holstein to show that it had no design on that duchy, and took up positions along the southern border of Slesvig – 40,000 men for a sixty-mile front. On February 1, 1864, an Austro-Prussian army of 60,000 men crossed the river Eider under the leadership of General Wrangel (who would be fighting against Austria two years later). The Danes, commanded by General de Meza, who as an artillery cadet had shown such fearlessness on the battlements when the English bombarded Kronborg castle as to be reprimanded for wasting gunpowder, were outnumbered and in an untenable position since the Dannevirke, their ancient line of defence, had long ago collapsed in many places or been washed away, while the bogs and marshland that protected it were dried up and at that season covered by firm ice. The Danes managed to defeat a couple of attacks; then, since General de Meza's orders were that he was to keep his army intact and ready to fight in the spring, they withdrew from the Dannevirke to the Dybbøl. It took the men eighteen hours to march to Flensburg – there was a train that could have transported them in one-tenth of the time, but the High Command was not yet trained to think in terms of railways – and the retreat had such an appalling effect in Copenhagen that General de Meza was made the scapegoat and dismissed.

The Danes were not only outnumbered but faced with superior weapons. The Prussian breech-loading rifles could fire a dozen rounds to the Danish muzzle-loader's one. While the Prussians advanced into Jutland the Danes at Dybbøl held out heroically for two months, until at last the fortifications were completely destroyed. Then they retired to the little island of Als. When the Prussians bombarded the small defenceless town of Sønderborg, Lord Shaftesbury declared in the House of Lords that this was one of the most shameful and cruel acts that had ever taken place 'not only in civilized, but even in uncivilized warfare'. Her Majesty's Government called him to order. Ingeborg Collin Drewsen's son Viggo, for whom Andersen had years ago written one of his most popular poems, 'Little Viggo', was wounded at Dybbøl and left for dead on the battlefield, where the Prussians picked him up still alive. To Andersen, as to many other Danes and Germans, the war seemed fratricidal. In his diary he wrote:

'I feel how much kindness people in Germany have shown me, acknowledge friends there, and feel as a Dane that I must completely break with them all; they are torn out of my heart; we can never meet again: a beautiful past will not be renewed.' His dreams were full of blood and wounds and he had Füssli-like nightmares. Fear and sorrow carried him into deep waters as his sense of security became every day more precarious. This time insanity seemed to him to be without as well as within him.

As the concept of the balance of power, in the sense that no European state should gain new territory without the agreement of all the other states, was still widely accepted in theory, Denmark appealed to England, France and Russia. The Danes had great hopes of England, since Christian IX's beautiful seventeen-year-old daughter Princess Alexandra had the previous year married the Prince of Wales and the marriage was popular in both countries. 'Firebrand' Palmerston was known to sympathize with the Danes, but the majority of the cabinet and the opposition were against taking action and Queen Victoria imagined that Prince Albert, who had died in 1861, would have championed Prussia. England's neutrality was deplored in Denmark, not only for personal reasons. Nine years later Bishop Martensen told young Edmund Gosse: 'Your ministers hesitated until the moment for action was past, and they have let loose in Europe forces which may be directed against themselves. We have seen the Germans at Fredericia: I pray God you may not see them at Gravesend.' Nor was help forthcoming elsewhere. Napoleon III was in no position to intervene since he was on bad terms with England, faced opposition at home, and had committed himself to sending troops to Mexico. Russia had been put under sedation the previous year by Bismarck's promise of support against the Polish insurrection. Volunteers came from Norway and Sweden but nothing officially except expressions of sympathy – to the fury of Ibsen, who in disgust went to live in Italy. Many Danes, including Andersen, began to fear that their country would be dismembered and their language fall into disuse and become merely 'an echo from the North'.

Throughout this period Andersen's diary reveals intense nervous depression. 'Outside Holmen's Church I met a wounded guards officer, Rosen. He took me to the mortuary to see his brother's body . . . The evening sun shone. The verger raised the lid of the coffin. Rosen lay there, gentle and still, like one asleep. He looked stronger and happier than his living brother. I burst into tears. I felt compelled to go to Edvard and talk to him, yet he was not what I wanted . . .' He felt 'godless and bitter', frequently felt faint in the streets, and to his dismay found himself becoming increasingly short-tempered, as his diary shows. 'Was at Madame Meergaard's. Took Madame Hammerich in to dinner. "Shall we soon have something new from you? I suppose you are not much affected by what is happening," she said. "Do you mean to insult me?" I cried out in anger, losing my temper. She tried to smooth it over, but I was so overcome that I felt quite sick and had to leave . . .' Small news items in the papers made him weep, and he wrote in his diary: 'I lost for a moment my hold on God and felt myself as wretched as a man can be. Days followed in which I cared for nobody and believed that nobody cared for me.' Even the seemingly timeless peace of the manor houses was spoilt for him. After arriving in Basnæs in June he wrote: '. . . the apple-trees covered with red-white blossoms, cowslips in the grass . . . But the times are not the same as when I last saw the spring. I have seen violence and heard lying prevail, longed for death . . .' Religion was of no help to him. He felt utterly wretched. 'I had no relief in speaking to anyone.'

At sea the Danes had the upper hand and partially succeeded in blockading Germany and hampering her trade, but it was on land that the war had to be decided, and after Denmark was overrun by the Germans she was forced to sign the Treaty of Vienna, by which she surrendered Slesvig, Holstein and Lauenburg to 'their Majesties the King of Prussia and the Emperor of Austria' – for after fighting on behalf of the Duke of Augustenburg, Bismarck produced 'legal proof' that the Augustenburg family had long since relinquished its claims to the duchies, which therefore belonged to Christian IX, who had forfeited them by being defeated. Two years later Prussia attacked Austria and secured the duchies for herself alone.

The war cost Denmark almost a third of her territory and a fifth of her population, including 200,000 Slesvig Danes. She was now one of the smallest nations in Europe and it was widely believed that she would eventually be divided up between Germany and Sweden. At first people were stupefied. Later Andersen wrote: 'The year 1864 was heavy and bitter, a year of war, when Denmark lost Slesvig to Germany. And who could think of anything else? It was more than a year and a day before I wrote any story. *The Will-o'-the-Wisps Are in Town* developed from the heavy mood I was in during the time of war. It is a leaf from "The Fairy Tale of Time". It was written at Basnæs Manor in June, 1865.' This story begins: 'There was a man who once had known a great many new fairy tales, but he had forgotten them, he said. The fairy tale that used to come and visit him of its own accord no longer came and knocked at his door; and why didn't it come any more? It's true that for a year and a day the man hadn't thought of it, hadn't really expected it to come and knock; and it certainly wouldn't have come anyway, for outside there was war, and inside, the misery and sorrow that war brings with it. The stork and the swallow returned from their long journey, for they had no thought of danger. But when they arrived they found the nests burned, people's houses burned, and the fences smashed, yes, and some even completely gone, and the horses of the enemy were trampling down the old grave mounds.'

Of all his stories it is perhaps the one in which historical and poetic truth are most clearly mingled.

16. The Storm Shifts the Signboards

1865-7

... his hearing was *too* fine. Not only could he hear the grass grow, but he could hear every man's heart beat, whether in sorrow or in joy. To him the whole world was like the great workshop of a clockmaker, with all the clocks going 'Tick, Tock', and all the tower clocks striking 'Ding, Dong'. The noise was unbearable.

Hans Christian Andersen, *The Stone of the Wise Man*

'I love you so much, dear, dear Hans Andersen.'

A Letter from Mary Livingstone.

*

THE PRUSSIAN INVASION had reminded Andersen of what he had seen of the Napoleonic war when he was a child in Odense, so one of his next pieces of writing was a romantic three-act play, *When the Spaniards Were Here*, in which he had the then novel idea of not allowing the principal character, the Spaniard, to appear. The audience was to hear Spanish voices and the sounds of castanets off stage, and a Spaniard dominated the play through the strong impression he had made on all the Danish characters who were constantly discussing him. The play was accepted for the Royal Theatre but its performance was delayed, and on December, 24 1865 Andersen wrote in his diary:

Dreamed this morning some strange nonsense. My end was near. I was to be executed; the King was angry with me – I did not know why. I was not in prison. I went to my barber, who said that I was to be executed with ten others. Thorvaldsen was one of them; everyone was running to the castle to pray for his reprieve. I saw how the ladies ran. Suddenly I myself stood in a river. They showed me ships at a distance, from which I was to be shot.

Henrik Stampe told me that when I was shot, a new play was to be performed, and at that point I woke. The dream has some little connection with my annoyance at being constantly disappointed about the promised performance of *The Spaniards*. I have this morning sent a letter to State Councillor Kranald [director of the Royal Theatre].'

Only through work could Andersen shake off his wartime mood. From Basnæs he went to Frijsenborg castle, where on June 10, 1866, he wrote in his diary: 'A strange depressing feeling came over me during the afternoon, and I took a walk through the wood all alone. The solitude of the wood, the blooming flower garden, and the pleasant rooms of the castle wove themselves through my memory into a story which blossomed forth like a flower. I went home and worked on *Golden Treasure*, and my spirits were high again.' This, like *When the Spaniards Were Here*, recalls his childhood. The father in it wants his son to become a soldier and the mother objects – ' "But if he should come back a general?" said the father. "Without any arms or legs?" said the mother. "No, thank you, I'd rather keep my Golden Treasure whole!" ' In Andersen's story the drummer-boy becomes a famous violinist – music enters into many of his stories – and returning to his old home to embrace his widowed mother, the boy sees his father's old drum and says to it, ' "Father would have beaten a welcome on you today; now I must do it instead." ' In addition Andersen wrote *In the Nursery* and, while in Christinelund, *The Storm Shifts the Signboards* in which he described some of the vanished pageantry of the Odense of his childhood.

Back in Copenhagen among the pictures, books and flowers of his comfortable rooms in Nyhavn, Andersen had for once no immediate plans for travelling. He had not been home long, however, before he received a letter from George O'Neill, then Danish consul in Lisbon, inviting him to stay with himself and his brother in Portugal. As children the O'Neills had been brought up in Copenhagen, where they lived with Admiral Wulff's family, and they and Andersen had been friends since boyhood. The part of Andersen that resembled Mr Micawber – 'It would be rash not to go on and see the cathedral' – urged him to accept immediately, but memories of the discomfort of travel in Spain made him hesitate. At this point his excellent landlady told him that she had promised her student son better rooms if he passed his examinations and she also wanted to take another young lodger, so Andersen decided that it was once again travel-time for him. As cholera was still spreading in Spain, he decided to make a trip to Sweden first and that autumn visited Fredrika Bremer and Baron Beskow in Stockholm.

As always, he was excited by the constantly increasing speed of travel. He could remember when it took a week to cross Sweden; now Sweden had the railway and 'At two o'clock in the afternoon the train starts from Malmö, and in the evening one is at Jönköping, where there is a good hotel, as well managed as if it were in Switzerland. Next morning one takes one's place in a carriage, and is at Stockholm in the afternoon. What a change! What a flight! Our children and our children's children will live in the time of conveniences. We old people have had the line of trouble midway between the two generations: we stand, so to speak, with one leg in one generation and one in the other, but that is very interesting.' (He was sixty when he wrote this, and today the journey from Copenhagen to Stockholm by air takes seventy minutes.)

In Stockholm Andersen found the Henriques, friends whom he had met around 1860 and who by cherishing him in his old age were to play as important and beneficial a part in his sunset as Siboni, Weyse and Jonas Collin had played in his sunrise. Just as love of singing had set him on the path to fame as a child, so love of music led him into friendship with the Henriques and above all with their relatives the Melchiors, both cultured old Jewish families of bankers, brokers and shipping magnates, known for their probity and philanthropy. Mrs Henriques was a brilliant pianist and artists met regularly at her house for chamber music. Their own sensibility enabled these families to understand Andersen, and their cosmopolitan outlook was restful to the experienced traveller that Andersen had become. The Henriques accompanied Andersen to Uppsala, where he saw the Northern Lights and met an old friend, Böttiger, and his wife Disa, the daughter of the poet Tegnér, whose songs, set to music by Lindblad, had been carried all over Europe by Jenny Lind. He also met once more Jenny Lind's godson, the composer Josephson. Andersen was particularly touched by the warm welcome Josephson gave to Mrs Henriques as a fellow musician.

On returning to Stockholm he found at his hotel an invitation from the King to visit him at the castle of Ulriksdal, near Stockholm. King Oscar I had died in 1859 and been succeeded by his thirty-three-year-old son, Charles XV. Andersen was received with marked friendliness, particularly by the young Crown Princess Louise, one of his most devoted readers, who was later to marry the Crown Prince of Denmark. A few days later Andersen was invited by the Queen Mother to dine at Drottningholm. Drottningholm, which means Queen's Island, is the Versailles of Sweden, situated on one of the many islands in Lake Malaren. Built at the end of the seventeenth century by the Tessins, father and son, it had French gardens and a magnificent park complete with a Chinese pavilion built in 1770 by King Adolphus Frederik as a surprise for his wife's birthday. But for Andersen the greatest beauty of Drottningholm was the eighteenth-century theatre built for Gustavus III, who had been a keen amateur dramatist and actor and often performed there in his own plays for the royal family, household and guests. This was Andersen's first meeting with the Queen Mother since the death of her husband, King Oscar, and they greeted each other with emotion.

Andersen had not seen Fredrika Bremer since she visited Denmark with the Marcus Springs, and talk of these American friends led them to more talk of Henriette Wulff, who had lived with the Springs in America after her brother's death. They talked too of Jenny Lind and the past to which they had all contributed. Twenty-six years had gone by since Andersen and Fredrika Bremer had met aboard a steamer crossing Lake Vänern. Although they were both much changed, the affection between them was old and true. Andersen, in particular, had changed for the better physically. The lines on his face had drawn there a map of spiritual beauty of a most unusual kind. Young Edmund Gosse was to write of him: 'There was an appeal in his physical appearance that claimed for him immunity from the rough ways of the world, a childlike trustfulness, a tremulous and con-

fiding affectionateness, that threw itself directly upon the sympathy
of those around. His personality was somewhat ungainly: a tall
body with arms of very unusual length, and features that recalled,
at the first instant, the usual blunt type of the blue-eyed, yellow-
haired Danish peasant. But it was impossible to hold this impression after a minute's observation. The eyes, somewhat deeply set
under arching eyebrows, were full of mysterious and changing
expression and a kind of exaltation which never left the face
entirely, though fading at times into reverie, gave a singular
charm to a countenance that had no pretension to outward
beauty. The innocence and delicacy, like the pure frank look of a
girl-child, that beamed from Andersen's face, gave it a unique
character hardly to be expressed in words; notwithstanding his
native shrewdness, he seemed to have gone through the world
not only undefiled by, but actually ignorant of, its shadowy side.'
As they took leave of each other Fredrika Bremer clasped his hand
and said, 'I am always a steadfast friend, Andersen.' They never
met again, for she died the following Christmas, aged sixty-four.

On the way home Andersen stopped at Lund. Twenty-five
years ago he had received his first public ovation from the students
here and now a new generation welcomed him with equal
fervour.

As he expected to be leaving Copenhagen again soon for Spain
and Portugal, Andersen went to the Hôtel d'Angleterre rather
than to look for new lodgings. Once more, however, he was
delayed by bad weather and by the news from Spain, where there
was a revolt against Isabella II, whom he had seen in Andalusia.
The leading spirit in the revolt, General Juan Prim y Prats, was
reported to be moving troops near Badajoz, which lay on
Andersen's route. While he lingered in Copenhagen the King
invited him to stay at Fredensborg and to read the royal family
his latest stories. All Christian IX's children – Crown Prince
Frederik, Prince George who had become King of Greece in
1863 when he was only eighteen, Princess Alexandra who was
now Princess of Wales, and Princess Dagmar who was to marry
Alexander III of Russia and live to see her son and daughter-in-
law and her grandchildren assassinated in the Bolshevik revolu-

tion – had been brought up on Andersen's stories. Now the two youngest, Princess Thyra and Prince Valdemar, were allowed to stay up half an hour later than usual in honour of Andersen's visit.

At last, after Christmas visits to Holsteinborg and Basnæs, he left Copenhagen, went through Fyn and the lost duchies, still occupied by Prussian troops, and so to his 'old home', the Hôtel de l'Europe in Hamburg. On February 4 he stopped at Celle, near Hanover, to visit the grave of the unfortunate Anglo-Danish Queen Caroline Mathilde, and when he reached the Rhine he was delayed in a hotel with poor service and stale bread, which reminded him of inns he had known as a young man – 'many call that the time of romance! I prefer the time of modern convenience.' He spent several weeks with friends in Amsterdam, which was built on piles in mud and water and described by Erasmus as 'a city whose inhabitants live like crows at the top of trees'. Two things shocked him here – that the orphanage children were obliged to wear particoloured uniforms similar to those of criminals in Denmark, and that Jews were not admitted to concert halls. Nor did he care to hear modern dance music played during intervals at the theatre to the accompaniment of shouting, whistling and noisy drinking of tea and beer. His most interesting encounters were with the Dutch poets Jan Jacob ten Kate and van Kneppelhout, who introduced him to most of the professors at Leyden University.

At last he reached Paris where there had recently been another outbreak of cholera. One of these virulent outbreaks is probably responsible for the well-known story of a young English girl who, on returning to her hotel in Paris, is told that no such person as her mother, with whom she is staying there, exists: during the girl's brief absence her mother has died of cholera and the body has been smuggled out of the hotel lest her death frighten off clients. The Crown Prince of Denmark was staying at the Hôtel Bristol in the Place Vendôme and on Andersen's first Sunday in Paris the Prince invited him to accompany him to the races at Vincennes. The royal party set off at one o'clock in three carriages with outriders and was applauded by the crowds along the boulevards and at the race-track, where a room with a fire, armchairs and sofas had been prepared for them in the Imperial Tribune. Soon after them arrived Murat's son and grandson. A singing crowd gazed up at the royal box, and, as often on similar occasions, Andersen was awed by the thought of how far he had come since the days when he went barefoot in Odense.

Next day, his sixty-first birthday, he was showered with telegrams. The Prince paid him a visit; the Danish consul gave a dinner for him; at his hotel he found a compatriot who, at Mrs Melchior's request, had brought him flowers on her behalf.

During this visit he met the young Swedish singer Christina Nilsson, who had made her debut in Paris the previous year, and the composer Rossini, who was seventy-four years old at this time. Hearing Rossini tell an Italian visitor that he was a German poet, Andersen corrected this to Danish, whereupon Rossini looked puzzled and said, 'But Denmark belongs to Germany.' A new admirer was Jules Sandeau, the writer and Academician, who had as a young man collaborated with George Sand in *Rose et Blanche* and who described Andersen as 'like Haydn in music'.

Andersen was to celebrate the King of Denmark's birthday with Mimi Holstein-Holsteinborg, daughter of the Danish Naval Minister, and his description of the difficulty of getting accross Paris to her house is applicable today: 'The place to which I was to go lay by the Porte Etoile, on the left side. I went from the Place de la Concorde an hour before the time, in order to look at the multitude promenading the Champs-Elysées. The crowd pressed on along the broad road, passing on both sides, one carriage followed another, elegant equipages from the drive in the Bois de Boulogne. They increased all the way up to the Porte Etoile, where it seemed to me impossible to cross without being run over, and yet I must get to the opposite side. For a whole hour I hunted for a good crossing place . . . I could see the house where I was to go, but not any possibility of reaching it. It was past the appointed time when my good genius again came to me, or rather was sent – a heavily laden wagon drawn by six horses, that was going across at a slow pace, and so made a bulwark, as it were, against all the dashing equipages.'

Just before leaving Paris, on April 13, Andersen received from

Vienna the Order of Notre Dame de Guadeloupe on behalf of the Emperor Maximilian, then in Mexico, where he was killed the following year. Andersen was touched by this token of remembrance from a prince whom he could remember seeing in Vienna twenty years ago as a boy of fourteen.

From Paris Andersen went to Bordeaux from which a steamer sailed once a month to Lisbon. He had already told the O'Neills to expect him on April 28, but as the sea was stormy, he hesitated. However, when he heard that Ristori was to appear in Bordeaux in *Medea* and *Mary Stuart*, he could not bear to miss this, so decided to wait and risk the overland journey to Portugal.

The first part of his journey, across the wild and lonely Basque country, was enlivened for him by his having a French translation of Basque legends that had been presented to him by the French scholar Francisque Michel. In Madrid he found the revolt in abeyance (it broke out afresh a few weeks after his arrival in Lisbon), but even so he had to wait five days for a place on a mail-coach, despite which his only travelling companion was a young doctor from Lisbon. They crossed the campagna by moonlight, the river Tagus next morning, and in the evening dined at Trujillo, which exhilarated Andersen as it was the birthplace of Pizarro, the great conquistador. But for the most part, since travellers could not be sure of procuring any food but chocolate, they ate the provisions they had brought with them. The carriage travelled slowly, lurching over rocky tracks and slumping into deep ruts, and by the time they reached the railway station at Mérida even Andersen's enthusiasm for sightseeing had waned and he 'looked with sleepy eyes on old stones' and found it 'much more delightful to hear the locomotive whistle'. From the frontier to Lisbon was a day and a night's journey, and very comfortable this seemed after Spain. Andersen noted: 'To go from Spain to Portugal is like flying from the Middle Ages into the present era. All about were whitewashed friendly-looking houses hedged about by trees; and at the larger stations refreshments could be had, while in the night we found a chance to rest in the roomy railway carriage.'

The O'Neills lived at Pinieros in the country outside Lisbon. Expecting him by sea, they had gone to the harbour to meet the

ship and found that all the Danish ships there had run up their
flags in his honour. From the first Andersen was charmed by
Portugal, especially by the gardens with their roses, geraniums,
red pomegranates, blue chicory and blossoming elder-trees. As
head of the firm Tolades O'Neill, George O'Neill had to spend
most of his days either at his counting-house or acting as Danish
consul, but Andersen had the company of O'Neill's wife and two
sons, George and Arthur. He was particularly interested by
Mrs O'Neill's reminiscences, which reached back to the days of
the notorious Don Miguel, who had first plotted with his mother
to overthrow his father's government and subsequently, as Regent,
seized the throne from his niece Maria, only to be chased out of
Portugal by his elder brother.

With the O'Neills Andersen met the Portuguese poet Feliciano
de Castilho, a remarkable man who, despite having been blinded
by smallpox at the age of six, had studied history, philosophy,
Greek and Latin, in which he had written his first poems at the
age of fourteen. His wife, Charlotte Vidal, was the daughter of
the consul at Elsinore, and with her help he translated a number
of Danish poets into Portuguese.

After some weeks with George O'Neill and his family, Andersen
went to stay with George's brother Carlos. Accompanied by his
hosts he sailed across the Tagus to Setubal, set among orange
groves overlooking the sea. There Carlos O'Neill's carriage drove
them over the old highway lined with flowering aloes to his villa,
Quinta dos Bonecos, not far from the ruined fortress of Palmela
and the lonely monastery Brancana. Andersen's room overlooked
a garden full of fountains, palms and pepper trees, and beyond
that orange groves, vineyards and the sea. Here he was again
able to enjoy sunshine and domesticity. The son of the house,
Carlos, a handsome youth with dark blue eyes and black hair,
took him riding through lemon groves where pomegranates and
magnolias were in flower, to deserted monasteries, and to
Palmela to see the view out over the great cork forests to the Tagus,
Lisbon and the Cintra mountains. They went to a bullfight in
Setubal, 'innocent and bloodless' compared with Spanish bull-
fights, and they sailed across to the grotto at Mount Arabida and
visited the buried city of Troja, founded by the Phoenicians and

later exploited by the Romans. Looking across the Atlantic, Andersen thought of America. He had been invited to go there, but, though he longed to see the country of Longfellow, Washington Irving and Fenimore Cooper, he dreaded the long sea voyage. Other thoughts of all he had not done assailed him here. A letter written in July mentions the heat that kept him indoors all day. 'Not till evening do I come into the garden to breathe, but the air is also like a bridal kiss. A bridal kiss I have to imagine, however – I don't know it. I imagine so much – and know so little' – a sentence which itself says so little and conveys so much.

After a month's stay at the Villa Quinta dos Bonecos he set off to visit Coimbra and Cintra. Coimbra was famous for its ancient university, which had been transferred there from Lisbon in 1306, and Andersen was fascinated by its narrow, steep, crooked streets full of students who still wore medieval clothes, long black gowns, short capes and Polish caps. At Cintra, described by Byron as 'the new paradise', Andersen was the guest of José O'Neill and found a friend in the English consul, Edward Robert Lytton, the son of the Byronic writer and politician Bulwer Lytton who was raised to the peerage that year. Young Lytton and Andersen, who had already met in Lisbon, had many friends in common in London, and Andersen very much enjoyed the rides in the countryside around Cintra for which Lytton and his beautiful young wife took him. The future Viceroy of India described Andersen as 'a perfect faun, half child, half god'.

By this time Andersen was anxious to leave lest he be cut off from his friends at home by the war that had just started in Germany. Bismarck was steadily proceeding with the long-term plans for Prussian dominance of Germany that he had set in motion by invading Denmark. In June 1866 he proposed that the Bundestag in Frankfurt be dissolved, the German Confederation be abolished and a special German assembly be elected to draft a new constitution excluding Austria and all Austrian lands. Austria immediately accused Prussia of breaking the Treaty of Vienna and the Convention of Gastein and called on the federal German states to mobilize against Prussia. Nine out of the fifteen states supported Austria, but since their armies were scattered,

Bismarck felt sure he could prevent them combining either with each other or with the main Austrian army in Bohemia. War began on June 16 and on July 3 the main Austrian army was decisively defeated at Sadowa. News still travelled slowly, and since many people around Andersen thought that France might yet be drawn into the war, he decided to leave for home as quickly as possible.

On August 14 he heard that the *Navarro* had just arrived from Rio de Janeiro and was taking passengers as well as goods aboard. George O'Neill introduced him to the captain of this 'great floating hotel' and he obtained a place on it. The crossing was a stormy one. The ship never stopped rolling, heaving and creaking, and although it was the largest vessel Andersen had ever travelled on, his berth was too small for his height and would hold 'only three-quarters' of him, so he sat alone in the dark dining-room thinking nauseatedly of fire and shipwreck until memories of Henriette Wulff made it impossible for him to keep still and he rushed out on deck, where the beauty of the phosphorescent waves calmed him. Next day the sea was smoother, and on the fourth day out he saw the lighthouse on the rocky heights at the entrance to the Gironde, and after a few hours' sailing up the river, reached Bordeaux.

As there was cholera again in Paris, Andersen stayed only a day and a night there before going on to Hamburg, where he soon discovered, however, that the cholera epidemic was even worse than in Paris. He left Hamburg early next morning and reached Odense in the afternoon. There he visited his old friend Bishop Engelslöft and the scenes of his childhood, before leaving for Sorø to pay a surprise visit to Mrs Ingemann. But on learning that she had only just undergone an operation on her eyes, he realized that she was in no state for surprise visits and went straight on to Copenhagen. He was so exhausted that, for the first time, he believed his travelling days to be over.

He was met by the Melchiors, who took him out to their country house, Rolighed, overlooking the Sound. Rolighed, which was to be the haven of Andersen's old age, was an eighteenth-century house, rebuilt by Moritz Melchior, a miniature of

Rosenborg Palace with a tower and high balconies. Rooms were always set apart for Andersen so that he could come and go as he pleased. Here he found the rest he needed. The evenings were so mild that he was able to spend them in the garden, where the candlelit tables attracted a multitude of fireflies.

Soon after his homecoming he received an invitation from the royal family, which enabled him to say a personal goodbye to nineteen-year-old Princess Dagmar, who was to marry the future Tsar. On the day of her departure Andersen went down to the wharf to see her sail. On her way to the ship, Princess Dagmar saw him among the crowd and stopped to shake hands with him. As though he could foresee the horrors this young girl would have to face, tears came into his eyes. In the magnificent Jean Hersholt Collection of Hans Christian Andersen in the Library of Congress, Washington, is a two-volume edition of Andersen's *Eventyr og Historier*, illustrated by V. Pedersen, bound in red and gold cloth, in a morocco case, and inscribed 'To Her Royal Highness The Grand Duchess Maria Feodorovna Dagmar – with all humility I ask you to accept these tales of your childhood home. With sincere gratitude and the very deepest respect. H. C. Andersen.'

When, after visits to Sorø and Holsteinborg, he returned to Copenhagen, he took rooms in Kongens Nytorv, near the Royal Theatre. A lawyer and a photographer lodged in the same building, which also contained a café, restaurant and club, so he had 'meat and drink near by, and no lack of company'. When he was in town he was always engaged for dinner, going usually to Edvard Collin's on Monday, to Edvard's sister Ingeborg on Tuesday, to Ørsted's widow and daughter on Wednesday, to the Melchiors on Thursday (formerly kept for old Jonas Collin), to Henriette Wulff's sister, Ida Koch, on Friday, to the Scavenius family on Saturday and on Sunday to the Henriques family. Only one unpleasant incident disturbed him. This year a man named Peter Hjort published a collection of old letters from well-known people. Among them was one written in 1827 by Hauch shortly after the publication of Andersen's *A Walking Tour from Holmens Canal to the Eastern Point of Amager*. It was a spiteful letter, accusing Andersen of licking people's boots and pushing himself forward. Hauch, who was now seventy-seven and had long been one of Andersen's true friends, was in despair at this resuscitation of an opinion altered long ago, but Andersen, whose first thought was of the probable effect on his old friend, immediately went, though in poor health himself, to visit and comfort Hauch, who burst into tears on seeing him.

Andersen wrote four stories this year, including the delightful *Aunty*. He seemed less restless than ever before, but his wanderlust was only dormant and less than a week after his sixty-second birthday – for which the Melchiors gave a party and he was laden with messages and presents – he was on his way to Paris to visit the Universal Exhibition of 1867.

This tremendous exhibition was held, like the first French Industrial Exhibition of 1798, in the Champ de Mars, the huge parade-ground that stretched from the Ecole Militaire to the Seine, covering the area where the Eiffel Tower now stands. (Young Gustave Eiffel was among those who contributed to the Gallery of Machinery.) The Imperial entrance, facing the Pont d'Iéna, was in the form of a triumphal arch from which pillars, banners and a covered way lined with green cashmere patterned with Napoleonic bees led to the exhibition ground with its central palace, its 'titanic creations of modern metallurgy', and its park where Andersen saw 'the royal palace of Egypt. The Bedouins from the land of the hot sun galloped past, and there were the Russian stables, with beautiful fiery horses from the steppes. Over there was the small thatched cottage of a Danish peasant, with Dannebrog, the flag of Denmark, next to Gustavus Vasa's beautifully carved wooden cottage from Dalarna, American log cabins, English cottages, French pavilions, mosques, churches and theatres were all spread about in a wonderful manner. And in the middle of all this was the fresh green turf, with clear running water, flowering shrubs, rare trees, and glass houses where one might imagine oneself in a tropical forest. Complete rose gardens, brought from Damascus, bloomed in glory under glass roofs . . . A burring and buzzing sounded from the hall of the machines, and chimes rang out from the towers, while the tones of organs sounded from the churches, mingled with hoarse, nasal strains from Oriental coffee houses. It was a Babel empire, a Babel language, a wonder of the world.' There were automatons –

monkeys who played the fiddle and bears at their harpsichords – there were toy soldiers from Germany, cricket bats, tennis racquets, croquet sets and dolls' houses from England, and even an American restaurant which served ice-cream sodas, 'corpse revivers', porterhouse steak, oyster stew and prairie hens.

Never had there been so resplendent an exhibition. There were 42,237 exhibitors – over three times as many as at the Crystal Palace – and the 11,000,000 visitors included two emperors and more than eighty other royal personages. 'Princes for months were as plentiful in Paris as blackberries,' reported George Augustus Sala in the *Daily Telegraph*. In retrospect the coming Franco-Prussian war is thought to have cast a shadow over the exhibition – Krupp of Essen exhibited guns in a setting of plush and aspidistras – but at the time these attracted less popular attention than the military bands that played daily in the Tuileries gardens, where the eleven-year-old Prince Imperial could be seen playing with his dog Nero.

Fascinated by the spectacle, Andersen went every day to the exhibition, and kept meeting friends and acquaintances from all over the world – 'It was as if a great rendez-vous had been appointed here'. One day a well-dressed woman recognized him from his portraits, spoke to him in a mixture of Swedish, English and German, and introduced him to her husband, Ira Aldridge, a Negro actor who was playing *Othello* at the Odéon. This was the first time Andersen had met one of his African readers and he greeted the actor with spontaneous pleasure. Another stimulating meeting was with Sir Samuel White Baker, the English explorer who had gone up the Nile with his Hungarian wife and in 1864 had discovered the great lake on the Congo-Uganda border which he named Albert Nyanza. It was at this Exhibition that Andersen saw George I of Greece for the first time since the young Danish prince had left Copenhagen for Athens.

He left Paris in May, intending to be home in time for the King and Queen's silver wedding, but at Le Locle, where he stayed with his old friends the Jürgensens, snow put a stop to travel and he had to celebrate the anniversary in Switzerland. During the return journey he had a saddening experience which he noted in his diary for June 1: 'At Giessen I discovered that the

Grand Duke Karl Alexander [whom he had not seen since the war] travelled by the same train as I; I also knew his gentleman-in-waiting. It was painful not to be able to fly out and press his hand. I did not know how he would receive me, nor how I should have liked it myself if he had responded to my feelings. I therefore drew the curtain over the window. At Hundeshausen our ways parted: he proceeded to Weimar; half an hour later I was in Kassel.' They never met again. As with Dickens, it was a case of 'Past – past – and so all stories end.'

When at last he reached home, he found that on the occasion of the King and Queen's silver wedding celebrations, the King had given him the rank of Councillor of State. He went out to Fredensborg to thank the King, and dined with the royal family, including Princess Dagmar who was visiting her parents and told him that since their last meeting she had read a Russian edition of his stories. The King seems to have had doubts as to the appropriateness of the rank he had chosen for Andersen, who noted, 'The King asked whether I objected to his having made me a Councillor of State; he was anxious to give me a proof of his high esteem. I said that in Denmark Professor was a fine title, which was appreciated, but abroad it did not signify much; Councillor of State would be much more useful there.' That the title meant something to him, gave him confidence, is shown by one of his still recurrent dreams about Meisling which he described to Edvard's wife, Henriette, later that year: 'I thought I was in Meisling's house; it was just the same down to the last detail, save that Meisling, amid all his bitter mockery, called me "Councillor of State". Yet a change had taken place within me: I got up from the school bench, threw my books at him, and left the room; but now something else characteristic occurred, which revealed how dispirited I was in those days: I was afraid to show myself in the presence of your father-in-law, and so I turned to Edvard first, but he began a stern lecture, in the course of which I fortunately awakened.'

In the calm of Rolighed he was able to write *Godfather's Picture-book*, a long, subtly condensed story of the life and times of Copenhagen, and *The Little Green Ones*; but *The Dryad*, a story about the exhibition, was still unfinished and this kept his thoughts towards Paris. August brought French visitors to Denmark – and after a talk with two of these, one of whom was writing a book about Denmark, he could not resist the impulse to visit the exhibition once again before completing *The Dryad*. He left on September 1, accompanied by Robert Watt, a Danish journalist, whom Andersen had met during his previous visit to the exhibition and liked for the adventurous spirit that had led him to Australia, where as a youth he had prospected for gold.

Never before had Andersen felt so much at home in Paris, and in addition he felt young again, 'as always on a journey'. There were new exhibits to be seen in the Champ de Mars since his last visit, and he received many invitations from French journalists and writers and was taken to the Bal Mabille. Originally a rustic tavern, where a dancing-master named Mabille organized a summer ball where clerks and shop-girls could amuse themselves for a cheap entrance fee, the Bal Mabille had during the July Monarchy and the Second Empire become one of the most famous places of amusement in Paris. By 1843 Mabille's son had added gardens, groves, lawns, a grotto and gas-light and its more notorious dancers included Céleste Mogador, who married the Comte de Chabrillan, and Rigolboche, who was the first to dance the can-can in 1843. This too Andersen described in *The Dryad*, a sixty-page story published by itself, of which he wrote in the notes to the 1874 edition of his collected stories: 'In the spring of 1867 I journeyed to Paris to attend the great World's Fair. No previous or later trips to Paris ever had charmed and impressed me with such delight as this timely event. It was a mighty and overwhelming sight. The newspapers in France and in all other countries spoke of its magnificence. A Danish reporter declared that no one with the exception of Charles Dickens would be able to describe it. However, I felt that it was particularly suited to my talents, and it would make me very happy if I performed this task in a way that would please both my countrymen and strangers. With this in mind, I saw one day a withered chestnut tree in the square outside the hotel where I lived. On a wagon close by was a young, fresh tree brought in from the country that very same morning to replace the discarded one. The idea of a story about the Paris World's Fair was related to me by way of this young tree. The Dryad beckoned me. Each day during my stay in Paris and following my return to Denmark, the story of the Dryad's life and its connection with the great World's Fair occupied my thoughts and began to take form. I felt that I ought to make another visit to the fair, as I had not seen enough of it to make my story a true and full picture. Therefore I went back in September. It was after my return to Copenhagen that I completed the story.'

He left Paris at the end of September and on the way home stayed for a few days at Baden-Baden, where he was pleased by the scenery but troubled by the atmosphere peculiar to places where gambling is the chief activity, an atmosphere perfectly described that same year by Dostoyevsky in *The Gambler*. Baden-Baden's reputation for dissipation was so widespread that the wife of a British diplomat felt she had given a complete description of a society adventuress when she said that the latter 'lived an untrammelled life in Baden-Baden'. Andersen's impression was that 'In Mabille there was gaiety; I knew what it was; at Baden-Baden there was a fine show, but the place had an unhappy, demoniacal look.'

On the way to Copenhagen he stopped for a day's rest in Odense. His arrival coincided with that of a battalion of soldiers taking up garrison duty there and he was invited to the welcome celebrations in the riding school and impressed by the friendliness of the townspeople's attitude towards the military, so different from the attitude he had observed in his childhood when soldiers were treated as riff-raff. Remembering how, as a child, he had seen a soldier forced to run the gauntlet in the riding school, he said, 'How bright and beautiful is our time in comparison with those old days I knew.' Several of his Odense friends reproached him for paying only flying visits to his birthplace, and those only because it lay on the route to somewhere else. He would soon, they said, be receiving an official invitation to visit Odense for celebrations in his honour. He laughed and advised them to wait until September 1869, which would be the fiftieth anniversary of his departure for Copenhagen. They were reluctant, however, to 'postpone good things' and that November the Odense Town Council wrote to him:

'We herewith have the honour to announce to your Excellency that we have elected you an honorary citizen of your home town; permit us to invite you to meet us here in Odense on Friday, the Sixth of December next ensuing, upon which day we wish to deliver to you the certificate of citizenship.'

17. *The Most Incredible Thing*

1867-70

His old age found life immensely interesting. It was as though sunrise and
sunset had changed places for him, and he advanced towards the former.

F. F. Roget, *Vaussore, A Son of Rousseau,* 1898

*

WHEN ANDERSEN reached Odense on December 5, 1867, the
weather was cold and stormy and, as often when he was nervous,
he had a raging toothache. Also he was suddenly possessed by 'a
strange insane fear' that some calamity would ruin the occasion,
even that he himself might be murdered. Memories of past
humiliations returned to torment him – the Dean's disdainful
reception of him at confirmation classes, the mockery of the Latin
schoolboys, his grandfather pursued through the streets by
jeering ragamuffins, and above all, of his father's delirious end,
raving of the Emperor Napoleon on his white horse, his father's
ever-seeking unbalanced mind to which he himself probably
owed the beautiful and alarming abnormality that is genius. He
spent the night before the ceremony as the guest of Bishop
Engelslöft. In pain and sleepless, he felt that he was being given
more than he deserved and – as if he had been suddenly transported back to school – could think only of his bad qualities, his
clumsiness, his failures.

Next morning, when he heard the town was decorated in his
honour and all the schoolchildren had been given a holiday, he
felt even unworthier than he had done during the night. At ten
o'clock the Chief of Police, State Councillor Moch, and the Mayor
escorted him to the City Hall. People had flocked in from the
surrounding countryside and the streets were full of Danish flags
and welcoming crowds, including community singers singing his

own songs. At the City Hall, which was elaborately decorated and packed with well-dressed women and officers from the garrison, the Mayor made a speech thanking Andersen for stories that had delighted old and young, in peace and in war, and that had brought Denmark honour and fame abroad.

Thoughts of his father dying young, poor and frustrated made it difficult for Andersen to reply without breaking down. Later he spoke of this moment to a young friend who had said that Andersen's father had been the root and he himself the tree. 'Why should he be only the root?' said Andersen. 'Oh, if he had only lived to see the celebrations in my honour at Odense, he would have died of joy!' In his speech of thanks he said that he felt like Oehlenschläger's Aladdin, looking out of the window of the castle created by his magic lamp and saying, 'I was down there when I was a poor boy.' In his expressions of gratitude he made particular mention of Jonas Collin and Ørsted.

In the afternoon there was a banquet at the City Hall. His bust stood on a pedestal in the middle of the hall surrounded by decorations and commemorative medallions. More of his songs were sung and by four o'clock the banqueting hall was packed. After the King's health had been drunk at dinner there were more speeches, including one by the Bishop calling Andersen 'the great man of our day' and linking his name with that of Tycho Brahe, Holberg and Ørsted. As he listened, Andersen remembered coming to the City Hall as a child to see a waxwork exhibition, and his astonishment at the sight of kings, queens and celebrities in effigy. Once, too, an old musician had taken him to the City Hall to see the celebrations for King Frederik VI's birthday – born at the end of Christian VII's reign, Andersen had lived under five Kings. He had never expected recognition at home on this scale and was seized by nervous dread that Copenhagen might jeer at Odense's enthusiasm – but his fears were dispelled as, throughout the banquet, telegrams poured in from all over the country. Afterwards more guests arrived, and before the dancing began, Andersen was seated in the middle of the room and the children surrounded him and sang a song written for the occasion, which began:

There, where the street **turns round**,
A little house is found,
And there, say the wise **men**,
The stork brought Andersen.
Ole came, the lively fellow,
And hoisted his umbrella;
What dreams about the baby flocked,
His cradle the Nis gladly rocked.

Here he sat by the river side,
And mermaids, mermen there he spied;
And when on the mossy bank he walked
With Elder Mother then he talked.
Christmas came, blustering, raw,
And the Snow Queen white he saw –
Whate'er it was that charmed his heart,
He let us freely have a part.

During the dancing that followed, a telegram from the King arrived which was greeted with cheers and applause.

Andersen thought the festivities were over, when suddenly, at eight o'clock, a torchlight procession of all the corporations in Odense marched into the square below with flying colours and sang in his honour. Called to the window, Andersen looked out and could scarcely believe what he saw – for in every window in sight a light was burning. He remembered the wise-woman telling his mother that he would be 'a wild high-flying bird, and one day all Odense will be illuminated in his honour'. With a grateful and aching heart he wished that his father and mother could have seen him join the rare company of the dreamers whose dreams come true. Almost half a century had passed since he told his mother, 'First you endure terrible hardship, then you become famous.'

Andersen need have had no fears that anyone would mock his home town for making much of him. Ørsted had told him long ago that he would one day be appreciated as truly at home as he was abroad, and at last that day had come. He was a national hero. Letters of admiration came to him from all over the world. One of the most charming of these was from a child and its only address was HANS ANDERSEN, DENMARK.

> *Ulva Cottage, Hamilton,*
> *Scotland, 1st January, 1869*

Dear Hans Andersen,

I do like your fairy tales so much, that I would like to go and see you, but I cannot do that, so I thought I would write to you. When papa comes home from Africa, I will ask him to take me to see you. My favourite stories in one book are: *The Galoshes of Fortune, The Snow Queen,* and some others. My papa's name is Dr Livingstone. I am sending my card and papa's autograph. I will say good-bye to you and a happy New Year.

I am your affectionate little friend,

ANNA MARY LIVINGSTONE

PS. Please write to me soon. My address is on the first page, and please send me your card.

Andersen answered this in Danish followed by an English translation in his own handwriting:

> *Copenhagen, 19th January, 1869*

My Dear Little Friend
   Anna Mary Livingstone,

Thank you, my dear, for your letter, for your carte de visite and Papa's autograph. I shall guard it well and thereby remember my little friend. What a nice idea thus to give me joy.

All of us know the name and the man Dr Livingstone, all of us were so sorry when we were told that he was dead, but now we are so happy to know that he lives, and now since little Anna Mary and H. C. Andersen know each other, I am sure the kindest regards from my warm sympathizing heart will reach Papa.

The Most Incredible Thing

In this letter you will find enclosed my carte de visite and I also send an English translation on the other side, as I fear little Anna Mary otherwise would not understand what I have written.

Tell me occasionally when Papa is expected home, tell me a little about mother, brothers and sisters on Ulva Cottage.

May God preserve and render happy my dear little friend. My love to all in your dear home from the friend

HANS CHRISTIAN ANDERSEN

In September 1869 the fiftieth anniversary of Andersen's arrival in Copenhagen was celebrated there. He was asked to give a reading at the Students' Club, after which Hauch made a speech and a bust of Andersen was unveiled and took its place in a niche beside busts of Ingemann and Heiberg. One by one all his old friends were turning into statues. Next day there was a banquet at the Hôtel d'Angleterre attended by two hundred and forty-four notabilities. Among the many presents Andersen received was a basket of roses and laurels containing a silver dock-leaf with a silver snail on it, in memory of his charming story of snails, *The Happy Family*, planned long ago at Glorup: 'A part of the garden was overgrown, as it had been for years, with great burdocks, planted for the large white snails which were once a delicacy. The burdock and the snail gave me material for the story, *The Happy Family*, which was written out later, during my first visit to London.' This story contains an irresistible account of the snobbery of two surviving snails. 'They themselves did not know how old they were, but they could remember very clearly that once there had been a great many more of them, that they had descended from a prominent foreign family, and they knew perfectly well that the whole forest had been planted just for them and their family. They had never been away from home, but they did know that somewhere there was something called a manor house, and that there you were boiled until you turned black, and were laid on a silver dish . . . they couldn't imagine what it would be like to be boiled and laid on a silver dish, but everyone said it must be very wonderful and a great distinction. Neither the cockchafer nor the toad nor the earthworm, whom

327

they asked about it, could give them any information. None of their families had ever been boiled and laid on silver dishes. So the old snails knew they were by far the most important people in the world.' Altogether the banquet for Andersen was so joyful that one of the guests said later, 'I thought I was in heaven, everyone there had become both good and happy; one felt like shaking every hand.'

Two days later he was invited to Bernstorff to receive the congratulations of the King, who made him Commander of the Dannebrog. Writing to his young American friend Horace Scudder, Andersen said: 'On Friday I left Copenhagen and came out here to the country seat of Basnæs. Like an afterglow of my festivities in the city was the lovely welcome which beamed here. I arrived in the evening, and before the castle bridge I saw a large and beautiful triumphal arch decorated with lights and the Danish flag waving. The wife and family of the estate, with several from neighbouring country seats, received me; Count Holstein-Holsteinborg made a handsome speech; and out in the park attractive fireworks showing my name were set off; and the many country folk gathered there greeted me with a resounding "Hurrah!" All of this is indeed too much kindness to show to one person, though it does not make one vain, but rather tender, reflective and humble.

'Towards the end of the week I shall go for a couple of days to stay at Holsteinborg, and from there for a similarly short stay to Glorup in Fyn for a visit with Count Moltke-Huitfeldt. After that I shall proceed southwards without delay via Dresden to Vienna and farther on later.'

This year of apotheosis also brought him the deep satisfaction of reading the finest analysis of his work that had yet been written. So far Danish critics had given him little pleasure or instruction. As a young writer, he had often been misunderstood at home and after he was famous whatever he produced was indiscriminately praised. So it was with astonished gratitude that, at the age of sixty-four, he read strong, brilliant and original criticism of his work. It came from a young Jewish writer, Georg Brandes, then twenty-seven years old and destined to be one of the greatest nineteenth-century critics in Europe, in the tradition of Sainte-

Beuve, who died this same year. Born into a cultured family of non-orthodox Danish Jews in Copenhagen, Georg Brandes had graduated from the university in 1864, writing the thesis for his doctorate on '*L'Esthétique Française Contemporaine*'. He was strongly influenced by Hegel's philosophy, as introduced into Denmark by Heiberg, and also by John Stuart Mill, whose *The Subjection of Woman* he translated; and he was one of the first to recognize the international importance of Kierkegaard who had died when Brandes himself was a boy of thirteen. He thought that Denmark was forty years behind the rest of Europe intellectually and he wanted to rouse a spirit of 'independent research'. One of the qualities that particularly impressed him in Andersen was the latter's imaginative grasp of the spiritual importance of science and material progress. The first part of his famous essay on Andersen appeared in the *Illustreted Tidende* in 1869:

'The nature of genius is an organically connected whole; its weakness in one direction is the condition of its strength in another; the development of this faculty causes that one to be checked in its growth, and it is impossible to alter any single particular without disturbing the entire machinery. We may wish that one quality or another was different from what it is, but we can readily comprehend that any decided change is out of the question. We may wish our poet had stronger personality, a more manly temperament, and more mental equilibrium; but we have no difficulty in understanding that the lack of defined personality and the incompleteness of the character whose acquaintance we make in *The Story of My Life*, stand in the most intimate relationship with the nature of his endowments. A less receptive mind would not be so susceptible to poetic impressions, a harder one would not unite so much flexibility with its more rigid attitude, one more susceptible to criticism and philosophy would not be so naive . . . There is not a single Danish poet who, to such a degree as Andersen, has scorned to produce effect through the romance of the past; even in the nursery story, which from the beginning has been handled by the Romantic School of Germany in a style comparable with that of the Middle Ages, he is always solely and entirely in the present. He, as well as Ørsted, dares to sacrifice the interesting element in his enthusiasm for

King John and his times and he heartily joins Ovid in exclaiming,
*Prisca juvent alios, ego me nunc denique natum
gratulor; haec aetas moribus apta meis.'*

Mental equilibrium in the conventional sense Andersen would never possess. Despite devoted friends, a comfortable income and deserved fame, all of which assured him that his end would not be as his beginning, the nervous vulnerability that had fed his talent when he was a young man made daily life increasingly difficult for him as he grew older. The anguish that had always been latent even in his times of joy broke out into a score of fragmentary and specific fears – of cholera, of trichinosis, of fire and shipwreck, of missing trains, of losing his passport, of putting letters in wrong envelopes, of leaving private papers in books, of forgetting to extinguish candles, of offending people, of taking the wrong dose of medicine, of crossing open spaces. Once a young friend with whom he was travelling was half an hour late for an appointment with Andersen and found him distraught: during that half hour he had imagined the young man first injured, then dead; he had broken the news to the grieving family, had arranged the funeral, and was almost as exhausted by the experience as an ordinary person would be by bereavement itself. That he knew these fears to be morbid did not help him. In his diary he wrote: 'I ought to talk to a doctor, but to whom? One who has insight, who could enlighten my sick mind.' He told Edvard's wife Henriette: 'I have imagination, yes, I live by it for the most part, of course, but it causes embarrassment now and then, especially when one thinks it's not working, and it's just then that its reactions are strongest.'

He continued to be tormented by nightmares in which he was jeered at by Meisling or caused disappointment to old Jonas Collin, and, most painful of all to him, he could not prevent himself flying into rages with Edvard Collin, during which he would relive humiliations and frustrations long past. At such times he would send for young Jonas Collin, who would find him weeping with horror of himself for harbouring ungrateful thoughts of his truest friends. The young man understood the old one better by this time, and although he could not free him from these painful attacks of sensibility, he helped him by listening to him and trying to lessen his feeling of guilt.

The kind of help Andersen needed did not exist. There was then no psychiatric treatment and his fears were attributed to his liver and his age – although he had suffered from precisely the same type of fears for as long as he could remember. Nowadays a psychiatrist would recognize that he had a psychasthenic constitution, a combination of hyper-sensitive nerves with a need to justify his existence by creative achievement that might have driven him into a madhouse had he been less gifted. As a boy, Andersen was undermined by a well-justified sense of insecurity that produced concomitant feelings of inadequacy, unworthiness and guilt; as a man, his lack of family ties and his failure to experience requited love and thereby found a family of his own made him utterly dependent on his friends for emotional sustenance. He was therefore constantly aware of a need, terrifying in its urgency, to please in both his private and his professional life. From this came his hunger for fame. Once a friend accused him of being either a great simpleton or a great rogue, to which he answered unself-consciously that he was a bit of both – 'But that is a good thing too, isn't it?' It was good in that it enabled him to maintain his fragile mental equilibrium, but he paid a heavy price for this – as Dag Hammarskjöld wrote in his diary for 1955: 'While performing the part which is truly ours, how exhausting it is to be obliged to play a role which is not ours; the person you must really be in order to fulfil your task, you must not appear to others to be, in order to be allowed by them to fulfil it. How exhausting – but unavoidable, since mankind has laid down once and for all the organized rules for social behaviour.'

Andersen is not essentially a writer for children, nor did he prefer children to adults, but he did remain in many respects a child himself, a child always ready to plunge into the forest through which the castle is to be reached and to confront the dragons that symbolize the elementary powers that bar access to the light. His path, like that of the haunting Norwegian painter Edvard Munch, 'always ran alongside an abyss' and his fears, as well as his hopes, his joys and his humour, enabled him to produce out of the depths of his unconscious fairy tales that are pure poetry and satisfy both the child's and the adult's need for magic. The part of Andersen that was dominated by feelings of inferiority believed, as Kafka did, that the artist is weaker than the average man; nevertheless, he had the strength to assume his destiny and provide, out of the richness and variety of his interior life, the magic that even the crudest people need to compensate them for what their own lives lack.

Although he showed these signs of emotional exhaustion, Andersen still, however, had the desire and energy for travel, and when his friends remonstrated he said, 'I suppose I must have been born under a star called Pendulum, so am bound to keep going to and fro, tic-tac, tic-tac.'

In the winter of 1869 he went to Germany, Austria, Switzerland and France with Jonas Collin. In January 1870 he wrote from Nice: 'I have now been in Nice six weeks and am feeling quite at home. I am living nicely and comfortably at the Pension Suisse, hard by the open rolling ocean. There are people from every country here, and we celebrated Christmas Eve by assembling in the large reception room of the hotel, where a mighty fir tree was set up and decorated with ornaments, candles, and the flags of all nations. In the midst of the festivities one of the company stepped forward and said: "We have with us a man to whom we all, whatever nation we may belong to, owe thanks for the many happy hours he has given us through his writings." And then a little girl handed me a laurel wreath wrapped with ribbons in the Danish colours and the entire gathering applauded . . . So you may see how much friendliness and sympathy I have met with here far from home, and moreover in a country where only three or four of my books are translated.' His pleasure in the most trifling tokens of admiration came neither from childishness nor vanity but from a sense of insecurity that he never lost. As a child, he had found some protection against the present in imagining his future castles, but now that his future was present, he was often ensnared by memories of the past. On June 4, 1870, he wrote in his diary: 'Slept badly last night. Once again I dreamt of subservience: I fled from Meisling, was frightened of old Collin as dissatisfaction with me prevailed in the new school. To think that I still have such dreams . . .' Although this and similar dreams occur again and again in Andersen's diary, always described in the same simple terms, repetition does not hide the fact that the awkward child who had lived what the distinguished old man dreamt was as bleakly isolated as one of Giacometti's figures, and the small icy schoolroom in which Andersen learnt to use the counters that are words still seemed to him as vast and shadow-filled as Piranesi's prisons.

That same June Dickens died suddenly at Gad's Hill at the age of fifty-eight. Andersen learnt the news through a newspaper and was strongly affected by it. He remembered seeing Dickens for the first time, youthful and ebullient, at the house of Lady Blessington, who had died in 1849 in Paris, to which she and the Count d'Orsay had fled to escape their debts – but it was his own debt to her that Andersen remembered as he saw again in imagination Gore House, its tropical birds, its cow on the lawn providing an artificially pastoral note, the glittering dinner with the Duke of Wellington's son toasting the Danish visitor beneath the eyes of Napoleon's portrait. He remembered the happy domestic scenes at Gad's Hill, the gaieties of amateur theatricals and the splendours of the Crystal Palace, all past now as every story must one day be.

18. *What Old Johanne Told*

1870-4

As long as human intelligence survives, there will surely exist some grateful memory of Hans Andersen. Edmund Gosse, *Two Visits to Denmark*, 1911

They [Hans Christian Andersen's fairy tales] have gone to forming the character and delighting the hearts of almost everyone now living in the European and European descended races.

Ford Madox Ford, *The March of Literature*

*

A MONTH LATER, on July 19, 1870, the Franco-Prussian war broke out, deliberately provoked by Bismarck. The modernized Prussian army was far stronger than was realized abroad, and after a series of defeats along the eastern front, the French were forced to surrender at Sedan on September 1. Danish sympathies were with France. At the beginning of the war a Danish newspaper published in North Slesvig rejoiced so openly at the possibility of Germany's being defeated that it was suppressed. Among those who distinguished themselves on the French side was a Danish volunteer, Wilhelm Dinesen, son of the Lieutenant Dinesen whom Andersen had liked so much in Paris in 1833 and the future father of Karen Blixen.

Although his health was failing, Andersen had not lost his capacity for work. In November 1870 Reitzel Forlag published his novel, *Lucky Peer*, the story of a poor boy's struggle to succeed, for which he drew on the happy parts of his own early life, omitting Meisling's torments, a significant omission, since in March of the following year he wrote in his diary:

March 1 Again last night I had attacks of my mad fantasies.

March 2 God has given me fantasy for my calling as a poet, but not so that I shall become a candidate for an asylum. What are these obsessions that so often torment me?

March 3   Lay on the sofa tormented by a fixed idea of insanity and calamities. Went to the theatre to see *The Jewess*. When I came home it was as if my curtain of insanity were raised.

In April 1871 Andersen moved to the Hôtel d'Angleterre, where he felt 'It was as if a nightmare had ended. I felt rejuvenated, as if I were travelling and back in my younger days . . .'

His increasing fits of melancholy did not, however, lessen his attentiveness to his friends. In May he found time to write to little Mary Livingstone:

> *Basnæs, near Skjelskør*
> *25 May 1871*
> *(Denmark)*

My dear little friend,

Many thanks for the dear nice letter you wrote to me the other day, many thanks for all what you told me about the pantomime in 'The Theatre Royal', it must have been a pleasant night. I know the tale about Sinbad, it is to be found in 'Thousand and one nights', that book you must read.

I am going to send you by the first opportunity a continuation of the tales and stories, which your Sister Miss Agnes brought you from me. My new book contains many tales you hardly know yet. I lived at a country-house near Copenhagen when your sister and some of her friends gave me the great pleasure of their visit and brought me little Mary's love, how friendly and considerate of her, give her and the old lady who accompanied her my kindest regards. Here in Denmark we often speak of your dear papa and his travels in Africa. The other day I read in a newspaper that he had left and was on his way home to Europe. Hurrah! – how splendid! Providence never gives up good men, who live in him and in performing noble deeds. What a heartfelt joy in the family, what festivity in all the country, when the dear energetic father, whom we all appreciate and honour, comes back to England. Then when he has kissed his little Mary many times, chatted and told her news, then remember my kind regards to him, whom Providence has guarded to our joy and our instruction. Remember me also to the aunts and to everybody in the family whose mind is kind towards little Mary's friend Hans Christian Andersen.

I am now in the country, close to the sea-coast at an old manor with high steeples, the garden plies towards the strand, and towards our splendid beechwood, which just now is delightfully fresh and green, the whole ground is like a carpet of violets and anemones, the doves are cooing and the cuckoo tells news. Here very likely I am writing a new story, which my little friend later shall read. After the holidays I again return to town to stay some time with my friends the Melchiors in the beautiful Villa where sister Agnes was so kind to call on me. When Papa returns I expect a little letter from his dear Mary. And now I say farewell! You do not forget the friend in Denmark.

HANS CHRISTIAN ANDERSEN

This year Henrik Ibsen, who was still living abroad, paid a visit to Denmark and was presented to Andersen. He was at this time forty-three and reputed to be a man of alarming temper. Molbech, who had known him in Rome in 1865, later told young Edmund Gosse: 'Oh, to be in Rome with Ibsen and Björnson together, my dear young friend, was a weary, weary thing! They could not keep apart; they were like two tom-cats parading and snarling and swearing at each other, yet each bored to death if the other were not present. They collected their adherents behind them; there were two well-defined parties. I assure you, if it amused the Norwegians, it was death to us easy-going Danes and Swedes. At last Björnson took himself off. Oh! what a sigh of relief we gave. And Ibsen came into the Club, and glanced round, and snarled, and there was no one to snarl back at him. Then followed the publication of *Brand*, and money came in, and Ibsen grew to be a celebrated character; so he smiled and stretched his legs and was quiet. But agreeable? Oh no! Let us use words in their true sense. Ibsen has never been an agreeable man and he never will be. But he is a great genius, and a very honest person.'

This being the case, Andersen approached the meeting with qualms. To his surprise, Ibsen proved mild, friendly, and asked to hear some of Andersen's latest work. A strange session it must have been when the author of *Lucky Peer* – 'His trust in mankind was never deceived; he had a child's soul and a man's endurance' – read aloud to the irascible author of *Peer Gynt*. Soon after meeting Ibsen, Andersen paid his first visit to Norway. On his way there, at Göteborg, he met Viktor Rydberg, a Swedish writer with as poor a background as his own, who had nevertheless founded the principal newspaper in his home town, acquired fame with his book *The Last Athenian* in 1859, and had in 1870 become deputy for Göteborg. He had been influenced by Andersen's *Ahasuerus* and was absorbed by religious problems, of which they talked at length. Andersen found Rydberg's point of view 'human and reasonable', but, despite his own instinct to love God as a Father, he could not believe in orthodox views. Indeed, his disbelief in the Trinity provoked one ardent follower of Grundtvig's to say that 'at best he could only be counted among the Jews'; and when his old friend Hauch died in March 1872, he wrote in his diary, 'Is he now dust and ashes, dead, extinguished; burnt out like the light that exists no more?'

Earlier Andersen had received a letter from Jenny Lind. In his diary he wrote; 'Received today a letter from Jenny Lind-Goldschmidt – for twenty years I have not heard from her. She wrote of Oberammergau [the 1870 performances of the Passion Play had been interrupted by the war, so it had been given again in 1871]: "The most holy scenes the world has witnessed ought never to be reproduced in a theatre." Said her health was better. "I gave too much of myself in my art; all my life's strength was on the point of being extinguished. But I would with joy have died for this my first and last, deepest and purest love. Nothing is more pure than art, as it lifts us to Him who gave us art. And God has thus, step by step, led me up Jacob's ladder, until my Saviour stood clearly before my eyes and taught me to understand *why* He came down in order to save the world by shedding His blood for us." ' It seemed to Andersen that there were two Jenny Linds, the middle-aged wife and mother, devoted to religion and domesticity, and the artist still so much nearer to him, the young girl who had been serenaded by the students and who had once shared a Christmas tree with him, the young girl whom he had hoped to marry. The two figures would not merge.

Everyone who saw Andersen at this time was impressed by his appearance. The odd-looking youth had grown into a beautiful old man. His features had not changed, but his expression, his noble forehead and his gaiety and unself-conscious originality, made him as spell-binding as his stories. He was no longer intimidated by people. As he told young Nikolaj Bøgh, 'I say . . . exactly what I think. They tell me I mustn't and I've tried not to, but I can't stop it, even if I make up my mind, out it comes directly afterwards.' The celebrated phrenologist, Dr Carl Gustav Carus of Dresden, once measured Andersen's head and concluded:

Love of children	: great
Sexuality	: small
Good nature	: very great
Hopefulness	: great
Idealism	: very great
Sense of wonder	: great
Creative power	: great
Affection	: great
Wit	: very great
Covetousness	: small

Nikolaj Bøgh and William Bloch were two young writers who became his friends during his last years, accompanying him on journeys, taking care of him, and showing him the most delicate understanding. It was during a journey to Venice in 1872 that he confided in Bloch the truth about Mrs Meisling's attempts to seduce him as a schoolboy, a subject he had touched on only lightly and evasively in *Only a Fiddler*. Everything about her had been distasteful to Andersen but he had been too impressionable not to be disturbed by her advances. Looking back, he regretted his ignorance and said to Bloch, 'Suppose I live to be eighty, which I shan't, even then I should have only thirteen years left. Oh God, oh God . . . it is nothing! . . . If only I were thirty and had my present development, *then* I should achieve something, I should really become famous – and I'd turn cartwheels the whole length of Østergade with sheer joy.' Cartwheels, however, were far behind him and a trip abroad which he made with William Bloch this year was cut short by an accident.

One night in Innsbruck Andersen could not make himself comfortable in bed. He had disarranged the bedclothes in his first sleep and, waking, got up to straighten them and the mattress. Reaching too far for a chair, he overbalanced and fell, knocking over a chair and a heavy candlestick. The noise awoke the people in near-by rooms and Bloch rushed in and found him on the floor, his nose badly bruised and contusions on kneecap, thighs, shoulders and temples. (Andersen described his kneecap as 'an orange surrounded by green, blue and black rings'.) He found it difficult to walk and ached all over. They went to Munich for medical advice, but despite headaches and spells of dizziness, Andersen insisted on showing Bloch the sights. He persisted in trying to provide entertainment for Bloch in Augsburg and Nuremberg, but for all his spirit he had suffered a severe physical shock. He still reacted to travel as a circus horse does to music, but he was now an old horse whose prancing days were almost ended. On October 23 he had moved into two rooms at 18 Nyhavn, the house where as a schoolboy of seventeen he had spent his Christmas holidays as the guest of warehouse-keeper Balling. These were to be his last rooms in Copenhagen.

This same year Andersen received a visit from the twenty-three-year-old Edmund Gosse who recorded it in his *Two Visits to Denmark*:

'My host had formed in secret the design of presenting me to the first notability of the country, one, indeed, of the most famous men at that time alive in Europe, Hans Christian Andersen. It was not within the reach of every visitor to Copenhagen to meet this admirable writer, who was old, feeble, and shielded by a bodyguard of friends against the incursions of the Philistine. Carl Andersen (no relation to H. C. Andersen) had taken me, in the course of our walk this morning, to the bachelor flat – I think in Havnegade, overlooking the so-called New Harbour [Nyhavn], close to Charlottenborg Palace – where H. C. Andersen lived in

Copenhagen. But here we were curtly told that he was "out of town". That phrase, however, is a flexible one, and Dr Fog, as it appeared, had discovered that Andersen was a very little way "out of town", namely no farther off than Rolighed, the house of his friends, the Melchiors. This house – I believe it has been since pulled down – lay close to the sea, with beautiful gardens around it, at no great distance beyond the northern fortifications. In fact, you traversed the fort called Kastellet, kept on along the terrace of the citadel, and reached Rolighed through the vague land of villas then skirting the old Limekilns [Kalkbrænderierne]. The Dean had obtained from Mr Melchior a cordial invitation to bring me out this afternoon, when Hans Andersen would be pleased to receive me. So little way was Rolighed "out of town" that we walked there from our house in a very short space of time.

'Andersen had gradually come to make this his second home. The name Rolighed means Quietude, and it was this quality about the place that had led his Jewish friends to suggest that he should accept their hospitality through part of every year. It was an eighteenth-century house, and had been the residence of a series of interesting people, among others of Rahbek, who died there in 1830, and afterwards of Hostrup, and then of Ørsted. It was owned (in 1872) by Mr Moritz Melchior, who had rebuilt it and who had turned it into a miniature of Rosenborg Palace, with a tower, and with high balconies overlooking the Sound. It was no longer the "hillside cottage" which Rahbek had celebrated eighty years before:

> That hence the way-worn traveller may detect
> Chains of white sails along the twinkling Sound
> And ancient Malmö set on Swedish ground,
> A belvedere my lowly roof hath decked;

but the same objects were still more advantageously to be observed from the anything but lowly turrets of Mr Melchior. At Rolighed Andersen was so constantly welcome that a portion of the house – three or four charming rooms – was set apart entirely for his service, and he came and went without restraint. "Rolighed" – with some play on the meanings of the word – is the subject of Andersen's latest poem, in which he says:

My home of homes, where behind the slope of elder-bushes,
My life regained its sunshine and my harp its tone,
To thee I bring with gratitude this blithe song of mine.

'Mr Moritz Gerson Melchior, who met us at the door, and
welcomed us in, was a handsome man of about sixty, a little deaf,
a little shy. He was one of the leading merchants and bankers of
the country, and perhaps its then wealthiest commoner. He held
at that time a seat in the Landsting, but I was told that he was
indifferent to politics, was a bad speaker and had not troubled
himself to make any mark in Parliament. On the other hand, he
was extremely energetic in civic and philanthropic work. Mrs
Melchior, who also entertained us, had been a Henriques; both
of them, and their children, spoke English to perfection. The
family conducted us over the grounds and through parts of the
house, but no word was said of the object of our visit. Suddenly,
however, as we were seated in the living-room, there appeared in
the doorway a very tall, elderly gentleman, dressed in a complete
suit of brown, and in a curly wig of the same shade of snuff-
colour. I was almost painfully struck, at the first moment, by the
grotesque ugliness of his face and hands, and by his enormously
long and swinging arms; but this impression passed away as soon
as he began to speak. His eyes, although they were small, had
great sweetness and vivacity of expression, while gentleness and
ingenuousness breathed from everything he said. He had been
prepared to expect a young English visitor, and he immediately
took my hand in his two big ones, patting and pressing it. Though
my hands have no delicacy to boast of, yet in those of Hans
Andersen they seemed like pebbles in a running brook, as
Elizabeth Barrett Browning might say.

'The face of Hans Andersen was a peasant's face, and a long
lifetime of sensibility and culture had not removed from it the
stamp of the soil. But it was astonishing how quickly this first
impression subsided, while a sense of his great inward distinction
took its place. He had but to speak, almost but to smile, and the
man of genius stood revealed. I experienced the feeling which I
have been told that many children felt in his company. All sense
of shyness and reserve fell away, and I was painfully and eagerly,
but with almost unprecedented success, endeavouring to express

my feelings to him in Danish. Andersen had at one time possessed considerable knowledge of English, and understood how to read it still, but had ceased to speak it with any ease. The rest of the company tactfully left us alone, and Andersen conversed about the many happy memories he had of England, his two bright visits to Charles Dickens, the shock of grief he had felt at Dickens's death, and his hope to come again some day to London.

'He then conducted me over the house, showing off its magnificence with a childlike enthusiasm, and finally he stopped in his own bright, high room open to the east. He took me out into the balcony and bade me notice the long caravan of ships going by in the Sound below – "They are like a flock of wild swans," he said – with the white towns of Malmö and Landskrona sparkling on the Swedish coast, and the sunlight falling on Tycho Brahe's island. Then he proposed to read to me a new fairy-tale he had just written. He read in a low voice, which presently sank almost to a hoarse whisper; he read slowly, out of mercy to my imperfect apprehension, and as he read he sat beside me, with his amazingly long and bony hand – a great brown hand, almost like that of a man of the woods – grasping my shoulder. As he read, the colour of everything, the twinkling sails, the sea, the opposing Swedish coast, the burnished sky above, kindled with sunset. It seemed as though Nature herself was flushing with ecstasy at the sound of Andersen's voice.

'When he had finished reading, he talked to me a little about the manuscript, and he confided to me that he intended this, *The Cripple*, to be his last work. He was very much pleased with it; he thought it summed up all his methods, and that in a certain sense it presented symbolically his lesson, his imaginative message, to mankind. The reader may not recollect this tale, which is far from being among the best known of Andersen's stories; nor is it really one of the most characteristic, for there is nothing supernatural or fantastic about it. It presents a little complicated episode of humble manners. A gardener and his wife have five children, of whom the eldest, an intelligent boy, has the misfortune to be a bedridden cripple. The parents, worthy narrow people, live engrossed in their materialistic interests, and when some one, from whom a present is expected, gives the cripple a book, they ungraciously say to one another, "He won't get fat on that." But it is a book of fairy-tales, and the boy's whole spiritual life is awakened by the vistas these open for him in every direction. He finds two simple and direct parables, which he reads over and over again to his parents, and their hearts, too, are humanised and melted. Finally, a little dark bird, like the Emperor of China's nightingale, is presented to him, and in a supreme nervous effort to save its life the cripple regains the use of his own limbs. Andersen intended in this story to sum up the defence of fairy-tales and of their teller. It was to be a sort of apologia for his whole poetical career, and he told me that it would be the latest of his writings. In this matter, however, his mind afterwards changed, for later in this same year – 1872 – he composed *Auntie Toothache*, inspired by his own sufferings, and it was with this story that the long series of his fairy-tales ultimately ended.

'As he was making these comments, Andersen's voice abruptly faded away, to my alarm. The bell was rung, and servants summoned the family, who looked at me as though I had blotted one of their black-letter volumes or dropped one of their splendid vases. It was, however, decided that the great man had lost his voice by the imprudence of reading aloud in the evening air, and he was conducted to his bed with infinite precautions. I could not help being amused at the languishing way in which Andersen lent himself to all this fuss, gazing silently at me while they supported him from the room. I supposed that we should now take our leave, but Danish hospitality is not to be restrained. On the contrary, the next two hours were vivaciously spent with the Melchior family in the garden. At supper, Hans Andersen reappeared; he occupied the seat of honour, and I was allowed to sit next to him. It was indicated to me, however, that he must be encouraged to talk but little, and soon after 10 p.m. the Dean rose and we excused ourselves. The sky was a vault of dark blue, cloudless, and all the stars keen and crystalline. We walked home along the outer edge of the rim of lakes that then bounded the city on the western side. Suddenly, out of the woods, the moon rose like a great luminous flower, a perfect globe of gold against the violet-blue. It shone out upon us in the midst of a metaphysical discussion, and transported us to silence.'

A very satisfying postscript to the story of Andersen's relations with the Melchiors is that when during the Second World War their granddaughter, Miss Melchior, was obliged to flee to Sweden with no time for packing, she took with her one of Andersen's letters to her grandparents and, thanks to this, was kept from immediate want.

Shortly before he left for what was to prove his last trip abroad, Andersen drove to the royal palace to say goodbye. As a boy staying in Amalienborg Square for the first time with the Wulff family, he had identified himself with Aladdin and gazed down from the windows with exaltation in his heart; now, more than half a century later, the prince of story-tellers was too weak to climb the royal staircase. So the King and Queen came down to him, accompanied by the Crown Prince and Princess and their infant sons, Prince Christian, who as King Christian X was to prove an outstandingly brave ruler of German-occupied Denmark in the Second World War, and Prince Carl, who as King Haakon VII was to head the Free Norwegian movement in England. (During the Second World War, incidentally, the Germans banned – quite uselessly since a volume containing it was already in most Danish homes – one of Andersen's earliest stories, *The Wicked Prince*, who 'thought only about how he might conquer all the nations of the world and make his name a terror to all mankind', despite which the wicked prince was finally 'defeated by a gnat'.) To the King and Queen and their children Andersen represented a magical national institution, just as they themselves did to him. The King gave Andersen the appropriate present of a portmanteau – which can now be seen in the Andersen Museum in Odense – and later, while Andersen was packing, the King made a s rprise visit to his rooms in Nyhavn, saying that he had been unable to resist seeing him once more before he left for Switzerland.

Friends insisted that he move to the Royal Hotel for a couple of days to see how he stood the change and when at last he did leave, an army of friends and admirers saw him off with his young friend Nikolaj Bøgh. They travelled by easy stages, via Frankfurt, to Switzerland, where Andersen had always felt well and hoped to get fresh medical advice. The first doctor they saw there said truthfully that Andersen's lungs and heart were sound, and his constitution good, but his nerves exceedingly fragile. A second doctor proved useless and Andersen took one of his rare dislikes to him. At last, on May 11, 1873, they settled at the Hôtel Righi Vaudois at Glion, one of Matthew Arnold's favourite places. Andersen and Bøgh had rooms with a superb view over the Lake of Geneva, the Dent du Midi and the Jura mountains. As a child Andersen had been taught to ask the cuckoo how long he would live, and this superstition returned to him now – 'The cuckoo is here too,' he wrote to Mrs Melchior, 'but is silent directly I ask him how long I have to live, yet it is so good to be alive, to have such friends and be able to enjoy such scenery.'

It was with the cuckoo's mute warning in mind that Andersen wrote to Edvard Collin: 'I have many friends, yes, some who take as lively an interest in me as they would if I were a member of their immediate family – the Melchiors, for example, but you, dear friend, are the oldest of my friends, from the time you helped me with my Latin compositions and were a little too much of a mentor towards me, until the most recent years, when our relationship became completely unclouded. You have also become so incomparably youthful and soft, in a good sense of the word, since that serious and dangerous operation of yours. [Edvard had recently undergone a successful operation for the removal of a tumour on his jaw.] All of your admirable qualities shine through every occasion, and I am not the only person who sees you thus, you are infinitely dear to me, for I cannot do without you. The words I write here come from my heart, you will understand me. It is wonderful to have friends in this world, friends such as I have.' Edvard did indeed understand these words. The days when he himself was an undemonstrative 'mentor' were long past, and he was to sum up his feeling for his oldest friend with 'I have looked into the depths of his soul . . . I know *that he was good.*'

Despite the cuckoo, Andersen's health quickly improved in Switzerland. He slept well and had a huge appetite. Indeed, he felt so much better that he agreed to give a public reading in Berne, his first in nine months. It was a great success, and when he left Berne the station was packed with children, many of whom insisted on being held up to the window of his carriage to wave goodbye. Encouraged by having succeeded in doing this with no ill results, he made up his mind to show his gratitude for Bøgh's care by giving the young man a glimpse of Italy.

They hired a carriage to cross the Splügen Pass, one of the great roads built after Napoleon's fall, when the perpetual neutrality of Switzerland had just been guaranteed. All went well until they were almost at Chiavenna, just across the Italian frontier. At this point the mosquito-maddened horse kicked the carriage almost to pieces and bolted, leaving them by the roadside in blazing sunlight. After this they gave up the idea of going to Italy and went to rest in the Engadine, one of the highest inhabited valleys in the Alps, and at this time a very peaceful and isolated region. There was a great deal of emigration among the native population, who could be found all over the Continent working as pastrycooks, confectioners, distillers, restaurant-keepers and chocolate vendors; pastures were let annually to shepherds from Bergamo, 'a wild, dark, scowling class of men, clad in brown or white blankets', and the mowing of meadows and the gathering of the harvest were done by seasonal Tyrolese workers. Tourists were few, since there was little accommodation for travellers except at St Mauritz (today's St Moritz), which was beginning to acquire a reputation as a spa. Here Andersen seemed to make a wonderfully quick recovery, and as soon as he could travel they set out for home. In Munich, however, he had a relapse and an attack of fever was followed by increasingly frequent fainting fits. He reached home worn out, and went straight to the Melchiors at Rolighed. Neither they nor he knew that he had cancer of the liver. There has been much discussion as to the nature of his last illness, but most medical evidence indicates this.

For the rest of 1873 and much of 1874 Andersen's outings when he was in Copenhagen were limited to trips from his rooms in Nyhavn to the Students' Union, and half-hour walks in Havnegade. Much of his time was spent on his enormous correspondence. In February he wrote to little Mary Livingstone, whose father had been reported dead, and who was indeed dead though a true report of this did not reach England until April:

Copenhagen, 17th February, 1874

My Dear Young Friend!

How glad I was to receive your letter, which was written and posted to me on January 25th. I was just then thinking of you, and was much grieved, but your letter has given me hope and joy again. You know, young as you are, that one must not always believe what the newspapers relate, there is often not a single grain of truth in it. More than once it has been announced that the Livingstone so highly prized by the world was dead, and – God be praised and thanked he still lives. A similar announcement of his death was published in the Danish newspapers before January 25th, and I, in common with the whole Danish nation, was grieved to hear that he had been called away from his great work for mankind just as he would be returning to his family and his country. Then I received your letter, dear Mary, and as you told me in it that he was coming home, and that you would perhaps visit Copenhagen with him, all the press news disappeared like fog, and I hoped, and hope, that he lives, and that he will see his children, relations, and friends again.

I have much to say and to write to you, but to-day I feel great anxiety as to the uncertainty of your father's destiny as mapped out by God.

Write me very soon. May it be an all-sunshiny letter!

With the most sincere sympathy and devotion,

H. O. ANDERSEN

Reading occupied as much of his time as ever, and he still enjoyed constructing things with his hands. From December 1873 to April 1874 he worked on a large folding screen for Mrs Melchior. This ingenious montage of coloured pictures of landscapes and famous people, grouped so that Denmark, Norway, England, France and Germany each had a section, was inspired by a screen given him by Countess Wanda Danneskjøld, and can be seen today in the Andersen Museum at Odense. It is the work of a born traveller at a time when photography was still so young an art that the untravelled had no moving pictures to give them a faint familiarity with what they were missing.

He was again invited to go to America, where, he was assured, he would have 'a greater reception than royalty', but he could no longer go even as far as to the Royal Theatre and this was one of his greatest deprivations. In *Aunty* he had written: 'Aunty deserved to live as long as the theatre itself, but she couldn't hold on that long; nor did she die in the theatre, but quietly and decently in her own bed. Her dying words were full of significance; she asked, "What are they playing tomorrow?" ' Andersen often wondered that as he sat in his rooms among his playbills and followed the play in his own mind, 'Now they have got to that part.' The actors and actresses visited him faithfully, bringing him all the latest theatre news and gossip.

He did not accept his immobility as final but with incredible resilience managed in June to go for a three weeks' visit to Holsteinborg, followed by a visit to Bregentved. The Countess Moltke-Huitfeldt's birthday was celebrated at Bregentved while he was there, and he managed not only to write thirty verses for the cotillon favours but attended the ball and took a lady down to the midnight supper. Despite these wonderful spurts of vitality, however, the power to write deserted him. 'It is as if I had filled up my wheel of life with fairy-tale spokes quite close together. If I go into the garden among the roses, what have they (and even the snails upon them) to tell me that they have not told me already? If I look at the broad water-lily leaves, I remember that *Thumbelina* has already finished her journey. If I listen to the wind, it has already told me about Valdemar Daae, and has no better story. In the wood, beneath the old oak, I recalled that the old oak has long ago told me its last dream. Thus I get no new impressions and that is sad.'

News of his illness had spread abroad and in America had given rise to a rumour that he was living in poverty, a rumour which he scotched promptly and with dignity in a letter to Gibson Peacock, publisher of the *Evening Bulletin*:

Copenhagen, 30th August, 1874

Honoured Sir,

You will accept my most sincere thanks for your kind

communication, and will hear with the same disposition what I have to say.

American papers have taken the occasion of my recent illness to discuss the outward circumstances under which I live, and to point out to parents and patrons the obligations which they owe me, after flattering expressions in relation to me as the author of *Fairy Tales and Stories*. I hear also, in addition, that a general subscription has begun in several places of the Union. You, my unknown friend, have already forwarded me some cash contributions.

The thought from which this movement had its origin touches me deeply. It has always been my joy and happiness that my tales have found readers far beyond the boundaries of my small fatherland, and its little-known language, and I cannot be more thankful for the bounties of Providence towards me, in that it has been granted me to influence such numberless child-souls, and, as I hope, to have implanted in so many childish hearts something of nobility and goodness. It moves me deeply, and I admit it most sincerely, that a feeling of obligation and gratitude has been expressed towards me. I feel it doubly in that you have sought me after severe illness, and under presumably narrow circumstances.

A gift of affection brought to me under such conditions I cannot thrust aside. Large or small, it bears a stamp which must make it dear to me. Deeply touched, I send the little ones my greeting and my thanks!

But it is due to myself, as well as the nation to which I belong, to clear up a possible misunderstanding. I am still weak after my illness, and am near the end of my seventieth year; but I do not find myself in pecuniary distress. My fatherland does not belong to those countries which allow their poets to suffer want. Without being in the service of the State, I receive yearly from it an honourable stipend, which covers all my expenses. My work as an author also brings me in an income, and although it is a truth that I have practically received no honorarium for the manifold translations of my books into foreign languages, yet I have here and there been paid an indemnification, as from America, for the so-called

'Author's Edition'. My sympathizing friends, therefore, must not think of me as a poor, forsaken old poet, who lives in anxiety for his daily bread, and can take no care of his feeble body. In this respect, also, God has been good towards me. Kind friends surround me. Great happiness, not to say fortune, has been my portion, and not the least of it is the pleasure which I experience, that in wide America many children have broken open their money-boxes, in order to share their contents with their old author, whom they believe to be in the deepest necessity.

The whole is to me an enchanted page in my life's history, but it must be understood that I can accept no gift sent to me by private individuals. However well meant they might be, they would still have a stamp, which would neither accord with the desire of the giver, nor with my sense of dignity. What would be to me an honour and a token of esteem, when presented by the American youth as a whole, would become a painful act of benevolence, if sent piece-meal in gifts from single persons, and that for which I ought really to feel pride and gratitude would be turned to humiliation.

I beg you, sir, who have already proved to me your kindly sympathy, to bring this, my explanation, to the knowledge of your readers, and I hope that your respected colleagues throughout the wide country will give publicity to the same.

I remain,

Your servant,

H. C. ANDERSEN

When he returned to Rolighed in the autumn, he was still able to take country walks and pay occasional visits to Copenhagen. Here he received an account of her father's funeral from Mary Livingstone:

Ulva Cottage,
Hamilton, 24th September, 1874

My dear Hans Andersen,

I have often thought of you since you wrote to me last, and wished to write to you, but never got to do so before. You

would see from the newspapers the great sorrow we have
had this year. I did so expect to have had papa take me to
see you in Denmark. Instead of going to the different places
I fully intended to with papa, I was obliged to take the sad
journey to London to see him buried in Westminster Abbey.
Both my aunts were there, and also my brothers and sister.
We all had wreaths of pure white flowers to put on his coffin.
At one o'clock the procession entered the abbey, and the
coffin was placed on velvet trestles. It was covered with a
black velvet pall edged with white silk, and the top of the
coffin was covered with white wreaths and palm leaves.
While the procession was moving along the organ played
most beautifully. Then we all sang that hymn:

> O God of Bethel, by whose hand
> Thy people still are fed,
> Who through this weary pilgrimage
> Hast all our fathers led.

Then the procession to the grave formed. Immediately
after the coffin came grandpapa [Dr Moffat] and my two
brothers, Thomas and Oswell. Next came my sister and
myself, and behind us my aunts, and then friends. When the
coffin was set down at the grave, which was all draped in
black, Agnes, my sister, and I had to lay our wreaths on the
coffin, and then my aunts laid theirs. One of my aunts from
the south of England laid a wreath of violets and primroses
from a lane that papa liked to walk in very much. We were
ranged round close to the grave, and a beautiful anthem was
sung, called: 'His body was buried in peace'. Then the Dean
read the funeral service, and all was over. The abbey was
crowded, and the vergers of the abbey said they had never
seen such a number of people in Westminster Abbey since
the death of the Prince Consort. There was a funeral service
preached in the abbey the next Sunday. The picture of me
that I send you is taken just as I stood at Papa's grave. It was
my first visit to London. Papa's two coloured servants were
here seeing us last week. They were telling us a great many
interesting things about papa; and one of them, called
Chumah, made a little model of the grass hut in which papa

died, and showed us the position of papa's bed in it. It is very interesting to us.

I was very, very sorry to hear you had been so ill, but I hope you are better now. I should so much like, if you are able, to get a letter from you. My brother has gone back to Egypt again.

I am going to a boarding-school next week, which will be a new experience to me altogether.

I forgot to tell you, when speaking of papa's funeral, that our beloved Queen sent a most lovely white wreath, and she and the Prince of Wales had their carriages at the abbey.

I think I have told you all I know, so with much love, I am your ever loving,

ANNA MARY LIVINGSTONE

He thought of David Livingstone who had gone so far afield in his sixty years on earth, of his own father who had died so much younger without having crossed a single frontier, and of how much Mary Livingstone's future – both she and her husband were to go as missionaries to Africa, the dark continent that held such a fascination for nineteenth-century explorers – and his own past as a writer might owe to their respective fathers. It was from his father that Andersen had learnt to love Shakespeare, and knowing himself near death – for sixty-nine meant extreme old age at that time – he remembered the beautiful words so mysteriously in harmony with the sea around him,

> Full fathom five thy father lies;
> Of his bones are coral made;
> Those are pearls that were his eyes:
> Nothing of him that doth fade,
> But doth suffer a sea-change
> Into something rich and strange. . . .

19. Finale

1874-5

Everyone was happy for him, everyone blessed him, and there was no one who was envious. And that was the most incredible thing.

Hans Christian Andersen, *The Most Incredible Thing*

*

IN 1874 the old Royal Theatre was abandoned for a new one with room for 1,600 spectators. Proud as they were of their new theatre, many people thought nostalgically of the memories bound up with the old building that had housed a hundred and sixty-six years of theatre-going. In his *Studies in the Literature of Northern Europe* Edmund Gosse wrote of this original Royal Theatre: 'Within its walls almost all that is really national and individual in the poetic literature of the country had found at one time or another its place and voice within the walls that now no more will ever display their faded roses and smoky garlands to the searching flare of the footlights. Almost every Danish poet of eminence with the exception of Grundtvig and Winther, perhaps everyone had been taken personally into the sympathy of the nation in a way no mere study-writer can be. Men who had seen the white sick face of Ewald grow whiter under the storms of applause . . . the next generation [who] saw Oehlenschläger, handsome and burly in his stall, receive the plaudits like a comfortable burgher, one of themselves; the younger men that knew the haughty, keen face of Heiberg, master of all the best aesthetic culture that his age could give, yet a Dane in every feature, and a type to every romantic youth of what a Dane should be – these men had a sense of being part and parcel of the national poetic life such as no citizens have had save at Athens and Florence and Weimar, and their sympathy has been so far wider than

353

these that it was not the emotion of a single city, however potent, but of a whole nation . . .'

Andersen was invited to the opening performance at the new theatre and insisted on going. He received a tremendous ovation as he took his seat, but the audience was awed by the signs of death in his face. He managed to visit the theatre once or twice more, and to keep up his regular visits to the Collins, and he was able to see beautiful Princess Alexandra when she came from England to visit her family. She already had four children, the ten-year-old Duke of Clarence, the nine-year-old Prince George (the future George V of England), the Princess Royal, and little Princess Victoria. He read more than ever now that he could no longer write, and was at pains to help young writers. His own early struggles had not developed in him any wish to see others rise the hard way. One of the last young writers he saw this year was, once again, Edmund Gosse, with whom he had corresponded since their previous meeting.

Gosse describes this in his account of his second visit to Denmark:

'As it happened it was the oldest of all my friends to whom I was summoned immediately after this bath in the earnest gaiety of youth. When I went into the study next morning, to greet my host after *smørrbrød*, he told me that Hans Christian Andersen had sent a servant round with a note asking if I were not arrived in Copenhagen, and saying that he wanted to see me. We gazed together, pensively, at the little piece of paper, tremulously scribbled over, and it was not needful that either of us should remark to the other on the evidence it gave of physical feebleness . . . I flew in response to his summons at once. When I arrived at the house on Nyhavn, the *entresol* of which he occupied whenever he was not with the Melchiors at Rolighed, the woman who opened the door made a long face. "Impossible," she said, "the Konferenceraad [Privy Councillor], for he was thus addressed, could see no one. He was very tired, very weak."

'Perceiving my great disappointment and anxiety, and learning that Andersen had summoned me himself, she finally withdrew to see her master, and returned, visibly displeased, to announce that the Konferenceraad insisted upon my coming in, but she privately added, "You must not stay more than two minutes; he is very ill." As I entered the bright, pretty sitting-room, Hans Christian Andersen was coming in from an opposite door. He leaned against a chair and could not proceed. I was infinitely shocked to see how extremely he had changed since I had found him so blithe and communicative, only two years before. He was wearing a close-fitting, snuff-coloured coat such as I remember to have seen Lord Beaconsfield wear as he went slowly up Whitehall, on Mr. Curry's arm, in the later 'sixties. This garment, besides being very old-fashioned, accentuated the extreme thinness of Andersen's tall figure, which was wasted, as people say, to a shadow. He was so afflicted by asthma that he could not utter a word, and between sorrow, embarrassment and helplessness, I wished myself miles away.

'The door at which he had entered remained open, and I supposed it to lead to his bedroom. I implored him to return to it, and to allow me to come at a more favourable moment. But, while he leaned heavily on my wrist, and stumbled back, I discovered that it was not a bedroom, but a library, in which he could easily be persuaded to sink upon a comfortable sofa. He now found his voice, and would by no means suffer me to go. I must take a chair at his side, and he held my hand affectionately in his. He explained, with great sweetness, that this was not the beginning, but was the end of a malady. He had suffered ever since the New Year from a most painful illness, as indeed I knew; but, although he was very weak, he declared that he was almost well. I had, till now, hardly perceived a third person in the room, a good-looking young fellow, with a very refined expression, to whom Andersen now presented me. "This is Nikolaj Bøgh. You read so much Danish, that I daresay you know his poems. He is like a son to me; God bless him!" He went on to say that Bøgh had never left him since his last severest attack of illness, and that he hoped he never would. "I should have died without him!" and still holding me by one hand, he affectionately pressed that of his young friend with the other.

'Two days before had been Midsummer Day, the great festival and holiday of Denmark, when the whole city of Copenhagen empties into the forest, and comes back in the evening laden with boughs of the national beech-tree, thus bringing "great Birnam

Wood to Dunsinane". Hans Andersen said that he had insisted on going out, too, although they had declared he must not. "Oh! I can still be very obstinate," he laughed; and in a carriage he and young Bøgh had driven far into the verdant recesses of Söndermarken, "far, far out – as far as to Valby", he said, as though this very suburban excursion had been made into fairy lands forlorn. Mr Bøgh, who had not hitherto spoken, looked at him reproachfully. "You ought not to have gone! It has tired you too much!" "No, no!" replied Andersen, "it was exquisite. I shall be the better for it; I am really better already." But I was conscience-stricken and eager to be gone. Mr Bøgh regarded me, it was plain, with unmitigated displeasure. Yet before I could leave, Hans Andersen, who was now certainly less feverish, insisted on rising, and, with his great emaciated hand laid again upon my wrist, accompanied me slowly into the outer room, where several boughs of sparkling young beech stood in a vase. He broke off a spray, and gave it to me, half solemnly, with his poet's blessing; and then Mr Bøgh came, peremptorily this time, and led him back again . . . This was a glimpse at the setting of a luminary of the first order of glory. As long as human intelligence survives, there will surely exist some grateful memory of Hans Andersen.'

At the end of 1874 Andersen had bronchitis and was given morphine to make him sleep. He then had a dream of Meisling that seemed to bring to an end, in a way strikingly characteristic of Andersen, the story of the unfortunate relationship that had started fifty-two years earlier. 'The morphine must have had a very strong effect,' the old man wrote in his diary; 'I had splendid dreams, one of them particularly pleasant. I was quick-witted in my examinations and Meisling came in, and I declared that he was not to listen while I was being examined, for in that case I should feel so self-conscious that I would answer stupidly – which I then proceeded to do. A little later I took a walk with Meisling, he made his usual jokes, I felt quick and lively, we soon began to talk about art and beauty, and *at last we became good friends*, he seemed to appreciate me and I him. When I woke I was heartily pleased with this conciliatory dream.'

Early in the new year Andersen decided to try the goat's milk cure at Glion again. He bought a new suit, had his furniture stored and booked rooms in Montreux. But his friends knew that he would never again be able to travel abroad. When he arrived at Rolighed, on March 4, he looked so ill that even the Melchiors' little daughter was alarmed. He continued, however, to fight his disease with astonishing courage and resilience and was back in Copenhagen for his seventieth birthday, which the Melchiors celebrated with a banquet at their town house at which every dish on the menu was in honour of one of his stories.

MENU

April 2, 1875

The Neighbouring Families	Oysters
Soup on a Sausage Peg	
Spin a Long Yarn about Nothing	Turkey
From the Barnyard	
Under the Willow Tree	Champignons
What One Can Invent	Frittered sweetbreads with
Five Peas from a Pod	green peas
Something	Salmon with asparagus
The Sweethearts	Wine jelly
The Wild Swans	Game
Everything in Its Proper Place	Danish open sandwiches,
Ask the Old Lady from Amager	cheese and radishes
The Ice Maiden and *The Snowman*	Dessert

WINES

Something from the Bottleneck

The Old House	(Château Guiraud)
From Spain	(Sherry, Champagne)
The Jumpers	(Champagne)
It's Quite True	(Bordeaux)
The World's Fairest Rose	(Château Larose)
She Was Good for Nothing	(Madeira)

The Wild Swan

Aunty	(Veuve Clicquot)
Kept Secret but Not Forgotten	(Old Madeira)
The Last Pearl	(Malvoisier)

Messages and presents poured in from all over the world and were dealt with by Dorothea Melchior and Henriette Collin. There was a message and a new decoration from the King, also from the Grand Duke of Weimar; from the Melchiors a velvet-bound announcement that the subscription lists for a statue to be raised to him in the King's Garden had been filled in record time.

There was a great deal of discussion as to the form this statue should take, and Andersen strongly objected to the designs submitted by Saabye. On June 6, 1875, he wrote to Jonas Collin: 'Saabye visited me again last night. My blood boiled, and so I spoke my mind in no uncertain terms, saying that none of the sculptors knew me, that none of their designs suggested that they had seen and known what was characteristic of me, that I could never read aloud when anybody was sitting behind me or close to me, still less when I had children on my knees or young Copenhageners leaning against me, that it was a mere phrase to call me the "children's poet". My goal was to be a poet for all ages, and children could not represent me. The naïve element was only part of the fairy tale, the humour was the salt of it, and my written language was based on popular speech . . .'

Yet he did rejoice in children's love of him, and in 1866, when he had for the first time bought some furniture instead of living in furnished rooms, he had written to Hartmann: 'I have now for the first time got my own bed, which I suppose will be my death-bed. I am now, as Madame Jette Collin so nicely puts it, "an elderly man", and so I must think of my death-bed. You attend to the funeral march! It will, of course, be the schools, the small schools, which will follow, not the big Latin ones. So arrange the music to suit children's steps.' From America the editor of the *New York Tribune* sent books subscribed for by the children of America. In his letter of thanks he wrote: 'My seventieth birthday was a day rich in sunshine and blessing. From every part of my beloved country and far away beyond its boundaries came beautiful presents, letters, and telegrams. For what an infinite amount of good I have to be thankful.' To the Grand Duke he confided that he had been so ill as to be barely able to receive all his visitors: 'God willing, I shall soon leave town. Only country quiet and summer warmth can help me now.'

Immediately afterwards the Melchiors took him back to Rolighed. There he was given his usual ideal rooms with a balcony overlooking the Sound, and one of the Melchiors' manservants to whom Andersen had in the past shown particular kindness volunteered to look after him night and day. At first he was able to walk in the garden. Sometimes he would sit in the sun and, just as when he was a child he had planned every detail of the castle he would build when grown up and famous, so now the old man who all his life had lived in lodgings and hotels would plan to build a villa for when he got well: a villa of his own, to be built in Moorish style, with a circular glass vestibule full of evergreens and palms, a fountain with goldfish in the centre, and round the walls busts of the great Danish artists. He could see himself sitting writing in the midst of them – 'I would turn out something worth reading.'

Gradually his state became somnolent. He wrote to the composer Hartmann, one of the remaining friends of his youth who was an exact contemporary: 'If I am to die, may it happen quickly – I cannot wait, I cannot lie and crumble up like a withered leaf.' At last he had to stay in his bedroom, getting up only for short spells on the balcony. He never complained and seemed at peace with his end. Once he murmured, 'How happy I am! How beautiful the world is! Life is so beautiful. It is as if I were sailing to a land far far away, where there is no pain, no sorrow.' He told Nikolaj Bøgh, 'I have never *wished* to do evil. I have always loved what is good, though I know very well that I have often been ill-tempered, bitter and absurd.'

His love of reading persisted and the last book he read was the *Pancha Tantra*, a collection of Hindu stories and fables attributed to Bidpay, who lived in the fourth or third century before Christ. As a child Andersen had delighted in the *Arabian Nights*, and as an old man he still responded to the pristine colours of fantasy.

On Saturday, June 19, he wrote for the last time in his diary: 'Today I intended to arrive at Bregentved, but I am still sitting here, and shall have to be extraordinarily glad if I can get there in eight days' time. This morning a letter from Robert Henriques, as well as from Mathilde Ørsted, who is leaving today with her mother for Fredensborg to stay with the Bournonvilles. Jonas Collin has come out here and promised to take care of all my things. Visit from Candidate Krohn. This afternoon I have written down almost all of this week's happenings . . . The sun is shining but in spite of that I feel cold and have a fire going in the stove.' After that the diary was dictated to members of the Melchior family. The final entry was for July 27: 'A good night, yet very tired . . . Clear but stormy weather. Letter from Miss Clara Heincke enclosing a clipping from an illustrated periodical. Have been sitting on the balcony for about three hours.' On July 29 he was unable to leave his bed, but when Mrs Melchior brought him a white rose he kissed it, pressed her hand, and whispered, 'If I were not so very tired I should feel quite well.'

Andersen had every reason to feel tired. He had come so far – *What the Old Man does is always right* had been painfully achieved, step by step of the way, and he looked back as if down a long avenue growing narrower and narrower towards the end, where a barefoot illiterate boy stood beside a little river, a child's ocean, singing for his supper to the Emperor of China and vying with the nightingale that was to be denied him, back, back, through the springtime woods, the stork's return and the cuckoo's cry, to a little house where a baby lay on a funereally draped home-made bed beside which a young cobbler read into his child's future the plays of Denmark's glorious Holberg. He had 'imagined so much and known so little', was indeed, for all his domestic pieties, a 'high wild-flying bird'.

His sense of time slid from him imperceptibly. When told it was August 1, he showed surprise and said, 'What a lot of trouble I am giving you. How tired you must be of me.' For the next two days he was half asleep, had to be roused to take food, and when spoken to said gently, 'Don't ask me how I am, I understand nothing more.' On the morning of August 4, Dorothea Melchior went in to see him as usual around eleven o'clock and found him sleeping peacefully. She left the room for a few minutes. Then the manservant came running to her. Andersen had just given a sigh and stopped breathing.

A telegram, now in the Odense Museum, was sent to Edvard Collin – 'At eleven o'clock this morning our beloved friend passed peacefully away' – and at the end of Andersen's diary Mrs Melchior wrote:

'Now the light has been extinguished.
What a happy death. At five minutes past eleven the dear
friend gave his last sigh.'

All the bells in Copenhagen tolled the day that Hans Christian Andersen went through its streets for the last time. The Church of Our Lady could not contain one tenth of the mourners. The whole city wanted to stay with him to the last, and for days afterwards his grave in the Assistens Cemetery was surrounded by crowds who had been unable to enter the church.

Today, nearly a hundred years later, his grave is never without flowers, his stories are never out of print, his home in Odense is never without visitors – all the signposts in Odense have an extra arm pointing towards *Andersens Hus* – and there is never a moment when there is not somewhere in the world a child who is reading Hans Christian Andersen for the first time.

BIBLIOGRAPHY
INDEX

Bibliography

BOOKS BY ANDERSEN

The Complete Andersen. All the 168 stories by Hans Christian Andersen (some never before translated into English, and a few never before published), translated by Jean Hersholt. The Heritage Illustrated Bookshelf, New York: The Heritage Press, 1942–8

Hans Christian Andersen's Fairy Tales translated by R. P. Keigwin, World Edition, edited by Svend Larsen, Odense, 1950

Andersen's novels: The Improvisatore, or: Life in Italy, translated by Mary Howitt, London, 1845

Only a Fiddler, translated by Mary Howitt, London, 1845

O.T., translated by Mary Howitt, London, New York, 1845

The Two Baronesses, translated by Charles Beckwith, London, 1848

To Be or Not to Be, translated by Mrs Bushby, London, 1857

Lucky Peer, included in the Jean Hersholt collection.

Andersen's travel books: A Poet's Bazaar, translated by Charles Beckwith, London, 1846

Rambles in the Romantic Regions of the Harz Mountains, Saxon Switzerland, etc., translated by Charles Beckwith, London, 1848

In Sweden, translated by K. R. K. Mackenzie, London, 1852

In Spain, translated by Mrs Bushby, London, 1864

Andersen's Autobiographies: The Fairy Tale of My Life, translated by W. Glyn Jones, Copenhagen, London and New York, 1954

The Story of My Life, Author's Edition, Boston and New York, Cambridge, 1871

The True Story of My Life, American-Scandinavian Foundation, 1926

BOOKS ABOUT ANDERSEN: (A) ENGLISH

'Andersen', Nos. 248–9 of year XXII of the International Review *Adam*

BAIN, R. N. NESBIT, *Hans Christian Andersen, a Biography*, London, 1895

BÖÖK, FREDRIK, *Hans Christian Andersen, a Biography*, translated from the Swedish by George C. Schoolfield. Norman, Okla., 1962

Bibliography

BOYESEN, H., 'An Acquaintance with Hans Christian Andersen', *Century*, New York, March 1892

BROBY-JOHANSEN, R., *and* KRAG, EILER, *Hans Andersen's Copenhagen*, Copenhagen, 1963

BROWNING, GEORGE, *A Few Personal Recollections of Hans Christian Andersen*, London, 1875

City of Odense Museums, udgivet af Odense Bys Museer, 1960

CRAWFORD, F. (ed.), *Hans Christian Andersen's Correspondence with the late Grand Duke of Saxe-Weimar, Dickens, etc.*, London, 1891

GODDEN, RUMER, *Hans Christian Andersen. A Great Life in Brief*, New York, 1955

HERSHOLT, JEAN, *and* WESTERGAARD, WALDEMAR, *Andersen-Scudder Letters*, Berkeley and Los Angeles, 1949

LARSEN, SVEND, *Hans Christian Andersen*, translated by Mabel Dyrup, Odense, 1961

REUMERT, ELITH, *Hans Christian Andersen the Man*, London, 1927

TOKSVIG, SIGNE, *The Life of Hans Christian Andersen*, London, 1934

A Book on the Danish Writer Hans Christian Andersen, His Life and Work, published on the 150th anniversary of his birth, by Det Berlingske Bogtrykkeri, Copenhagen, 1955

With Hans Christian Andersen as our Guide through the Collections in Odense, published by the Hans Christian Andersen Museum, Odense

Hans Christian Andersen's visit to Charles Dickens, as described in his letters, published with 6 of Dickens's letters in facsimile by Ejnar Munksgaard, Copenhagen, 1937

(B) DANISH

H. C. Andersens Samlede Skrifter I-XXXIII, Copenhagen, 1853-1879. (Normally 2nd edition is quoted, because this first edition is seldom obtainable complete.)

H. C. Andersens Eventyr, vol. II, by ERIK DAL, ERLING NIELSEN, Copenhagen, 1964

H. C. Andersens Levnedsbog, Foreword by HANS BRIX, Copenhagen, 1926

BEHREND, C., *and* H. TOPSØE-JENSEN, *H. C. Andersens Brevveksling med Edvard og Henriette Collin*, I-VI, Copenhagen, 1934-7

BIRGER, FRANK NIELSEN, *H. C. Andersen Bibliografi*, Copenhagen, 1942

BLOCH, WILLIAM, *Paa Rejse med H. C. Andersen*, Copenhagen, 1942

COLLIN, EDVARD, *H. C. Andersen og det Collinske Hus*, Copenhagen, 1882

DAL, ESTRID og ERIK, *Fra H. C. Andersens Boghylde; Hans Bogsamling belyst gennem Breve, Kataloger og bevarede Bøger*, Copenhagen, 1961

FRIIS, AAGE, *Fra det Heibergske Hjem*, Copenhagen, 1940

FRIIS, FINN T. B., *H. C. Andersen og Schweiz*, Copenhagen, 1949

HELWEG, HJALMAR, *H. C. Andersen: en psykiatrisk Studie*, Copenhagen, 1927

Bibliography

HETCH, G., *H. C. Andersen og Musiken*, Copenhagen, 1930

HØEG, EILER, *Om H. C. Andersens 'Afreageren'*, Copenhagen, 1940

HUDE, ELISABETH, *Henriette Hanck og H. C. Andersen, Fynske Studier I*, Odense, 1958

LARSEN, SVEND, *and* H. TOPSØE-JENSEN, *H.C. Andersens eget Eventyr i Billeder*, Copenhagen, 1952

LEBECH, MOGENS, *Gamle københavnske Billeder*, Copenhagen

LEHMANN, EDVARD, *Almueliv og Eventyr* (The chapter: H.C.A. – Hin Primitive), Copenhagen, 1910

LUND, AXELINE, *Spredte Erindringer*, Copenhagen, 1917

LUND, OLE, *Smaabilleder fra Helsingør 1800–30* by cand. Theol. Oscar Geismar, Copenhagen, 1900

NEERGAARD, BODIL (born Hartmann), *Spredte Træk af mit Liv*, Copenhagen, 1941

NIELSEN, SVEN, *En Tur paa Assistens*, Copenhagen, 1960

OLRIK, H. G., *Hans Christian Andersen. Undersøgelser og Kroniker 1925–1944*, Copenhagen, 1945

PORTMAN, ARNE, *H. C. Andersens sidste Dage*, Copenhagen, 1952

REUMERT, ELITH, *H. C. Andersen og det Melchiorske Hjem*, Copenhagen, 1924

ROSENKILDE, VOLMER, *Gamle danske Bøger af international Berømmelse*, Copenhagen, 1935

RUBOW, PAUL V., *H. C. Andersen og det Collinske Hus*, Copenhagen, 1929

SCHMIDT, KARL, *Meddelelser om Skuespil og Theaterforhold i Odense*, Odense, 1896

SCHWANENFLÜGEL, H., *Hans Christian Andersen. Et Digterliv*, Copenhagen, 1905

STAMPE, RIGMOR, *H. C. Andersen og hans naermeste Omgang*, Copenhagen, 1918

SØRENSEN, VILLY, *Digtere og Daemoner*, Copenhagen, 1959

TOPSØE-JENSEN, H., *H. C. Andersens Brevveksling med Jonas Collin den ældre og andre Medlemmer af det Collinske Hus, I–III*, Copenhagen, 1945–8

H. C. Andersen i Livets Aldre, Copenhagen, 1955

Mit eget Eventyr uden Digtning. En Studie over H.C.A. som Selvbiograf, Copenhagen, 1940

Omkring Levnedsbogen, Copenhagen, 1943

H. C. Andersen og Henriette Wulff. En Brevveksling I–III, Odense, 1959

WAD, GUSTAV LUDVIG, *Om Hans Christian Andersens Slægt*, Odense, 1905

WILDE, ALEXANDER, *Erindringer fra før jeg blev Løjtnant*, Copenhagen, 1885

WOEL, CAI M., *H. C. Andersens Liv og Digtning, I–II*, Copenhagen, 1949 (also published in I–IV, but it is the same)

Much valuable information on Andersen is also contained in various periodicals published in Denmark and elsewhere. These include *Anderseniana, Berlingske Tidende, Dagens Nyheder, Aftenbladet, Politiken, Illustreret Tidende*, and many others.

Bibliography

OTHER BOOKS CONSULTED

D'ANDLAU, B., *Madame de Staël*, Coppet, Switzerland, 1963

ARNAUD, ODETTE, *Pêcheur de Rêves*, Paris, 1936

BAILHOCHE, JEAN, *Danemark*, Paris, 1959

BAINVILLE, JACQUES, *Louis II de Bavière*, Paris, 1964

BAUDELAIRE, CHARLES, *L'Art Romantique*, Paris, 1964

BÉGUIN, ALBERT, *L'Ame Romantique et le Rêve*, Paris, 1960

BERLIN, ISAIAH, *Karl Marx, His Life and Environment*, London, 1963

BRAIBANT, CHARLES, *Histoire de la Tour Eiffel*, Paris, 1964

BRANDES, GEORG, *Wolfgang Goethe*, New York, 1924
   Main Currents in Nineteenth Century Literature, London, 1923
   Lord Beaconsfield, London, 1880
   Creative Spirits of the Nineteenth Century, New York, 1923

BREDSDORFF, ELIAS, *Danish Literature in English Translation, a Bibliography*,
   Copenhagen, 1950
   Hans Andersen and Charles Dickens: A Friendship and Its Dissolution, Copen-
   hagen, 1956

BREDSDORFF, ELIAS, MORTENSEN, BRITA, and POPPERWELL, RONALD,
   Scandinavian Literature from the Earliest Time to Our Day, Copenhagen and
   London, 1951

BREMER, CHARLOTTE (ed.), *Life, Letters and Posthumous Works of Fredrika
   Bremer*, London, 1868

BRIGGS, ASA, *Victorian People*, London, 1954

BRION, MARCEL, *L'Allemagne Romantique*, Paris, 1962
   Art Fantastique, Paris, 1961

BRØNSTED, JOHANNES, *The Vikings*, Harmondsworth, 1960

BROOKS, VAN WYCK, *The Dream of Arcadia*, New York, 1958

BROWNING, ROBERT and ELIZABETH, *The Letters of Robert Browning and
   Elizabeth Barrett Browning*, John Murray, London, 1923

BRUUN, G., *Nineteenth Century European Civilization, 1815–1914*, London, 1959

BULMAN, JOAN, *Jenny Lind*, London, 1956

CANNON, HENRY, *The Ludwigs of Bavaria*, London, 1933

CLOUGH, ARTHUR HUGH, *Amours de Voyage*, London, 1888

CRUIKSHANK, R. J., *Roaring Century, 1846–1946*, London, 1946

DAHL, ARTHUR, *Søren Kierkegaard's Pilgrimage to Jutland*, Danish Tourist
   Association, 1948

DANSTRUP, JOHN, *A History of Denmark*, Copenhagen, 1947

DELACROIX, EUGENE, *Journal (1822–63)*, Union Générale d'Editions, 1963

ECKERMANN, JOHANN PETER, *Conversations with Goethe*, translated by Margaret
   Fuller, 1839

EISELEY, LOREN, *Darwin's Century*, Garden City, New York, 1961

Bibliography

FISHER, H. A. L., *History of Europe*, London, 1962

FORD, FORD MADOX, *The March of Literature*, London, 1947

GERNSHEIM, HELMUT and ALISON, *L. J. M. Daguerre*, London, 1956

GOETHE, J. W. VON, *Goethe présenté par lui-même*, edited by Marguerite Ancelot-Hustache, Paris, 1956

GOSSE, EDMUND, *Two Visits to Denmark*, London, 1911
Studies in the Literature of Northern Europe, London, 1879

GREEN, ROGER LANCELYN, *The Saga of Asgard*, London, 1960

GRELET, PIERRE, *La Suisse des Diligences*, Lausanne, 1947

GUSDORF, GEORGES, *Kierkegaard*, Paris, 1963

HAUSER, ARNOLD, *The Social History of Art*, New York, 1958

HAZARD, PAUL, *Les Livres, les Enfants et les Hommes*, Paris, 1949

HERSHOLT, JEAN, *Catalogue of the Jean Hersholt Collection of Hans Christian Andersen*, Washington, 1954

HOFFMANN, E. T. A., *Le Chat Mure*, translated by Albert Béguin, Paris, 1943

HOHLENBERG, JOHANNES, *L'Oeuvre de Søren Kierkegaard*, Paris, 1960
Søren Kierkegaard, a Biography, New York, 1954

HOWITT, MARY, *An Autobiography*, edited by her daughter Margaret Howitt, London, 1889

HOWITT, WILLIAM and MARY, *The Literature and Romance of Northern Europe*, London, 1852

HURTON, WILLIAM, *Leith to Lapland*, London, 1852

JAMES, HENRY, *William Wetmore Story and His Friends*, London, originally published 1903

JANSEN, F. J. BILLESKOV, *Anthologie de la Littérature Danoise*, Paris, 1964

JEMIMA, MISS, *Miss Jemima's Swiss Journal, the first conducted tour of Switzerland*, London, 1963

KIERKEGAARD, SØREN, *Journals 1834–1854*, London, 1958
Kierkegaard par lui-même, edited by Marguerite Grimault, Paris, 1962

LAURING, PALLE, *A History of the Kingdom of Denmark*, Copenhagen, 1960

LOWRIE, WALTER, *A Short Life of Kierkegaard*, Garden City, New York, 1961

MARRYATT, HORACE, *A Residence in Jutland, the Danish Isles and Copenhagen*, London, 1860

MITCHELL, P. M., *A Bibliographical Guide to Danish Literature*, Copenhagen, 1951

MORAND, PAUL, *La Dame Blanche des Habsburgs*, Paris, 1963

MORRISON, HELEN BARBARA, *The Golden Age of Travel*, New York, 1951

MORTON, H. V., *A Traveller in Rome*, London, 1957

NAMIER, SIR LEWIS, *Vanished Supremacies*, London, 1962

NEIIENDAM, ROBERT, *Teatermuseet ved Christiansborg*

NERVAL, GÉRARD DE, *Oeuvres*, Paris, 1956

OGRIZEK, DORÉ, *Les Pays Nordiques*, Paris, 1951

PACA, LILLIAN GRACE, *The Royal Birds*, New York, 1963

POPE-HENNESSY, JAMES, *Monckton Milnes*, New York, 1955

ROHDE, PETER, *Søren Kierkegaard*, London, 1960

Romantiques Allemands (Jean-Paul, Novalis, Schlegel, Tieck, E. T. A. Hoffmann, von Kleist, de la Motte-Fouqué), Paris, 1963

SALA, GEORGE AUGUSTUS, *Notes and Sketches of the Paris Exhibition*, London, 1868

SAUNDERS, EDITH, *The Age of Worth*, London, 1954

SITWELL, SACHEVERELL, *Denmark*, London, 1956

SPINK, REGINALD, *The Land and People of Denmark*, London, 1957

STAËL, MADAME DE, *De l'Allemagne*, 5 vols., Paris, 1960

STORY, W. WETMORE, *Roba di Roma*, Boston, 1893

THOMSON, DAVID, *Europe since Napoleon*, London, 1963

VALLENTIN, ANTONINA, *Henri Heine*, Paris, 1956

WILLEY, BASIL, *Nineteenth Century Studies*, London, 1964

WILLOUGHBY, L.A., *The Romantic Movement in Germany*, London, 1930

YOUNG, G. M., *Portrait of an Age*, London, 1954

Index

Index

Index

375

Index

Index

Index

379

Index

Index

Index

Index

Index